THE KNOWLEDGE ECONOMY AND LIFELONG LEARNING

The Knowledge Economy and Education
Volume 4

Series Editors:
David W. Livingstone, *Ontario Institute for Studies in Education*
David Guile, *Faculty of Policy and Society, Institute of Education, University of London*

Editorial Board:
Stephen Billett, *Griffiths University, Australia*
Zhou Zuoyu, *Normal University, Beijing, China*
Emery Hyslop-Margison, *Concordia University, Canada*
Karen Jensen, *University of Oslo, Norway*
Johan Muller, *University of Cape Town, South Africa*
Yoko Watanabe, *University of Kyoto, Japan*

Scope:
The aim of this series is to provide a focus for writers and readers interested in exploring the relation between the knowledge economy and education or an aspect of that relation, for example, vocational and professional education theorised critically.

It seeks authors who are keen to question conceptually and empirically the causal link that policymakers globally assume exists between education and the knowledge economy by raising: (i) epistemological issues as regards the concepts and types of and the relations between knowledge, the knowledge economy and education; (ii) sociological and political economic issues as regards the changing nature of work, the role of learning in workplaces, the relation between work, formal and informal learning and competing and contending visions of what a knowledge economy/knowledge society might look like; and (iii) pedagogic issues as regards the relationship between knowledge and learning in educational, community and workplace contexts.

The series is particularly aimed at researchers, policymakers, practitioners and students who wish to read texts and engage with researchers who call into question the current conventional wisdom that the knowledge economy is a new global reality to which all individuals and societies must adjust, and that lifelong learning is the strategy to secure such an adjustment. The series hopes to stimulate debate amongst this diverse audience by publishing books that: (i) articulate alternative visions of the relation between education and the knowledge economy; (ii) offer new insights into the extent, modes, and effectiveness of people's acquisition of knowledge and skill in the new circumstances that they face in the developed and developing world, (iii) and suggest how changes in both work conditions and curriculum and pedagogy can led to new relations between work and education.

The Knowledge Economy and Lifelong Learning

A Critical Reader

Edited by

D.W. Livingstone
University of Toronto, Canada

and

David Guile
University of London, UK

SENSE PUBLISHERS
ROTTERDAM / BOSTON / TAIPEI

A C.I.P. record for this book is available from the Library of Congress.

ISBN 978-94-6091-913-8 (paperback)
ISBN 978-94-6091-914-5 (hardback)
ISBN 978-94-6091-915-2 (e-book)

Published by: Sense Publishers,
P.O. Box 21858, 3001 AW Rotterdam, The Netherlands
https://www.sensepublishers.com

Cover picture with credit to "goodluz."

Printed on acid-free paper

Endorsements for *The Knowledge Economy and Lifelong Learning: A Critical Reader*

Given all of the discussion about a knowledge economy in both academic and popular writing, we need a volume that helps us understand both what is actually happening in the real world and what the implications of all this are for education. *The Knowledge Economy and Lifelong Learning* is a substantive and insightful treatment of both of these sets of issues. I strongly recommend it.

Michael W. Apple, John Bascom Professor of Curriculum and Instruction and Educational Policy Studies, University of Wisconsin

This book is a timely and powerful antidote to the half-aware writing about knowledge economies that is wafting around the globe. It shines penetrating lights on assumptions about unilinear trends and illuminates the darker recesses of the power politics involved. In so doing, it expands and reformulates conceptions of knowledge-based economies in ways that can fundamentally reshape the future of lifelong learning.

Karen Evans, Chair in Education (Lifelong Learning) Institute of Education, University of London

It is high time that the notion of knowledge economy is submitted to critical scrutiny. Commoditization and privatization of knowledge and learning need to be overcome by means of careful analysis and viable alternatives. This book takes an important step in that direction. It brings together a rich set of conceptual tools and research insights for the rediscovery of knowledge as use value and common good in service of global solidarity.

Yrjö Engeström, Professor of Adult Education and Director of CRADLE, University of Helsinki

TABLE OF CONTENTS

SECTION TWO: SPECIFIC CHALLENGES

ACKNOWLEDGEMENTS

The editors and publisher are grateful to the following publishers and authors for permission to reproduce previously published material:

John Wiley & Sons and Kenneth Carlaw, Les Oxley, Paul Walker, David Thorns, and Michael Nuth for 'Beyond the Hype: Intellectual Property and the Knowledge Society/Knowledge Economy,' *Journal of Economic Surveys* (2006), *20*(4), 633–658.

Sense Publishers and Bob Jessop for 'A Cultural Political Economy of Competitiveness and Its Implications for Higher Education.' In B. Jessop, N. Fairclough, & R. Wodak (Eds.), *Education and the Knowledge-Based Economy in Europe*, Rotterdam (2008), pp. 13–39.

Sage Publications, Chris Warhurst, and Paul Thompson for 'Mapping Knowledge in Work: Proxies or Practices?' *Work, Employment and Society* (2006), *20*(4), 787–800.

Taylor & Francis, Phillip Brown, and Hugh Lauder for 'Globalisation, Knowledge and the Myth of the Magnet Economy.' *Globalisation, Societies and Education* (2006, March), *4*(1), 25–57.

University of Toronto Press and D.W. Livingstone for 'Debunking the Knowledge Economy.' In *The Education-Jobs Gap: Underemployment or Economic Democracy*, Toronto: Garamond (2004, 2nd ed.), pp. 133-172.

Taylor & Francis and Paul Duguid for 'The Art of Knowing': Social and Tacit Dimensions of Knowledge and the Limits of the Community of Practice.' *The Information Society* (2005), *21*: 109–118.

Taylor & Francis and Alison Fuller, Lorna Unwin, Alan Felstead, Nick Jewson, and Konstantinos Kakavelakis for 'Creating and Using Knowledge: An Analysis of the Differentiated Nature of Workplace Learning Environments.' *British Educational Research Journal* (2007), 33(5), 743–759.

Sense Publishers and Monica Nerland for 'Professions as Knowledge Cultures.' In K. Jensen, L. Chr. Lahn & M. Nerland (Eds.), *Professional Learning in the Knowledge Society*, Rotterdam (2012).

University of Chicago Press and Beth Bechky for 'Object Lessons: Workplace Artifacts as Representations of Occupational Jurisdiction.' *American Journal of Sociology* (2003, November), *109*(3), 720–52.

Taylor & Francis and Arthur Bakker, Celia Hoyles, Phillip Kent, and Richard Noss for 'Improving Work Processes by Making the Invisible Visible.' *Journal of Education and Work* (2006, September), *19*(4), 343–361.

Taylor & Francis and Catherine Casey for 'The Learning Worker, Organizations and Democracy.' *International Journal of Lifelong Education* (2003, November–December), *22*(6), 620–634.

Taylor & Francis and Michael Young for Education, Globalisation and the 'Voice of Knowledge.' *Journal of Education and Work* (2009, July), *22*(3), 193–204.

ABOUT THE AUTHORS

Arthur Bakker, Freudenthal Institute for Science and Mathematics Education, Utrecht University

Beth A. Bechky, Graduate School of Management, University of California, Davis

Phillip Brown, School of Social Sciences, Cardiff University

Kenneth Carlaw, Department of Economics, University of British Columbia

Catherine Casey, School of Management, University of Leicester

Paul Duguid, School of Information, University of California, Berkeley

Alan Felstead, School of Social Sciences, University of Cardiff

Alison Fuller, Education School, University of Southampton

David Guile, Centre for Learning and Life-chances in Knowledge Economies and Societies, Institute of Education, University of London

Celia Hoyles, Department of Culture, Communication and Media, Institute of Education, University of London

Bob Jessop, Department of Sociology, Lancaster University

Nick Jewson, School of Social Sciences, University of Cardiff

Konstantinos Kakavelakis, Organisational Behaviour, University of Bedfordshire

Peter Kennedy, School of Business for Society, Glasgow Caledonian University

Phillip Kent, The Knowledge Lab, Institute of Education, University of London

Hugh Lauder, Department of Education, University of Bath

D.W. Livingstone, Ontario Institute for Studies in Education, University of Toronto

Monika Nerland, Faculty of Education, University of Oslo

ABOUT THE AUTHORS

Richard Noss, The Knowledge Lab, Institute of Education, University of London

Michael Nuth, School of Sociology and Anthropology, University of Canterbury

Les Oxley, Department of Economics, University of Canterbury

Peter H. Sawchuk, Ontario Institute for Studies in Education, University of Toronto

Paul Thompson, Business School, University of Strathclyde

David Thorns, School of Sociology and Anthropology, University of Canterbury

Lorna Unwin, Centre for Learning and Life-chances in Knowledge Economies and Societies, Institute of Education, University of London

Paul Walker, Department of Economics, University of Canterbury

Chris Warhurst, Business School, University of Sydney

Michael Young, Institute of Education, University of London

PREFACE

This book grew out of a discussion between the editors and the publisher about the need for a book that provided an overview of critical studies of the emergent knowledge economy and learning activities. We are grateful to many colleagues who offered suggestions as we sought out representative authors and writings from this field of studies. We are especially indebted to the contributing authors, all of whom readily agreed to be included in this reader and many of whom provided updates on previously published material. We thank the publishers who agreed to have papers reprinted here, as indicated in the list of acknowledgements. Stephan Dobson should be complimented on his highly professional editing and formatting of the final manuscripts.

Whether or not a knowledge economy becomes a new global reality and whether or not lifelong learning proves to be an effective strategy to cope with it are the central questions. There are no easy answers and much contestation and debate ahead. We hope this set of readings will contribute to more clearly framing the debate.

DWL   DG
Toronto London

GENERAL INTRODUCTION

The focus of this book is on a critical appraisal of dominant claims about a 'knowledge-based economy (KBE),' or 'knowledge economy,' and empirical investigations of the presumed relations between work requirements and learning in this economy. We conclude by suggesting new principles policy makers could use to ensure that policies for lifelong learning (LLL) articulate more purposefully with the expanded conception of the knowledge-based economy that emerges from this collection. Our book therefore differs significantly from another recent published edited collection, *Educating for the knowledge economy: Critical perspectives* (Lauder, Young, Daniels, Balarin, & Lowe, 2012), which focuses critically on the relation between educational policy, provision, and the knowledge economy. Both books nevertheless offer fresh insights into the debate about the relationship between education and the economies of advanced industrial societies.

We start by noting that the existence of a 'knowledge-based economy' is widely taken for granted by governments, mass media, public opinion, and most scholars today. The common view is that a transformation from earlier economies has occurred since around the end of the 1960s (see David & Foray, 2002) in terms of: (1) an unprecedented acceleration of the speed of creation and accumulation of knowledge; (2) a revolution in the instruments of knowledge production including information and communications technologies generally and the internet in particular; and (3) a growing relative importance of intangible capital (investment in research and development; training and education for knowledge production; investment in sustaining the physical stock and health of human capital compared to tangible capital (i.e., physical infrastructure; equipment; inventories; natural resources). The basic notion is that an ever-increasing speed of innovation in new knowledge-intensive commodities is needed for economies to survive in globally competitive markets. An essential corollary of this view is that the current and prospective labour force must engage in greater learning efforts throughout their lives in order to respond to this economic imperative. A primary solution to the demands of this knowledge-based economy is therefore presumed to be the development of a 'learning society,' or 'knowledge society' in which increasing lifelong learning enables further innovation and more knowledge-intensive products.

The basic purpose of the book is to bring together some of the most insightful critical assessments of these widespread assumptions. Taken cumulatively, the chapters in this book suggest that these assumptions are either exaggerated or plainly wrong. Section One offers general critiques of the distinctiveness of the most widely assumed features of the knowledge-based economy and of the general need for greater learning efforts; contrary evidence and arguments are provided for each of these features. Section Two looks more closely at an array of workplaces in which the transformation is presumed to be taking place. The basic finding is that the multiple forms of knowledge being used to facilitate improvements or innovation to products and services as well as processes of learning in the context of workplace change are both richer and more complex than advocates of the knowledge-based economy ever intimate.

All these authors agree on two basic points. First, knowledge cannot be reduced to a commodity and is not reduced but increased by use. The more we use it, the more there is – in contrast to the nature of most other commodities. Secondly, all authors display keen awareness of the reductionist effects of the efforts of knowledge economy theorists, large employers, and governments to control and manage knowledge. All the contributors to this reader, irrespective of their different theoretical perspectives, shed light on manifestations of these two points.

As many of our contributors suggest, all human economies are knowledge based. The most distinctive feature of our species has been the gathering of information from our environment and processing it into useful knowledge to cope effectively with changes in this environment. These forms of knowledge have ranged from basic language elements to highly sophisticated theories of life. All human civilizations have exhibited a wide range of forms of knowledge. The more we study both ancient and modern societies, the more we appreciate the depth of the knowledge they have relied upon to survive, including informal and tacit knowledge as well as formally documented knowledge systems. Contemporary advocates of knowledge-based economies have tended to focus on cognitive, rationalist, formalist aspects of knowledge and their relevance for production of new knowledge-intensive commodities. Daniel Bell (1973) has argued most influentially that theoretical knowledge, particularly as generated by science, technology, engineering, and mathematical (STEM) research, must be the pre-eminent form of knowledge in modern economies. Some other advocates of a knowledge economy (e.g., Lundvall, 1996), however, have argued that tacit knowledge, by dint of its inaccessibility to standardization, is becoming the most important form of knowledge.

Indeed, it has become increasingly strategic for production of new knowledge-intensive commodities to try to capture knowledge generated in more informal learning environments, or 'learning organizations.' This is merely to recognize workplace learning that has been ongoing since time immemorial, taken for granted, unrecognized, and unrewarded. So-called 'high performance' organizations now try to facilitate the interaction of formal and informal learning activities among their employees to enhance productivity. Such attempts at knowledge management run up against the fact that explicit formal knowledge is always limited in principle. Consequently, as one proponent of a new division of knowledge as the fundamental working principle of the knowledge-based economy recognizes:

> The unique human ability to perceive and act in complex situations without referring to explicit rules, therefore, is indispensably needed in order to make sense of this limited abstract knowledge and in order to make it usable for practical innovations. This basic fact of skill development and knowledge formation makes systematic personnel development and lifelong learning a

permanent management task in knowledge-intensive processes of value creation ... [M]ost of the skills and competences needed are embodied and cannot be expropriated, but must be maintained and developed in and through the work processes in which they are used. All managerial activities ... therefore, are directed to achieve this. (Brödner, 2000, pp. 15, 22)

This permanent knowledge management task continually contends with the expansive embodied nature of workers' knowledge and with workers' individual and collective motivation to share (or not share) it. This has been a familiar story in industrial societies.

The tendency for knowledge held in workers heads to be seen by managers as more strategic for commodity production, as well as the emergence of knowledge-based economy theorists advocating this view, can be traced to the rapid decline of employment in the manufacturing sector that began around the end of the 1960s. This is probably the most significant economic shift since the decline of agricultural employment. The development of industrial machinery in the nineteenth century stimulated both massive labour declines in agriculture as well as the massive expansion of manufacturing of all sorts. Many of those forced off the land were drawn into factories. The expansion of manufacturing continued into the mid-twentieth century. Steel, auto, petrochemical, and electrical industries created new mass-produced commodities that quickly became essential needs for urbanizing workforces. Similar processes of devising a marketable product and an efficient division of labour, then an expansion of product markets and labour forces, were replicated for many manufactured goods across the globe. But in recent generations, as automation has increased and market capacity has been exceeded, a spiral of mass layoffs of workers and the mergers or failures of remaining firms have occurred in many manufacturing industries. Between 1970 and the early twenty-first century, the advanced industrial countries lost massive numbers of manufacturing jobs and even most newly industrialized countries have now joined this declining trend (International Labour Organization, 2003; Pilat et al., 2006). We have witnessed the general decline of employment in manufacturing in a much more rapid way than the decline in agriculture in the previous two centuries. But in what sense is this shift indicative of a transformation?

The growth of employment in service sectors coincident with the decline of manufacturing, and the growing focus on non-material service commodities over material goods commodities, have given some credence to the claims that production is becoming more knowledge-based. But knowledge workers such as engineers and other professionals were just as fundamental to early twentieth-century manufacturing as computer programmers and other information technologists are to new knowledge industries today. Growing proportions of jobs explicitly involve information processing. But information is not necessarily knowledge. Information is raw material that may be processed by knowledgeable workers to produce valuable goods and services. It is arguable that a growing proportion of jobs have more explicitly design-based aspects that could be construed as 'intangible capital' (to be discussed further in the book's Conclusion). But whether or not this is true generally or for the newest information-based industries, it does not necessarily lead to the conclusion made by KBE theorists that today's workers must make greater efforts in relation to the knowledge required to produce today's non-material services.

The increasing prominence of information processing has led many who conflate information with knowledge to conclude that we now live in a well developed 'knowledge economy.' The debate over the extent of transformation still rages among scholars, including those in this book. Most would probably agree with the following social facts pertaining to all advanced market economies:

1. as noted above, declining minorities of jobs are in manufacturing and materials processing occupations, and growing majorities of jobs and of tasks in jobs involve information processing with increasing amounts of the information being mediated by use of computers;

2. growing proportions of jobs in advanced industrial societies are designated as professional and technical occupations distinguished by forms of specialized formal knowledge;

3. growing proportions of labour forces are attaining post-secondary formal education;

4. participation in adult education courses is also increasing throughout the life course;

5. as more married women have entered the paid labour force, the significance of previously hidden unpaid household and community labours is increasingly recognized; and

6. with increasing recognition of information processing as a component of so many peoples' paid and unpaid work, recognition of the importance of informal as well as formal aspects of lifelong learning in work have also increased and knowledge management has become a high declared priority of private corporations and governments.[1]

Most advocates of the knowledge economy presume that knowledge workers are becoming more influential in shaping its future direction and at least imply that capitalism will become more benign and sustainable as a result. None have explicitly suggested the demise of capitalism as an economic system. However material or immaterial its products may be, the capitalist mode of production is distinguished by constantly turning spheres of activity into commodities for sale with the aid of hired wage labour. There is continual change driven by three basic underlying relationships: (1) inter-firm competition to make and sell more and more goods and services commodities at lower cost for greater profits; (2) negotiations between business owners and paid workers over the conditions of employment and knowledge requirements, including their relative shares of net output; and (3) continual modification of the techniques of production to achieve greater efficiency in terms of labour time per commodity, leading to higher profits, better employment conditions, or both. Approaches such as knowledge economy theories that have not attended to these underlying contradictory dynamics of advanced capitalism – including conflicting aspects of the interest relationship between owners and paid workers – have misunderstood the nature and extent of changes occurring in both work and learning processes. As Livingstone (2009) states:

> A continual reorganization of the factors of production to increase productivity is the consequence of inter-firm competition as well as the productivity increases generated endogenously by a workforce as it learns to labour and produce more efficiently with given tools and techniques. The forces of production, including tools and techniques and their combination with the capacities of labour, have experienced extraordinary growth throughout the relatively short history of industrial capitalism. Such technological developments, from the water mill to the steam mill to interconnected mechanical and electronic networks, continually serve to expand private commodity production and exchange, while also making relevant knowledge more widely accessible. On the one hand, private ownership of production and the attendant wealth become increasingly concentrated in a smaller number of larger corporations, from the joint stock companies of the 1880s to the massive global corporations of the present. Owners strive to control knowledge of specific commodity production techniques for advantage over competitors (e.g., patents, licences, industrial secrets). On the other hand, workers and the general public gain ever-greater access (via public education systems and such forums as public libraries, public radio and television, and the Internet) to knowledge previously restricted for commodity production by private firms, as well as to diverse sources of knowledge for everyday life. In the context of inter-firm competition and labour contracts that cannot specify what workers know, the expansion of publicly accessible knowledge continues to be greater than any enterprise owner's ability to appropriate such knowledge for private gain. (pp. 59–60)

As virtually all authors in this book indicate in their own terms, this opposition between most peoples' widening access to valued knowledge and the efforts by business owners and managers to control knowledge as discrete intellectual property is a central feature of the times. Some express this opposition in terms of a contrast between aspirations for a 'knowledge society' in which there is increasingly equal access to higher education, and a 'knowledge economy' in which exclusive development and sale of intellectual products is an increasing preoccupation of paid work. Whatever the terms, most of these authors see the contest between democratic access to and use of knowledge versus its privatized control as a vexed issue with no easy path toward the dominance of one or the other in the foreseeable future. In terms of widening access to valued knowledge, Kennedy in Section One refers to the general 'logic of labour,' while in Section Two, Fuller et al. refer to 'expansive learning environments' in some workplaces and Sawchuk identifies extensive learning directly related to human needs or 'use-values.' All identify extensive learning efforts and working knowledge among employees that many contemporary paid workplaces as currently organized are unable to effectively utilize. This conflictual view contrasts to the more starry-eyed visions of those who see the rapid development of either tendency, particularly knowledge economy theorists who envisage full utilization of workers' knowledge for enhanced production of more knowledge-intensive commodities. As long as capitalism survives, this opposition is most likely to persist.

Whether the focal commodities are material or non-material, the quintessential motor of capitalism is competition between firms, which ensures that each of them must grow and reinvest its profits to survive. As Foster et al. (2010) remind us: 'By its nature, capital is 'self-expanding, and accumulation is its sole aim ... The earth and human labour are systematically exploited/robbed to fuel this juggernaut' (p. 109). However much knowledge economy advocates and other mainstream economists focus on non-material aspects of the economy, it is clear that the scale of damage to the earth from continuing material production has reached unprecedented levels, as has the massive polarization of wealth and poverty around the globe. One of the deepest ironies of knowledge economy discourse is that there has been precious little attention in it to the kinds of knowledge of our environment that is needed to aid human survival in the wake of the negative environmental effects of the continual expansion of capitalist production. The knowledge that counts in this context is that which can be applied to producing material or non-material commodities for continuing profit, and anything else − including human and ecosystem survival − remains secondary.

Aside from the indifference in knowledge economy discourse to issues of survival, there is a large contradiction between the widespread assumption in this discourse of skill deficits of current labour forces and their consequent need for lifelong learning and, conversely, the social facts of unprecedented levels of participation in higher education and adult education. Human capital theorists have long argued that investment in formal education leads to economic growth. But we have experienced a generation of unprecedented growth of advanced formal education along with economic stagnation and high unemployment. Many empirical researchers have also documented the existence of growing underemployment of formal knowledge attained in comparison to educational requirements for available jobs (see Livingstone, 2009). In particular, while the ability to use computers and the internet are the most often required competencies for new labour market entrants, these are also the competencies where there is the greatest surplus of underutilized skills (Allen & van der Velden, 2009). If the dominant tendency is for workers to have both unprecedented levels of formal knowledge/qualifications and increasingly recognized extensive embodied informal knowledge, and there is increasing evidence of underemployment and/or underutilization of their abilities, then surely the assumption of a major skill deficit as a significant barrier to further development of a knowledge economy is highly questionable. As some of the authors in this book suggest, the deficit is more likely to reside in the organization of paid work that inhibits many workers from fully using their substantial abilities.

On the basic question of continuity and change in the prevailing economic system, most of the authors in this book would probably agree that the contradictory dynamics of advanced capitalism are still at play in driving both knowledge management of twenty-first century firms and the lifelong learning of current and prospective workers. Numerous specific features of firms, workers, and their strategic relations have been changing significantly, as the case studies in Section Two amply illustrate. But overall, the following chapters should at least provoke scepticism about the defining claims of knowledge economy discourse, as well as reflection about the most beneficial of these changes and whether alternative ways of organizing economic life should be put on the agenda to utilize our knowledge for a sustainable future.

NOTES

1 For documentation of most of these facts as well as discussion of the distinction between formal and informal learning, see Livingstone (2010). On knowledge management, see Luque (2001).

REFERENCES

Allen, J. & van der Velden, R. (2009, December). Report on the large-scale graduate survey: Competencies and early labour market careers of higher education graduates. Lifelong Learning Program, European Commission. Ljubljana: Faculty of Social Sciences, University of Ljubljana.

Bell, D. (1973). The coming of post-industrial society: A venture in social forecasting. New York: Basic Books.

Brödner, P. (2000, February 24–25). The future of work in a knowledge-based economy. ICT/CIREM International Seminar on 'Economy and Work in the Knowledge Society.' Barcelona.

Foster, J.B., Clark, B., & York, R. (2010). *The ecological rift: Capitalism's war on the earth*. New York: Monthly Review.

International Labour Organization (OECD). (2003). Key indicators of the labour market: Employment by sector. Retrieved from http://ilo.org/public/english/employment/stat/kilm04.htm.

David, P.A. & Foray, D. (2002). An introduction to the economy of the knowledge society. *International Social Science Journal, 54*(171), 9–23.

Lauder, H., Young, M., Daniels, H., Balarin, M., & Lowe, J. (Eds.). (2012). *Educating for the knowledge economy: Critical perspectives*. London: Routledge.

Livingstone, D.W. (Ed.). (2009). *Education and jobs: Exploring the gaps*. Toronto: University of Toronto Press.

Livingstone, D.W. (Ed.). (2010). *Lifelong learning in paid and unpaid work*. New York: Routledge.

Lundvall, B.-Å. (1996). *The social dimensions of the learning economy*. Working papers. Copenhagen: DRUID: Department of Industrial Economics and Strategy, Copenhagen Business School & Department of Business Studies, Aalborg University.

Luque, E. (2001). Whose knowledge (economy)? *Social Epistemology, 15*(3), 187–200.

Pilat, D., Cimper, A., Olsen, K., & Webb, C. (2006). *The changing nature of manufacturing in OECD economies*. STI Working Paper 2006/9. Directorate for Science, Technology and Industry. Paris: Organisation for Economic Co-operation and Development.

SECTION ONE: GENERAL CRITIQUES

SECTION ONE

General Critiques

INTRODUCTION

As suggested in the General Introduction, the notion of the emergence of a knowledge economy has become so widespread that it is now commonly assumed in both policy discussions and the mass media. Many advocates have heralded the knowledge economy as transforming the nature of both work and learning. A shift from materials handling to processing of information aided by global electronic technology is seen to be converting much of the labour force into knowledge workers; a direct consequence is that workers must devote more of their efforts to pursuit of lifelong learning to meet the growing knowledge demands of their jobs. The problem, as the chapters in this section make clear, is that this notion remains far from reality.

Carlaw and his colleagues extensively explore the debates across both economics and sociology around the extent of movement into a new knowledge economy and/or knowledge society. They find little clarity or consistency. They then move on to a more specific comparative historical analysis of how intellectual property has been protected and controlled in both the industrial revolution and in contemporary societies through patents, copyright, secrecy, and other means. They conclude that the role of intellectual property remains central to innovation, but that its protection and control has become a harder global challenge with the rise of new forms of communication.

Warhurst and Thompson find that most academic and policy debate about the knowledge economy tends to be prescriptive and inattentive to economic and workplace realities, particularly in terms of the use of knowledge in different levels of the workplace. Much of their critical attention is devoted to discussing the limits of the most common general proxy measures used to demonstrate the purportedly 'knowledge-driven' character of contemporary economies. These are: information and communications technologies (ICT); investment in research and development; formal qualifications of the labour force; and imputation of increasing knowledge from changing occupational composition. In each respect, they find these proxies are misleadingly insensitive to underlying variations and developments. They then go on to suggest a conceptual frame that might more effectively map workplace knowledge with reference to practice.

Jessop takes a broader cultural political economy approach to tracing the development of the knowledge-based economy and its predecessor, the post-industrial economy, as the hegemonic 'imaginary' or dominant frame for interpreting contemporary capitalism and higher education. He traces ways in which Daniel Bell's optimistic projections of democratization of knowledge have been controverted by its reduction to a factor of production oriented to an

D.W. Livingstone and D. Guile (eds.), The Knowledge Economy and Lifelong Learning: A Critical Reader, 3–5.

economizing logic of profit and loss, both in material production generally and in the operation of universities. Jessop offers several case studies to illustrate the construction of the knowledge economy as a very successful economic imaginary. He shows that the rise of the knowledge economy as a dominant frame resulted from competition between social forces in a particular complex historical period. He also delineates differences between economists' approach to the knowledge economy and a sociological approach to the knowledge society as well as between theoretical and policy frames reflecting these phenomena. Finally, he examines the reorganization of education on a world scale, the increasing construal of education as a directly economic factor and – even where it remains beyond the market – the treatment of education in terms of its effect on economic competitiveness. Perhaps most importantly, Jessop's chapter strongly suggests that the categories, structures, and processes repeatedly referred to by advocates of knowledge economy as natural are indeed partial constructions of reality.

Livingstone sees knowledge economy theories as an example of the general evolutionary progress paradigm and assesses their basic claims in their own terms. Empirical evidence indicates only incremental gains in skill requirements and the proportions of the labour force in jobs recognized as requiring specialized knowledge. This contrasts with much larger increases of advanced schooling and adult education. Human capital theory has provided the most compelling rationale for expecting emergence of the knowledge economy and continued economic growth through individual and aggregate investment in education. But increasing numbers of highly qualified people are unemployed or underemployed and most experience decreasing marginal returns for their formal education. Thus, human capital theory may have reached its limit as an explanatory frame; the growing education–jobs gap may be better understood in terms of conflict theories.

Brown and Lauder sceptically assess the now-dominant view that, in the global knowledge economy, developed countries can resolve issues of individual aspirations, economic efficiency, and social justice through the creation of high-skills, high-wage 'magnet' economies. The authors find four key claims to be seriously deficient, namely: high skilled jobs do not necessarily lead to high wages; the bond between education, jobs, and rewards is loosening, not tightening; an anticipated power shift from employers to knowledge workers has not happened; and increased emphasis on individual employability and raising the educational standards of all ignores an oversupply of graduates for good jobs and exacerbates the problem of equality of educational opportunity at a global level. Their analysis seriously challenges both the notion of a 'magnet' economy and the major tenets of the dominant discourse of education, knowledge, and the global economy.

Duguid takes a more general approach to the nature of knowledge in modern societies. He suggests that individualist approaches to knowledge, particularly in mainstream economics, tend to reduce it to calculable units of information to be codified, exchanged, and controlled. He compares the approach of 'community of practice' (CoP, a.k.a. situated learning theory), which recognizes that much knowledge is generated and continues to reside tacitly in social contexts. Duguid counters economists' arguments to substitute tacit with more explicit knowledge by stressing that the impact of knowing how to do something is at least as important as knowing cognitive details about it. Most pungently, he observes that: 'A brief list of all that is involved in tying a shoelace would overwhelm a learner.' He concludes with cautionary notes about essential tacit aspects of social networks that continue to be ignored by social capital theorists preoccupied with information exchanges between individuals – a caution that could be equally applied to most knowledge economy theorists as well as to theorists of lifelong learning who reduce learning to its most formal, individual dimensions.

Kennedy counterpoises two logics of development: (1) the familiar dominant logic of late modern capitalism that the 'knowledge economy' is evidence of the expansion of capital into new products and services in a search to generate surplus value, with 'life-long learning' responding by supplying the working population with the requisite skills for capital to exploit in the course of this expansion; and (2) a 'logic of labour' argument which accords primacy to understanding the shift towards the knowledge worker and the 'lifelong learner' in terms of the development of the general social power of labour. In line with autonomist labour theorists, he sees surplus value becoming more difficult to locate and control in immaterial forms of labour power because its increasingly socialized character is being drawn into global interconnection via information technology. Kennedy recognizes capital–labour relations as a moving contradictory process. But he discerns an emerging capacity for labour power to become social power, not only limiting necessary labour used for capitalist profits but expanding free labour, identifying, defining, and ultimately controlling production for social need.

Taken together, the chapters in Section One present a compelling argument that a knowledge-based economy in which the existing knowledge and learning abilities of the labour force are being effectively utilized in current forms of employment remains far from reality in advanced industrial societies generally. These chapters also puncture the common assumption that greater lifelong learning effort by this labour force is both required and a most appropriate solution to current economic problems. The second section will look more closely at how these basic claims of knowledge economy advocates apply in diverse contemporary paid workplaces, including in those that such advocates see as the leading edge of transformation to a new economy.

KENNETH CARLAW, LES OXLEY, PAUL WALKER,
DAVID THORNS, & MICHAEL NUTH

BEYOND THE HYPE

Intellectual Property and the Knowledge Society/Knowledge Economy

INTRODUCTION

Much has been made about whether anything is 'new' about the 'New Economy,' with the conclusion being that we now *are* a knowledge-based society. But in what sense, if at all, are we any more of a knowledge society now than we were in Neolithic times, the Renaissance, and th1e Industrial Revolution? What is the role of intellectual property (IP) and the intellectual commons in the process of innovation, growth and economic development? What role does technology and technological knowledge play both in the process of innovation and economic growth and in the protection of IP itself? To answer some of these questions requires a clear understanding of 'the nature of the beast,' what we mean by the New Economy, how we measure the level and growth of innovations, how we test for association/causation between knowledge (both embodied in human capital and disembodied) and any consequences it might generate (both good and bad), and how we protect IP.

Foss (2002) argues that 'Whatever we think of this journalistic concept [of the knowledge economy], it arguably does capture real tendencies and complementary changes' (p. 62). What might these 'new' tendencies be?

> We define the knowledge economy as production and services based on knowledge-intensive activities that contribute to an accelerated pace of technical and scientific advance, as well as rapid obsolescence. The key component of a knowledge economy is a greater reliance on intellectual capabilities than on physical inputs or natural resources. (Powell & Snellman, 2004, p. 199)

Here the 'modern' emphasis seems to be on 'knowledge' (yes) 'accelerated technical and scientific advance' (yes) and 'greater reliance on intellectual capabilities than physical inputs or natural resources' (yes). Is this all new? Marshall (1890) states that 'Knowledge is our most powerful engine of production' (p. IV.1.2). MacLeod (1988) argues that: 'The unreformed [pre-1852] patent system was at best ineffective, or at worst, a brake on invention and its dissemination' (p. 200). Furthermore Ashton (1955) suggests that 'If Watt's Fire Engine Act had not extended the life of his steam engine patent we would have had a railway system earlier' (p. 107), and Boehm and Silbertson (1967) state that

*D.W. Livingstone and D. Guile (eds.), The Knowledge Economy and Lifelong Learning:
A Critical Reader, 7–42.*

'Evidence placed before the 1851 Select Committee ... certainly throws doubt on a strong causal connection between our early patent system and the British industrial revolution' (p. 26).

In this chapter, we will emphasize a *historically grounded* approach to consider what, if anything, is fundamentally 'new' about the knowledge economy/society and whether it constitutes a modern economic and social 'revolution.' The themes we will investigate mirror some of the issues raised above as potential indicators of a 'changed world' and include: (1) *the role of entrepreneurship, technological knowledge creation and obsolescence*; (2) *intellectual capabilities and intellectual knowledge*; and (3) *the role of science and research and development*. In order to consider whether the modern world is 'fundamentally' different we will, through the lens of history, consider these issues with a view to then analysing what the current literature on the knowledge economy/society really has to say.

In particular, in the second section, we explore characteristics of the British Industrial Revolution of the nineteenth and nineteenth centuries and similar episodes in Europe with a view to 'setting the historical scene' for subsequent comparisons with the 'modern eras' of the 'new' 'information' and 'knowledge' societies emerging in the latter half of the twentieth and the beginning of the twenty-first centuries. Section 3 focuses on the role of the *entrepreneur* as risk taker and innovator in a world characterized by uncertainty, complementarities and elective affinities. The analysis is illustrated with references to a range of developments that led to and potentially 'caused' the Industrial Revolution. This section continues to 'set the scene' to allow us to consider whether the world is 'fundamentally different' now to then. In section 4, four particular forms of IP and its protection are considered including patents, secrecy, 'first-to-the-market,' and copyright in order to identify their historical origins, historical developments and their potential roles in the two epochs contrasted here.

Section 5 presents the case for the critical role of *science and research and development* in the European Industrial Revolutions to allow an historical comparison with current debates on the assumed primacy of such elements in 'New Economy' and the potentially changing role of IP that modern developments and ownership create. With this historical background in place, section 6 undertakes a detailed analysis of what might now define a modern knowledge economy/society via extensive reference to what others have said on such matters. The evidence from this section is that 'quantifiable, non-circular' definitions are frustratingly absent; however, 'knowledge' and the resultant role of IP creation and protection are a key component in all the cited authors' discussions. Whether IP and knowledge are 'uniquely' key to the 'New Economy' will be an issue we return to in the concluding section. Section 7 extends discussion of the role of IP in the knowledge society, emphasizing the fundamental role of the Information and Communication Technologies (ICTs), where innovation is increasingly seen as the fuel of the New Economy, with the internet the 'electricity,' and section 8 concludes by looking forward to identify key research questions and methodological challenges to progress these debates.

HISTORICAL BACKGROUND

One of the key questions we try to address relates to whether we are currently living through a period of fundamental change, as radical and extensive as the 'great transformation'[1] (Polanyi, 1944) of the eighteenth and nineteenth centuries. This 'transformation' comprised changes to the technological, economic, political and values base of societies.

To explore this question, we will examine the two historical periods that have been identified as ones of dramatic change. The first created the 'industrial/modern society,' replacing the agrarian period, whereas the second is attributed to creating what many typically call the 'information/knowledge society' (Toffler, 1980).[2] Considerable controversy still lingers around both these claims, with some seeing linear progress (Hirst & Thompson, 1996) and gradual change rather than sharp discontinuities, whereas others subscribe to more radical transformations and argue for difference rather than continuity. Drawing on economic, sociological and historical traditions and critique, we seek to take stock of the debates and identify the key questions still to be addressed in an ongoing research program.

Knowledge has always been important for the development of economic and social life.[3] In the eighteenth- and nineteenth-century industrial revolution, and in the more recent post-1960s information revolution, we see an age-old tension between the desire for an openness to innovation and change and the spread of information that would assist this activity and the need to control the access to knowledge in order to enable those who have created new IP to gain some economic return. Without protection of some kind, it is often suggested that there would be no incentive for a continued investment in the time, energy and capital that is necessary for the creation of yet more ideas. However, sorting out what if anything is different in the two time periods with respect to the role of knowledge has not proven straightforward for most authors. We would argue, however, that it is simply a matter of identifying the *specific types of knowledge* in use in the relevant periods and suggesting how the legal systems are forced to adapt their 'rules of the game' as these technologies emerge and evolve.

A considerable volume of research by both sociologists and economists has been devoted to examining the industrial revolutions that took place in the eighteenth and nineteenth centuries. A substantial change came from the use of new technologies and motive power – from water to coal, electricity and oil. Such technologies allowed new forms of production to take place, expanding the industrial base of these societies. It also changed how things were made, moving products from small craft shops to factories and assembly lines. Human labour was deskilled from craft working and 're-skilled' to skilled and semi-skilled production line work (Hobsbawm, 1975). Larger units of labour required different settlement patterns encouraging the growth of new cities. For example, in the United Kingdom in 1801 there was only one city, London, that had a population of over 100,000, but by 1901 this number had increased to 35 cities of more than 100,000 and containing 25.9 per cent of the population of the United Kingdom (Thorns, 2002). The initial development of industrial cities was marked by tenement housing and crowded conditions that allowed workers to live close to their work, but was associated with poor living and health outcomes,[4] reflecting the unequal distribution of the cost and benefits of the new system.

Economic changes associated with the development of the industrial system were profound. The source of wealth creation shifted from land-based and raw commodity trading to products of the industrial system. The accumulation of capital from the production and sale of commodities produced by increasing large-scale manufacturing became the key driver of economic life.[5] This led to the formation of the 'Fordist' system whereby reducing the cost of commodities through mass production, paying a wage that allowed workers to consume, and regulating working hours[6] to create leisure became a recipe for expansion (Amin, 1994). The labour process was changed with the growth of scientific management – 'Taylorism.' This created an ongoing debate as to what created increased efficiency and worker satisfaction (Braverman, 1975). Was it through streamlining that the production process (time and motion study) was improved or was it through creating a strong collegial bond between workers and management and developing more of a team approach (Roethlesberger & Dickson, 1939)?

In industrial societies the principal source of value was human labour allied to new technologies of production. A key social change that was suggested as critical to the creation of this new system of economic activity was the 'spirit' of capitalism (Weber, 1930, 1947); a change took place in values as a result of the Protestant reformation emphasizing a more individual understanding of faith and religious work. Weber argued that it was the Calvinist idea of predestination and 'election' that encouraged hard work and the achievement of economic prosperity that then indicated that persons were part of the 'elect.' Weber identified what he termed an 'elective affinity' between the economic, social and religious changes which created a climate that allowed the industrial system to develop extremely rapidly (Gerth & Mills, 1946, pp. 284–285).

However, Lipsey et al. (2005) see the Protestant work ethic as a sub-evolution following the invention of the printing press rather than as a major theme. In particular they identify five key differences between Europe and the rest of the world. The first is pluralism of authority and control. The second is the corporation, in the forms of the church, guilds and universities. Third is the adoption of natural philosophy in place of the doctrine of occasionalism that leads directly into the fourth difference, Newtonian science, that cannot exist without natural laws, and fifth, a legal system that evolves out of canon law. Therefore, lacking these elements, the economies of India and China fell behind in terms of their rates of economic growth. What this shows is that technology on its own is insufficient to create economic growth; therefore, such growth comes from a combination of influences including *changes to the values and ideas* underpinning a particular society.

INDUSTRIAL REVOLUTION AND THE ROLE OF UNCERTAINTY, TECHNOLOGY IDEAS, COMPLEMENTARITIES AND ELECTIVE AFFINITIES

It is broadly recognized (see, e.g., Suatet, 2000) that innovative entrepreneurship is a significant engine of technological knowledge creation, which itself is recognized as the fundamental engine of long-run economic growth.[7] Innovative – typically profit seeking – entrepreneurs have been responsible historically for a large proportion of the innovation necessary to make new technologies commercially viable. For example, much of the mapping of the globe and the refinements to the technology of three-masted sailing ships in the fifteenth and sixteenth centuries occurred because individuals were seeking new ways (routes) to obtain economic profit.[8] This entrepreneurial activity led to the development of complementary technologies in the form of the joint stock company[9] and many other related financial innovations. In fact, *economic incentives* have driven a significant number of major technological innovations throughout history. Writing was invented as a result of a desire to keep records for the purposes of taxation to fund public works.[10] The steam engine was invented to pump water out of mines. Furthermore, while other such general purpose technologies (GPTs) have found their inspiration from non-economic motives (e.g., the computer and internet were originally developed as military technologies), their development and diffusion has been the direct result of entrepreneurs exploiting economic opportunities.

To the extent that economic growth is desirable, it is necessary to understand this entrepreneurial engine of economic growth. In order to do this we must understand how technological knowledge manifests and develops and how it relates to other knowledge, pre-existing technologies and economic structures such as institutions, laws and capital (physical and human). We must also understand the incentives and motivation of the entrepreneurs who drive the process of technological change. Consider the process of economic growth driven by technological change. The critical feature of this process is that it is pervaded by uncertainty. Individual pieces of technological knowledge are complementary with other pieces of technological knowledge and with the economic structure into which they get embodied. The economic growth process exploits complementarities through combinations and re-combinations of technological knowledge. Decision-makers (including entrepreneurs) of the system must form expectations with respect to investment decisions that take into account these features of technological change.

Because innovation implies doing something that has not been done before, uncertainty pervades the process of technological change.

It is often impossible even to enumerate in advance the full set of outcomes of a particular line of research. Time and money are often spent investigating specific research questions to discover whether the alley they lead up is blind or rich in potential. As a result, massive sums are sometimes spent with no positive return, while trivial expenditures sometimes produce results of great value. Furthermore, the search for one technological advance often produces different, unforeseen advances. (Lipsey & Carlaw, 2000)

Uncertainty implies that different agents may make different innovative choices with respect to the same technology, resulting in different outcomes. Sociologists have drawn attention to the unintended as well as intended consequences from technological and other innovations, which also create uncertainty as we are unable to fully predict the associated or down-stream affects. The environmental effects of chemical fertilizer applications and dioxin-based sprays are good examples in which the unintended consequences of these new ways of enhancing farm production have had major unforeseen consequences upon the health and well-being of local populations. Yet, it is still possible for all outcomes of technology to generate economic value because each outcome can result in a commercially viable product or service. One important point is that while some outcomes may generate more value than others, there is no uniquely optimal outcome that should be chosen above all others, nor do we always measure the long-term effects in making these calculations. Another important point is that no single individual can know in advance all of the potential applications for a given technology. The set of applications that is realized after this fact is the result of many diverse experiments (resulting in innovation) conducted by many different agents.

As an illustration of the importance of complementarities, consider the following thought experiment. How much would a group or groups within society be willing to pay not to have an identifiable technology such as electricity or the computer taken away for a given period, say a year? Think about conducting this experiment for several iterations, replacing the previously removed technology and taking out another. Now contemplate how many times this experiment must be conducted before the entire annual GDP of that national state (i.e., its ability to pay) is exhausted. Our conjecture is that the number of technologies that need to be individually removed to exhaust total GDP is smaller than the total number currently in use creating that national state's GDP.

Why does this occur? It is because of technological complementarities. The removal of electricity from the production system renders several (or most) other technologies in that system useless. There would be no electric light, no telephones, faxes or email, no internet in computers, and so on. The subsequent replacement of electricity and removal of the computer or internet means that the willingness-to-pay calculation has double counted the value of these technologies.

These observations about technological complementarities reveal that there is a major issue of attributing value to *individual pieces of knowledge*, about which we say more shortly. The complementary structure of technological knowledge leads directly to another observation about the innovation process. Elements of technological knowledge can be combined and recombined to make different technologies. For example, many of the components for the Wright Brothers airplane were derived from bicycle parts. Another example is found in the sequence of power technologies: water wheels were displaced by steam, which in turn was replaced by electricity. However, hydroelectricity generation uses a water wheel. This is the characteristic of knowledge that leads to the optimistic view that economic growth driven by technological change is sustainable because the combinatoric possibilities with new and existing knowledge are boundless. These combinatoric possibilities circumvent diminishing returns in the creation of knowledge. In making such combinations and adaptations of technologies to new conditions, the social and cultural conditions are a major factor. In Kobe, Japan, the local Rugby Union team imported a scrum machine from New Zealand and decided to 'improve the technology' by making the machine work with less friction. However, by doing so they completely defeated the purpose of the technology. Clearly there was no transfer of the complementary cultural information about the purpose and use of the machine!

There are two important aspects of entrepreneurial behaviour with respect to innovation that must concern us. First, given the characteristics (uncertainty and complementarity) of the technological growth process, the entrepreneur plays a critical role in identifying and exploiting the innovation opportunities that new technologies present. Second, entrepreneurs are the economic mechanism which transforms technological knowledge into economic value.

Entrepreneurs are the decision-making force that generates both continuous innovation and economic value from that innovation. The innovative entrepreneur is the opportunist who recognizes the opportunities inherent in new technologies; 'In that sense, the entrepreneur gives life to the implicit [in some cases explicit] demand on the part of consumers' (Sautet, 2000, p. 60). In almost all cases it is impossible to attach probabilities to outcomes and expectations are in many cases best guesses. Thus, entrepreneurs are the risk takers who form a vital linkage in the process of technological change and economic growth, converting technology into commercial value.

With such pervasive uncertainty, how do we appraise the economic value of the IP generated from innovative entrepreneurship and contemplate mechanisms to protect such property? Both are difficult issues. Appraisal requires assigning value often to individual pieces of technological knowledge. The problem exists because the economic value of the individual pieces of knowledge is only generated when they are combined with other pieces of knowledge to form commercially valuable products and processes. Protection provides the incentive to individuals to undertake innovative research, thus overcoming the positive spill over associated with the non-rivalrous characteristic of knowledge.[11] However, it also limits the exploitation of the protected technology by subsequent innovative entrepreneurs who will themselves create innovations by applying the technology in novel ways. Thus, protection slows the diffusion of new technology and limits the value extractable from it.

Economists' accounts of how technical change arises in market economies are influenced by Schumpeter's (1942) work that recognizes the need for profit in 'rivalrous' competition. In contrast, sociological accounts have featured the social and professional aspects of this process and have given more attention to the social actors involved (Nelson, 1989). Increasingly both have recognized the need for an evolutionary approach that takes account of the inter-relationship of the private (market-based) imperatives and the 'public' knowledge creation and application-based aspects of innovation. Evolutionary paths, however, are not smooth. They may have significant spikes when major technological innovation occurs, as is clearly shown by the work on GPTs.

What was the value of the printing press when Gutenberg first introduced the technology (i.e., before the standardization of the vernaculars of Europe)? The press became much more valuable after the standardization of spelling and dialect. Should we then appraise Gutenberg's IP before or after the standardization of languages? Our problem with appraising the value of Gutenberg's IP is a problem that pervades all of IP over technological knowledge. How should we appraise the value of the individual pieces of knowledge contained in the printing press, many of which Gutenberg did not create himself? For example, movable type was invented in China long before the European version of the printing press was created. Other critical pieces of knowledge, such as the alphabet and language, were also used by Gutenberg but not invented by him. This provides support for the way that ideas and technologies interact with the social and political conditions of particular nation states in specific time periods.

The ability to associate economic value with a particular piece of knowledge is made difficult by the very nature of technological knowledge and the processes that create it. However, if we are trying to get incentives for these agents of change such that they create as much economic value from new technologies as possible,[12] we face some major issues. Some of the value will come from giving agents the incentive to expand the set of application technologies associated with a particular enabling technology as quickly as possible, which implies the need for diffusion. Some of this value implies giving agents the incentive to create the enabling technologies in the first place. (These incentives may take the form of IP protection.) The critical issue is the amount these agents must receive in order for each type to undertake innovative entrepreneurial activities. This amount need not be nearly as large as the appraised value of the technology at any given stage of production. In fact, economic theory tells us that the number need only be sufficient to cover the resource and development costs (including the entrepreneur's opportunity costs and risk premium) of innovation. This minimum reward is sufficient to induce the desired behaviour and in all cases where the innovation is commercially viable it must be less than the total value of the technology over its useful life. The problem then is to appraise IP to get incentives correct for innovative entrepreneurs, which means appraising the costs of innovation and not the total potential value.

INTELLECTUAL PROPERTY PROTECTION AND CONTROLS

1. Patents

In exploring the role of ideas and innovation, the issue of IP is a central one as it concerns the way in which ideas can be diffused (Rogers, 1962). In thinking about innovation, clearly one component is the creation of new ideas, such as the creation of new technical processors, and new ways of organizing and managing work. One way of controlling the flow of ideas and information is to subject these to patents and copyright restrictions (see, e.g., Liebowitz and Watt, 2006; Ramello, 2006; Towse, 2006). Economists see IP protection as desirable because it gives inventors the incentive to create new technologies in the first instance. However, such protection is potentially a double-edged sword in that it restricts the creation of innovative technologies that exploit the initial technology. For example, Watt's patent on his atmospheric steam engine effectively delayed technological innovation in the form of high-pressure steam engines for 80 years (the length of his patent).

Historically, property rights, especially with respect to IP, have played a major role in technological and economic growth. However, it is important to note that the development of property rights is as often driven by technological change as it is a cause of such change. For example, rights to water access were established only after the need for fast-flowing water to run water wheels to power textile and other manufacturing factories were put in place. A modern example of this problem is the internet's impact on privacy and copyright for music (see Liebowitz & Watt, 2006). The important lesson is that well-defined property rights may help to facilitate the creation of new technologies, but new technologies may also require changes to existing property right regimes. IP comes in a variety of forms and this variety is actually a reflection of the technological knowledge being protected.

On the surface a *patent* seems to be a fairly straightforward way to ensure IP protection. However, in practice patents have little enforcement value for many holders. Pharmaceutical and chemical innovations enjoy nearly complete property right protection from patents, while computer software innovations obtain very little protection. There is a fundamentally different characteristic between these technologies that relates to the technological characteristics of complementarities and combinatorics. Pharmaceutical and chemical innovations are new combinations of complementary components of knowledge that take the form of molecules. The critical feature of pharmaceuticals and chemicals is that there is a unique mapping between the particular molecular combination and the output generated by the combination. Therefore, any marginal variation to the molecular combination will result in a completely different output. This is not the case for computer software (or most other technologies). Variations in computer code can produce virtually the same output. For example, consider the number of different word processors available to consumers. Thus, patents appear to be a useful protection mechanism only for technologies where there is a unique relationship between the combination of pieces of technological knowledge and the output of the technology.

Patenting does, however, have a long history. Machlup and Penrose (1950) note that a rather well-developed patent system existed in Venice in the fifteenth century, and that the practice of granting monopoly privileges by the Crown or by local governments to inventors was widely followed in many parts of Europe in the sixteenth and seventeenth centuries. In England, the policy of granting the privilege of monopoly under royal prerogative culminated in the Statute of Monopolies of 1624, providing the first patent law of a modern nation. Other countries followed, after a gap of more than a century, with France and the United States enacting patent laws in 1791 and 1793 respectively.

The role of patenting during the British Industrial Revolution, however, is a controversial one. On the one hand, controlling the flow of new innovations through patenting copyrighting and use of trademarks was prevalent and some analysts see this as a factor that limited innovative activity during the industrial revolution; for example, 'Evidence placed before the 1851 Select Committee … certainly throws doubt on a strong causal connection between our early patent system and the British industrial revolution' (Boehm & Silbertson, 1967, p. 26). However, many economists have argued that innovators are 'rational profit maximizers' and as such without the protections of IP laws there would have been little incentive for them to spend time in the research and development that creates new innovations, as they would be unsure as to whether or not they would have an economic return (Drahos, 2005).

Historians' judgements of the consequences for economic development of the precocious English patent system are mixed. Some, including Fox (1947), simply associate the origins of the modern patent system in England with the location of the British Industrial Revolution. MacLeod (1988, p. 198) takes a more cautious approach. She notes that the concept of 'intellectual property' in regard of technical invention was a late development.[13] It was mentioned first in a pamphlet of 1712, and after that the term re-appears sporadically in the patent applications later in the eighteenth century, before being enshrined in the Act extending James Watt's patent in 1775, 'his property in the said application secured.' However, MacLeod argues that the unreformed (pre-1852) patent system was at best ineffective, or at worst, a brake on invention and its dissemination. Ashton (1955, p. 107) suggests that if Watt's Fire Engine Act had not extended the life of his steam engine patent, we would have had a railway system earlier.

Ironically, Dutton (1984, p. 204) argues that the imperfect nature of the British patent system during the Industrial Revolution may have in practice approached the ideal. Inventors paid heavily and separately in England, Scotland and Ireland for the temporary, 14 years in the first instance, and uncertain privileges of patent protection, because property rights were dependent on decisions made by the Courts, not by the Patent Office. Nevertheless, British patents offered a degree of property protection to inventors, but did not provide complete barriers to access and use by others, and this, according to Dutton, was in all probability the most appropriate for the economy as a whole during the Industrial Revolution. The balance eventually swung in the favour of patentees. Sullivan (1989, p. 436) argues that part of the increased patent activity after 1830 was a response to the increased value of patent rights due to favourable treatment of patentees in the courts. Even so, in 1850 the system, according to Boehm and Silbertson (1967, p. 19), was enormously cumbersome, and involved ten stages, stages that involved obtaining the sovereign's signature twice. The Patent Law Amendment Act of 1852, which simplified the process and cheapened the price of patenting, was the outcome of the persistent lobbying by inventors in the years since 1780.

For the period 1780–1851, Dutton's instinct that an imperfect patent system approached the ideal receives the support of classical economists from Smith to Mill, the latter stating categorically that the condemnation of monopolies ought not to extend to patents. Sentiments in favour of abolishing the patent system were not entirely absent in an era that saw the end of Bank of England and East India Company monopolies in the 1830s. Machlup and Penrose (1950, p. 15), for example, cite an editorial from the *Economist* in 1850, which argues that inventors, to establish a right of property in their invention, should give up all the knowledge and inventions of others, which is impossible. Nevertheless in Europe only the Netherlands, in 1869, abolished patents, although its citizens could take out patents in foreign countries, while Switzerland did not enact patent legislation, after torturous debate, until 1888. Schiff (1971) argues that industrialization flourished in these two countries in the absence of a patent system. Whether the property rights afforded to inventors during the Industrial Revolution were a lever to technological and industrial progress is, on the basis of the historiography, unclear. Indeed, Boehm and Silbertson (1967), cite Rogers' (1863) view of the debates of a century earlier, 'that the arguments have not gone further than a *post hoc ergo propter hoc* discussion,' and express doubt there has been much subsequent advance in thinking. The reverse interpretation, that the growth of patenting after 1760 followed industrial development, does appear in the literature. Ashton (1948) postulates that the timing and the direction of Industrial Revolution patenting activity was influenced by economic conditions, including prices, costs and interest rates.

Historians remain divided on the sectoral pervasiveness of Industrial Revolution technological progress. O'Brien (1993), Harley (1993) and Crafts (1985) argue that technological progress was localized in the cotton and iron industries. Alternatively, Temin (1997) and Landes (1969) see the Industrial Revolution as broadly based. McCloskey (1988) adopted an intermediate position, claiming that around 46 per cent of economy-wide productivity growth arose outside the 'modernized sectors.' The linkages between patents, as a measure of 'protected' inventive activity, and the disaggregate records of British industrial growth between 1780 and 1851, have the potential to inform the debates surrounding historians' conceptualizations of the Industrial Revolution. The extent, if any, to which the effects of patented inventions spilled through the industrial economy, will shed light on whether protecting inventors' property rights impinged on the economy-wide adoption of new technology. Conversely, the statistical causality tests will also show if patenting activity was stimulated by particular industrial sectors.

In a series of papers, Greasley & Oxley (1994, 1996, 1997a) use modern times-series econometric methods and macro-level real total industrial production data to identify the origins and likely 'end' of the British Industrial Revolution, dating the period as 1780–1851. Their work uses the Crafts and Harley (1992) amended version of the Hoffman (1955) data set. Using traditional Granger-type and more recent Toda and Phillips (1991) and Toda and Yamamoto (1995) methods, Greasley and Oxley (1997b) and Oxley and Greasley (1997) also consider possible causal linkages between industrial production (output) and other aggregate level data that have traditionally been identified in the economic history literature as potential candidates for 'drivers/engines of growth.' The candidates included real wages, imports, exports, population and *patents* and affected production *processes*. In that work, bi-directional causality between patents/processes (levels or growth rates) and industrial production (levels or growth rates) was identified. Their work is the only published work we know of that considers the causal relationship between British industrial production and patent activity over the period of the Industrial Revolution.

In related work, however, Sullivan (1989) assumes that because increased growth of patenting *preceded* increased growth of total factor productivity (TFP), a causal relationship can be inferred. However, he does not test for causality or, importantly, consider the effects of the non-stationary nature of the data that would affect the form of chosen causality test. Greasley and Oxley (2000) also consider the sectoral inter-relatedness of the growth of industrial output, and thus of the pervasiveness of technological progress during the Industrial Revolution period, applying co-integrating relationship methods and tests for common stochastic trends, to Hoffman's disaggregate, sector-level data. They conclude that Industrial Revolution technological progress spread widely, but unevenly. From their perspective, the productivity shocks shaping cotton and iron goods output defined the profile of early British industrialization. These two key industries shared a common stochastic trend with a wide group of mining and metal industries, and had long-run causal links to shipbuilding, paper, malt and sugar. The output trends in other important industries, notably woollens, linens, flour and bread, were isolated from the technological progress driving the cotton and iron goods industries. In Greasley and Oxley (2007), they add to the debates surrounding the pervasiveness and the forces shaping Industrial Revolution technological progress by investigating the causal links between patenting activity and industrial output at the sectoral level during the period 1780–1851. Using time-series methods applied to the Hoffman (1955) data set they consider the existence of bi-and multivariate causality between patents and 16 sectors of the British economy comprising copper, copper ore, beer, coal, iron and steel, woollens, worsted, tobacco products, tin, sugar, shipbuilding, malt, linen yarn, cotton yarn, cotton pieces and hemp products. Broadly, their results show that the rise in patented inventions after 1780 was a consequence, not a cause, of the Industrial Revolution.

Because patenting procedures did not change materially in the period to 1851, the simple implication is that the value of protecting the IP embodied in technical inventions rose sharply during the Industrial Revolution. These findings offer support to those historians, including MacLeod (1988), who argue that inventors 'rediscovered' the patent system after 1760 and learned to use it to their best effect. Before this date, inventors did not figure prominently in the debates surrounding IP, which centred largely on the rights of authors, publishers and printers. In contrast, post-1780 the engineering lobby was the most vociferous in the campaigns for patents reform and for cheaper and more certain protection of IP. Interestingly, the results show that patenting activity was associated particularly with the 'new' fast growth sectors of the Industrial Revolution, notably cotton and iron. Inventors responded to the specific opportunities of the Industrial Revolution, a result that coincides with Ashton's (1948) interpretation of the direction of patenting activity.

2. Secrecy

Secrecy is another illustration of how the particular characteristics of a technology imply which IP protection mechanism is best suited. IP used internally in a particular production process is often usefully protected using secrecy. Using data on 4,688 English innovations at the 1851 Crystal Palace Exhibition, Moser (2005) demonstrates that industries such as watchmakers relying on alternatives to patenting to protect IP (that is, utilizing secrecy), tend to be more geographically concentrated than those that do. Those industries that subsequently shift to patent protection experience a tendency to geographic diffusion. Close proximity is required to enforce secrecy and minimize 'leaks.' Similarly, in the lean (or 'just-in-time') production created in modern Japanese automobile manufacturing firms (particularly Toyota), the technological knowledge was completely internal to the firm's production activities. Even when American automobile manufacturing firms first visited Japanese plants to uncover the secrets of the Japanese success, they misunderstood the technology. The many failed experiments in robotics and complete automation of the assembly line in the United States are a testament to this.

3. First-to-the-Market

Being 'first-to-the-market' is an especially effective protection mechanism for technologies that are complementary to human capital that must be acquired by the user to extract any value from the technology. For example, computer software requires a human capital investment by the user in order to be able to generate output by using the software. In this case, being first-to-the-market means that owners of software capture large segments of the market because there is a cost for consumers to switch to any competing technology that subsequently enters the market. Technologies that require users to invest in complementary human capital in order to use them are most likely to find protection by being first-to-the-market.

4. Copyright

Historically copyright has been a relatively effective mechanism for protecting IP that is stored in a physical medium. For example, owners of IP stored in books, records, cassette tapes and CDs have been able to appropriate much of the value of their property. However, with the new technology of digitally recording music, the physical medium is no longer needed and, thus, we observe the current debate about the rights of internet web sites such as Napster in terms of violation of copyright law (see, e.g., Liebowitz & Watt, 2006 for a fuller discussion of this particular issue). There are various other mechanisms for IP protection in use today, but the above discussion is sufficient to illustrate the point that the effectiveness of the mechanism depends on the type of technology to which it is applied. This should not be surprising given what has already been said about the complementary nature of technological knowledge. *Intellectual property protection mechanisms are a kind of technological knowledge themselves that are complementary to the particular technology to which it is applied.* Given what we know about complementarities and combinatorics, it should be obvious that these complementarities will manifest in different forms just as different technologies do.

It should also be obvious that the protection mechanisms will co-evolve with technology. Furthermore, as has already been noted, some technological changes undermine existing IP protection mechanisms. In a sense, the technology of these protection mechanisms is rendered obsolete by Schumpeterian creative destruction. Just like technologies themselves, new IP protection mechanisms must be invented and in many cases the inventors of such mechanisms will be entrepreneurs trying to protect research investments and profits they perceive to be available from the opportunities present in the new technologies.

THE ROLE OF SCIENCE AND RESEARCH AND DEVELOPMENT

A further critical component of the 'great transformation' was the role of science. The adoption of a natural philosophy (rather than occasionalism) within the Christian religion brought a challenge to existing authority systems and epistemologies creating a belief in 'scientific knowledge' and exploration. The basis for this was systematic enquiry based on the new methods of science – observation, objectivity, classification, and theory development. The world could be better explained through these means and once understood would be easier to shape and control. Reason was to dominate over the belief in other forms of knowledge. Science expanded and as it did, so too did the demands on it by the growing industrial economy and society. The growth of new applied disciplines of engineering, metallurgy and mining became important and new universities based around delivering these areas of study arose – often in the new industrial cities (e.g., Manchester, Leeds and Sheffield) – and were supported by public funds and civic investment. In part, the rise of these new, more technologically focused institutions occurred because the older established institutions were less sympathetic to these new areas of knowledge. This raises a further interesting question that impinges on our interest in IP and the way ideas flow, which is, how far is growth in knowledge limited by the institutional structures that exist at the time?

In an important contribution to the understanding of how science advances, Kuhn (1962) suggested that this was through paradigm shifts. Kuhn argued that science and technology grew not through the falsification of existing paradigms, but in fact by making a move to a new paradigm. Movements in ideas therefore occurred through 'scientific revolutions' when a new paradigm overthrows an existing one – rather than paradigms being defeated through careful and systematic study. During non-revolutionary periods, 'normal' science takes place within the dominant paradigm. The work of Kuhn drew attention to the social conditions and institutional restrictions of innovation that can occur through the ways in which disciplines and areas of knowledge become dominated by powerful elites who, as the gatekeepers of knowledge, attest to the quality of work, shape the journals and decide on orthodoxy. Such systems would also strongly support a more restrictive approach to IP transfer and availability. The role of research and development is a critical component of the innovation system and one that impinges on debates around IP rights. In many countries there is substantial public investment in R&D, and this raises the issue of the new subjects and sub-disciplines within science and technology, the rise of more applied subjects and the growth of the social sciences. It also raises the issue of the ownership of knowledge created via public investment (Nelson, 1989). Knowledge, though a commodity, is different from other commodities, in that many can make use of it without degrading it. However, it can also be used to create new wealth-generating activity and thus limitations on its dissemination have attractions. The New Zealand New Economies Research Fund (NERF) is an example of where public money is available to support research, which it is hoped will have possible commercial applications that will stimulate new economic activity. In such cases the release of research results can be restricted and can therefore conflict with the right of the public to know the outcome of funded research activity.

David (2005) identifies three principal institutional devices employed by states to encourage the provision of public R&D – these are patronage, property and procurement. Patronage is where publicly financed research is awarded on the basis of a competitive process, such as the way that the NZ Foundation of Science and Technology administers the Public Good Science Fund of $460 million. Here the assumption would be that the results are in the public domain and are available for wide distribution. However since the 1990s, as the science system has increasingly been based around Crown Research Institutes (CRIs) that operate as profit making concerns and with universities also being encouraged to adopt a more business-like model, holding onto the IP by the research organization has become more attractive and significant for their overall economic performance.[14] Procurement is where the state contracts with a preferred research organization or individual and the decision as to whether or not the information is made available tends to be a decision of the contracting party rather than the researcher. This model has increasingly been adopted within the New Zealand government, especially as the public sector reforms of the 1980s led to the downsizing of the internal research capacity within departments and ministries (Pool, 1999; Thorns, 2000, 2003). Here research can be 'buried' when it is of a sensitive nature and at odds with current policy directions. Release here is often dependent on the nature of Freedom of Information legislation and Statutes of Limitation. The final arrangement is that whereby private producers of new knowledge are granted exclusive property rights that allow them to collect fees and other forms of return for the use of their knowledge. The increasing importance of information, and the new ways that this can now be accessed, sets the context for new struggles over IP rights and controls within the second period of transition that we are considering in this chapter – the 'information and knowledge revolution.'

INFORMATION/KNOWLEDGE ECONOMY/SOCIETY

So far we have considered a number of themes – that is, the role of entrepreneurship, technological knowledge creation and obsolescence; intellectual capabilities and intellectual knowledge; and the role of science and research and development – in our historical comparisons to set the scene. Up to this point we have not considered the modern meanings and origins of the period that is (currently) referred to as (variously) the information/knowledge economy/society in any systematic or rigorous way. However, if we are to critically and, importantly, fairly to address the fundamental question of whether we are any more of a knowledge society now than we were in the Neolithic, the Renaissance and the Industrial Revolution, we have to be sure that we are talking the same language of those authors we seek to review.

In this section, we will undertake a thorough critical analysis of what current authors appear to mean when they refer to the information/knowledge economy/society and what they identify as the unique characteristics of this period, with a view to ascertaining whether, based upon 'their' definitions of the beast, the world is fundamentally different.

The foreshadowing of the 'new' information/knowledge economy/society can be found in the revival and development of the economies and most of the societies of the protagonists in the Second World War built around a continuation of the pre-war pattern. The basic industries were still mining, steel production and manufacture of commodities within a 'Fordist' system of production. This system was one based around mass commodity production and strong welfare states that ensured full employment and basic social provisions such as health, education and social security (Jessop, 2000). Economic growth was assisted by the recovery required after the destruction of wartime, with strong growth in population as a result of disruptions and delays to marriage and childbirth through war. Growth in population also stimulated housing and the growth of consumer spending on household appliances and motor cars, which became an increasingly significant mode of transport. However, by the 1960s the boom times were ending and the restructuring of the industrial economies was beginning, changes that had far-reaching effects in the 1970s and 1980s. This was a time of 'deindustrialization' in the economies of North America and Western Europe (Bluestone & Harrison, 1983; Massey, 1984; Lash and Urry, 1987). Manufacturing was reduced as a component of the economies and in a number of cases shifted to cheaper labour markets in Southern Europe (e.g., Spain), Central and South America (e.g., Mexico), and into Asia (including the Asian 'tiger' economies). This began the formation of a 'new international division of labour,' and was one of the factors that stimulated the debate as to whether a new 'epochal' transformation was taking place and what the central drivers of the former industrial manufacturing economies would be (Froebel et al., 1980; Smith & Feagin, 1987; Thorns, 1992).

The idea that the industrial manufacturing society was starting to be transformed into an 'information society' was initiated by, among others, Peter Drucker (1959, 1969, 1994) and Alvin Toffler (1980) and was part of a debate about the role of information and service workers within the changing economy of the time. New areas of activity emerged and new areas of expertise were called upon to run the modern corporation. Strong growth occurred in information management, finance, marketing, and sales. Also, the expansion of the welfare systems created an expanding 'service' population engaged in government work, including education, administration, social welfare services and urban and regional planning. In many of these positions, information was a more significant requirement than it had been in the past. Analysis of the growth of 'services,' as part of a shift from a 'secondary' to a tertiary economy and workforce, was often difficult, as separating out whether the activities of service workers were new rather than an extension of previous forms of work proved very difficult due to the way that occupations were classified and recorded in national statistical databases.

By the 1970s, the understanding of the changes taking place shifted from information (which remains data without human processing of it) alone to a greater emphasis on knowledge (which is processes information embodied in human capital). However, the bulk of the shift occurred in the 1980s and 1990s at a time when the institutional environment was one of deregulation and liberalization that encouraged government to dismantle border controls and other forms of economic regulation.

Thus we see that technological and economic change has been allied with political and social change as it was in the 'great transformation.' This supports the argument that we are living through a time of far-reaching changes to the basis of societies. The key to understanding these changes is being ascribed to the place occupied by knowledge, but what exactly is this role and is it uniquely 'new?'

Central to Stehr's thesis is his argument that 'the origin, social structure and development of knowledge societies is linked first and foremost to a radical transformation to the structure of the economy' (Stehr, 1994, p. 122):

> The economy of the industrial society is initially and primarily a material economy and then changes gradually to a monetary economy … and then becomes as evident recently, a symbolic economy. (1994, p. 123)

Economists as well as sociologists have also identified knowledge as a key driver of contemporary economies. Economists, however, present a wide set of definitions/characteristics of what they believe constitutes a knowledge economy and hence its drivers. Smith (2002) summarizes succinctly the problem one faces with such attempts:

> What does it mean to speak of the 'knowledge economy' however? At the outset, it must be said that *there is no coherent definition* [emphasis added], let alone theoretical concept, of this term: it is at best a widely-used metaphor, rather than a clear concept. The OECD has spoken of knowledge-

based economies in very general terms, as meaning 'those which are directly based on the production, distribution and use of knowledge and information.' This definition is a good example of the problems of the term, for it seems to cover everything and nothing: all economies are in some way based on knowledge, but it is hard to think that any are directly based on knowledge, if that means the production and distribution of knowledge and information products. (pp. 6–7)

Economists tend to focus on the idea of knowledge-based economies (KBEs), which could be seen as a subset of the knowledge society, and limit the focus to the changed role of knowledge in economic activity. For example, the OECD (1996) defined a KBE as 'Economies which are directly based on the production, distribution and use of knowledge and information' (p. 7). In the Asia-Pacific Economic Co-operation (APEC, 2000) definition, this idea is broadened somewhat to talk about how in such an economy all sectors are being reconstituted around a higher input of 'knowledge,' but fundamentally the circularity persists.

In a series of papers, Quah (2002a, 2002b) and Coyle and Quah (2002) raise the idea of the New Economy as a *weightless economy*. This terminology is inherently 'Quah' and has not been widely adopted even though it has more concreteness than several other leading brands:

The weightless economy[15] comprises four main elements: 1. Information and communications technology (ICT), the Internet. 2. Intellectual assets: Not only patents and copyrights but also, more broadly, name brands, trademarks, advertising, financial and consulting services, and education. 3. Electronic libraries and databases: Including new media, video entertainment, and broadcasting. 4. Biotechnology: Carbon-based libraries and databases, pharmaceuticals. (Quah, 2003, p. 2)

Central to many authors' views on the New Economy is the importance of digital technologies, the internet, computers, and information and the globalized networks these technologies enable. For Talero and Gaudette (1996),

the information economy is emerging where trade and investment are global and firms compete with knowledge, networking and agility on a global basis. A corresponding new society is also emerging with pervasive information capabilities that make it substantially different from an industrial society: much more competitive, more democratic, less centralized, less stable, better able to address individual needs, and friendlier to the environment.

Where does all this take us in our understanding of what the knowledge economy is and whether it is a fundamentally different economic form as compared to past ones? All current definitions/ideas explicitly or implicitly have a central role for 'knowledge' in economic activity. We would suggest, however, that historically this is not *fundamentally* 'new.' The entrepreneurs of the Industrial Revolution used 'knowledge' to create new products. Fundamental constraints on the quantity and quality of these products during this and later industrial periods included, importantly, land, raw material and production technologies (factories and machines) governed by scarcity, rivalry and diminishing returns. However, what is 'new' now is the type of technologies that exist and interact in the current economy and society – digital technologies, built around ICTs. The issue for economists is whether these technologies create a fundamentally new technical environment where, for example, diminishing returns and inflationary tendencies are 'a thing of the past.'[16] According to Gordon (1998), this has led to the growth of the 'Goldilocks Economy:'

> Freed from the restraint of restrictive monetary policy that had choked earlier expansions, and with its fires stoked by the lowest medium-term and long-term nominal interest rates in three decades, the economy charged ahead and achieved a state of high growth-noninflationary bliss that some have dubbed the 'Goldilocks economy' (neither too hot nor too cold, but just right).

Although it is clear that economists talk of knowledge, Stehr criticizes them for not giving the role of knowledge sufficient attention in their work:

> A close examination of the literature in economics indicates, however, that the function of knowledge and information in economic activity is, for the most part, ignored by economists. Either that, or they introduce knowledge as an exogenous variable, as an expense and generally treat it as a black box. (1994, p. 123)

However, although there has been considerable recent growth in the study of knowledge, the view of Adhikari and Sales (2001, pp. 2–3) is that concepts such as the knowledge society are also incomplete and imprecise, for they are found wanting in terms of exact meaning and are of partial and sectarian relevance. McLennan (2003, p. 4) notes that in much of the literature concerning the knowledge society, there has been an absence of a sustained discussion concerning definitional issues. Others, such as Ungar (2003), argue that the idea of the knowledge society is itself a gloss, as it is frequently evoked but rarely ever defined or explored in a systematic way. Moreover, Ungar continues, it is used merely as an extension of the 'more concrete' concept of the knowledge economy. Indeed, it seems apparent that the concept of the knowledge society needs additional clarity so as to differentiate it from other, similar concepts. In the view of Knorr Cetina (cited in Adhikari & Sales, 2001, p. 15), there is a need for a sociological concept of knowledge growth that brings into focus knowledge itself, 'breaking open and specifying the processes that make up the "it."' In other words, a more sociological approach to knowledge needs to identify the social processes in which knowledge is generated and from which it is turned into a commodity.

If the term 'knowledge economy' is primarily concerned with knowledge as a commodity and the value of intellectual labour in the creation of wealth, then the term 'knowledge society' should concern the social climate in which the knowledge economy resides. In other words, the knowledge society concept should relate to the much broader social context that both motivates and mediates the development and exchange of knowledge. This point is elucidated by McLennan

(2003, p. 7), who notes that while some persistently equate the knowledge economy with the knowledge society, in actuality they are concepts that run in two different directions. McLennan notes that while the concept of the knowledge economy involves a 'strenuous reductionism,' the concept of the knowledge society generally accepts that there are broader social and cultural factors that underlie the techno-economic momentum central to the post-industrial order and that the concept acknowledges knowledge's intrinsic value beyond its worth as a commodity.[17] This conceptual position is antithetical to that of the knowledge economy conceived of merely as knowledge as an object of economic value. Knorr Cetina and Preda (2001, p. 30) refer to this an as exteriorized perspective of knowledge, whereby knowledge viewed as a commodity is regarded merely as a product or a research finding. Such an approach to knowledge growth overlooks social and cultural factors, which may be pertinent to how knowledge is generated and valued. This, on the other hand, appears to be what the concept of the knowledge society is attempting to address. Rather than viewing knowledge growth in purely reductionist terms, the concept of the knowledge society acknowledges that there are social and cultural factors that may influence knowledge growth at any point of time. As Thorlindsson and Vilhjalmsson (2003, p. 99) note, although the concept of the knowledge society is not yet well developed, it generally acknowledges that while science, innovation and expertise are the moving forces of economic development, social forces may intervene at any stage. This often relates to issues of power – conferring it on those who own knowledge and those involved in the politics of knowledge-exchange.

In the discussion of the current 'transformation of capitalism' knowledge is viewed as a key driver of production. Typical of this view is that:

> Capitalism is undergoing a transformation from a mass production system, where the principal source of value was human labour to a new era of innovation mediated production, where the principal component of value creation productivity and economic growth is knowledge. (Houghton & Sheehan, 2003, p. 2)

The key element in the transformative properties of the knowledge society is identified as 'information,' and here the major factor has been the ICT revolution and, in particular, the growth of the internet and more recently digitization. This makes the access to information easier and quicker, extends its global reach and makes it considerably harder to control. For all these reasons, Castells (2000a) has suggested that:

> What is new in our age is a new set of information technologies. I contend they represent a greater change in the history of technology than the technologies associated with the Industrial Revolution, or with previous Information Revolution (printing). (p. 10)

Castells has further suggested that the internet is the 'electricity of the information age' (2001, 2004). There has been a phenomenal increase in the expansion of the internet within a very short space of time. In 1989 there were 159,000 internet hosts and this had grown to 43 million by 2000 (Houghton & Sheehan, 2003, p. 2).[18] However, one must not ignore the fact that there have also been massive gains in computational capacity through Complementary Metal Oxide Semiconductor (CMOS) logic design. This has been far more rapid and for a much longer period of time than the expansion of the internet. Some would argue that the expansion of the internet would not have been possible without the efficiency advances of microchips. What the IT revolution has brought about is the ability to manipulate, store and transmit large quantities of information at very low cost (Houghton and Sheehan, 2003). ICT and digital technology through the power of the modern computer and the next generation of high-speed computers – with storage in terabytes rather than gigabytes – have created new possibilities in the storage, surveillance, linking and processing of data sets that previously were unconnected. This extends possibilities from the tracking of criminals and terrorists across the globe, to profiling markets for products by small geographical areas (Geographic Information Systems [GIS] and other applications) to tracing benefit frauds (Lyon, 2003). New networking opportunities are created through this enhanced connectivity that generates new forms of knowledge and leads to a whole range of new economic activities associated with the creation, storage and retrieval of information.

The new computer and digital technologies have started to transform the way that work gets done across all sectors, but particularly within the 'knowledge generating' areas of science and technology. We can see here the growing impact in the last decade of e-Science and e-Social Science based on collaborations built around shared information transmitted via the new fibre optic superhighways and satellites – creating a much more globally connected world. These transformations are at least partially attributable to particular characteristics of the technology, namely, the sending and receiving capabilities of communication at a very large number of dispersed nodes, generating both a network externality and the non-rivalrous nature of the commodity being exchanged, namely, *information*. This stimulates the demand for new software products and creates new networks, information clusters and incubators that have become key nodes of innovation. The managing of these new information systems has led to knowledge management becoming a critical area of contemporary business development and practice.

We need here to distinguish between the data – which are the units recorded, information which is processed data – and knowledge which is what can be created from the information. What this indicates is that in 'knowledge societies' some would argue that we have a new principle, 'knowledge,' that creates a new source of added value. This leads into the wider debate that has emerged about different forms of capital. Bourdieu (1986) has extended our understanding of capital to include symbolic and cultural capital, and subsequently social capital has also been distinguished (Putnam, 2000; Cunningham, 2005; Pillay, 2005; Marinova & Raven, 2006).

Human capital in knowledge societies has also been reinterpreted and seen to be of increased importance. Knowledge is now a commodity to exchange and for creating new wealth-generating opportunities; thus, those with desired 'human capital' and access to 'social capital' become sought after. Bell (1973) sees this shift leading to the end of the industrial working class and its gradual replacement by a post-industrial proletariat consisting of poorly unionized, part time, casual workers. Such a core-periphery pattern of employment creates new patterns of social inequalities with the new 'knowledge' class as one of its significant components. Such a class is global in its importance and it significantly increases the value of and need for new skills and capabilities that in turn has altered the way education is thought of and delivered. Drucker (1969) drew attention to the importance of teamwork in a knowledge society, and he drew a distinction between people who work with their hands and people who worked with their minds. Increasingly in the knowledge society, he argues, the dominant class of people is likely to be those who work with their minds.

Contemporary society is coming to *depend more and more* on knowledge in economic production, political regulation and everyday life (Stehr, 1994; Castells, 1997). With the spread of knowledge and the demonstrated loss of scientific legitimacy through a growing realization that there are many areas where there is still limited understanding, a greater questioning and scepticism towards experts is becoming more prevalent. This is part of the wider post-modern critique of the enlightenment scientific paradigm and a move away from meta-narratives and linear theories that embrace a greater range of understandings about how social change takes place. Many now see path-dependent and complexity theories providing greater insights into change than more determinist approaches, either technologically driven explanations or ones that assumed a linear pathway such as forms of modernization theory (Urry, 2003; Law & Urry, 2004). The idea of the knowledge society is not a new form of technological determinism, but rather a new argument about 'elective affinity' (i.e., connections between beliefs, actions, and the unintended consequences of action). Social actors have greater capacities for self-interpretation and action than have been acknowledged in past theories of change (Giddens, 2001). For Castells, 'the information technology revolution did not create the network society. But without information technology, the Network Society would not exist' (Castells, 2000a, p. 139). It is suggested that in a knowledge society the wealth of a company is increasingly embodied in its creativity and information. The place of the creative industries cannot be relegated to a footnote, but now it needs to be seen as an integral component of the 'knowledge'-based industries (O' Brien et al., 2002).

Alongside these views that information technology has generated new social and economic conditions – thus creating a social transformation – are a range of sceptics who consider that there is insufficient evidence for such an assertion (May, 2002). Much of this critique turns on the view that the argument is based on technological determinism through the assertion that 'technological changes bring in their wake major shifts in societies which use them' (May, 2002, p. 24). Bimber (1995) draws attention to three strands of technological determinism: the normative, the nomological and the unintended. Most accounts of the shift to the information society stress the first two rather than the unintended as they are stressing the positive move towards a new social and economic organization of knowledge and practice of accumulation. Sociological work adopting less determinist views has stressed continuity rather than rupture; thus the information 'revolution' becomes part of the continuing development and utilization of technologies to change the ways that we do things both intentionally and unintentionally (Mumford, 1966; May, 2002). This suggests that we should adopt an approach to the 'knowledge society and economy' that sees it as part of a continuingly evolving history of connection between specific national and international contexts, technological innovations and economic, social, political and cultural opportunities that either facilitate or resist innovation and change.

The other strong link that has been made is between the knowledge society and globalization. The definition of globalization, rather like the knowledge society, is subject to controversy (Scholte, 2000; Holton, 2005). There is some agreement that what we are now seeing is a much greater connectedness across the globe created by the possibilities arising from the IT revolution. This compresses time and space and enables new ways of working, drawing upon globally connected workers. This makes national boundaries and forms of control much more difficult and potentially creates challenges to local and national cultures through the penetration of globalized entertainment, information, ideas and practices. Global communication through a range of new media has now become accessible and available as never before. Competitiveness is now occurring within a global environment that emphasizes free trade and weaker national borders, allowing for the freer flow of capital and labour. A greater importance is attached to flexibility in labour markets, a flexibility that brings an end to stable employment and the predictability of career paths. Growing inequality at both the global and local levels has resulted, with a growing gap between rich and poor at the national and individual levels.

INTELLECTUAL PROPERTY IN THE KNOWLEDGE SOCIETY

One of the major themes that runs through the current literature on the knowledge economy/society is the role of innovation created via human capital with '*a greater reliance on intellectual capabilities*' in production and consumption. These issues are increasingly seen by some as the 'fuel' of the New Economy, with the internet, *enabled by electricity*, as the 'energy/motive power.' In this section we will focus upon the role of IP in modern societies, an area that is typically ignored or subsumed in simple *economy*-based discussions. For advanced societies a greater emphasis appears to be placed upon a culture of innovation and a focus on how this can be generated. The power of the internet and the connectivity that it allows poses new threats to the control of IP and for some raises an issue as to whether it is still possible to protect the flow of information at all. Computer systems are vulnerable to security breaches, and ensuring the security of such systems has become a significant growth industry in itself as web-based activity extends into all aspects of life – from work to shopping, banking, recreational and leisure activities, including gambling and downloading music and video MP3 files onto iPods (see, e.g., Liebowitz & Watt, 2006).

The speed of innovation also raises further questions with respect to the protection of IP in the contemporary environment in which, in some areas, with the current speed of diffusion, the shelf life of new products may be only a matter of months. Computer systems and software are subject to frequent upgrades and changes, making it potentially a 'greedy technology' that constantly demands investment to keep it 'current.'

The importance of networks and clusters within the new environment has led to the creation of new territorial and virtual clusters of innovation as with, for example, Silicon Valley in California and Manhattan's Silicon Alley (see Graham, 2004). Knowledge can now thus be created in 'virtual' research communities that can gain intellectual capital through the participation of cross-national teams working through computer-based collaborative technologies. Such innovations have led to new linkages between universities and commercial enterprises looking to make use of new knowledge areas such as genetics and genetic engineering, biotechnology and nanotechnology. Universities now operate in the new 'enterprise and business environment' in which they are also interested in the commercialization of the IP of their researchers (see Verspagen, 2006). This raises questions as to who owns the IP created (Delanty, 2001). Digital access, broadband and internet connectivity become the key aspects of inclusion in the new knowledge-creating activities and thus become of increased importance. Being part of the 'advanced networks' that allow for fast and extended linkages across national systems and globally are now seen as keys to research and development and maintaining global competitiveness. For example, the NZ government's decisions to invest in the Advanced Network Group Ltd. providing gigabytes of connectivity across universities and CRIs was stimulated by the desire to keep the New Zealand R&D sector globally competitive. Similar networks are now present in 40 other countries, so the absence within New Zealand creates problems for our scientists – the Advanced Network Group Ltd. will 'ensure our scientists are able to catch up with their partners and participate in the exciting world of modern science' (Jarvie, 2005, p. 2). However, there is still a digital divide with the levels of connectivity across and within nations differing that creates a new set of inequalities, as noted in a recent United Nations Centre on Human Settlement (UNCHS) report that talks about

> Enclaves of 'super connected' people, firms and institutions, with their increasingly broadband connections to elsewhere via the internet, mobile phones and satellite TVs and their easy access to information services, often cheek by jowl with much larger numbers of people with at most rudimentary access to modern communications technologies and electronic information. (UNCHS, 2001, p. 6)

The OECD countries have the highest rates of telephone and mobile phone subscribers and internet and broadband connections and, as with many other forms of technology, those with the lowest incomes, globally and locally, have the most restricted access to the benefits of the technology (UNCHS, 2001).

Sociologists have typically focused on the issues associated with power and the limitation of access and the reasons why material might be withheld. Do such restrictions assist in maintaining the power and position of the dominant sectors within society and thus contribute to the maintenance or creation of social inequalities? Information on the new superhighway of the internet is mostly public and therefore freely available as long as the potential user is connected. Although the originators of the internet such as ARPANET shared information among their users, open source software was central for the development of the internet open to a more general public, facilitating open interchange and reducing restrictions on access to information. Acknowledging the power issues is crucial to a sociological understanding of the role of knowledge in society and therefore to the understanding of IP. The concept of IP refers to a number of protections for human creations including patents, trademarks and copyrights (amongst others).

In the shift to a knowledge-based economy, whereby ideas gain economic value, it is believed that the existence of intellectual property rights (IPRs) is absolutely vital in order to prevent others from producing and selling copies of your own ideas (Kenny, 1996, p. 701). Owing to their abstract nature, intellectual technologies are difficult to control and may 'escape' the clutches of their creators to become public goods, to be used and manipulated by others (Kenny, 1996, p. 702). Acknowledging this, it is apparent that assigning IPRs is an exercise in knowledge management aimed at restricting the accessibility of knowledge in order to preserve or enhance its value as a commodity; or in Fuller's words (2001, p. 188), with the assignment of IPRs, knowledge is 'captured' and then delivered as a service. IPRs, in this case, are directly concerned with the privatization of knowledge for monetary gain.

Globally there is a significant digital divide with levels of connectivity that are very different across nations and within nations (Mansell, Samarajiva, & Mahan 2002). One of the changes to IP under the knowledge society is that knowledge has itself increasingly become a commodity, a product that can be traded. The ideas as well as the people creating them are valuable. The cost of excluding people from information can also be high as it can limit innovation or can result in the appropriation of information by the few. The shift to greater emphasis upon ideas and their creators increases the value of the well-educated and trained section of the population, giving rise to 'brain drains and brain gains.' The declining and ageing of the intellectual workforce in the European economies is one of the growing pressures facilitating migration of innovative and highly qualified and trained people from the less developed countries. This has implications for the digital and other aspects of the knowledge divide and is one factor in the continuing inequalities between the wealthier and poorer nations.

One of the key differences 'knowledge as a commodity' has with other commodities is that it is not reduced by use; rather, there is evidence that it is a collective product that is enhanced by many users. This raises a further challenge to determining IP as many of the 'innovations' and 'inventions' within a knowledge society are the products of large international, multidisciplinary teams; thus, ascribing IP to individuals becomes increasingly difficult. Research and development funding has also had to adjust to these new times and there has been a move towards longer funding cycles and a greater emphasis on inter-and multi-disciplinarity that crosses not only the boundaries of the traditional sciences but also recognizes the contribution of the social science and humanities.

The forms of protection include both statutory systems of protection such as patents from the fifteenth century and, later, copyright, trademark and design protection. The new global environment has focused attention increasingly on international agreements as a new way of trying to enforce IP protection. Examples here are the passing of a directive on the legal protection of databases by the European Union (EU) in 1996. Since then the EU has continued to work for a treaty on this issue. The World Intellectual Property Organization (WIPO) currently administers 23 treaties on intellectual property and WTO members are required to abide by the standards set out in the agreement on the Trade-Related Aspects of Intellectual Property Rights (TRIPS) (David, 2005; Drahos, 2005). These various agreements and statutes have given rise to the growth of national and international bureaucracies and forms of administration. In all these contemporary debates we can see the interconnection of economic, legal and political arguments and decision-making surrounding the need for and ways to control the flow of ideas.

The globalization of IP protection has largely benefited the advanced economies, particularly the United States and the European Union. Such protections are part of the ways that these countries and the corporations based in them (but operating globally) seek to maintain their dominance. Here the increased prominence of transnational companies – many of which have greater annual revenue than the annual GDP of many nation states – as key global players is increasingly significant (Held, 2000). The awareness of the value of IP amongst developing countries and indigenous peoples has also stimulated attention to the protection of such IP from the activities of global corporations. An example here would be the recent UNESCO convention on cultural indigenous knowledge protection (see Marinova & Raven, 2006). Some of these attempts at protection, however, come up against WTO free trade agendas and the desire of the advanced countries to include trade in services and ideas. Interestingly, the development of the internet, especially in its earliest stages, was not through commercial imperatives, but more as a result of the work of researchers and enthusiasts exploring the possibilities of a new form of communication. The ethos of this group was about openness, hence the open source nature of much of the internet. It is interesting to note that high-tech developments in ICT have occurred largely in the absence of IP protections.

As David (2005) notes, there has also been a long-running moral argument about the accessibility of information. Advocates for the openness of government and commercial activity to public scrutiny suggest this is best achieved by the free flow of information and the encouragement of debate on social improvement. Those who support a more open system of exchange generally favour a move towards a greater balance between the interests of the IP holders and users. Drahos argues that:

The current problem facing knowledge economies is that their law-making processes have been heavily influenced by owners of intellectual property. As a result the rights of owners have strengthened. (2005, p. 149)

Thus, the debate about openness and free dispersal of knowledge versus restriction and exclusivity is not new. In recent times, however, international law has focused on strengthening exclusivity of IP rights rather than making knowledge more accessible, as with, for example, the American Digital Millennium Copyright Act (DMCA) (1998). Prosecuting and policing the increasingly borderless transmission of information is proving difficult. The solution that is being sought is the harmonization of IP rights laws. However, this is likely to provide the greatest advantage to the developed countries. Alternatively the rights and participation of users could be strengthened, creating a more even contest around the access to and use of knowledge. Increasing knowledge becomes the key resource for future economic growth. As a consequence, the struggle over IPRs will intensify, making it even more important that we undertake robust analysis of whether IP protection facilitates or restricts the flow of new innovations and creative activities in twenty-first century societies.

CONCLUSIONS

The concepts of knowledge society and economy are clearly related as both leverage off the idea of transformation to create fundamentally different features of society and economy. Both see information as having a special and significantly different place. Speed and forms of storage and transmission emerge as key elements in its newness. Information as a central driver of production requires new forms of organization favouring the more flexible and responsive idea of networks rather than institutional structures. Thus we see a new form of society emerging, one characterized as a 'network' society, where flows and movement and less certainty are characteristic. Forms of explanation have shifted from linear causality to a greater appreciation of path dependency and complexity. Combinations of technologies and social and cultural practices mediated by local and global political relations are now part of what has to be considered to explain the growth of new forms of technological and economic activity. This favours explanations that explore the past as a way of understanding the present. It requires a sustained empirical analysis, one deeper than is seen in much of the debate about either the knowledge society, knowledge economy or information society. There are substantial challenges facing work in this area. These are at both the theoretical and methodological level. A more consistent set of definitions is required and more robust measures are derived from the theory rather than from what is currently or conveniently available. For an economist the question has been: is the 'knowledge economy' a *fundamentally* new economic paradigm, with new drivers, or is it just '*hype?*' Whereas sociologists have asked: is the 'knowledge society' fundamentally different from what preceded it? The first issue we face is one of potentially viewing a *process* rather than an *outcome*. The period of the 'great transformation' has occurred and although one might debate the relative importance of patents as a cause or effect of the Industrial Revolution, in the absence of new evidence the historical events have occurred. For those studying the 'knowledge society,' the twin problems of definitional limitations and potential lack of a complete historical lens complicate analysis. We may simply conclude that 'the world is no different than the past' simply because change is incomplete.

Assuming, for the moment, that we can resolve the definitional issues of what constitutes the knowledge economy or the knowledge society and what set of changes is 'fundamental,' what evidence could we call upon to test such hypotheses, in particular the role and consequences of innovation, IP, its creation and protection?

Innovative entrepreneurship operating in a world of uncertainty, where profit seeking innovation creation leads to new product creation with and from new technologies, where IP has an important role to play, could equally describe the Industrial Revolution or the Information Revolution. The technologies differ and the relative mix of land, labour, capital and knowledge differs, but the general paradigm has explanatory power. The historical forms of IP protection remain in place although the mix of users differs. It is interesting to note that one of the simplest and less formal – secrecy, with resultant geographic proximity – has made a comeback when faced with the challenges of protecting digital goods. New challenges for IP protection arise with the rise of 'digital goods,' but this technology generated the need for a technologically new IP protection system that is not, in itself, new. The actual goods produced differ, the *relative* role of knowledge-led produced goods differs; but is the economic world *fundamentally* different?

What has the weightless economy done to workers, firms, ownership and control? The traditional neoclassical theory of the firm (Grossman, Hart, Moore) puts ownership of physical capital to the fore. Do we have a robust theory of the firm in a knowledge economy? We would suggest not. Fully rejecting the notion that the knowledge economy represents a fundamentally new economic paradigm where the 'old rules' do not apply must await a traditional theory of the firm explanation of knowledge-only-driven, weightless goods production.

In the old economy, reading, writing and the access to books was what divided the 'haves' from the 'have-nots.' Those with these basic skills were identifiably different from those without. Here access to a knowledge base of trusted information was potentially 'exclusive' – the knowledge was typically expensive to acquire (books or education), but the knowledge itself was 'trustworthy.' The modern analogy is access to the internet and ICTs more generally. The 'digital divide' is in part about access and acquisition of information, much as it always was. However, the added dimension, above simple access, is about the trustworthiness of the available information. Information is cheap to acquire, but the trustworthiness of its content is low. As in the past, information remains data without the human capital ('wisdom') to create knowledge from combination. Reputation of the provider acts as a screen, with the role of trademarks and brands coming to the fore as they have in the past.

Digital technologies and new forms of connectedness are creating fundamental societal transformations in work, leisure and other relationships across a whole range of aspects of life. Here speed and availability via computers, internet and cellular technologies are potentially transformative, opening up new ways of knowing and choosing and organizing aspects of life from shopping, to travel, to working practices to dating, gambling and selecting and listening to music on the iPod. The technologies in their broadest sense also create new means of sifting and sorting populations, from the web-based 'Up My Street' systems in the United Kingdom to the marketers' databases on tastes and preferences to police and social welfare databases on where at-risk populations are concentrated (Burrows and Ellison, 2004). The new technologies of storage and retrieval also raise issues around protection and authentication of material; we now have the Wiki encyclopaedia, alongside more established ones, claiming its place as a repository of knowledge. Such sources create new challenges to the establishment of authenticity and accuracy of the text. The growth of more 'open source' ways of discovery also poses challenges to established gatekeepers of knowledge and have been seen to open the way to more democratic practices of knowledge dissemination and use. However, will these constrain innovation by undermining its commercial value or enhance it? This is the old debate in the new clothes of the twenty-first century digital and internet world. To move forward, we need a clear understanding of the key elements of change in past transformations to guide us in determining the present and possible future transformations. In finding a way forward it is important to acknowledge both the continuities and discontinuities with the past and to further see how technological innovations and economic, social, political and cultural opportunities both facilitate or resist innovation and change.

ACKNOWLEDGEMENT

The authors acknowledge funding from the New Zealand Marsden Fund for the research that contributed to this chapter.

NOTES

[1] One might argue with this terminology of 'great transformation' in that it may have been no 'greater' than the move to settled agriculture in Neolithic times or the transformation that ensued with the invention of writing.

[2] Again, one might challenge this rather contrived demarcation of history if we identify the creation of writing and the printing press as the 'first information society.'

[3] Lipsey et al. (2005) argue that the evolution of technological knowledge has driven economic growth and social transformation since at least the Neolithic agricultural revolution.

[4] However, there is a body of literature that would argue that the lowest classes of serfs and roaming labour were far better off in industrial working activities than they were in the feudal agricultural system.

[5] 'When a man's wages went up in the eighteenth century the first beneficial effects might be expected to occur in the brewing industry, and in the commercialisation of sport and leisure ... gambling, boxing, horse racing and the like. When a woman's wages went up the first commercial

effects would be expected in the clothing industries, which provided consumer goods for the home. Her increased earnings released her desire to compete with her social superiors – a desire pent up for centuries or at least restricted to a very occasional excess' (McKendrick, 1974).

[6] In 1767, Steuart wrote: 'workers that had once been forced to work out of poverty or coercion ... now men are forced to labour because they are the slaves to their own wants' (Steuart, 1966).

[7] Other engines of technological change include basic science, public and to some extent privately funded research.

[8] Though much was state sponsored.

[9] Here technological innovation is being used more broadly than simply 'physical' technologies (see Lipsey et al., 2005).

[10] One could also argue that this shows the importance of the political process linked ultimately to the development of the nation-state.

[11] Knowledge is non-rivalrous in the sense that one individual's use of knowledge does not preclude another's use of the same knowledge in the same way that one person's consumption of a loaf of bread precludes another's consumption of the same loaf of bread.

[12] This assumes that economic and social objectives are themselves aligned – a heroic assumption.

[13] Intellectual property laws and patents are synonymous in these earlier periods, but this is certainly not the case today when IP is protected via a range of other legal means.

[14] See Verspagen (2006).

[15] The 'weightless economy,' as compared with the label 'weighty economy' of the industrial era.

[16] The view of Lipsey et al. (2005) is that it is the ongoing creation of new technologies that frees us from diminishing returns and not any specific technology in any period of time. ICTs may be a sufficient technology to achieve this at this point in time, but it is not necessary in the light of other new GPTs that might arrive.

[17] However, it is easy to conceive of the knowledge economy as simply being encompassed, or nested within, the concept of the knowledge society.

[18] Between 2000 to 2011, internet usage worldwide has grown 480.4 per cent (Internet World Stats, 2011).

REFERENCES

Abramovitz, M. & David, P.A. (2001, August). *Two centuries of American macroeconomic growth: From exploitation of resource abundance to knowledge-driven development*. SIEPR discussion paper, 01-05. Stanford: Stanford Institute for Economic Policy Research.

Adhikari, K. & Sales, A. (2001). Introduction: New directions in the study of knowledge, economy and society. *Current Sociology, 49*(4), 1–25.

Amin, A. (Ed.). (1994). *Post-Fordism: A reader*. Oxford: Blackwell.

Ashton, T.S. (1948). Some statistics of the industrial revolution in Britain. *Manchester School, 16*, 214–223.

Ashton, T.S. (1955). *An economic history of England*. London: Meuthen.

Asia-Pacific Economic Cooperation (APEC). (2000, November). *Towards knowledge-based economies in APEC*. Singapore: APEC.

Bell, D. (1973). *The coming of post industrial society*. New York: Basic Books.

Bimber, B. (1995). Three faces of technological determinism. In Smith, M.R. & Marx, L. (Eds.), *Does technology drive history: The dilemma of technological determinism* (pp. 79–100). Cambridge, MA: MIT Press.

Block, F. (1985). Postindustrial development and the obsolescence of economic categories. *Politics and Society, 14*, 71–104, 416–441.

Bluestone, B. & Harrison, B. (1983). *The deindustrialisation of America*. New York: Basic Books.

Boehm, K. & Silberstson, A. (1967). *The British patent system*. Cambridge: Cambridge University Press.

Bohme, G. & Stehr, N. (Eds.). (1986). *The knowledge society.* Dordrecht: Reidel.

Bourdieu, P. (1986). The forms of capital. In Richardson, J.G. (Ed.), *Handbook of theory and research for the sociology of education* (pp. 241–258). New York: Greenwood.

Braverman, H. (1975). *Labor and monopoly capital: The degradation of work in the twentieth century.* New York: Monthly Review.

Brint, S. (2001). Professionals and the 'knowledge economy': Rethinking the theory of postindustrial society. *Current Sociology, 49*(4), 101–132.

Browne, F. (2000). Discussing the papers of Gordon and Felderer. Oesterreichische Nationalbank. Volkswirtschaftliche Tagung 2000. *Das neue Millennium: Zeit für ein neues ökonomisches Paradigma?* OeNB, 28.

Burrows, R. & Ellison, N. (2004, March). *Towards a social politics of neighbourhood informatization.* Paper presented to the British Sociological Association Conference (BSAC). University of York.

Castells, M. (1996). *The rise of the network society* (Vol. 1: The information age). Oxford: Blackwell.

Castells, M. (1997). *The power of identity.* Oxford: Blackwell.

Castells, M. (2000a). Material for an exploratory theory of the network society. *British Journal of Sociology, 51*(1), 5–24.

Castells, M. (2000b). The contours of the network society. *Foresight: The Journal of Futures Studies, Strategic Thinking and Policy, 2*(2), 151–157.

Castells, M. (2001). *The internet galaxy.* Oxford: Oxford University Press.

Castells, M. (2004). *The network society: A cross cultural perspective.* Northampton, MA: Edward Elgar.

Choi, S.Y. & Whinston, A.B. (2000). *The internet economy: Technology and practice.* Austin, TX: SmartEcon.

Council of Economic Advisors (CEA) (2002). *Economic report to the president 2002.* Washington, DC: US Government Printing Office.

Coyle, D. & Quah, D. (2002). *Getting the measure of the new economy.* London: ISociety.

Crafts, N.F.R. (1985). *British economic growth during the industrial revolution.* Oxford: Oxford University Press.

Crafts, N.F.R. & Harley, C.K. (1992). Output growth and the British industrial revolution. *Economic History Review, 45*, 703–730.

Cunningham, S. (2005). Knowledge and cultural capital. In Rooney, D., Hearn, G., & Ninan, A. (Eds.), *Handbook on the knowledge economy* (pp. 93–101). Northampton, MA: Edward Elgar.

Danabalan, D.V. (1999, November). *Knowledge economy and knowledge society: Challenge and opportunities for human resource management.* Paper presented at the Workshop on Human Resource Management organised by the Public Service Department, Malaysia, in co-operation with the Commonwealth Secretariat Langkai.

David, P. (2005). Does the new economy need all the old IPR institutions and more? In Soete, L. & ter Weel, B. (Eds.), *The economics of the digital society* (pp. 113–151). Northampton, MA: Edward Elgar.

David, P. & Foray, D. (2002). Economic fundamentals of the knowledge society. *Policy Futures in Education, 1*(1), 20–49.

Delanty, G. (2001). *Challenging knowledge: The university in the knowledge society.* Philadelphia: Open University Press.

Drahos, P. (2005). Intellectual property rights in the knowledge economy. In Rooney, D., Hearn, G., & Ninan, A. (Eds.), *Handbook on the knowledge economy* (pp. 139–151). Northampton, MA: Edward Elgar.

Drucker, P. (1959). *Landmarks of tomorrow.* London: Heineman.

Drucker, P. (1969). *The age of discontinuity: Guidelines to our changing society.* London: Heineman.

Drucker, P. (1994). The age of social transformation. *Atlantic Monthly, 174*, 53–80.

Dutton, H.I. (1984). *The patent system and inventive activity during the industrial revolution.* Oxford: Oxford University Press.

Elmeskov, J. (2000). New sources of economic growth in Europe? Oesterreichische Nationalbank. Volkswirtschaftliche Tagung 2000. *Das neue Millennium: Zeit für ein neues ökonomisches Paradigma?* OeNB, 28.

Enterprise Development, The. (2005). Web site. The knowledge economy. Retrieved from www.enterweb.org/know.htm.

European Commission (EC). (2000). *European competitiveness report 2000*. Luxembourg: EC.

European Commission (EC). (2001). *European competitiveness report 2001*. Luxembourg: EC.

Foray, D. (2004). *The economics of knowledge*. Cambridge: Cambridge University Press.

Foss, N.J. (2002). Economic organization in the knowledge economy: An Austrian perspective. In Foss, N.J. & Klein, P.G. (Eds.), *Entrepreneurism and the firm: Austrian perspectives on economic organization* (pp. 48–71). Cheltenham: Edward Elgar.

Foss, N.J. (2005). *Strategy, economic organization, and the knowledge economy: The co-ordination of firms and resources*. Oxford: Oxford University Press.

Froebel, F., Heinrichs, J., & Kreye, D. (1980). *The new international division of labour*. Cambridge: Cambridge University Press.

Fuller, S. (2001). A critical guide to knowledge society newspeak: Or, how not to take the great leap backward. *Current Sociology, 49*(4), 177–201.

Fox, H.G. (1947). *Monopolies and patents*. Toronto: University of Toronto Press.

Giddens, A. (1982). Sociology: A brief but critical introduction. London: Macmillan.

Giddens, A. (2001). *The global third way debate*. Cambridge: Polity.

Gordon, R.J. (1998). Foundations of the Goldilocks economy: Supply shocks and time-varying NAIRU. *Brookings Papers on Economic Activity, 2*, 21–40.

Gordon, R. (2000). Does the new economy measure up to the great inventions of the past? *Journal of Economic Perspectives, 14*(4), 49–74.

Graham, S. (Ed.). (2004). *The cybercities reader*. London: Routledge.

Greasley, D. & Oxley, L. (1994). Rehabilitation sustained: The industrial revolution as a macroeconomic epoch. *Economic History Review, 47*, 760–768.

Greasley, D. & Oxley, L. (1996). Technological epochs and British industrial production, 1700–1992. *Scottish Journal of Political Economy, 43*, 258–274.

Greasley, D. & Oxley, L. (1997a). Endogenous growth or big bang: Two views of the first industrial revolution. *Journal of Economic History, 57*, 935–949.

Greasley, D. & Oxley, L. (1997b). Causality and the first industrial revolution. *Industrial and Corporate Change, 7*, 33–47.

Greasley, D. & Oxley, L. (2000). British industrialization 1816–1860: A disaggregate time series perspective. *Explorations in Economic History, 37*, 98–119.

Greasley, D. & Oxley, L. (2007). Patenting, intellectual property rights and sectoral outputs in Industrial Revolution Britain, 1780–1851. *Journal of Econometrics, 139*, 340–354.

Harley, C.K. (1993). Reassessing the industrial revolution: A macro view. In Mokyr, J. (Ed.), *The British industrial revolution: An economic perspective* (pp. 171–226). Boulder, CO: Westview.

Harris, R. (2001). The knowledge-based economy: Intellectual origins and new economic perspectives. *International Journal of Management Reviews, 3*(1), 21–40.

Held, D. (2000) A globalizing world? *Culture, economics, politics*. London: Routledge.

Hirst, P. & Thompson, G. (1996). *Globalization in question*. Cambridge: Polity.

Hobsbawm, E. (1975). *Age of capital*. London: Weidenfeld and Nicholson.

Hoffmann, W.H. (1955). *British industry 1700–1950*. Oxford: Blackwell.

Holton, R. (2005). *Making globalization*. Basingstoke: Palgrave Macmillan.

Houghton, J. & Sheehan, P. (2003). *A primer in the knowledge economy*. Melbourne: Centre for Strategic Economic Studies, Victoria University of Technology.

Internet World Stats. (2011). World internet usage and population statistics: March 31, 2011. Retrieved from www.internetworldstats.com/stats.htm.

Ittner, C.D., Lambert, R.A., & Larcker, D.F. (2003). The structure and performance consequences of equity grants to employees of new economy firms. *Journal of Accounting and Economics, 34*, 89–127.

Jarvie, C. (2005). *The advanced network*. Wellington: Ministry of Science and Technology.

Jessop, B. (2000). The state and the contradictions of the knowledge-driven economy. In Bryson, J.R., Henry, N.D., & Pollard, J. (Eds.), *Knowledge, space, economy* (pp. 63–78). London: Routledge.

Kenny, M. (1996). The role of information, knowledge and value in the late 20th century. *Futures, 28*(8), 696–707.

Kling, R. & Lamb, R. (2000). IT and organizational change in digital economies: A sociotechnical approach. In Brynjolfsson, E. & Kahin, B. (Eds.), *Understanding the digital economy: Data, tools, and research*. Cambridge, MA: MIT Press.

Knorr Cetina, K. (1999). *Epistemic cultures: How the sciences make knowledge*. Cambridge, MA: Harvard University Press.

Knorr Cetina, K. & Preda, A. (2001). The epistemization of economic transactions. *Current Sociology, 49*(4), 27–44.

Kuhn, T. (1962). *The structure of scientific revolutions*. Chicago: University of Chicago Press.

Landes, D.S. (1969). *Prometheus unbound*. Cambridge: Cambridge University Press.

Lane, R.E. (1966). The decline of politics and ideology in a knowledge society. *American Sociological Review, 31*, 649–662.

Lash, S. & Urry, J. (1987). *The end of organised capitalism*. Oxford: Polity Press.

Law, S. & Urry, J. (2004). Enacting the social. *Economy and Society, 33*(1), 390–410.

Leadbeater, C. (1999). *Living on thin air: The new economy*. Harmondsworth: Penguin.

Liebowitz, S. & Watt, R. (2006). How to best ensure remuneration from creators in the market for music. *Journal of Economic Surveys, 20*: 513–545.

Lipsey, R.G. & Carlaw, K.I. (2000). Technology policy: Basic concepts. In Edquist, C. & McKelvey, M. (Eds.), *Systems of innovation: Growth, competitiveness and employment* (pp. 421–455). Northampton, MA: Edward Elgar.

Lipsey, R.G., Carlaw, K.I., & Bekar, C. (2005). *Economic transformations: General purpose technologies and long term economic growth*. Oxford: Oxford University Press.

Lyon, D. (2003). *Surveillance after September 11*. Cambridge: Polity.

Machlup, F. & Penrose, E. (1950). The patent controversy in the nineteenth century. *Journal of Economic History, 10*, 1–29.

MacLeod, C. (1988). *Inventing the industrial revolution*. Cambridge: Cambridge University Press.

Makarov, V. (2004). The knowledge economy: Lessons for Russia. *Social Sciences, 35*(1), 19–30.

Mansell, R., Samarajiva, R. & Mahan, A. (2002). *Networking knowledge for information societies: Institutions and intervention*. Delft, the Netherlands: Delft University Press.

Marginson, S. (2006). Putting the 'public' back into the public university. *Thesis Eleven, 84*, 44–59.

Marinova, D. & Raven, M. (2006). Indigenous knowledge and intellectual property: A sustainability agenda. *Journal of Economic Surveys, 20*, 587–605.

Marshall, A. (1890). *Principles of economics* (Vol. 1). London: Macmillan.

Massey, D. (1984). *Spatial divisions of labour*. London: Macmillan.

May, C. (2002). The information society: A sceptical view. Cambridge: Polity.

McCloskey, D.N. (1988). Bourgeois virtue and the history of P and S. *Journal of Economic History, 58*, 297–317.

McKendrick, N. (1974). Home demand and economic growth: A new view of the role of women and children in the Industrial Revolution. In McKendrick, N. (Ed.), *Historical perspectives: Studies in English thought and society in honour of J.H. Plumb* (pp. 152–210). London: Europa.

McKenna, B. & Rooney, D. (2005, November 28–29). *Wisdom management: Tensions between theory and practice in practice*. A paper given at the Second Annual International Conference on Knowledge Management in Asia Pacific – Building a Knowledge Society: Linking Government, Business, Academia and the Community, Wellington.

McGuckin, R.H. & van Ark, B. (2002, January). *Performance 2001: Productivity, employment, and income in the world's economies.* Conference Board of Canada, Report no. 13. Ottawa: Conference Board of Canada.

McLennan, G. (2003). *Sociologists in/on 'knowledge society.'* A paper based upon a presentation given for the Sociological Associated of Aotearoa/New Zealand Sociological Conference, Auckland.

Micklethwait, J. & Wooldridge, A. (2003). *A future perfect: The challenge and promise of globalization.* New York: Random House.

Moser, P. (2005). Do patent laws help to diffuse innovations? Evidence from the geographic localization of innovation in production in 19th century England. MIT Sloan & NBER working paper.

Mumford, L. (1966). *Myth of the Machine* (Vol. 1: Technics and human development). London: Secker & Warburg.

Munro, D. (2000). The knowledge economy. *Journal of Australian Political Economy, 45,* 5–17.

Nassehi, A. (2004, Summer). What do we know about knowledge: An essay on the knowledge society. *Canadian Journal of Sociology,* 439–450.

Neef, D. (1998). The knowledge economy: An introduction. In Neef, D. (Ed.), *The knowledge economy* (pp. 1–12). Boston: Butterworth-Heinemann.

Nelson, R. (1989). What is private and what is public about technology? *Science, Technology, and Human Values, 14*(3), 229–241.

Nokkala, T. (2004, December). Knowledge economy discourse: Dominant reality in higher education? *ESIB European Student LINK, 3*(28). Retrieved from www.esip.org/newsletter/link/2004-03/knowledge.php.

Notes. (2001). Antitrust and the information age: Section 2: Monopolization analyses in the new economy. *Harvard Law Review, 114*(5), 1623–1646.

Nowotny, H., Scott, P., & Gibbons, M. (2001). Rethinking science: Knowledge and the public in an age of uncertainty. Cambridge: Polity.

O'Brien, L., Opie, B., & Wallace, D. (2002). *Knowledge, innovation and creativity: Designing a knowledge society for a small country.* Wellington: Ministry of Research Science and Technology.

O'Brien, P.K. (1993). Introduction: Modern conceptions of the industrial revolution. In O'Brien, P.K. & Quinault, R. (Eds.), *The industrial revolution and British society* (pp. 1–20). Cambridge: Cambridge University Press.

Organisation for Economic Co-operation and Development (OECD). (1996). *The knowledge-based economy.* Paris: OECD.

Organisation for Economic Co-operation and Development (OECD). (2000, July 3). *A new economy? The changing role of innovation and information technology in growth.* Paris: OECD.

Oxley, L. & Greasley, D. (1997). Vector autoregression, cointegration and causality: Testing for causes of the British industrial revolution. *Applied Economics, 30,* 1387–1397.

Piazolo, D. (2001). The digital divide. *CESifo Forum, 2*(3), 29–34.

Pillay, H. (2005). Knowledge and social capital. In Rooney, D., Hearn, G., & Ninan, A. (Eds.), *Handbook on the knowledge economy* (pp. 82–90). Northampton: Edward Elgar.

Polanyi, K. (1944). The great transformation: The political and economic origins of our time. New York: Rinehart.

Pool, I. (1999). *Social sciences and an evidence-based public policy.* Wellington: Royal Society New Zealand miscellaneous series 54, pp. 62–73.

Powell, W.W. & Snellman, K. (2004). The knowledge economy. *Annual Review of Sociology, 30,* 199–220.

Progressive Policy Institute. (Nd). The new economy index. Retrieved from www.neweconomyindex.org.

Putnam, R.D. (2000). Bowling alone: The collapse and revival of American community. New York: Simon & Schuster.

Quah, D. (2002a, December). *Digital goods and the new economy.* London: Economics Department, London School of Economics.

Quah, D. (2002b, January). *Technological dissemination and economic growth: Some lessons for the new economy*. London: Economics Department, London School of Economics.

Quah, D. (2003). The weightless economy. Retrieved from http://econ.lse.ac.uk/staff/dquah/ tweirl0. html.

Ramello, G. (2006). What's in a sign? Trademark law and the economic theory. *Journal of Economic Surveys, 20*: 547–565.

Roethlisberger, F.J. & Dickson, W.J. (1939). *Management and the worker*. Cambridge, MA: Harvard University Press.

Rogers, E.M. (1962). *Diffusion of innovations*. New York: Free Press.

Rogers, J.E.T. (1863). On the rationale and working of the patent laws. *Journal of the London Statistical Society, 26*, 121–142.

Rooney, D., Hearn, G., Mandeville, T., & Joseph, R. (2003). *Public policy in knowledge-based economies: Foundations and frameworks*. Cheltenham: Edward Elgar.

Samuelson, P. & Varian, H.R. (2001, July 18). *The 'new economy' and information technology policy*. Berkeley: University of California at Berkeley.

Sautet, F.E. (2000). *An entrepreneurial theory of the firm*. London: Routledge.

Schiff, E. (1971). *Industrialisation without patents: The Netherlands, 1869–1912, Switzerland 1850– 1907*. Princeton, NJ: Princeton University Press.

Schiller, H.I. (1991). *Who knows: Information in the age of the Fortune 500*. Norwood, NJ: Ablex.

Scholte, J.A. (2000). *Globalization: A critical introduction*. Basingstoke: Palgrave Macmillan.

Schumpter, J.A. (1942). *Capitalism, socialism and democracy*. New York: Harper.

Smith, K. (2002, June). *What is the 'knowledge economy?' Knowledge intensity and distributed knowledge bases*. Discussion paper series, 2002–2006. Maastricht: Institute for New Technologies, United Nations University.

Smith, P.S. & Feagin, J.R. (1987). *The capitalist city: Global restructuring and community politics*. Oxford: Basil Blackwell.

Stehr, N. (1994). *Knowledge societies*. London: Sage.

Stehr, N. (2001). *The fragility of modern societies: Knowledge, and risk in the information age*. London: Sage.

Steuart, J. (1966 [1767]). *An inquiry into the principles of political economy*. London. Rpt. Skinner, A.S. (Ed.). Edinburgh: Oliver and Boyd.

Sullivan, R.J. (1989). England's 'Age of Invention:' The acceleration of patents and patentable invention during the industrial revolution. *Explorations in Economic History, 26*, 424–452.

Talero, E. & Gaudette, P. (1996). Harnessing information for development: A proposal for a World Bank group strategy. Retrieved from www.worldbank.org/html/fpd/harnessing/index.html#contents.

Temin, P. (1997). Two views of the British industrial revolution. *Journal of Economic History, 57*, 63–82.

Thompson, G.F. (2004). Getting to know the knowledge economy: ICTs, networks and governance. *Economy and Society, 33*(4), 562–581.

Thorlindsson, T. & Vilhjalmsson, R. (2003). Introduction to the special issue: Science, knowledge and society. *Acta Sociologica, 46*(2), 99–105.

Thorns, D C. (1992). *Fragmenting societies*. London: Routledge.

Thorns, D.C. (2002). *The transformation of cities*. Basingstoke: Palgrave Macmillan.

Thorns, D.C. (2003). The challenge of doing sociology in a global world: The case of Aotearoa/New Zealand. *Current Sociology, 51*(6), 689–708.

Toda, H.Y. & Phillips, P.C.B. (1991). *Vector autoregression and causality: A theoretical overview and simulation study*. Working paper, 977. New Haven, CT: Cowles Foundation.

Toda, H.Y. & Yamomoto, T. (1995). Statistical inference in vector autoregressions with possibly integrated processes. *Journal of Econometrics, 66*, 225–250.

Tofler, A. (1980). *The third wave*. London: Collins.

Towse, R. (2006). Copyright and artists: A view from cultural economics. *Journal of Economic Surveys, 20*, 567–585.

Ungar, S. (2003). Misplaced metaphor: A critical analysis of the 'knowledge society.' *Canadian Review of Sociology and Anthropology, 40*(3), 331–347.

United Nations Centre for Human Settlements (Habitat) (UNCHS Habitat). (2001). *Cities in a globalizing world.* London: Earthscan.

Urry, J. (2003). *Global complexity.* Cambridge: Polity.

Verspagen, B. (2006). University research, intellectual property rights and European innovation systems. *Journal of Economic Surveys, 20*, 607–632.

Wadhwani, S.B. (2001, March 20). *The new economy: Myths and realities.* Travers Lecture, London Guildhall University.

Weber, M. (1930). The protestant ethic and spirit of capitalism. London: Allen & Unwin.

Weber, M. (1946). *From Marx to Weber: Essays in sociology.* Gerth, H. & Mills, C.W. (Eds.). London: Routledge & Kegan Paul.

Weber, M. (1947). *The theory of economic and social organisation.* New York: Free Press.

Webster, K. (1995). *Theories of the information society.* London: Routledge.

CHRIS WARHURST & PAUL THOMPSON

MAPPING KNOWLEDGE IN WORK

Proxies or Practices?

INTRODUCTION

Governments and firms are exhorted, on pain of relegation to the lower divisions of (un-)competitiveness, to embrace the idea of a knowledge economy (Department for Trade and Industry, 1998; European Communities, 2004; Hamel & Prahalad, 1996; Nonaka & Takeuchi, 1995; OECD, 2001a; Reich, 1993; World Bank, 2002). However, this mainstream academic and policy debate tends to be prescriptive and insensitive to real developments in the economy and workplace. It also fails to provide the necessary conceptual definitions and distinctions concerning the use of knowledge in the workplace. Moreover, there is insufficient disentangling of firm strategies and structures, occupational changes and the content of work. With these critiques in mind, this chapter focuses on two main issues: first, how being 'knowledge-driven' is currently measured, focusing on the proxies employed in such assessments; second, how the mapping of workplace knowledge might be undertaken better by reference to practice. This approach builds on existing critical research, including our own earlier work that has argued for a disentangling of knowledge work and knowledgeability in work (Thompson, 2004; Thompson et al., 2001; Warhurst & Thompson, 1998).

There are many types of knowledge with differing workplace usage and purpose, but the central characteristics of knowledge work are that it draws on a body of theoretical (specialized and abstract) knowledge that is utilized, under conditions of comparative autonomy, to innovate products and processes. This is similar to Frenkel et al.'s (1995) definition of a knowledge worker as someone whose work requires high levels of creativity, intellective skills and theoretical rather than purely contextual knowledge. So, while all work is knowledgeable, in that there is at least experiential understanding of it often involving tacit knowledge, only a smaller range of activities (and therefore, occupational and professional groups) meet the aforementioned criteria. That knowledge-intensive jobs are limited in extent does not mean that we are dismissing the 'knowledge issue.' Instead, alternatives are required that can provide more conceptually and empirically robust accounts of knowledge and knowledge work.

D.W. Livingstone and D. Guile (eds.), The Knowledge Economy and Lifelong Learning:
A Critical Reader, 43–55.

THE MAINSTREAM AGENDA

If mainstream thinking is interrogated, three assumptions relevant to this article can be distinguished. First, it is argued that the economy is characterized by growing knowledge intensity. This assumption has wide governmental support (see World Bank, 2002). According to the OECD (2001a), the knowledge economy is one in which 'Symbolic resources are replacing physical resources, mental exertion is replacing physical exertion and knowledge capital is beginning to challenge money and all other forms of capital' (p. 148). In what has become known as the Lisbon strategy and 'transitioning' itself, the European Union (EU) has declared that it aims to be 'the most dynamic and competitive knowledge-based economy in the world by 2010' (European Communities, 2004, p. 6). The idea that knowledge displaces traditional factors of production such as land, labour and capital has been around for at least 30 years (e.g., Bell, 1973). However, it is now legitimized by influential social theorists (Castells, 1996; Lash, 2002), policy entrepreneurs (Leadbetter, 1999) and pop management writers (Kelly, 1999). The enduring theme is the intangible, weightless, immaterial nature of knowledge and knowledge work.

The second assumption is that firms need to change their mode of management to adapt to creating, capturing and capitalizing on knowledge (Ichijo et al., 1998). One reason why the commercialization of knowledge is regarded as so difficult rests with its nature and location – inside employees' heads, as the inherent property of the producer (Despres & Hiltrop, 1995). Firms need to facilitate and encourage employee learning and experimentation, communication and trust in order to generate and enable the sharing of ideas and knowledge.

Finally, it is assumed that public policy too must be fundamentally reshaped. While certainly not suggesting intra-firm intervention, the OECD and World Bank are keen for governments to have a proactive, strategic role in stimulating the conditions outside the firm that will foster the knowledge economy. This involves support for the innovative capacities of knowledge-intensive firms, including incentives for creative interaction within high-tech clusters of businesses and universities (Department for Trade and Industry, 1998; European Communities, 2004; Scottish Executive, 2004). In addition, there is a focus on investment that enhances the quality of human capital, with education becoming the priority as governments intervene in and/or 'reform' the supply side of the labour market to improve the quality of labour through its attainment of qualifications (Department for Education and Skills, 2005; European Communities, 2004; HM Treasury, 2004; OECD, 2001a; World Bank, 2002). One key feature of this policy is the creation of more graduates through expanded higher education. Mass higher education creates a mass of potential knowledge workers (Brown et al., 2003) who then stimulate demand for better jobs from employers (Layard, 1997).

CRITIQUE: PROXY MEASURES AND THEIR LIMITS

Given the economic and political imperatives that follow from these assumptions, robust measures might be expected to exist in order to assess the growth of knowledge and knowledge workers in the economy. Unfortunately, they do not. Although there is an increasingly rich literature on the different types of knowledge used in work and trends identified in which some types of knowledge are becoming more salient (see, e.g., Blackler et al., 1998), this recognition has had limited impact. Instead, measurement rests on a series of general proxies. Ironically, although it is suggested that the knowledge economy is based upon intangible factors of production, assessment in mainstream accounts tends to rely on tangible measures. It is not possible to examine all the relevant dimensions in one short article. Here we critique the four most frequently cited and overlapping proxies; ones used particularly by bodies such as the OECD, EU and the U.K. Government. We should make clear that this is not a rejection of proxies in principle or for all purposes. Their deployment may be inevitable for assessing certain macro-level phenomena such as broad indicators of industrial evolution. What we want to explore is whether these particular proxies can bear the theoretical and policy weight resting on them, particularly with reference to work and employment.

Proxy 1: ICT

The first proxy is information and communications technology (ICT), with an assumption that if an industry relies heavily on ICT, then it must be knowledge-intensive, and that the introduction and use of ICT requires high skill employees (Department for Trade and Industry, 1998; European Communities, 2004). The OECD (2004) makes an explicit link between ICT and improved economic performance when combined with investment in skills but, within the nine countries from which research was reported, the nature of the linkages is unclear. Such inconveniences have not stopped claims that ICT advances require enhanced skills use with a shift to knowledge management (Burton-Jones, 1999).

There is U.K. evidence that the number of jobs involving ICT has dramatically increased since the mid-1980s and, relatedly, that the use of computer skills by employees has increased. Over 70 percent of respondents in the Work Skills in Britain 1986–2001 survey (Felstead et al., 2002) reported using some type of automated or computerized equipment, with 40 percent saying that the use of the latter is now essential to their work. A key issue, however, is the sophistication and purpose of these computer skills. Call centres, for example, are regarded as part of the 'new economy' because of their ICT-intensive operations. Yet their employees use few thinking skills: ICT is required for (customer) information transfer and input based on keyboard and screen template usage rather than knowledge-driven innovation of either product or process (Thompson et al., 2001). In the United States, Appelbaum et al. (2003) note greater computer use among workers but, also, how little training is required to acquire the requisite computer skills. Felstead et al. (2002) observe that U.K. workers in clerical and related service work who have high dependency on ICT have only moderate levels of job complexity, a finding supported by Fleming et al.'s (2004) Australian research. Second, technological determinism is an issue. Skill outcomes from new technology must be examined in relation to managerial strategy. De-skilling is one other possible outcome of workplace ICT usage. Management may be encouraged to use computer systems to sub-divide organizational tasks into 'component processes' that enable the use of less skilled workers (Kanevsky & Housel, 1998, p. 281). As Livingstone and Scholtz (2006) note, with reference to Canada, while new technologies and digital networks have been incorporated by large numbers of enterprises, even the most optimistic estimates put knowledge workers as a quarter of the labour force. Third, any upskilling that might arise from ICT usage appears to be complemented by deteriorations in other work aspects, namely autonomy and discretion (Felstead et al., 2002).

Finally, the introduction and use of new ICT systems should not be simply assumed to involve technical skills. Instead, other, 'new' skills are required of employees, such as adaptability and having the right attitude (Rubery & Grimshaw, 2001). Little wonder that the OECD (2004, p. 80) admits that 'better measurement [of ICT's impact] remains a challenge,' related as it is to other variables such as management practices and work organization.

Proxy 2: R&D

Investment in research and development (R&D) is supposed to indicate the extent of being knowledge-driven (European Communities, 2004; OECD, 2001b). In this context, the EC notes that implementation of the Lisbon strategy has been undermined by inadequate R&D spending across most of the EU. While acknowledging that investment in R&D to stimulate the knowledge economy can be publicly as well as privately-funded (European Communities, 2004; World Bank, 2002), this approach inordinately focuses on manufacturing and so-called 'knowledge-intensive industries,' but again there are problems.

First, as a measurement it can distort the analysis. Industries may invest heavily in R&D, but not all firms operating in these industries are knowledge intensive. The computer manufacturing industry is constantly innovating its products based on continuous R&D. However, manufacturing of these products, such as PCs, can involve routine, repetitive, low skill, low-value added work. Countries that attract such assembly work are mislabelled as knowledge economies because this activity is encompassed within the overall industry categorization (McNicholl et al., 2002). Moreover, it is an approach that conveniently omits any analysis of the content of the work of those employed in R&D. As we have pointed out elsewhere (Warhurst & Thompson, 1998), the capacity for R&D workers to undertake 'blue skies' research is diminishing under the weight of commercial pressures and managerial imposition. Randle's (1995) research on technical workers in the pharmaceuticals industry is a case in point. Here, these employees' discretionary activity, such as their 'ten per cent time' or one–half day per week intended to enable 'a greater degree of creative and independent thinking' on new projects became subsumed into ordinary working time on 'goals emphasised by line managers' (pp. 13–14). More broadly, it is worth noting that the previously-mentioned decline in employee autonomy and discretion at work reported in the Work Skills in Britain 1986–2001 survey findings is experienced most by professional workers and that decline has become sharper in recent years (Felstead et al., 2002).

To overcome the problems with the first two proxies, McNicholl et al. (2002) suggest that a better measure is the level and type of skills embodied in the production of a good or service. Two measures are used to assess this skill: qualification (as a measure of accumulated skills) and occupational position (as a signal of skill usage). These two measures feature prominently in characterizations of knowledge-driven economies and we will deal with them separately and in more detail.

Proxy 3: Qualifications

Qualification is perhaps the widest used proxy for both skills and knowledge, and the most specious. A more and better-qualified workforce is required, it is argued, to meet the assumed high-skill needs of the knowledge economy. The Scottish Executive (2004) overtly cites the number of graduates in its list of measurements of progress towards creating 'a smart, successful Scotland.'

However, the relationship between qualification and skill can be problematic. HM Treasury acknowledges that it is possible to be skilled without a formal qualification and vice versa, and certainly some of the aforementioned new skills are difficult to accredit as qualifications (Grugulis et al., 2004). As a recent twist, the U.K. government has suggested that attainment of a qualification can act as a 'signal' of the possession of these new skills (HM Treasury, 2004). An equally valid signal, however, might be parental class (Nickson & Warhurst, 2007). There is also the issue of whether the qualifications acquired relate to the job being done by an employee. If not, a skills mismatch can occur, raising issues about the relevance of qualifications. A graduate of history might be employed in health management, for example. It might be argued that both the qualification and occupational position involve the same level of skill, but such a belief rests on an untested assumption that all higher education degrees across all institutions produce common levels of 'graduateness.' Brown and Hesketh (2004) note the propensity for 'blue-chip' employers to select graduate training candidates from a restricted number of universities in the United Kingdom. In addition, there is some evidence that qualification inflation is occurring, by which some learning necessary to do a job that was previously sub-degree is now being re-badged as degree level (Rodgers & Waters, 2001). It is just as well, therefore, that employers are less concerned with the knowledge possessed by their graduate employees than their 'new' skills (again), such as 'work ethic' and 'ability to work as part of a team' (National Centre for Vocational Education Research, 2001).

With a bountiful supply of highly qualified labour, firms simply raise the entry tariff to employment without changing the work undertaken by these employees. Since the 1980s, 'credentialism' has risen at graduate (Green, 2004) and other levels in the United Kingdom (Felstead et al., 2002) and in other countries (Brynin, 2002; OECD, 1994). This under-employment reflects a mismatch between the supply and demand for graduates. Using data from the U.K.'s Association of

Graduate Recruiters, Brown and Hesketh (2004) calculate that the ratio of available graduates to available graduate jobs ranges from 7:1 to as high as 20:1. Contrary to government expectations, having more graduates in the labour market does not result in employers creating better jobs to satisfy supply. Instead, having a degree has become an entry ticket to employment rather than a requisite of work. This issue has begun to receive further attention, notably from Purcell et al. (2003), who suggest that it is more useful to acknowledge that there is now a range of 'jobs that graduates do' rather than 'graduate jobs.'[1]

Proxy 4: Occupation and Skill

On skill and occupation, there are two questionable assumptions. First, policy makers, in particular, are quick to conflate knowledge and skill (HM Treasury, 2004; Scottish Executive, 2004), with 'thinking skills' the bridge. Cully (2003) does flag the issue of whether or not skill can be equated with knowledge but argues that 'There is no established literature yet which clearly conceptualises knowledge work,' a point with which we would agree; but he then continues: 'In lieu of this, treating the skills required to do a job as equivalent to the knowledge required to do it seems a reasonable basis on which to begin' (p. 14). In other words, because an attempt to disentangle skill and knowledge has yet to be made, there is no point in doing it – with which we do not agree. Instead, although often interdependent in work, knowledge and skill can and should be practically and conceptually disentangled. A university professor, for example, may have extensive knowledge of mediaeval literature but almost no communication skills that would allow the effective (and required) dissemination of that knowledge to students.

Second, the typicality claim about knowledge workers rests on a particular reading of occupational categorization weightings – that is, economic change is assumed from aggregate occupational change. This is a mis-reading of such changes that has three facets. First, substantive change in the nature of the economy is assumed because the numbers employed in these occupations is rising. We have noted elsewhere (Warhurst & Thompson, 1998) the practice of casually re-labelling many existing and very disparate occupations as knowledge workers. Simply using or applying knowledge in a job is enough for some to be regarded as a knowledge worker. Davenport et al. (1996) note how even front-line workers in restaurants in some accounts can be viewed as knowledge workers. Second, it is a partial reading, ignoring the fact that, while management, professional and technical jobs are expanding, so too are routine services jobs, particularly in personal services and retail and hospitality. Brown and Hesketh (2004) suggest that such trends indicate a polarization of high skill 'knowledge work' jobs and low skill 'routine' jobs – the U.K. hourglass economy identified by Nolan (2001). Fleming et al. (2004) make the same claim for Australian skills and jobs. Third, it equates knowledge workers with these managerial, professional and technical occupations. Statistics Canada is one such example (see Baldwin & Beckstead,

2003). Yet, as even knowledge economy advocate Reich (1993) acknowledges, not all professional workers are knowledge workers.

Such lumpy aggregations obscure more than they illuminate. More sensitive readings of aggregate government data, for example of Australian professional job content by Fleming et al. (2004), suggest that it is important to differentiate between different types of professional jobs. Analysis 'below the surface of the growth in professional employment' reveals that most growth has occurred in jobs 'associated with knowledge handling and servicing' rather than those that are considered to be 'autonomous and empowered knowledge productive jobs' (p. 735). Furthermore, analysis of the job content of Associate Professions in Australia reveals these jobs to be not dissimilar from administrative occupations that have existed for most of the twentieth century and so 'not ... particularly distinctive' (p. 738). This outcome is not unique to Australia. Associate Professional and Technical Occupations have increased and are projected to increase most as a percentage of the U.K. employment to 2012 (Wilson et al., 2004). However, a research brief for the U.K.'s Department for Education and Skills (Rodgers & Waters, 2001) admits that the emergence of some private and public sector Associate Professional jobs is simply a result of a reclassification of these jobs, with these jobs incorporating a variety of tasks from occupations traditionally rated at a lower level.

Thus, although policy makers and academics across the United States, Europe and elsewhere have been quick to trumpet the emergence of the knowledge economy, the most frequently used proxy measures are problematic; such measures are too often centred on broad-brush assumptions and aggregate measures that are insufficiently sensitive to underlying sector, industry and occupational variations and developments.

KNOWLEDGE AT WORK: TOWARDS A NEW RESEARCH AGENDA

Instead of being an evidence-driven policy, the knowledge economy is a policy increasingly at odds with the evidence. Its persistence speaks more to the needs of policy-makers for 'an optimistic story that legitimises smaller government in an age of globalisation and low taxes' (Thompson, 2004, p. 51). In the search for data, a range of substitutes for knowledge usage are invoked for measurement purposes. Our argument has been that these measures are often deeply flawed.

In particular, labour or product market measures have been used to sustain claims that ultimately need to be validated in analysis of the labour process. We accept that proxies may serve a more effective purpose when used as measures of broader processes such as knowledge flows in particular industry sectors (see Smith, 2000). More care, we suggest, needs to be taken about the term 'knowledge intensive.' Industries can be knowledge intensive through investment in ICT and R&D, but given that the outcomes of such investment may be the development of expert systems, such investment might not be reflected in the growth of knowledge work characterized, as indicated earlier, by theoretical knowledge, creativity and intellective skills. These proxies may be acceptable if re-directed specifically towards terrains such as industry knowledge flows. We remain much more sceptical of the use of occupation and qualification as proxies, as these are used to draw direct inferences about knowledge work.

We also accept that as a legitimate feature of public policy, there is a case for better quantitative measures of skill and occupations, as Brown and Hesketh (2004) have begun to undertake. However, there is also a need for research to examine the issues more concretely in relation to the dynamics of different categories of knowledge and labour, and this kind of orientation needs to inform that more complex reading of occupational data. If this is not done, public policy will be mis-directed towards labour markets and human capital rather than the 'under-employment' issue – in other words 'how successfully current labour processes utilize the existing skills of workers' (Livingstone & Scholtz, 2006).

Drawing on work elsewhere (Thompson, 2004; Thompson et al., 2001), we would summarize some of the basic trends as follows. Although routine and expert labour continue to differ significantly in content and context, both have undergone significant changes. A central focus in both instances has been on attempts to enhance the conversion of tacit to explicit knowledge.

The contested politics of knowledge has always been central to the workplace (Jacques, 1996) and became the focal point of conflict through Taylorism's attempts to appropriate the knowledgeable practice of craft workers. Firms are keen to introduce organizational structures and practices that facilitate initiative and innovation in the form of creativity and continuous improvement on the part of routine workers. Such changes are marked primarily by a shift from explicit to tacit knowledge. Explicit knowledge was held either by management through Taylorism or by workers through apprenticeships and related training. As is well known, formal employee knowledge and craft skills development through apprenticeships has been in long-term decline. Teamwork, which provides a collective framework for workers to share knowledge and solve problems, is the preferred alternative.

Admittedly, many of the new forms through which informal expertise is mobilized have proved to be faddish, superficial and compatible with elements of Taylorism. For all these limitations, the search for ways of identifying and utilizing knowledgeability is real and unlikely to disappear from corporate agendas. Though such arguments largely reflect the experience of manufacturing, there is an equivalent direction for interactive services. Increased competition in expanded, heterogeneous and de-regulated markets has led companies to focus their attention on the management of 'front-line' work (Frenkel et al., 1999). Though the form varies according to the work context, attention focuses on control and cost efficiency, with employees selected and trained to deliver consistent service quality and required to take on expanded, delegated responsibilities.

In addition to the move from explicit to tacit knowledge, there is also a shift from the technical to the social. Technical here refers to the abstract and practical pre-conditions in skills and knowledge for workers to be effective in the tasks that they undertake. What is happening is a shift towards 'person-to-person' social competencies, or to what in the past might have been regarded as personal characteristics. Research from France, the United Kingdom, and the United States has found that attitudes, dispositions and appearance are frequently more important than level of education and training (Mounier, 2001; Grugulis et al., 2004; Lafer, 2004 respectively). As a result, employers may be choosing to invest more in recruitment and selection processes that can identify workers with the appropriate personal characteristics than in skill development and learning. This is particularly the case in service work as studies of call centres, retail and hospitality demonstrate (Callaghan & Thompson, 2002; Nickson et al., 2005). As a U.S. manager in industry remarked: 'It's much more of a challenge to engineer change with people than to hire in new people' (Moss et al., 2003, p. 13).

In contrast, expert labour is generally taken to mean professional or other groups whose position in the division of labour is defined by the existence and use of their specialist knowledge. High-level skills, core strategic knowledge and organizational competencies in manufacturing and services are concentrated in small sub-sections of expert labour and senior management. Nevertheless, the wider category of 'real knowledge workers' is clearly important to individual firms and the wider economy as sources of design, research and innovation. It is also fairly obvious that knowledge-intensive work requires much higher levels of autonomy and trust for particular groups of technical and professional employees.

Admittedly, the newness of much of this emphasis is debatable. The tension between creativity, commodification and control has always been at the heart of knowledge work (see Barrett, 2004, for a recent illustration). What can be said is that this tension has become sharper. There are two main sources. Knowledge-intensive firms are under strong competitive pressures to reduce the life cycle of 'molecule to market' projects (McKinlay, 2002). Meanwhile, public sector knowledge workers have increased constraints on their professional autonomy as a result of a combination of bureaucratic regulation and managerial control of their work, and the introduction of internal markets and associated forms of competition. This is the real meaning of knowledge management with its attendant language of 'capturing,' 'leveraging' or 'converting' knowledge for commercial gain (see, e.g., Nonaka & Takeuchi, 1995). It is, therefore, at the very heart of knowledge management to 'separate knowledge from the knower.'

These trends are by no means exhaustive across occupations and sectors. Compared to routine and expert labour, contemporary research has a less detailed picture of other groups such as the Associate Professionals and Intermediate Occupations (though this latter grouping is emerging as a key concern – see Department for Education and Skills, 2005). In developing such an expanded agenda, we would suggest some key differentiating criteria and research questions related to any exploration of workplace knowledge:

1. Input issues: what, if anything, needs to be known prior to, or as a condition of entry to the job?
2. Output issues: what opportunities are available to use, modify or add to the stock of job-related knowledge?
3. Process issues: what needs to be known to enable a job to be performed appropriately; what degree of learning, training and progression are available to advance access to and acquisition of knowledge?

With respect to input issues, a key research question is to examine whether there is an increasing disconnection between theoretical knowledge and job characteristics, reflecting the view of a Chief Executive of a City financial services company that they are moving towards a workforce where a 'guy with an O level in woodwork sits next to a guy with a PhD in mathematics' (quoted in *The Economist*, 2004, p. 12). Even if an employee enters a job with a body of knowledge, we need to know the extent to which that knowledge is expected to be and can be utilized. For example, schoolteachers may be constrained from using and adding to their knowledge by externally directed syllabi and examinations. More awareness is needed too of the form of knowledge use in the workplace, not just that 'knowledge' is being used. On the process terrain, it is frequently observed that there is a decline in traditional career structures and internal labour markets (Cappelli, 2001; International Labour Organization, 1997). While such trends may be exaggerated, more research is needed on the effects of changes in career prospects and perceptions on opportunities for learning and advancing knowledge.

It is important not merely to map the content of knowledge at work but also its context. Theory and research needs to address the parameters to, and determinants of, access to and use of workplace knowledge. We would suggest that the following represent the key factors:

1. Organizational hierarchy and control systems;
2. Work intensity, effort bargain and reward systems;
3. Skill formation systems;
4. Internal and external labour markets;
5. Professional or occupation structures and cultures; and
6. State, political economy and other institutional factors.

The literatures on knowledge and its management too often give the impression that the pre-conditions and opportunities for knowledge utilization depend solely on the motives and commitment of individual workplace actors when there are wider contextual issues too. For example, the recent (2004) Agenda for Change plans in the U.K.'s National Health Service offer enhanced opportunities of knowledge use and acquisition for nurses, but the pressures on management to keep down or even drive down costs and increase patient throughput places limits on the capacity and willingness of employees to embrace such changes. We do need fine-grained studies of the workplace practices of occupational groups such as technical workers (Barley, 2005) but 'communities of practice' are not islands. Knowledge and skills are formed through broader institutional processes, ranging from labour markets to the variety of capitalism within which the workplace is embedded. Mapping this context suggests that both a critique of and alternative to the current mainstream are needed to better understand knowledge in work, shifting the emphasis away from a concern with proxies and onto embedded workplace practice.

ACKNOWLEDGEMENT

The authors would like to thank Rachel Parker for her comments and suggestions on an early draft of this article.

NOTES

[1] Purcell et al. (2003) offer a five-category classification that identifies 'traditional graduate' jobs such as solicitors and scientists and 'modern graduate' jobs involving the newer professions such as accountants and teachers. The incumbents of both types of jobs are predominantly graduates. Other jobs, 'new graduate' – such as marketing managers and welfare officers, 'niche graduate' – sports and hotel managers for example – and 'non graduate occupations' – such as clerks and sales assistants – are increasingly employing graduates. In the latter two categories 'the majority of incumbents are not graduates' and 'are likely to constitute under-utilization of [graduates'] higher education skills and knowledge' (p. 4).

REFERENCES

Appelbaum, E., Bernhardt, A., & Murnane, R. (2003). Low-wage America: An overview. In Appelbaum, E., Bernhardt, A., & Murnane, R. (Eds.), *Low-wage America* (pp. 1–29). New York: Russell Sage Foundation.

Baldwin, J.R. & Beckstead, D. (2003). *Knowledge workers in Canada's economy 1971–2001*. Ottawa: Statistics Canada.

Barley, S. (2005). What we know and mostly don't know about technical workers. In Ackroyd, S., Batt, R., Thompson, P., & Tolbert, P. (Eds.), *The handbook of work and organizations*. Oxford: Oxford University Press.

Barrett, R. (2004). Working at Webboyz: An analysis of control over the software development labour process. *Work, Employment and Society, 38*(4), 777–794.

Bell, D. (1973). *The coming of post-industrial society*. New York: Basic Books.

Blackler, F., Crump, N. & McDonald, S. (1998). Knowledge, organisations and competition. In von Krogh, G., Roos, J., & Kleine, D. (Eds.), *Knowing in firms*. London: Sage.

Brown, P. & Hesketh, A. (2004). *The mismanagement of talent*. Oxford: Oxford University Press.

Brown, P., Hesketh, A., & Williams, S. (2003). Employability in a knowledge-driven economy. *Journal of Education and Work, 16*(2), 107–126.

Brynin, M. (2002). Over-qualification in employment. *Work, Employment and Society, 16*(4), 637–654.

Burton-Jones, A. (1999). *Knowledge capitalism*. Oxford: Oxford University Press.

Callaghan, G. & Thompson, P. (2002). 'We recruit attitude:' The selection and shaping of call centre labour. *Journal of Management Studies, 39*(2), 233–254.

Cappelli, P. (2001). Assessing the decline of internal labor markets. In Berg, I. & Kalleberg, A. (Eds.), *Sourcebook of labor markets*. New York: Plenum.

Castells, M. (1996). *The rise of the network society*. Oxford: Blackwell.

Cully, M. (2003). *Pathways to knowledge work*. Leabrook: National Centre for Vocational Education Research.

Davenport, T.H., Jarvenpaa, S.L., & Beers, M.C. (1996, Summer). Improving knowledge work processes. *Sloan Management Review*, 53–65.

Despres, C. & Hiltrop, J-M. (1995). Human resource management in the knowledge age: Current practice and perspectives in the future. *Employee Relations, 17*(1), 9–23.

Department for Education and Skills (DfES). (2005). *Skills: Getting on in business, getting on in work*. Norwich: Her Majesty's Stationary Office.

Department for Trade and Industry (DTI). (1998). *Our competitive future*. London: Her Majesty's Stationary Office.

Economist. (2004, January 15). *What's it worth?*

European Communities (EC). (2004). *Facing the challenge.* Luxembourg: Office for Official Publications of the European Communities.

Felstead, A., Gallie, D., & Green, F. (2002). *Work skills in Britain 1986–2001.* London: Department for Education and Skills.

Fleming, P., Harley, B., & Sewell, G. (2004). A little knowledge is a dangerous thing: Getting below the surface of the growth of 'knowledge work' in Australia. *Work, Employment and Society, 18*(4), 725–747.

Frenkel, S.J., Korczynski, M., Donoghue, L. & Shire, K. (1995). Re-constituting work. *Work, Employment and Society, 9*(4), 773–796.

Frenkel, S., Korczynski, M., Shire, K., & Tam, M. (1999). *On the front line.* Ithaca, NY: Cornell University Press.

Green, F. (2004). *Over-education.* Paper presented at the SKOPE Conference, Lumley Castle, Durham.

Grugulis, I., Warhurst, C., & Keep, E. (2004). What's happening to 'skill?' In Warhurst, C., Grugulis, I., & Keep, E. (Eds.), *The skills that matter.* London: Palgrave.

Hamel, G. & Prahalad, C.K. (1996). Competing in the New Economy: Managing out of bounds. *Strategic Management Journal, 17,* 237–242.

HM Treasury. (2004). *Skills in the global economy.* Norwich: Her Majesty's Stationary Office.

Ichijo, K., von Krogh, G., & Nonaka, I. (1998). Knowledge enablers. In von Krogh, G., Roos, J., & Kleine, D. (Eds.), *Knowing in firms.* London: Sage.

International Labour Organization (ILO). (1997). *World Labour Report 1997–8.* Geneva: ILO.

Jacques, R. (1996). *Manufacturing the employee.* London: Sage.

Kanevsky, V. & Housel, T. (1998). The learning–knowledge–value cycle. In von Krogh, G., Roos, J., & Kleine, D. (Eds.), *Knowing in firms.* London: Sage.

Kelly, K. (1999). *New rules for the new economy.* London: Fourth Estate.

Lafer, G. (2004). What is 'skill?' Training for discipline in the low-wage labour market. In Warhurst, C., Grugulis, I., & Keep, E. (Eds.), *The skills that matter.* London: Palgrave.

Lash, S. (2002). *Critique of information.* London: Sage.

Layard, R. (1997). *What labour can do.* London: Warner.

Leadbetter, C. (1999). *Living on thin air.* London: Viking.

Livingstone, D.W. & Scholtz, A. (2006). Contradictions of labour processes and worker's use of skills in advanced capitalist economies. In Shalla, V. & Clement, W. (Eds.), *Work in tumultuous times.* Montreal: McGill–Queen's University Press.

McKinlay, A. (2002). The limits of knowledge management. *New Technology, Work and Employment, 17*(2), 76–88.

McNicholl, I., Kelly, U., Marsh, R., & McLay, D. (2002). *Defining and identifying the knowledge economy in Scotland.* Glasgow: University of Strathclyde.

Moss, P., Salzman, H., & Tilly, C. (2003). *Under construction: The continuing evolution of job structures in call centers.* Center for Industrial Competitiveness, University of Massachusetts-Lowell.

Mounier, A. (2001). The three logics of skills in the French literature. Sydney: NSW BVET.

National Centre for Vocational Education Research (NCVER). (2001). *Statistics 2001: Survey of employer views on vocational education and training.* Leabrook: National Centre for Vocational Education Research.

Nickson, D. & Warhurst, C. (2007). Opening Pandora's Box: Aesthetic labour and hospitality. In Morrison, A., Lashley, C., & Lynch, P. (Eds.), *Critical hospitality studies.* London: Elsevier.

Nickson, D., Warhurst, C., & Dutton, E. (2005). The importance of attitude and appearance in the service encounter in retail hospitality. *Managing Service Quality, 15*(2), 195–208.

Nolan, P. (2001, December 27). Shaping things to come. *People Management,* 30–31.

Nonaka, I, & Takeuchi, H. (1995). *The knowledge-creating company.* Oxford: Oxford University Press.

Organisation for Economic Co-operation and Development (OECD). (1994). *Jobs study: Evidence and explanations.* Paris: OECD.

Organisation for Economic Co-operation and Development (OECD). (2001a). *Devolution and globalisation*. Paris: OECD.

Organisation for Economic Co-operation and Development (OECD). (2001b). *Science, technology and industry scoreboard: Towards a knowledge-based economy*. Paris: OECD.

Organisation for Economic Co-operation and Development (OECD). (2004). *Economic impact of ICT: Measurement, evidence and implications*. Paris: OECD.

Purcell, K., Wilton, N., & Elias, P. (2003). *'What is a graduate job?' An examination of the skills used in the workplace by graduates*. Paper to the 21st Annual International Labour Process Conference, University of the West of England.

Randle, K. (1995). *The whitecoated worker: Professional autonomy in a period of change*. Paper to the 13th Annual International Labour Process Conference, University of Central Lancashire.

Reich, R. (1993). *The work of nations*. London: Simon & Schuster.

Rodgers, R. & Waters, R. (2001). *The skills dynamics of business and public service associate professionals*. DfES Research Report, RR302. Norwich: Her Majesty's Stationary Office.

Rubery, J. & Grimshaw, D. (2001). ICTS and employment: The problem of job quality. *International Labour Review, 140*(2), 165–192.

Scottish Executive. (2004). *A smart, successful Scotland*. Rev. Edinburgh: Stationery Office.

Smith, K. (2000). What is the 'knowledge economy?' Knowledge-intensive industries and distributed knowledge bases. Rebild: DRUID Summer Conference on the Learning Economy.

Thompson, P. (2004). *Skating on thin ice*. Glasgow: Big Thinking.

Thompson, P., Warhurst, C., & Callaghan, G. (2001). Ignorant theory and knowledgeable workers: Interrogating the connections between knowledge, skills and services. *Journal of Management Studies, 38*(7), 923–942.

Warhurst, C. & Thompson, P. (1998). Hands, hearts and minds: Changing work and workers at the end of the century. In Thompson, P. & Warhurst, C. (Eds.), *Workplaces of the future*. London: Macmillan.

Wilson, R., Homenidou, K., & Dickerson, A. (2004). *Working futures: National report 2003–4*. Institute for Employment Research, University of Warwick.

World Bank. (2002). Building knowledge economies: Opportunities and challenges for EU accession countries. Paris: World Bank.

55

BOB JESSOP

A CULTURAL POLITICAL ECONOMY OF COMPETITIVENESS

And Its Implications for Higher Education

INTRODUCTION

In his widely-acclaimed book, *The Coming of Post-Industrial Society: A Venture in Social Forecasting* (1973), Daniel Bell made three predictions that, if fully realised, would have major implications for the nature and role of universities in the contemporary economic and social order. His first forecast was that, whereas capital had been the dominant factor of production in industrial societies, in post-industrial societies that place would be occupied by knowledge. Second, while industrialism was characterized by the dominance of mechanical technologies and of economic calculation based on cost-reduction and cost-recovery, intellectual technologies and a 'sociologizing' orientation concerned with intellectual planning and the public good would prevail in post-industrial societies. Third, he predicted that, whereas the industrial enterprise had been the dominant organization in industrialism, in post-industrial societies this position would be ceded to the university. These predictions have only been partially confirmed at best – with the first being the most widely, if still erroneously, accepted as having been fulfilled. Considering the nature and reasons for their theoretical inadequacy and/or empirical disconfirmation should tell us much about the contemporary economy and the current role of universities.[1]

The first prediction is certainly part of conventional wisdom as the knowledge-based economy has become the hegemonic representation or self-description of the economy as an emerging reality, an object of calculation, and object of governance in contemporary world society. But this does not mean that it adequately describes the dynamics of today's world market or the role of knowledge in world society. For it misrepresents knowledge as a 'factor of production,' understates the extent to which every economy is a knowledge economy, and thereby mistakes one societal self-description for a more complex discursive-material reality.

The second prediction has been stood on its head by the dynamic of the world market. For the production and uses of knowledge have become increasingly subordinate to an 'economizing' logic oriented to profit-and-loss calculation in contrast to Bell's optimistic prediction that the organization and purposes of material production would become subject to a sociologizing concern with the public good. Indeed, it is a telling indicator of this inversion that the hegemonic

D.W. Livingstone and D. Guile (eds.), The Knowledge Economy and Lifelong Learning: A Critical Reader, 57–83.

imaginary (or societal self-description) today is the 'knowledge-based *economy*' (KBE) rather than information *society*, learning *society*, or knowledge *society* (see below). It may also help to explain the drive to 'economics imperialism' in the changing hierarchy of disciplines in the social sciences as the profit-oriented, market-mediated logic of capital extends further in the real world into what had earlier been regarded as in one way or another 'extra-economic.'

The third prediction has been controverted in turn by the extent to which universities are now tending, in different ways and subject to greater or lesser financial, administrative, and ideological pressures, to act more like economic enterprises that aim to maximize revenues, market their education, research, and knowledge transfer capacities, position themselves competitively vis-à-vis other types of supplier of these services at home and abroad, and, additionally, serve the demands of various local, urban, regional, national, or even supranational knowledge-based economies. Thus, challenging, albeit indirectly, Bell's emphasis on the sociologization of knowledge, Castells and Hall (1994) write that universities, as major producers of knowledge, have the same role in the 'information economy' as coal mines had in the industrial economy (p. 231). We should also note that, while Bell wrote from within a primarily national perspective, universities now aim to meet not only local, urban, regional, or national demand, but also to serve supranational knowledge-based economic and political interests. And, while lip service is often paid to 'quality of life' as well, this is generally interpreted in terms of minimizing the adverse impact of market-driven economic activities on private, social and cultural life.

This chapter interprets these three predictions and their relative failure from the perspective of cultural political economy – a transdisciplinary approach that combines critical discourse analysis (CDA) with critical political economy of capitalism – and explains why the reality is much closer to a subordination of information, knowledge, and learning to the demands of the expanded reproduction of the globalizing knowledge economy than it is to Bell's expectation that we would see the widening and deepening of a democratic knowledge society. The chapter identifies three interrelated sets of economic, political, and socio-cultural changes. The first of these is the nature and dynamic of the contemporary world market as a crucial context for the transformation of universities; the second change is the development of a new logic of governance that links the reorganization and reorientation of higher education to its changing economic and political environment; and the third concerns the specific aims and objectives of higher education. In addressing these three sets of issues in their interconnection, I use cultural political economy (hereafter CPE) as an innovative evolutionary and institutional approach to the semiotic and material dynamics of contemporary capitalism (see Fairclough et al., 2004; Jessop, 2004, 2009; Jessop & Sum, 2001; Sum, 2009; Sum & Jessop, 2003). I draw heavily on the cultural (or, more accurately, *semiotic*) arguments of CPE in discussing hegemonic economic imaginaries and their role in orienting economic, political, and socio-cultural strategies, especially since the mid-1970s. In this context, an imaginary can be defined, briefly, as a more or less coherent set of ideas and expectations that simplify, and thereby frame, a complex social reality from a particular perspective, a set that is typically associated with a distinctive set of social technologies and practices broadly conceived that provide support and reinforcement to this imaginary (analogous terms that may be more familiar to readers are frame, mental map, model, paradigm, or self-description; for further discussion, see Jessop, 2009; and, on their translation into knowledge brands, Sum, 2009). I draw on the semiotic and material moments of CPE in my account of the changing dynamic of competition and competitiveness in the KBE, including the changing articulation of the economic and extra-economic conditions that sustain competitiveness in the world market. And, albeit this time drawing more on its material than its semiotic moment, I use CPE to consider the implications of contemporary economic change for the nature and purposes of (higher) education.

ON ECONOMIC IMAGINARIES

The approach to these interrelated issues suggested here is based on the concept of economic (and other kinds of) imaginaries that is central to recent work on cultural political economy. CPE is a broad post-disciplinary current in institutional and evolutionary political economy that makes a 'cultural turn' in economic and political studies to enhance their interpretive and explanatory power. The cultural turn is used here as an 'umbrella' concept for the wide range of (re-) discoveries in the humanities and social sciences of the role of semiosis in social life: the cultural turn, the narrative turn, the rhetorical turn, the discursive turn, the argumentative turn, the performative turn, the reflexive turn, the visual turn, and so on. *Semiosis* is the most comprehensive term to cover all of these cultural turns because it refers to all forms of social production of intersubjective meaning (which includes oral, textual, visual, musical, practical performance, etc.). In this sense, CPE might perhaps have been better termed Semiotic Political Economy. This would at least avoid the mistaken view that CPE involves no more than adding an interest in a separate realm of 'culture' to existing concerns with politics and economics that are also considered in turn as distinct spheres of social life, with the result that CPE is held to comprise a simple, mechanical addition of arguments drawn from the disciplines corresponding to these fields. Yet, as discourse theorists, mainstream and critical alike, have long recognized, semiosis cannot be confined to some arbitrarily abstracted or isolated sphere of 'culture,' but is a universal and critical dimension of all social life.[2]

Turning to CPE as currently understood, in previous work, Fairclough, Jessop, and Sayer (2004) have approached the cultural turn in the social sciences from the viewpoint of critical semiosis. They argue that semiosis is causally effective as well as meaningful. Events and processes and their emergent effects can be interpreted *and*, at least in part, *explained* by semiosis. Thus it is important to study the role of semiosis in the *construal* and *construction* of economic and political realities, hence in making and remaking the social world. A key feature of CPE in this context is its application of the evolutionary mechanisms of variation, selection, and retention to the analysis of economic imaginaries in regard to theoretical paradigms, policy paradigms, and their interaction as well as its concern with the form-determined, socially-mediated institutional dynamics of (different stages and varieties of) capitalism in a changing world market (see also Jessop, 2004; Sum & Jessop, 2003).

Informing this approach is recognition of the *hypercomplexity* of the natural and social worlds and the impossibility of observing and explaining these worlds (and their interaction) in real time. This requires continuing processes of *complexity reduction* as a condition of 'going on in the world' – with each process entailing a focus on selected aspects of the world, leading to different kinds of lived experience, and entailing different chances of ignoring other aspects of reality that are crucial to the success of specific strategies, projects, or policies (on complexity and, especially, complexity reduction, see Jessop, 2007b; Luhmann, 1995; Rescher, 1998). Applied to economic analysis, for example, at what orthodox economics misleadingly describes as the macro-level, CPE distinguishes the 'actually existing economy' as the chaotic sum of all economic activities (broadly defined as concerned with the social appropriation and transformation of nature for the purposes of material provisioning) from the 'economy' (or, better, 'economies' in the plural) as an imaginatively narrated, more or less coherent subset of these activities. The totality of economic activities is so unstructured and complex that it cannot be an object of calculation, management, governance, or guidance. Instead, such practices are always oriented to subsets of economic relations (economic systems or subsystems) that have been discursively – and perhaps organizationally and institutionally – fixed as objects of intervention. This involves 'economic imaginaries' that rely on semiosis to constitute these subsets. Moreover, if they are to prove more than 'arbitrary, rationalistic, and willed' (Gramsci, 1971, pp. 376–377), these imaginaries must have some significant, albeit necessarily partial, correspondence to real material interdependencies in the actually existing economy and/or in relations between economic and extra-economic activities. These subsets are always selectively defined – due both to limited cognitive capacities and to the discursive and material biases of specific epistemes and economic paradigms. They typically exclude elements – usually unintentionally – that are vital to the overall performance of the subset of economic (and extra-economic) relations that have been identified. Such exclusions limit in turn the efficacy of economic forecasting, management, planning, guidance, governance, et cetera, because such practices do not (indeed, cannot) take account of excluded elements and their impact. Similar arguments would apply, with appropriate changes, to so-called meso- or micro-level economic phenomena, such as industrial districts or individual enterprises.

Imagined economies are discursively constituted and materially reproduced on many sites and scales, in different spatio-temporal contexts, and over various spatio-temporal horizons. They extend from one-off transactions through to stable economic organizations, networks and clusters to 'macro-economic' regimes. While massive scope for variation typically exists at an individual transactional level, the medium- to long-term semiotic and material reproduction requirements of meso-complexes and macro-economic regimes narrow this scope considerably. The recursive selection of semiotic practices and extra-semiotic processes at these scales tends to reduce inappropriate variation and to secure thereby the 'requisite variety' (constrained heterogeneity rather than simple uniformity) that supports the always relative structural coherence of economic activities. Indeed stable semiotic orders, discursive selectivities, social learning, path-dependencies, power relations, patterned complementarities, and material selectivities all become more significant, the more that material interdependencies and/or issues of spatial and intertemporal articulation tend to increase within and across diverse functional systems and the lifeworld. Yet this growing set of constraints also reveals the fragility and, indeed, improbability of the smooth reproduction of complex social orders. This highlights the importance of retaining an appropriate repertoire of semiotic and material resources and practices that can be flexibly and reflexively deployed in response to emerging disturbances and crises (cf. Grabher, 1994; Jessop, 2003).

Economic imaginaries at the meso- and macro-levels emerge as economic, political, and intellectual forces seek to (re-) define specific subsets of economic activities as subjects, sites, and stakes of competition and/or as objects of regulation and to articulate strategies, projects and visions oriented to these imagined economies. Among the main forces involved in such efforts are political parties, think tanks, bodies such as the OECD and World Bank, organized interests such as business associations and trade unions, and social movements; the mass media are also crucial intermediaries in mobilizing elite and/or popular support behind competing imaginaries.[3] These forces tend to manipulate power and knowledge to secure recognition of the boundaries, geometries, temporalities, typical economic agents, tendencies and counter-tendencies, distinctive overall dynamic, and reproduction requirements of different imagined economies (Daly, 1991; Miller & Rose, 1993). They also seek to establish new structural and organizational forms that will help to institutionalize these boundaries, geometries, and temporalities in an appropriate spatio-temporal fix that can displace and/or defer capital's inherent contradictions and crisis-tendencies. However, because of rival economic imaginaries, competing efforts to institute them materially, and an inevitable incompleteness in specifying and securing their respective economic and extra-economic preconditions, each 'imagined economy' is only ever partially constituted. There are always interstitial, residual, marginal, irrelevant, recalcitrant and plain contradictory elements that escape any attempt to identify, govern, and stabilize a given 'economic arrangement' or broader 'economic order' (Malpas & Wickham, 1995; Jessop, 2002).

Nonetheless, relatively successful economic imaginaries have a performative, constitutive force.[4] On the one hand, their operation presupposes a substratum of substantive economic relations and instrumentalities as their elements; on the other, where an imaginary is successfully operationalized and institutionalized, it transforms and naturalizes these elements and instrumentalities into the moments of a specific economy with specific emergent properties. For economic imaginaries identify, privilege, and seek to stabilize some economic activities from the totality of economic relations and transform them into objects of observation, calculation, and governance. Technologies of economic governance, operating sometimes more semiotically, sometimes more materially,[5] constitute their own objects of governance rather than emerging in order to, or operating with the effect that, they govern already pre-constituted objects. Following the crisis of Fordism, two imaginaries gained influence. The first was neo-liberalism, which was also associated with the rise of finance-dominated accumulation and privileged financial innovation; the second was the knowledge-based economy, which had a number of inflections, including a neo-liberal one, and promoted innovation more generally. This chapter focuses on the hegemonic economic imaginary in contemporary capitalism – the knowledge-based economy – and explores its implications for theoretical and policy paradigms, especially its translation into policies for skills and higher education.

THEORETICAL AND POLICY INFLECTIONS OF THE 'KBE'

Discussion of the knowledge-based economy as an economic imaginary and/or economic reality is complicated by two theoretical and practical issues. First, different disciplines draw on different theoretical or disciplinary frameworks to discuss it. This is reflected, for example, in the contrasting concepts of knowledge economy and knowledge society, which draw respectively on economics and sociology. The knowledge economy and knowledge society are each associated with a broader set of cognate concepts that produce distinctive types of imaginary. The former considers knowledge in terms of factors of production, intellectual property, the skills-based economy, national systems of innovation, the knowledge base, the knowledge-driven economy, knowledge management, knowledge transfer, the learning economy, the learning organization, the learning region, and so on. The latter sees it in terms of a collective social resource, the intellectual commons, the division of manual and mental labour, technical and organic intellectuals, the information society, post-industrial society, lifelong learning, the learning society, et cetera (cf. Jessop, 2002, 2007a; and, for a general survey that contains 57 definitions of knowledge economy, KBE, knowledge society, and cognate terms, see the appendices in Carlaw et al., 2006).

Second, cross-cutting the distinction between knowledge economy and knowledge society as alternative, perhaps competing, economic imaginaries is the distinction between theoretical and policy paradigms. Wallis and Dollery (1999) differentiate them as follows:

> Policy paradigms derive from theoretical paradigms but possess much less sophisticated and rigorous evaluations of the intellectual underpinnings of their conceptual frameworks. In essence, policy advisers differentiate policy paradigms from theoretical paradigms by screening out the ambiguities and blurring the fine distinctions characteristic of theoretical paradigms. In a Lakatosian sense, policy paradigms can be likened to the positive heuristics surrounding theoretical paradigms. Accordingly, shifts between policy paradigms will be discontinuous, follow theoretical paradigm shifts, but occur more frequently than theoretical paradigms since they do not require fundamental changes in a negative heuristic.[6] (p. 5)

That this distinction is recognized by persons situated at the interface of the academic and policy worlds is evident from the complaint of a key independent scholar and OECD policy adviser, Bengt-Åke Lundvall, lamenting, in relation to his concept of 'national innovation system,' 'how it has "degenerated," how it has been "abused" and "distorted" while travelling from the academic to the policy world, compared with the connotations he originally intended for it' (cited in Ekland, 2007, p. 17).

This distinction (and its conflation) helps us to situate and understand the explosive interest in the KBE. For this theme is not just a matter of theoretical and empirical curiosity for disinterested observers, but is being actively translated into a wide range of policies and this, in turn, affects the ways in which the contemporary economy is described, examined, and explained. Indeed, as Godin (2006) shows, the concept of the KBE, as developed above all by the Organisation for Economic Co-operation and Development (hereafter OECD), has suggested that:

The concept of a knowledge-based economy is simply [one] that serves to direct the attention of policy-makers to science and technology issues and to their role in the economy and, to this end, a concept that allows one to talk about any issue of science and technology and generate a large set of statistics under one roof. This kind of concept I will call an umbrella concept. A related, but less controversial, thesis ... is that the (resurgence of the) concept of a knowledge-based economy in the 1990s owes a large debt to the OECD – and to the consultants it supported. ... [Indeed,] viewing the OECD as a think-tank is the key to understanding the popularity of the concept among member countries. (2006, pp. 17–18; cf. Miettinen, 2002; Eklund, 2007; Jones, 2008)

These remarks on the transfer of ideas and arguments between the theoretical and policy worlds reinforce the importance of distinguishing between them in order to avoid misunderstandings about the nature and role of discourses about the knowledge-based economy. Indeed, in the absence of this distinction, two complementary fallacies can arise. The first is that the theoretical status of the concept of the KBE imaginary, when viewed largely from the perspective of the ideas that inform the policy world, will be dismissed on the grounds that it is merely a political concept or, worse still, an essentially incoherent buzzword (cf. Godin, 2006) The second is that, when assessed in terms of the demands for analytical rigour appropriate to a scientific concept, the policies proposed to promote the KBE will be dismissed as inconsistent efforts at 'muddling through' and as bound to fail on these grounds alone. What gets missed here is the constitutive or performative force of the corresponding 'policy paradigm' (as a distinctive manifestation of the KBE imaginary) in helping to shape the emergence, provisional stabilization, and eventual consolidation (if any) of the knowledge-based economy as an actually existing phenomenon. This confirms the overall importance of the potential disjunction, mutual influence, and, indeed, interpenetration of theoretical and policy paradigms as alternative modes of

63

expressing, advocating, or translating the KBE imaginary – a topic particularly suited to a CPE analysis.

The significance of this distinction for present purposes is seen in a recent paper by Peters (2006) who, in noting that concepts have histories and family resemblances, argues that this also applies to the 'knowledge society' and 'knowledge economy:'

> These twin concepts while displaying similar characteristics – among them the attempt to describe society or economy in terms of dominant axial principle from which other societal or economic trends can be inferred – belong to different disciplines and discourses. To all intents and purposes these are separate and parallel discourses that are not cross-threading – in each case the trajectories of the disciplines seem to be powered by their own problematics, by the set of problems thrown up by the discipline rather than any external pressures, and they seem particularly impervious to radical cross-disciplinary borrowing or analysis. Where they do come together is in the area of policy, in policy studies, in actual policies or policy discourse, where the master concepts borrowed from the sociology and economics of knowledge have come to help shape and define policy templates for economic and social development and well being. At the level of policy the same demands for theoretical consistency or disciplinary rigor or internal consistency do not seem to operate; rather the easy dualism of the knowledge society and the knowledge economy is embraced without difficulty or contradiction. While there is, of course, some analysis of trends and even the collection of relevant data, these twin concepts are empirically underdetermined. They operate more like performative ideologies with constitutive effects at the level of public policy. And there are a whole series of self-legitimating sibling concepts spawned by policy analysts and think tanks that now roll off the tongue of any sociology undergraduate: 'information society,' 'learning society,' 'information economy,' and, more recently, 'learning economy.' (p. 1)

Three interrelated conclusions follow from the above discussion. First, having accepted the *prima facie* usefulness of the distinction between possible theoretical and policy expressions of the KBE imaginary, it is important not to conflate them or reduce one to the other but to explore their changing articulation in different contexts. Second, we must resist the temptation to derive immediate policy lessons from theoretical accounts of the KBE and/or to subject policy models to a purely theoretical critique. Third, from a CPE perspective, the distinction poses interesting questions about (a) the relative hegemony or dominance of different theoretical and policy expressions of economic imaginaries; (b) the discursive and material factors and forces that introduce variation, shape the selection, and consolidate the retention of hegemonic, subhegemonic, counter-hegemonic, or marginal accounts of the economy, its dynamic, and its conditions of existence; and (c) the performative force of economic imaginaries in shaping the actually existing economic realm. On the last of these issues, the performative force of ideas about the knowledge economy has been reinforced by its appropriation and promotion as a 'knowledge brand' for marketing purposes (see Sum, 2009, and the role of the Global Knowledge Economics Council, below). Together these issues will affect the changing discursive and material boundaries of the economic and extra-economic and their changing implications for economic performance. This could well be reflected in turn in changes in the scope, scale, and relative primacy of different policy fields. This has particular significance, as we will see, for the role of education, knowledge creation, and knowledge transfer to competitiveness.

THREE EXAMPLES

The idea of the 'information economy' as a distinct stage in economic development may well have emerged first in Japan. The term was introduced there by Tadeo Umesao in the 1960s, but it did not really take off until the late 1970s, by which time 'information economy' and analogous ideas had also been firmly established elsewhere in East Asia and in many advanced Western capitalist societies (cf. Dordick & Wang, 1993; Masuda, 1981; May, 2002). The use of such terms was based largely on the *speculative extrapolation* of contemporary trends into the future, focusing on trends in the most advanced national economies as if other economies would simply follow their path with a greater or lesser time lag. So we find references to the information economy, post-industrial economy, knowledge economy, and so forth (for a comprehensive list of 75 such terms, which were introduced at various times from 1950 to 1984, see Beniger, 1986; cf. Carlaw et al., 2006). In turn the first wave of information economy strategies were mainly focused on investment in information and communication technologies (ICTs) rather than the move to a knowledge-driven or knowledge-based economy. Typical of these was the American National Information Infrastructure programme launched in 1991, which was rapidly followed by many Western European economies and the European Union.

A broader notion of information economy developed in Japan and other East Asian economies. This was linked to the exhaustion of export-led growth based on catch-up dynamics, which prompted various intellectuals, think tanks, business leaders, and policy makers[7] to search for new bases for competition. The solution was not only to invest in information and communication technologies, but also to upgrade to an innovative, information-based economy; in later discourses and strategies, this idea would be expanded to the more encompassing notion of the knowledge economy. The first explicit information economy and/or KBE strategies in East Asia were the 'Intelligent Island' strategy in Singapore and Malaysia's '2020 Vision' – both of which were presented in 1991. Other East Asian countries followed, including Japan's High Performance National Information Infrastructure [NII] Plan (1994), Taiwan's NII 2005 (1994), South Korea's NII 2003 (1994), Vietnam's IT 2000 plan (1995), and Smart Philippines (2000). Despite the similar timing in East and West, Asian models and strategies tended to be more comprehensive, going beyond ICTs to broader economic and, even more importantly, extra-economic dimensions of innovation-led growth (for an outline of information economy strategies in this period, see Ducatel, Webster, & Herrmann, 2000). Nonetheless, the overriding conclusion to be drawn from this period is the key role of economic narratives and associated imaginaries in identifying turning points and/or crises and in reorienting technology, industrial, and wider-ranging economic policies.

To illustrate this conclusion and the earlier arguments about economic imaginaries, I present three brief case studies drawn from Western experience. The first concerns the growing sensitivity of U.S. policy makers and stakeholders to the importance of innovation and knowledge as strategic assets. The second is the 'National System of Innovation' (NSI), which was the precursor of the KBE as the dominant economic imaginary in the OECD and its transfer to member states and other economies. Its significance for our purposes is that, although 'the OECD always looked for conceptual frameworks to catch the attention of policy-makers' (Godin, 2006, p. 18), the National System of Innovation failed in this regard. So the third case turns to the knowledge economy and knowledge-based economy, which has proved very successful as an economic imaginary.

From Industrial Competitiveness to Knowledge-Based Economy

Almost as soon as it became the undisputed hegemonic power in the capitalist world following World War II, the United States has experienced agitated and ongoing debates about its alleged lack of economic competitiveness. These have co-existed with equally angst-ridden concerns about threats to its national military security, whether from the Soviet Bloc, China, or, most recently, asymmetric warfare waged by terrorist networks (on the role of these twin myths in legitimating government support for industry in a regime officially opposed to 'socialistic' or 'communistic' state intervention in the market economy, see Belabes, 1999). Worries about competitiveness prompted Congress to establish in 1978 the Office of Technology Assessment (OTA) to monitor the competitiveness of American industries. Its remit covered industry and market structures, the nature of work forces, availability of materials and components, supporting infrastructures, the environment for innovation and technology diffusion, business and economic conditions, government policies and interactions with the private sector, and international trade relations.

In 1983, in response to the perceived threat of 'Japan as Number One' and other indicators of technological, industrial, and financial decline, President Reagan set up the President's Commission on Industrial Competitiveness. Two key outcomes were the Young Report (President's Commission, 1986; see also Young, 1988) and a 'Council of Competitiveness', which was established in 1986, to act as a national 'forum for elevating national competitiveness to the forefront of national consciousness' (Council on Competitiveness, 2007). Commissions on competitiveness have continued to report regularly since 1983, with the most recent being the twenty-fifth anniversary report of the Council on Competitiveness' *Make* (2011) (for other reports, see www.compete.org). The Council is also very active, focusing on national innovation and identifying the importance of action to promote this in three main fields: talent, investment, and infrastructure. Regarding talent, the focus is on education and training to enable 'talented people' to acquire 'cutting-edge skills' so that they can create 'new ideas and innovative technologies' and 'keep the economy strong and growing stronger.' A particular concern has been lack of competitiveness in 'such critical fields as science, engineering, math and technical skills' and hence on measures to build 'a world-class workforce by initiating programs to encourage diversity in the S&E (i.e., science and engineering) pipelines and excellence in math and science education in America's schools at all levels' (Council on Competitiveness, 2001). This in turn is reflected in a whole series of policy recommendations concerning the reorganization of grade school education, further and higher education, and lifelong learning (see below). In addition, at all levels from the North American Free Trade Area down through the federal state, regional blocs of states, states, metropolitan regions, and cities to towns and neighbourhoods, we find concerted efforts to promote competitiveness in these and other areas.

National System of Innovation

'National System of Innovation' (or, sometimes, 'National Innovation System') is a paradigm that is actively promoted internationally by, even if it did not originate in, the OECD (cf. Albert & Laberge, 2007; Ekland, 2007; Freeman, 1995). It refers to the flow of technology and information among people, enterprises and institutions that is held to be central to continuing innovation on the national level. The concept emphasizes the contribution of a complex web of relations among private, public, and third sector actors in the NSI, including enterprises, universities and government research institutes at national, regional, and local levels that contribute to the production and, even more importantly, diffusion of new technologies and the wider knowledge base that supports their adoption in economically useful ways (cf. Freeman, 1995; Lundvall, 1992; Nelson, 1992; OECD, 1997). It has been closely linked in the work of the OECD with the concepts of learning economy and learning region (Foray & Lundvall, 1996; Lundvall, 1992; Lundvall & Johnson, 1994; Maillat & Kebir, 1999).

In a study of Finland in the OECD context with implications extending beyond the Finnish case, Miettinen (2002) has explored 'national system of innovation' as a metaphor performing several rhetorical functions. He argues that it simplifies, persuades and reorients thinking about the interrelationships between science and society; it incorporates tacit value schemes and promotes a vision; helps forge consensus, mobilizing various actors in particular ways; and it contributes to shaping events along lines prescribed by model. He adds that these functions can be performed in part because the definition of the NIS is loose, allowing different actors to impute different meanings to the term. At the same time, the associated vision of increasing the country's economic competitiveness often resonates with broader political trends in society. After presenting the Finnish case, Miettinen developed an 'epistemology of transdiscursive terms, that is, terms with significant rhetorical functions that flourish at the interface between science, public discourse, and politics and thereby provide the basis for textual interlacing and circulation of self-referentiality. In the language deployed above, these are terms that have a key bridging role in linking theoretical and policy paradigms, facilitating the translation between them but also disguising important differences in their form and function. In particular, he identified six key functions that they perform:

1. They must have a minimal traditional epistemic function in the sense of providing a representation or empirically anchored account of aspects of reality;
2. They serve as epistemic organizers, synthesizing earlier accounts and providing a new angle on things. Suitable terms and metaphors are used in organizing one's perspective, integrating various themes that formerly were separated. They provide a sense of inter-connection or holism;
3. They supply a world-view or a diagnosis of an era, a function that is also central to the integrative power of the conceptual framework;
4. They serve as boundary-crossers by engaging various social groups and institutions in shared discussion. That is why they are called transdiscursive (they cross between and link different discourses);
5. They serve ideological and consensus-creating (or vision-carrying) functions; and
6. They help mobilize and empower a multiplicity of actors under what the participants themselves come to perceive as a common banner. (adapted and expanded from Miettinen, 2002, p. 137)

Having framed the problem in this manner, Miettinen argues that transdiscursive terms must be loose to provide the interpretative flexibility needed to accommodate different interests expressed by actors across different domains, such as government, university and industry. The credibility of a term will in part depend on linkages with scientific communities because political viability derives from the semblance of scientific credibility. It follows that the tension between the epistemic reality-representing function of the term and its future-oriented rhetorical and discursive organizing functions has to be contained to prevent the puncturing and consequent collapse of the metaphor. This risk is illustrated from the OECD's (2002) admission in a review paper, that 'there are still concerns in the policy making community that the NIS [sic] approach has too little operational value and is difficult to implement' (cited in Godin, 2006, p. 19). This failure is one factor behind the rise of the KBE as an alternative concept. Thus Dominique Foray, one of the OECD consultants behind the new term, criticized the concept of National System of Innovation as 'neither strikingly original, nor rhetorically stirring' (David & Foray, 1995, p. 14) and for placing too much stress on national institutions and economic growth and not enough on the distribution of knowledge.

Knowledge-Based Economy

Every economy is a knowledge economy, but not every economy has been called a knowledge economy, let alone finds itself so labelled by its most prominent spokespersons as one of its most significant contemporary self-descriptions (on the polyvocal nature of self-descriptions of society, see Luhmann, 1987, 1990, 1995). Indeed, as indicated above, this label is relatively new. In many cases, especially early on, emphasis fell more on the role of information than of knowledge. More recent uses of the terms 'knowledge economy' and 'knowledge-based economy' (plus related abbreviations and acronyms such as the K-economy and KBE) are less concerned with forecasting the future than with the *empirical description* and *quasi-prescriptive benchmarking* of central features of actually existing economies. Related theoretical paradigms seek to establish the novelty of the KBE by identifying its distinguishing features in terms of some combination of the reflexive application of knowledge to the production of knowledge, the key role of innovation, learning, and knowledge transfer in economic performance, and the increasing importance of the intellectual commons and/or intellectual property rights in contemporary competition. In turn, the hegemonic policy paradigm is especially concerned to establish the reality of the KBE through the compilation and repetition of statistical indicators, through the development of benchmarks and league tables, and through the elaboration of an interwoven set of useful concepts, slogans, and buzzwords. These can then be applied to generate a relatively simple set of policy prescriptions and legitimations to be applied to many sectors, many scales, and many countries.

The key document was published by the OECD in 1996 under the title *The Knowledge-Based Economy*. This was followed in 1997 by guidelines for competitiveness in the form of *National Innovation Systems*. This prompted institution-building within and across the public and private sectors at many scales and in regard to many spheres bearing more or less directly on competitiveness in a knowledge-based economy. Within larger firms, knowledge management became a key discipline and knowledge audits were conducted regularly to identify strategic knowledge assets (Malhotra, 2000); governments established knowledge ministries, departments and agencies; national states began to map their 'national innovation systems' (NIS) and take measures to strengthen them; standardized vocabularies were promoted in the early 2000s to guide public and private sector debate with the engagement of various national standard agencies under the 'not-for-profit' auspices of the Global Knowledge Economics Council. This was taken further with the production of competitiveness indexes, such as the Global Competitiveness Report (World Economic Forum) from 1979 onwards and the *World Competitiveness Yearbook* (published by the Institute for Management Development in Geneva from 1989 onwards).[8] This highlighted 'the softer side of competition' in a KBE, that is, the role of value-adding through the creation, the management and the transfer of information and knowledge (American National Standards Institute & Global Knowledge Economics Council, 2001, p. 4). There is now a global growth industry that produces multiple competitiveness rankings for countries, regions, cities, and so on, each of which employs different statistical and other sources, directed at economic actors and policy makers around the world (for discussion, see Lall, 2001; Bristow, 2005; Oxley et al., 2007).

Godin has identified the leading role of the OECD in promoting the KBE as the key site of competition and the key focus of competitive strategies. He explains this in terms of the OECD's efforts to respond to the inadequate rhetorical appeal of 'national system of innovation' and 'learning economy' by reviving and consolidating the idea of the knowledge-based economy and, on this basis, identifying the importance of knowledge management and knowledge transfer. He notes above all the OECD's enrolment of the promoters of the KBE concept (e.g., Lundvall and Foray) as consultants and, even more importantly, the production of statistics to give the concept some empirical content and plausibility (Godin, 2006, p. 19). He emphasizes that a new approach was needed in order that the OECD could influence the policy process and notes that the rhetorical appeal of the KBE concept depends on its 'easy translation of readily available academic fads into keywords (or buzzwords), then into slogans in order to catch the attention of policy-makers.' In addition, the OECD and policy makers in its member states are under continuing pressure to publish:

> The OECD publishes biannual, yearly and biennial reports, among them those for ministers' conferences, where timeframes are very tight. Umbrella concepts are very fertile for producing documents. They synthesize what is already available, what comes from day-to-day work conducted in other contexts and, above all, what is fashionable, often at the price of original work. (Godin, 2006, p. 24)

A key factor in reinforcing the ability of memorable buzzwords and slogans to sell ideas is their association with 'a plethora of figures and graphs' (Godin, 2004, p. 684). These have a spurious scientific authority as well as intuitive persuasive force even though the OECD itself occasionally concedes that its indicators did not adequately capture the complex, dynamic nature of knowledge development and acquisition (e.g., OECD, 1995). For, as Godin notes, this presentational strategy appeals to the typical OECD readership: ministers, policy makers, journalists, et cetera. Thus, writing on the OECD's promotion of the idea of the 'New Economy,' Godin (2004) argues that:

> The strategy developed at the DSTI [i.e., Directorate for Science, Technology, and Industry] to integrate productivity into its statistics and reports was three-fold. First, digest all available academic work in order to imitate their methodology. Second, internationalise the (academic and national) statistics to make a convincing case for its member countries. Third, organise the discourse into a policy-oriented framework, using buzzwords. In the present case, it was new growth theories and the New Economy that were the buzzwords. But over the OECD history the latter also shared their popularity with others: high technology, national system of innovation, globalisation, knowledge-based economy, and information economy. (p. 688)

These three studies, illustrative of many other economic imaginaries, suggest four key conclusions on the power of economic imaginaries in the emergence, selection, and retention of theoretical and policy paradigms. First, during any period of economic discontinuity, many alternative economic imaginaries may be proposed, each based on a specific ensemble of economic categories linked in turn to wider vocabularies. Second, some of these economic imaginaries may be more resonant than others in a given conjuncture. This will depend in part on the ease of any interchange between theoretical and policy paradigms – reflecting the need both for scientific authority and for easy communicability to lay decision-makers – and in part on the centrality of the organizations and institutions that mediate between these worlds and undertake the necessary translation. Only when the theoretical and policy paradigms promoted by central organizations and institutions lack resonance and/or are held to have manifestly failed when pursued for significant periods does it become possible for marginal or counter-hegemonic forces to provide alternative economic imaginaries. Even here, if the central organizations and institutions are sufficiently powerful, they may persist in their error(s) and seek to repress or, at least, marginalize alternative imaginaries and policy proposals.[9] Third, where, as in the case of the KBE, theoretical and policy paradigms tend to reinforce each other because theoretically-justified policy paradigms are widely adopted and, more importantly, acquire a performative and constitutive character, then the relevant economic imaginary will be retained through normalization and institutionalization. But this will depend on the capacity of the economic imaginary to envisage potentialities in a relatively fluid conjuncture, to orient the actions of critical social forces towards their realization, and to provide means to consolidate this movement once it is initiated. And, fourth, from the viewpoint of a critical cultural political economy, this depends in turn on the capacity of the economic imaginary, once translated into economic strategies and appropriate economic and extra-economic policies, to regularize and stabilize the course of capital accumulation within specific spatio-temporal fixes, including their facilitation of the displacement and/or deferral of associated contradictions, conflicts, and crisis tendencies elsewhere and/or into the future (cf. Jessop, 2002, 2004).

STAGES OF CAPITALISM

As part of the general CPE approach, competition is regarded as a complex process that cannot be fully grasped in real time by market actors or economic observers. Indeed, this is implied in the very notion of an 'invisible hand.' Accordingly, the factors and forces bearing on competitiveness may be construed quite differently from the viewpoint of different economic imaginaries, as may the relations among relevant economic and extra-economic factors. CPE also claims that those economic imaginaries that get selected and retained also have a constitutive power in shaping economic orders and the manner of their embedding in wider ensembles of social relations (or social formations), that is, that they can involve not only construal but also construction. These claims are especially important for theoretical and policy paradigms concerned with the KBE and the conditions making for competitiveness in this 'new' form of capitalist accumulation regime. For economic competitiveness is an essentially contested, inherently relational, and politically controversial concept. There are many ways to define it, many modalities of competition, and many sites of competition. Definitions of competitiveness and their associated discourses are liable to change. Thus mercantilist notions from the seventeenth century can be contrasted with 1890s imperialism or recent worries about structural competitiveness or innovation-competitiveness (see Reinert, 1995; Cho & Moon, 2000; Porter, 1990). Indeed, as these examples suggest, different ideas of competitiveness are linked with different economic imaginaries. During the mercantilist period, for example, economics was regarded strongly as a matter of political calculation because it concerned state policies to control trade in order to increase financial reserves and because the economy was not yet seen (rightly or wrongly) as a distinct system with its own economic logic (Magnusson, 1994). In the classical imperialist period, global economic competition was mediated through state enclosure of territory abroad for military-political as well as geo-economic purposes (ten Brink, 2008). In the transition from classical imperialism to a more liberal post-war order (in the shadow of U.S. hegemony), competition focused more on domestic growth and multinational foreign investment, leading to conflicts between techno-nationalism and techno-globalism (Ostry & Nelson, 1995; Ruggie, 1982). And, with the rise of the neo-liberal transnational financial order and the reorientation of economic and political strategies to the opportunities and constraints of a globalizing knowledge-based economy, competition has been restructured again, this time over innovation policies and how best to subordinate the extra-economic to the 'demands' of economic competition (Jessop, 2002).

The rise of the KBE as the hegemonic economic imaginary was neither a fateful necessity nor an arbitrary act of will. It resulted from the operation of the usual evolutionary mechanisms of variation, selection, and retention as the social forces backing one or another economic imaginary compete for support in a particular, complex conjuncture. This was the crisis of the dominant post-war accumulation regimes, including Atlantic Fordism, East Asian exportism, Latin American import substitution, and, albeit less obviously capitalist, state socialism in the Soviet Bloc and in mainland China. Economic crises normally disorient social forces and lead to great *variation* in discourses addressed to their nature, causes, responsibilities, management, and possible long-term solutions. In some cases this involved efforts to define the crisis in political as well as economic terms, requiring a radical break in the form of political regime in order to radically modify the balance of forces and pursue 'necessary' structural reforms (e.g., Thatcherism); in others, it was sufficient for the economic crisis to be defined in terms of a loss of competitiveness in a changing world market that required new economic strategies supported by appropriate policy adjustments (e.g., the Nordic economies). These crisis interpretations are subject in turn to both semiotic and material *selection*, in terms of the initial resonance among personal, organizational, and meta-narratives as well as social forces' differential capacity to access and control the key sites and media in and through which competing discourses are communicated. Resonant discourses that are also widely disseminated to key social forces and get translated into effective strategies and policies will eventually be *retained*. This involves even more important material mediation in so far as these strategies and policies must be (seen to be) effective within the spatio-temporal horizons of the social forces who matter in a given social formation. Where economic imaginaries satisfy these semiotic and material tests, they are likely to be retained in three key areas: (a) incorporation in habitus, hexis, personal identity, organizational routines, institutional rules; (b) objectification in built environment, material and intellectual technologies; and (c) continuing expression in economic strategies, state projects, and hegemonic visions. In general, the wider the range of sites (horizontal and vertical) where resonant discourses are retained, the greater is the potential for effective institutionalization. This in turn should lead to relative structured coherence across institutional orders and modes of thought and in relatively durable patterns of social compromise among key actors.

Seen in these terms, three sets of changes have occurred in the transition from the economic imaginaries associated with Atlantic Fordism, Asian exportism, import substitution industrialisation, and state socialism to the currently hegemonic economic imaginaries that are oriented in different ways to a globalizing knowledge-based economy:

1. The first change is a shift from imaginaries that treat macro-economics mainly in national terms to imaginaries that are oriented to multiple, interpenetrating scales of economic organization up to and including the world market;
2. The second change concerns the expansion of the 'economic' to include an increasing array of factors and forces that were previously considered 'economically irrelevant;' and
3. The third change involves the widening of 'extra-economic' factors and forces that are now considered 'economically relevant.'

The education system figures in all three areas, for it is increasingly construed in post-national terms and is being reorganized on this basis at various scales. It is increasingly construed as a directly economic factor (education is now located within the profit-oriented, market-mediated economic or, at least, subject to commodification and/or evaluation in terms of market proxies); and, where it is located outside the market or quasi-market economy, it is nonetheless increasingly seen as an extra-economic factor that bears directly and ever-more critically on economic competitiveness (cf. Ball, 2007).

The OECD has had a key role in linking and promoting all three sets of changes so that they tend to be mutually reinforcing within the limits of a world market that is still governed in the shadow of sovereign national states, some of which are, of course, more powerful than others. It is primarily concerned with securing an appropriate balance between competition and co-operation between developed capitalist economies in regard to the economic strategies of enterprises as well as the economic and economically relevant policies pursued by governments at different scales. Established as part of the post-war international regime of embedded liberalism, the OECD faced problems in the late 1960s and early 1970s around the declining economic performance of advanced capitalist economies and the best ways to insert emerging economies into the world market. Its initial response to the unfolding economic crisis was to call for greater flexibility compared to the rigidities of an Atlantic Fordism based on mass production and mass consumption, big business, powerful unions, and big government; it then called for greater structural and/or systemic competitiveness[10] in terms of extra-economic as well as economic institutional arrangements (although this was framed primarily within the old economic imaginary); it shifted again, this time to recommendations about how to improve national systems of innovation (the start of a shift towards the KBE), to subsequent calls for a learning economy (an even stronger shift in this direction), and, finally, for measures to effect the transition to the knowledge-based economy as the next stage in capitalist development. At each step, the nature, scope, and significance of the extra-economic as well as economic factors making for competitiveness has tended to expand. This holds not only for firms as they seek to identify an ever-widening range of sources of dynamic competitive advantage (and disadvantage) and to capitalize upon the former and eliminate the latter; but also for the economic and extra-economic policies to be pursued by policy makers and associated stakeholders on all scales, from industrial or central business districts through cities and regions to nations and supranational blocs. A key element in all areas is the promotion of entrepreneurialism and an entrepreneurial culture supported, in more recent policy paradigms, by calls for investment in social capital and for the promotion of good governance. The wide range of indicators of competitiveness that are now included in benchmarks for technological, structural, systemic, and future-oriented growth competitiveness is a good index of this transformation in theoretical and policy paradigms.

SOME IMPLICATIONS FOR EDUCATION

The initial crisis in/of Fordism prompted a critique of education as failing to meet the needs of a changing economy and redefined labour market. This was associated with an increased emphasis on inculcating flexibility and adaptability as a short-term response to the vagaries of the business cycle and greater volatility in the labour market (Robins & Webster, 1989). Flexibility and flexible learning were also linked to organizational change, especially with the rise of open and distance learning enabled by new ICTs and new methods of context-situated and problem-oriented teaching and learning. Later, there was a broader emphasis on the role of education in promoting the globalizing, knowledge-based economy through the development of human capital. This was linked to growing concern with the certification of transferable as well as specific skills in schools, post-compulsory education, and on-the-job training. Training and lifelong learning became a central component of economic as well as social policy in all advanced capitalist economies, and they were tied to the growing consensus that successful competition depends on building the knowledge base and human capital.

These trends are evident at all levels of education, from schools through further and higher education to on-the-job training and career-linked lifelong learning and thence to 'universities of the third age' for older people. A cross-national survey some ten years ago of general discourses and proposals for educational reform identified a new orthodoxy based on:

(1) improving national economies by tightening the connection between schooling, employment, productivity, and trade; (2) enhancing student

outcomes in employment-related skills and competencies; (3) attaining more direct control over curriculum content and assessment; (4) reducing the costs to government of education; and (5) increasing community input to education by more direct involvement in school decision-making and pressure of market choice. (Carter & O'Neill summarized by Ball, 1998, p. 122)

Thus, schools were increasingly expected to enable children to become enterprising subjects and to develop their personal skills and capacity for team-working. They were also expected to provide the basis for the transition to work and to forge closer links with future employers. As Mulderrig (2008) indicates for the British case, a growing emphasis was placed on the development of technical, personal, and life skills that would be useful in employment. This is reflected in a proliferation of programmes to integrate education and work through more vocational training, partnerships, work experience, training credits, and so on. Linked to this is the extension of the new managerialism and audit culture into schools (as well as universities) with its emphasis on quasi-markets, internal cost centres, performativity, targets, benchmarking, staff appraisal, etc. (Clarke & Newman, 1997; Fairclough, 1993; Mautner, 2005; Power, 1997).

The tightened connection between schooling, employment, productivity and trade is reflected in a cross-national reorientation of the notion of skill, with increasing emphasis on key skills, lifelong learning and employability, as technology, corporate restructuring and volatile markets are believed to have ended the Fordist fantasy of jobs for life (Lauder et al., 2001). Education has become integrated into the workfarist project that downgrades the Keynesian state's commitment to full employment and now emphasizes its contribution to creating conditions for full employability. Thus, responsibility for becoming employable is devolved to individual members of the labour force who should acquire the individual skills, competencies, flexibility, adaptability and personal dispositions to enable them to compete for jobs in national and global labour markets. They may be largely responsible for this as enterprising individuals investing in their own human capital or as equal citizens entitled to support from the state and social partners to improve their skills. In all cases there should be increasing co-operation between colleges, universities and other learning providers and the world of work. Thus, employers and practitioners are involved in curriculum development, managers are drawn into educational governance and agenda-setting, mobility between the academy and non-academic worlds is encouraged, and colleges and universities deliver lifelong learning through advanced professional programmes, continuing professional development, part-time, evening, and distance teaching, remedial and second-chance courses, and so on (Teichler, 1999, p. 85).

Notwithstanding this cross-national policy discourse convergence, there are still marked differences in take-up and implementation. Brown et al. (2001) report, for example, that, where economies were dominated by a belief that the future lay in a post-industrial service economy, there was a polarization between education and training for high-skilled elites and for a flexible, low-skilled service sector. The latter sector also had relatively low investment and generated output more through long working hours than increasing productivity. Conversely, where manufacturing was still accorded a key role in accumulation strategies, the state emphasized intermediate skills and the need for education and training to link industry and services. This was coupled with high capital investment to harness skills for a high productivity economy. The United States and United Kingdom exemplify the first model; the second is illustrated by Germany.

Turning more directly to further and higher education, there has been a great emphasis on shifting university teaching and research from its ivory-towered intellectual isolation back into closer and more continuous contact with the economy, the state and the community as vital co-producers and consumers of useful knowledge. This is especially clear in technology, the sciences and medicine, and has also penetrated the social sciences so that it is not merely graduates but faculty members themselves who are expected to develop extensive links with users in industry, business, the professions, government and local communities. There is growing emphasis on external fund-raising, patenting, technology transfer, research parks, commercial spin-offs, science and technology parks, incubators, consultancy services – amounting to the emergence of a veritable 'academic capitalism' in liberal economies that encourages entrepreneurial universities and transforms faculty members into enterprising bearers of intellectual capital (Slaughter & Leslie, 1997). This change was encouraged in the United Sates (the principal cheerleader for the knowledge-based economy in the 1990s as a response to the perception of declining industrial competitiveness) through changes in federal funding for research, enabling universities to keep the intellectual property in their discoveries, as well as through the more general extension of the scope and duration of intellectual property rights. Universities are also encouraged to commercialize their research. This was intended to encourage academic entrepreneurialism, to subsidize corporate R&D, and to facilitate regional economic development. Similar patterns can be found in other university systems. Overall, in the words of Etzkowitz (1994), a leading researcher on the 'triple helix' interface between university, business and the state, writing at an early stage in this transformation:

> Virtually every country that has a university, whether it was founded for reasons of education or prestige, is now attempting to organise knowledge-based economic development. ... As the university becomes more dependent upon industry and government, so have industry and government become more dependent upon the university. In the course of the 'second academic revolution' a new social contract is being drawn up between the university and the wider society, in which public funding for the university is made contingent upon a more direct contribution to the economy. (pp. 149, 151)

Two apparently contrary but actually complementary strategies are being adopted here. On the one hand, the state is asserting the importance of education in the realization of national economic interests; and, on the other hand, it is conceding greater autonomy to educational institutions in how they serve these interests (Marginson, 1999). But this autonomy is being exercised in the context of the hegemony of knowledge-based accumulation strategies, the growing participation of the bearers of this strategy in the shaping of education mission statements, the increasing financial dependence of further and higher education on third-party revenues that do not derive from the state or, in cases where student fee income has been a significant source of income, from students, and, in all cases, the growing dependence of university revenues on student fees (which have, for example, risen dramatically in the United States and have also been rising in the United Kingdom), business research contracts, third mission activities, and university branding strategies relative to the share of income as block grants from government agencies. The first strategy 'involves a reaffirmation of the state functions of education as a "public good," while the second subjects education to the disciplines of the market and the methods and values of business and redefines it as a competitive private good' (Marginson, 1999, p. 122). Together, these strategies serve to reinforce the primacy of accumulation within the organization of education and to promote differentiation in the higher education sector between top research universities at the cutting-edge of the knowledge-based economy that engage in world-class international research co-operation and others that tend to specialize in cost-effective mass credentialization and opportunities for life-long learning at a more local or regional scale. At both ends of this increasingly stretched-out spectrum, however, there is emphasis on close links to the users of research and education to ensure, as far as possible, that economic needs are being served.

Again, there are different routes to this reconfiguration. In the United States, universities have long been encouraged to operate as business firms and to be entrepreneurial. Pressures in this direction have nonetheless been reinforced from the 1980s onwards, with the result that many universities have reoriented their activities from teaching towards research to generate patents and royalties. Moreover, because they must still teach, American universities must resort to continuing efforts to cut costs and boost efficiency by standardizing and commoditizing education, casualizing and flexibilizing intellectual labour, and selling on-line lecture courses. In Europe, the European Round Table is promoting a neo-liberal agenda that sees education and training as 'strategic investments vital for the future success of industry,' and has proposed measures to strengthen the comparatively weak influence of business on the curriculum and adapt it to the needs of industry through the development of private–public partnerships (Levidow, 2001). This has also been encouraged by the EU itself in the hope of increasing the international market share of EU education and to reduce the duration and costs as well as the inefficiencies in mass higher education (Bologna Declaration, 1999; see also Fairclough & Wodak, 2008). Overall, there is now a much enhanced global competition for talent – from recruitment of students at all levels through researchers in universities, research centres, and enterprises to skilled knowledge workers, the 'creative class,' and high-flying and effective entrepreneurs. All of this has important consequences for university governance in relation to internal management, accounting, audit, learning modes, incentives, career tracks, and so on as well as in relation to external partnerships, knowledge transfer, political guidance, and government controls. Thus, the traditional model of university governance, depicted most famously in the Humboldt model (on which, see Ash, 2008), is being challenged by demands for greater accountability to a multi-tiered state system, all manner of business interests from small- and medium-sized firms to national and international champions, and, more generally, to the treadmill of competitiveness across a wide range of scales and in relation to an ever-expanding range of economic and extra-economic factors.

CONCLUSIONS

This chapter has pursued three main objectives. First, it aimed to introduce a new approach to the political economy of the restructuring and reorientation of universities in advanced capitalist social formations. This approach has been presented as 'cultural political economy' and draws on several variants of critical discourse analysis and critical political economy. Its key innovation from the viewpoint of CDA is its emphasis on the variation, selection, and retention over time of alternative economic imaginaries and their contribution to the construction as well as construal of actually existing economies and their extra-economic conditions and supports. Conversely, its key innovation from the viewpoint of political economy is to resist the naturalization of economic categories, structures, and processes at the same time as showing the continued importance of the historically specific economic logic of an economic order that is primarily organized as a profit-oriented, market-mediated system with all that this implies for the modes of competition, the changing forms of economic competitiveness, and the continuing struggle to secure the extra-economic as well as economic conditions for competitiveness within and between economic spaces. Second, it has applied the cultural political economy approach to the emergence of the knowledge-based economy as the hegemonic economic imaginary of the current stage of capitalism – locating this in relation to the crisis of the main forms of economic growth in the post-war period, not only within the advanced capitalist economies but also in Latin America, East Asia, the Soviet bloc, and Mainland China, as well as in relation to the role of organizations and institutions charged with developing theoretical and policy paradigms that draw on and contribute to new economic imaginaries. And, third, it has indicated some of the implications of this transformation in economic imaginaries and their translation into economic policies and new forms of competitiveness for the education system in general and higher education in particular.[11] It remains, therefore, to invite readers to consider the implications of the rise of the KBE imaginary and its translation into business strategies, state policies, and 'common sense' for the increasing primacy of economic goals in the education sector.

NOTES

[1] I have benefitted from comments by Eva Hartmann, Norman Fairclough, D.W. Livingstone, Ngai-Ling Sum, and Ruth Wodak. The usual disclaimers hold.

[2]   Previous work in CPE by the present author and his colleagues has drawn mostly on the dialectical relational discourse approach associated with Norman Fairclough (e.g., 1992, 2003; see also Wodak & Meyer, 2001). But its evolutionary and institutional orientation also means that CPE can be linked to conceptual history in its German variants (*Begriffsgeschichte*, historical semantics) concerned with the selective co-evolution of discursive and structural changes over long periods (e.g., Koselleck, 1982) as well as its Cambridge (Skinnerian) variant concerned with the use of concepts in specific historical contexts to achieve particular purposes (e.g., Skinner, 1987).

[3]   I am not suggesting here that mass media can be completely disentangled from the broader networks of social relations in which they operate but I do want to highlight the diminished role of an autonomous public sphere in shaping semiosis.

[4]   Indeed, there is no economic imaginary without materiality (Bayart, 1994, pp. 20–21). On other accounts of the imaginary, see Castoriadis (1979) and Taylor (2004).

[5]   Although all practices are semiotic *and* material, the relative causal efficacy of these elements varies.

[6]   For Imre Lakatos (1978), a research programme provided rules about what paths of inquiry to pursue (positive heuristic) and which to avoid (negative heuristic).

[7]   Key figures here, in addition to East Asian intellectuals, think tanks, business strategists, and officials, were two Western thinkers, Alvin Toffler (1980) and Daniel Bell (1973, 1989).

[8]   The WEF and IMD published a joint report for a time but decided to separate reports because of measurement differences.

[9]   Thus Karl Deutsch (1963) notes that one measure of power is the ability not to have to learn from one's mistakes.

[10]   On structural competitiveness, see Chesnais (1987); on systemic competitiveness, Messner (1996; Esser et al., 1996). See also *STI Review* (published by the OECD).

[11]   For more detailed discussion of these implications, see other contributions in Jessop, Fairclough, & Wodak (2008).

REFERENCES

Albert, M. & Laberge, S. (2007). The legitimation and dissemination processes of the innovation system approach: The case of the Canadian and Québec science and technology policy. *Science, Technology & Human Values, 11*(2), 221–249.

American National Standards Institute & Global Knowledge Economics Council. (2001). Knowledge management – Vocabulary. Proposed American National Standard. Standards Committee working documents. Tucson: Global Knowledge Economics Council. [A draft can be retrieved from www.pwsb.pl/files/Pliki/PDF/English.pdf.]

Ash, M.G. (2008). From 'Humboldt' to 'Bologna:' History as discourse in higher education reform debates in German-speaking Europe. In Jessop, B., Fairclough, N., & Wodak, R. (Eds.), *Education and the knowledge-based economy in Europe* (pp. 41–61). Rotterdam: Sense.

Ball, S.J. (1998). Big policies/small world: An introduction to international perspectives in education policy. *Comparative Education, 34*(2), 119–130.

Ball, S.J. (2007). Education plc: Understanding private sector participation in public sector education. London: Routledge.

Bayart, J.-F. (1994). L'invention paradoxale de la mode économique. In Bayart, J.-F. (Ed.), *La réinvention du capitalisme* (pp. 9–43). Paris: Editions Karthala.

Belabes, A. (1999). Myth and paradox of 'U.S. competitiveness' debate from the end of World War II to nowadays. Retrieved from www.greqam.fr/IMG/working_papers/1999/99c07.pdf.

Bell, D. (1973). *The coming of post-industrial society.* New York: Basic Books.

Bell, D. (1989). The third technological revolution. *Dissent, 36,* 164–176.

Beniger, J.R. (1986). *The control revolution: Technological and economic origins of the information society.* Cambridge, MA: Harvard University Press.

Bologna Declaration. (1999, June 19). *Bologna Declaration.* Retrieved from www.bmbf.de/en/3336.php.

Bristow, G. (2005). Everyone's a 'winner:' Problematising the discourse of regional competitiveness. *Journal of Economic Geography, 5*(3), 285–304.

Brown, H., Green, A., & Lauder, H. (2001). *High skills: Globalization, competitiveness, and skill formation.* Oxford: Oxford University Press.

Carlaw, K., Nuth, M., Oxley, L., Thorns, D., & Walker, P. (2006). Beyond the hype: Intellectual property and the knowledge society/knowledge economy. *Journal of Economic Surveys, 20*(4), 633–690.

Castells, M. & Hall, P. (1994). *Technopoles of the world: The making of twenty-first-century industrial complexes.* London: Routledge.

Castoriadis, C. (1987). *The imaginary institution of society: Creativity and autonomy in the social-historical world.* Cambridge, MA: MIT Press.

Chesnais, F. (1987). Science, technology and competitiveness. *STI Review, 1*, 85–129.

Cho, D.S. & Moon, H.C. (2000). From Adam Smith to Michael Porter: Evolution of competitiveness theory. Singapore: World Scientific.

Clarke, J. & Newman, J. (1997). *The managerial state: Power, politics and ideology in the remaking of social welfare.* London: Sage.

Council on Competitiveness. (2011). *Make: An American manufacturing movement.* Washington DC: Council on Competitiveness. Retrieved from www.compete.org/images/uploads/File/PDF%20Files/USMCI_Make.pdf.

Daly, G. (1991). The discursive construction of economic space. *Economy and Society, 20*(1), 79–102.

David, P. & Foray, D. (1995). Assessing and expanding the science and technology knowledge base. *STI Review, 16*, 13–68.

Deutsch, K.W. (1963). *The nerves of government: Models of political communication and control.* New York: Free Press.

Dollery, B.E. & Wallis, J. (1999). *Market failure, government failure, leadership and public policy.* Basingstoke: Macmillan.

Dordick, H.S. & Wang, G. (1993). *The information society: A retrospective view.* London: Sage.

Ducatel, K., Webster, J., & Herrmann, W. (2000). Information infrastructures or societies. In Ducatel, K., Webster, J., & Herrmann, W. (Eds.), *The information society in Europe* (pp. 1–17). Lanham, MD: Rowman & Littlefield.

Ekland, M. (2007). *Adoption of the innovation system concept in Sweden.* Uppsala: Uppsala University.

Esser, K., Hillebrand, W., Messner, D., & Meyer-Stamer, J. (1996). *Systemic competitiveness: New governance patterns for industrial development.* London: Cass.

Etzkowitz, H. (1994). Academic-industry relations: A sociological paradigm for economic development. In Leydesdorff, L. & van den Desselaar, P. (Eds.), *Evolutionary economics and chaos theory* (pp. 139–151). London: Pinter.

Fairclough, N. (1992). *Discourse and social change.* Cambridge: Polity.

Fairclough, N. (1993). Critical discourse analysis and the marketization of public discourse: The universities. *Discourse and Society, 4*(2), 133–168.

Fairclough, N. (2003). Analysing discourse: Textual analysis for social research. London: Routledge.

Fairclough, N., Jessop, B., & Sayer, A. (2004). Critical realism and semiosis. In Joseph, J. & Roberts, M. (Eds.), *Realism, discourse and deconstruction* (pp. 23–42). London: Routledge.

Fairclough, N. & Wodak, R. (2008). The Bologna Process and the knowledge-based economy: a critical discourse analysis approach. In Jessop, B., Fairclough, N., & Wodak, R. (Eds.), *Education and the knowledge-based economy in Europe* (pp. 109–126), Rotterdam: Sense.

Foray, D. (2001). *Terms of reference for a project on design, implementation and exploitation of an international survey of knowledge management in the private sector.* DSTI/ICCP/IIS/RD (2001) 5. Paris: OECD.

Foray, D. & Lundvall, B.-Å. (1996). The knowledge-based economy: From the economics of knowledge to the learning economy. In Foray, D. & Lundvall, B.-Å. (Eds.), *Employment and growth in the knowledge-based economy* (pp. 11–32). Paris: OECD.

Freeman, C. (1995). The 'national system of innovation' in historical perspective. *Cambridge Journal of Economics, 19*(1), 5–24.

Godin, B. (2004). The new economy: What the concept owes to the OECD. *Research Policy, 33*, 679–690.

Godin, B. (2006). The knowledge-based economy: conceptual framework or buzzword? *Journal of Technology Transfer, 31*(1), 17–30.

Grabher, G. (1994). *Lob der Verschwendung: Redundanz in der regionalentwicklung: Ein socioökonomisches Plädoyer*. Berlin: Sigma.

Gramsci, A. (1971). *Selections from the prison notebooks*. London: Lawrence & Wishart.

Jessop, B. (2002). *The future of the capitalist state*. Cambridge: Polity.

Jessop, B. (2003). Governance and meta-governance. On reflexivity, requisite variety, and requisite irony. In Bang, H. (Ed.), *Governance as social and political communication* (pp. 101–166). Manchester: Manchester University Press.

Jessop, B. (2004). Critical semiotic analysis and cultural political economy. *Critical Discourse Studies, 1*(2), 159–174.

Jessop, B. (2007a). Knowledge as a fictitious commodity: Insights and limits of a Polanyian analysis. In Bugra, A. & Agartan, K. (Eds.), *Reading Karl Polanyi for the 21st century* (pp. 115–133). New York: Palgrave.

Jessop, B. (2007b). *State power: A strategic-relational approach*. Cambridge: Polity.

Jessop, B. (2009) Cultural political economy and critical policy studies, *Critical Policy Studies, 3*(3–4), 336–356.

Jessop, B., & Sum, N.L. (2001). Pre-disciplinary and post-disciplinary perspectives in political economy. *New Political Economy, 6*(1), 89–101.

Jessop, B., Fairclough, N., & Wodak, R. (Eds.). (2008). *Education and the knowledge-based economy in Europe*. Rotterdam: Sense.

Jones, P.D. (2008) Requisite irony' and 'the knowledge-based economy': A critical discourse analysis of the drafting of education policy in the European Union. In Jessop, B., Fairclough, N., & Wodak, R. (Eds.), *Education and the knowledge-based economy in Europe* (pp. 127–146). Rotterdam: Sense.

Koselleck, R. (1982). *Begriffsgeschichte* and social history. *Economy and Society, 11*(4), 409–427.

Lakatos, I. (1978). *The methodology of scientific research programmes*. Vol. 1: Philosophical papers. Cambridge: Cambridge University Press.

Lall, S. (2001). Competitive indices and developing countries: An economic evaluation of the *Global Competitiveness Report*. *World Development, 29*(9), 1501–1525.

Lauder, H., Brown, P., & Green, A.D. (2001). *Education and training for a high skills economy: A comparative study*. Swindon: Economic and Social Research Council.

Levidow, L. (2001). Marketizing higher education: Neoliberal strategies and counter-strategies. *Education and Social Justice, 3*(2). Retrieved from http://users.skynet.be/aped/babel/english/000eng.html.

Luhmann, N. (1987). The representation of society within society. *Current Sociology, 35*(2), 101–108.

Luhmann, N. (1990). *Essays in self-reference*. New York: Columbia University Press.

Luhmann, N. (1995). *Social systems*. Stanford: Stanford University Press.

Lundvall, B.-Å. (Ed.). (1992). *National systems of innovation: Towards a theory of innovation and interactive learning*. London: Pinter.

Lundvall, B.-Å. & Johnson, B. (1994). The learning economy. *Journal of Industry Studies, 1*(2), 23–42.

Magnusson, L. (1994). *Mercantilism: The shaping of an economic language*. London: Routledge.

Maillat, D. & Kebir, L. (1999). 'Learning region' et systèmes territoriaux de production. *Revue d'économie regionale et urbaine, 3*, 430–448.

Malhotra, Y. (2000). Knowledge management and new organizational forms: A framework for business model innovation. *Information Resources Management Journal, 13*(1), 5–14.

Malpas, J. & Wickham, G. (1995). Governance and failure: On the limits of sociology. *Australian and New Zealand Journal of Sociology, 31*(3), 37–50.

Marginson, S. (1999). After globalisation: Emerging politics of education. *Journal of Education Policy, 14*(1), 19–31.

Masuda, Y. (1981). *The information society as post-industrial society*. Washington, DC: World Future.

May, C. (2002). *The information society: A sceptical view*. Cambridge: Polity.

Miettinen, R. (2002). *National innovation system: Scientific concept or political rhetoric*. Helsinki: Edita.

Messner, D. (1996). *The network society*. London: Cass.

Miller, P. & Rose, N. (1993). Governing economic life. *Economy and Society, 19*(1), 1–31.

Mulderigg, J. (2008) Using keywords analysis in CDA: Evolving discourses of the knowledge economy in education. In Jessop, B., Fairclough, N., & Wodak, R. (Eds.), *Education and the knowledge-based economy in Europe* (pp. 149–170). Rotterdam: Sense.

Nelson, R.R. (1992). National innovation systems: A retrospective on a study. *Industrial and Corporate Change, 1*(2), 347–374.

Organisation for Economic Co-operation and Development (OECD). (1996). *The knowledge-based economy*. Paris: OECD.

Organisation for Economic Co-operation and Development (OECD). (1997). *National systems of innovation*. Paris: OECD.

Organisation for Economic Co-operation and Development (OECD). (2002). *Dynamising national innovation systems*. Paris: OECD.

Ostry, S. & Nelson, R.R. (1995). *Techno-nationalism and techno-globalism: Conflict and cooperation*. Washington, DC: Brookings Institute.

Oxley, L., Walker, P., Thorns, D., & Wang, H. (2007). *Exploring the knowledge economy/society: Another example of measurement without theory*. Working paper, University of Canterbury at Christchurch, New Zealand.

Peters, M.A. (2006, December 9). *Knowledge societies and knowledge economies*. Panel on the knowledge society at the New Zealand Sociology conference.

Porter, M.E. (1990). *The competitive advantage of nations*. Basingstoke: Macmillan.

Power, M. (1997). *The audit society: Rituals of verification*. Oxford: Oxford University Press.

President's Commission on Industrial Competitiveness. (1986). *Global competition: The new reality*. Washington, DC: Government Printing Office.

Reinert, E.S. (1995). Competitiveness and its predecessors: A 500-year cross-national perspective. *Structural Change and Economic Dynamics, 6*(1), 23–42.

Rescher, N. (1998). *Complexity: A philosophical overview*. Brunswick, NJ: Transaction.

Robins, K. & Webster, F. (1989). *The technical fix: Education, computers and industry*. London: Routledge.

Ruggie, J.G. (1982). International regimes, transactions, and change: Embedded liberalism in the postwar economic order. *International Organization, 36*(2), 379–415.

Skinner, Q. (1987). *The foundations of modern political thought*. 2 vols. Cambridge: Cambridge University Press.

Slaughter, S. & Leslie, L.L. (1997). *Academic capitalism: Politics, policies, and the entrepreneurial university*. Baltimore: Johns Hopkins University Press.

Sum, N.L. (2009). The production of hegemonic policy discourses: 'Competitiveness' as a knowledge brand and its (re-) contextualizations. *Critical Political Studies, 3*(2), 184-203.

Sum, N.L. & Jessop, B. (2003). Pre- and post-disciplinary perspectives in (cultural) political economy. *Économies et sociétés, 37*(6), 993–1015.

Taylor, C. (2004). *Modern social imaginaries*. Durham, NC: Duke University Press.

Teichler, U. (1998). The role of the European Union in the internationalization of higher education. In Scott, P. (Ed.), *The globalization of higher education* (pp. 88–99). Buckingham: Open University Press.

ten Brink, T. (2008). Geopolitik: Geschichte und Gegenwart kapitalistischer Staatenkonkurrenz. Münster: Westfälisches Dampfboot.

Toffler, A. (1980). *The third wave.* New York: William Morrow.

Webster, F. (1999). *Theories of the information society.* London: Routledge.

Wodak, R. & Meyer, M. (Eds.), (2001). *Methods of critical discourse analysis.* London: Sage.

Young, J.A. (1988). Technology and competitiveness: A key to the economic future of the United States. *Science, 241*, 313–316.

D.W. LIVINGSTONE

DEBUNKING THE 'KNOWLEDGE ECONOMY'

The Limits of Human Capital Theory

INTRODUCTION

If the common response of so many people to conditions of their own underemployment is to seek still more education, there must be some substantial bases for this response. In this chapter, I will look critically at two of these bases: (1) the widespread belief that jobs in the emerging future economy will require vastly increased numbers of highly educated workers; and (2) the relationship between more education and increased earnings which is widely presumed to apply not only to individuals but to societies.

Most of the chapter focuses on the claims of those scholars who have constructed the image of a '*post-industrial economy*' or a '*knowledge economy*,' which has become a common article of faith in public discourse. If, as these scholars claim, most of the emergent jobs in private market-driven economies will probably need an advanced education, then pursuing more education while one endures current underemployment is a reasonable response. Most of these prevalent theories of employment-related knowledge development are based at least loosely on notions of evolutionary progress. I will examine the actual knowledge and skill requirements for paid work in advanced private market economies, particularly the United States and Canada, and find some of these theories' claims to be illusory.

Investment in formal education has been associated with both higher individual earnings and growing societal wealth. These relationships have been most fully conceptualized and documented by *human capital theory* which stresses the value of peoples' learning capacities as a factor of economic productivity.[1] This perspective is built on the intellectual foundations of neo-classical market theory and the generally optimistic assumptions of the evolutionary progress paradigm. It reflected the post-World War II conditions of simultaneous expansion of employment and education fairly well, even though Berg (1970) and others documented the existence of a significant performance gap in the 1950s. The 'learning–earning' link is still valid at the individual level, although with diminishing marginal utility. But it is disintegrating at the aggregate or societal level and this disintegration is occurring beyond the margins of the market returns perspective of human capital theory.

D.W. Livingstone and D. Guile (eds.), The Knowledge Economy and Lifelong Learning: A Critical Reader, 85–116.
© 2012 *Sense Publishers. All rights reserved.*

THE EVOLUTIONARY PROGRESS PARADIGM: 'KNOWLEDGE ECONOMY' THEORIES

Robert Nisbet (1970), the conservative social historian, suggested that all theories of social change are based on the metaphor of organic growth and/or the analogy of the life cycle. Certainly the theories of social evolution and continual progress that have been prevalent for most of the past century and a half in Western societies have been grounded in organic growth metaphors: from Social Darwinism, to Weber's rationalization/bureaucratization, to Parsons' structural differentiation, to 'post-industrial'/'knowledge economy' theories. There is a rudimentary explanatory mechanism at the root of most evolutionary theories, namely Charles Darwin's notion of random variation/selective survival in a seldom-kindly environment. But the biological survival of the fittest has frequently resulted in species extinctions, while modern social evolutionary theories have been mainly optimistic extrapolations of the most positive recent trends.

Optimistic extrapolation is also surely the case with 'post-industrial'/'knowledge economy' theories. As promoted most notably by Daniel Bell (1964, 1973) in the United States, John Porter (1971) in Canada, Alain Touraine (1969) in France and Radovan Richta (1969) in eastern Europe,[2] post-industrial theory anticipated the growing centrality of theoretical knowledge, continuing expansion of tertiary-level occupations, the increasing eminence of a professional and technical class, and a general upgrading of the skills needed for work, as well as greater leisure time. As I have noted elsewhere (Livingstone, 1983), the creation of the future in this largely technocratic mode of thought

> apparently means discovering trends and then using further technical ingenuity to either mute or facilitate them. However sophisticated they become, such approaches are based on a presumption that the future really depends on forces that are beyond human capacity to control in any significant way. The enduring image of the future left by all such writings is one of irreversible technocratic trends remote from whatever social and political capacities ordinary people might retain. (p. 181)

This mode of thought serves to glorify the capacities of technocrats/experts themselves and resonates with increasing attempts by professional experts in many fields to monopolize knowledge that many others are capable of mastering and using (Derber, Schwartz, & Magrass 1990; Perkins, 1996; Parenti, 1996). This is surely one reason why, in spite of demonstrated empirical inadequacies and withering critiques from other researchers, post-industrial/knowledge economy advocates continue to assert the increasing pervasiveness of scientific knowledge and upgraded skills in the workplace.[3]

There is ample empirical warrant for describing contemporary advanced private market societies in terms of people's increasing pursuit of knowledge.[4] But we have also seen that the capacity of paid workplaces to utilize people's knowledge has become increasingly problematic. As a consequence of their presumption of the increasing centrality of scientific/technological knowledge and general skill upgrading of the workplace, post-industrial/knowledge economy theorists have continued to ignore most aspects of underemployment, most notably the performance gap.[5] With increasing underemployment, knowledge economy theorists' claims for the workplace have become less credible in relation to most people's experience. I will examine these claims more closely in the following section.

The overly optimistic character of the evolutionary theories of modernization and industrialization of the entire globe along Western society lines that emerged in the immediate post-World War II expansionary period has now been shown by the absolute and relative economic impoverishment of much of the 'underdeveloped' world, as well as by the reassertion of alternative models of society in some of these regions (Latouche, 1993; World Bank, 1997). There has been a common intellectual tendency in periods of widespread social malaise for theories of progress to be challenged by theories of decline.

The decline theories that have contested linear progress versions of societal growth in periods of widespread unemployment – from Nietzsche and Spengler through Sorokin to the more diffuse reflections of current post-modernists – also usually rely on implicit analogies of the life cycle of birth–growth–decline–death–rebirth. Pitirim Sorokin (1937–41), in his *Social and Cultural Dynamics*, produced at the end of the 1930s Depression, has provided one of the most elaborate taxonomic *descriptions* of long-term social change based on this life cycle analogy.

Among social theorists of the post-1970 era, optimistic projections of progress have again been challenged, this time by post-modernist eclecticism and post-structuralist ambiguity. While much of post-modernist theory celebrates social differences and the subjective identities of subordinated people, the underlying model of societal change is typically some version of decline or death of one form of society, often coupled with the nascent emergence of another.[6] Neither Sorokin nor current post-modernist theorists have suggested an alternative *explanatory* dynamic for societal change in general or education–work relations in particular.[7] Whether the world is deemed to be getting better or worse, most influential theories of social change have continued to be grounded, as Nisbet suggested, in simple analogies of growth and decline, and to regard such trends as largely beyond the control of collective social agency. But even in the present period of pervasive underemployment, revised theories of evolutionary progress tend to prevail in the public spheres of life, as evidenced by popular acceptance of the general view that continual economic growth remains necessary to ensure a healthy society.

THE 'KNOWLEDGE ECONOMY' AND WORKPLACE REALITIES

The emergence of a 'post-industrial' workplace dominated by highly educated information service workers has been heralded since the early 1960s (see especially Bell, 1964, 1973). The theories of post-industrialism have promoted the belief that the prevalence of information processing over material handling in the mode of production would necessitate skill upgrading and greater creativity and critical thinking of workers. In short, post-industrial/knowledge economy theories generally assume or assert that *workers increasingly require more skill, become more involved in planning their own work, and increasingly constitute a professional class*. We will examine the empirical evidence for each of these three basic claims below.

There have certainly been substantial changes in the *composition* of the employed workforce over the past generation in nearly all market economies. Most obviously, there has been sectoral decline of manufacturing and relative growth of personal, financial and social service employment. This is the pivot point for most 'post-industrial' projections. Other evident compositional shifts have been the relative increase of part-time and temporary jobs, and greater participation of married women in paid employment (see OECD, 1994a). But in relation to these compositional shifts, empirical researchers have been at least as likely to posit deskilling, less planning involvement and poorer compensation as their post-industrial opposites. Indeed, for virtually every aspect of contemporary paid work, advocates of degradation theses rather than post-industrial upgrading trends can be easily found in the research literature. Part of the difficulty in assessing levels and changes in actual work requirements has been that our customary ways of thinking about these requirements do not clearly distinguish between the technical tasks involved and the people doing them.

From Adam Smith (1982 [1776]) to the present, most theorists and researchers of divisions of labour have confounded the *technical division of tasks* and the *social division of workers*. From Smith's famous analysis of the pin factory (pp. 109–110) onward, there has been a widespread presumption that the separation of a work process into distinct steps for productive efficiency – task specialization – naturally leads to a detailed social division of labour among workers. But, as some observers of the more minute divisions of contemporary work within and between occupations have recognized, identified technical tasks can be efficiently allocated among workers in a variety of ways, not necessarily social divisions based on single tasks (e.g., Drucker, 1954; Braverman, 1974, p. 72). The fact that surgeons now perform a wide array of manual tasks while factory assembly workers perform only a few is a *social construction* rather than an inherent feature of these forms of work per se. As James Murphy (1993) insightfully observes of relations between technical and social divisions of labour:

> Any concrete account of the division of tasks, of occupations, of castes, presupposes the distinction between the division of functions and the division of persons. The specialization of legal, political, military, educational, and religious functions does not logically entail the social monopoly of these functions by specialists. It is well known that lay people can perform many of these functions for themselves perfectly well. How these functions have been historically appropriated by specialists is a fundamental question for the theory of the division of labor. Just as the technical division of tasks in the factory does not account for the detailed social division of workers, so the technical division of functions in society does not account for the social division of professionals and the laity. (p. 23)

As new machines and routines have been devised for work tasks, work theorists from Smith on have generally assumed that their implementation in a more detailed social division of labour would increase general productive efficiency, as long as workers could be motivated to use them as designed. The factory assembly line of simple technical tasks presented the classic motivational problem here, which industrial design specialists have attempted to resolve through incentives ranging from wage and benefit increases to various consultation processes among workers. This tendency to see the social division of labour as essentially determined by and necessarily adapting to available task techniques has been quite pervasive.[8] But in cases of highly automated production, the detailed division of labour has become so segmented and mind-numbing for line workers that industrial designers have had to resort to technical task recombinations, in the process illustrating that technologies are actually the *interaction* of technical divisions of tasks and social divisions of workers rather than machine-driven imperatives. In contrast, the post-industrial theorists' solution to the question of changing work requirements has been to simply assume rapidly increasing automation of most manual tasks and their replacement by professional and technical jobs based on theoretical knowledge.

A balanced assessment of the contemporary character of and trends in work requirements should directly consider: (1) the *technical division of labour* in terms of the allocation of simple and complex tasks between jobs; (2) the *social division of labour* in terms of the respective participation of various workers in planning the execution of tasks; and (3) their consequential effects on the *class structure of work*.[9]

DIVISION OF TECHNICAL SKILLS

Over the past generation, notably since the publication of Harry Braverman's (1974) 'deskilling thesis,' there has been a massive amount of research literature arguing for and documenting both deskilling and upgrading trends in the technical skill levels of labour processes in advanced industrial economies (see Wood, 1989). Braverman's study represented the first major challenge to the post-industrial upgrading thesis. It generated several waves of empirical case studies, the first documenting deskilling trends, followed by others on worker resistance to deskilling, and then more nuanced studies of negotiations between employers and employees over technical task divisions (V. Smith, 1994). Such case studies certainly confirm that upgrading has not been a universal trend.

Aggregate data to determine the actual extent of upgrading and deskilling in the workforce as a whole are difficult to find. A first approximation for the United States and Canada is provided by applying the technical skill requirements estimated by government job analysts in dictionaries of occupational titles to large-scale sample surveys. The two most commonly used indicators of skill levels in both countries have been the general educational development (GED) and specific vocational preparation (SVP) scales. The GED scale is intended to embrace those aspects of knowledge which are required of the worker for satisfactory job performance. The different levels of this scale on each of three dimensions (reasoning, mathematical and language development) range from carrying out simple instructions on elementary tasks to applying abstract principles to a wide range of problems.

The major division in this scale is between the first three levels, which involve primarily executing concrete tasks, and the other three levels which entail more complex problem-solving functions. I have applied standard GED ratings of respective U.S. and Canadian occupational classifications to the annual surveys of the National Opinion Research Centre (NORC) between 1972 and 1990, and to the OISE surveys in Ontario between 1980 and 1996.[10] These findings, based on mid-point splits for each of the six GED levels,[11] suggest a gradual overall upgrading of the technical skill level required in jobs over the past twenty-five years. The more detailed distributions indicate that very few jobs (less than one per cent) have been rated at the lowest skill level throughout this period, while jobs rated at the highest skill level have increased from about three per cent to five or six per cent. Similar conclusions have been drawn by Howell and Wolff (1991) for the United States over the 1960 to 1985 period and by John Myles (1988) for Canada as a whole over the 1961 to 1981 period, based on GED scores and other related measures with census data.

A longer general historical comparison for the United States can be constructed by drawing on the earlier aggregate GED estimates produced by Eckhaus (1964) for 1940 and Berg (1970) for 1950 and 1960.[12] These general estimates suggest that there may have been a substantial upgrading of technical skill requirements between 1940 and 1960 with a reduction in simple instruction, level one jobs from almost ten per cent to less than one per cent, while problem-solving jobs with skill levels of 4 or greater increased from under 30 per cent to over half of all jobs. This is a period that saw first the growth of a war economy – an economy which drew massive numbers of rural people from traditional small commodity forms of production work into military and factory employment – followed by rapid post-war growth of public and service sector employment. In contrast, the post-1960 period, the widely heralded era of the new knowledge economy, has experienced less dramatic sectoral shifts, with comparatively stable and gradually increasing required technical skill levels in the overall job structure. Indeed, the most extensive U.S. study finds that the upgrading effects of changes in the industry and occupational composition of employment on technical skill levels appears to have steadily declined during the 1960–85 period (Howell & Wolff, 1991, pp. 490–491).

The pattern of gradual upgrading of the U.S. and Canadian labour forces in the post-1960s period is further confirmed by analyses of the SVP scale,[13] which estimates the specific vocational preparation required for each job simply in terms of the amount of time needed to learn the techniques, acquire information and develop facility for average performance. This time estimate includes any relevant vocational education, apprenticeship training, further education courses, on-the-job training and/or essential experience in other jobs. The U.S. analyses indicate that, compared with the 1940–50 period, there are now very few jobs in which adequate performance can be achieved with less than a month of specific vocational training; the small proportion of jobs that require more than four years of preparatory training, as well as the proportion needing over a year of training, have increased somewhat since 1950. A small and very gradually increasing majority of the labour force have required more than a year of vocational preparation throughout the 1972–90 period. The SVP scores are very strongly correlated with the GED scores; virtually all jobs with GED scores over 4 require more than a year of training, while very few jobs with lower GED ratings need more than a year of vocational training. The analysis of Myles (1988) of the SVP scores of the Canadian labour force based on census data has found similar trends for the 1961–81 period. Jobs requiring less than 30 days of training decreased during this period, while jobs needing over two years of training increased. Comparing these findings suggests that the Canadian occupational structure may have had somewhat more jobs requiring very little training time than the United States. In any case, the overall post-1960 pattern of changes in required training time in both economies suggests a gradual decline of low skill jobs and a gradual increase of high skill jobs.

There are numerous limitations to occupational dictionary-based skill ratings. As Sidney Fine (1968), one of the designers of the GED scale, has noted: 'one should hardly become wedded to the absolute estimates ... the estimates for any given job are only significant relative to estimates for other jobs' (p. 370). More specific problems include selection biases, limited updating of ratings, and limited capacity to consider both skill level changes related to occupational composition as well as those within individual jobs in trend analyses. The number of job titles rated in these occupational dictionaries increased from 4,000 in 1956 to over 23,000 in 1993 (US Department of Labor, 1993). The initial selection of titles was far from inclusive of all types of jobs. While post-1960 versions have become much more inclusive, the selections are still not necessarily representative of all current jobs and the varying inclusiveness makes comparisons over time somewhat suspect. General updating of the job ratings has only been done a few times, while the re-rating of individual jobs has occurred on a more ad hoc basis. The rating scales are therefore always both somewhat selective and out of date in their applicability to the current workforce. Both the occupational composition of the workforce and the skill levels of individual existing jobs continue to change more rapidly than these rating scales are able to reflect.

In terms of changing skill content *within* specific jobs, Berg's (1970, pp. 47–48) comparison of the first two United States general dictionary GED ratings published in 1956 and 1966 found that 54 per cent of the original 4,000 job titles retained the same GED level in the later year, while 31 per cent were rated higher and 15 per cent were rated lower. He also noted that this set of titles had been reduced by about a third through consolidation. He suggested that a net upward trend in the skill level of these individual jobs was at least partly an artefact of the grouping itself, in which the GED for the new consolidated title had to be as high as the highest of the old titles. He also speculated that employers may have expanded the scope of some of these jobs in response to the supply of better-educated workers.

In any event, this painstaking analysis cannot address what was happening with the other 10,000 individual titles available in the 1966 dictionary, to say nothing of the compositional effects of the distribution of people in these jobs on the overall skill level of the workforce. Other and subsequent assessments using successive editions of these same occupational dictionaries have also found that there have been substantial changes in skill content in both directions within existing jobs. But the net effect is small (Horowitz & Herrnstadt, 1966; Spenner, 1983).

In contrast to Berg's analysis of GED changes, my analyses from the 1970s to the present are based on sample surveys that rely on skill ratings of jobs conducted at an early point in this period. These survey results may reflect changes in skill levels related to changes in the distribution of occupations fairly well; but these estimates provide no reading of changes in the skill levels within existing jobs over this period. In this regard, it should also be noted here that Myles' (1988, pp. 350–351) supplementary survey analysis found that respondents' self-reports generated significantly more polarized estimates of required training times for the Canadian labour force in the early 1980s than SVP scores did. The safest conclusion is that there was substantially more upgrading *and* deskilling occurring within specific occupations than measures based on invariant GED and SVP scores capture, but no definitive evidence for a dominant upgrading trend within existing jobs.

But the gradual *overall* skill upgrading trend in technical skill requirements of jobs since 1960 suggested by the above analyses is corroborated by the most extensive prior reviews of both compositional and within-job effects in other research based on U.S. population surveys and census dictionary job titles (Spenner, 1983, 1990), as well as by other recent large-scale studies using different data and measures. Cappelli (1995) uses a measure of skill developed by Hay Associates, the world's largest compensation consulting firm, a composite measure which includes 'know how' (capabilities, knowledge and techniques needed to do the job, ranked according to complexity); 'problem solving' (how well defined and predictable job tasks are); and 'accountability' (autonomy in decision-making). He analyses Hay's extensive records for U.S. jobs in manufacturing from 1978 to 1986, and in clerical work from 1978 and 1988. Taking account of both occupational composition and job content changes, he finds a discernible upskilling of most of the remaining production jobs within the declining manufacturing sector, while both upskilling and deskilling are evident within the expanding clerical sector. Howell and Wolff (1991) found similar trends for 1960–85 using census-based data and measures. Applying both conventional GED/SVP scores and other measures of cognitive complexity and routine activity to census data, Myles (1988, pp. 342–345) found the reverse pattern for the Canadian labour force between 1961 and 1981; that is, he found no change in the skill composition of industrial workers' jobs but substantial upgrading of service workers' jobs. In all of these instances, the aggregate trend for the entire labour force was gradual skill upgrading.

Assessments of technical skill requirements should distinguish between *enlargement* of the number of technical tasks to be performed and *enrichment* of the level of technical knowledge needed for the job. Manufacturing jobs have generally become more complex in terms of the array of technical tasks to be performed in a given time. This has occurred through job amalgamation, multi-tasking, multi-crafting and speed-ups in the context of early retirements and lay-offs, as well as new tasks associated with technological change. But neither task intensification nor new job tasks necessarily require higher knowledge. When work organizations downsize, restructure and computerize, the remaining workers are forced to learn a *wider* array of technical tasks rather than higher order, more complex or creative ones. As a skilled trades worker interviewed for our case study of workplace changes in the steel industry (Livingstone 1996) observed:

> There's just less guys [sic] to do the job faster. There's also more responsibility because there's less senior guys to talk to when there's a problem ... We're running with seventy per cent less men and we're still putting out the same amount of product here. So you tell me that's not efficiency! [The steel company] has become more trades-oriented with the trades doing more labour work too. Trades have really crossed over and are doing more labour work than the art of the trade, because they can get rid of a janitor and you can sweep your own floor. (p. 50)

The Report of the Commission on the Skills of the American Workforce (National Center on Education and the Economy, 1990) concluded that:

> 95 percent of American companies still cling to old forms of work organization. Because most American employers organize work in a way that does not require high skills, they report no shortage of people who have such skills and foresee no such shortage ... Most employers we interviewed do not expect their skill requirements to change. Despite the widespread presumption that advancing technology and the evolving service economy will create jobs demanding higher skills, only five percent of employers were concerned about a skills shortage. (p. 3)

The surplus of qualified workers is probably an even larger factor in employers' lack of concern about a skills shortage than 'old forms of work organization.' In any case, there is little evidence of any general and persistent technical skill deficiency among employed workers (see National Center on the Educational Quality of the Workforce, 1995) An Ontario survey (Livingstone, Hart, & Davie, 1995) found that 95 per cent of employees consider themselves to be at least adequately qualified for their current jobs. Also, underqualified employees are most likely to be involved in further learning activities to upgrade their technical skills and retain their jobs.

The most obvious recent change in the technical division of work has been the rapid, widespread introduction of computer-based technologies. For example, a Canada-wide longitudinal survey found that the proportion of employees working directly with computer technologies increased from about 15 per cent in 1985 to 37 per cent in 1991 (Betcherman, 1994). A 1994 U.S. survey (National Center on the Educational Quality of the Workforce, 1995) found that over 40 per cent of production and non-supervisory employees were using computers in their jobs. But this shift from material production to data processing does not necessarily translate into higher technical skill requirements for jobs. For most employees, more of the general control of the work process has tended to become computer-based rather than human-centred. A variety of sectoral studies of the effects of information technology and new production arrangements have found few gains in either most workers' need for higher order skills or opportunities to exercise discretionary control in task performance (Dawson & Webb, 1989; Beirne & Ramsay, 1992; Menzies, 1996). Again, whatever skill increases may be involved appear to have been far exceeded by rapid increases in the computer literacy of the workforce (Lowe, 1996; Livingstone, 1997).

Even in the most advanced 'high tech' production firms, recent case studies have found that only low levels of basic skills are required for successful performance of assembly work. The much vaunted training and testing programs of Motorola Corporation have been found to be an expensive way to upgrade hourly employees who never use their new skills because they remain in traditional handwork jobs (Brown, Reich, & Stern 1990). In California's Silicon Valley, a case study of four successful high tech companies found that there was no assembly work that actually required more than a solid eighth-grade education (Levn, Rumberger, & Finnan, 1990).

Overall, the weight of available empirical evidence suggests that there has indeed been a net upgrading of the technical skill requirements of the North American job structure since the 1940s. But the most substantial gains occurred prior to 1960 and the slight upgrading that is discernible since then reveals the related upgrading claims of most post-industrial/knowledge economy theorists to be quite exaggerated.

SOCIAL DIVISION OF LABOUR

At least in the United States and Canada since the 1960s, it is evident that this gradual technical upgrading of jobs has been greatly exceeded by the rapid expansion of the educational qualifications of the workforce. This condition appears to have provoked both increased disaffection with the inherent technical limitations of their jobs among workers, and heightened concern among corporate leaders and management consultants about enhancing worker commitment to the firm. As James O'Toole, author of the *Work in America* report for the U.S. Secretary of Health, Education and Welfare in 1972, which offered one of the first documented accounts of this disaffection, later observed:

> No industrialized nation has been able to produce an adequate number of jobs that provide the status, and require the skills and educational levels, that their workforces are achieving … [T]he situation is nearly Malthusian in its proportions: levels of educational attainment have tended to grow in almost geometric progression, while the number of jobs that require highly qualified persons has risen much more slowly … What is clear from almost every study of job dissatisfaction is that the placing of intelligent and highly

qualified workers in dull and unchallenging jobs is a prescription for pathology – for the worker, the employer, and the society. (1977, pp. 38, 60)

The most obvious expressions of this disaffection were rebellions by young workers on highly automated assembly lines such as the Lordstown, Ohio, auto plant (Aronowitz, 1973). There have been some widely publicized subsequent attempts to redesign the technical division of labour to give workers more integrated sets of tasks, as in Volvo's experiments with whole auto assembly teams at its now closed Uddevalla plant (Berggren, 1992, 1994). But a far more frequent response has been to offer workers a more consultative role in decisions about the allocation, evaluation and modification of technical tasks without reversing the detailed technical division of labour. This is what is now commonly called the 'high performance workplace.' There are multitudes of alternative models available for enhancing worker participation in organizational decision-making, the defining feature being somewhat greater voice for workers in some of the firm's affairs. But in North America to date there has been much more advocacy than implementation of such consultative models.

In spite of much management hoopla about corporate cultures, learning organizations and teamwork, surveys of U.S. and Canadian business executives indicate that the vast majority of enterprises have made no major organizational changes in response to the increasing educational calibre of recent graduates (Harris, 1991; Betcherman, 1994). The most extensive U.S. surveys of actual changes in workplace practices have found that only about a third of private sector firms have made substantial use of *any* of the most widely heralded innovative consultative practices (i.e., teams, job rotation, quality circles and Total Quality Management [TQM]), and that such practices do not cluster together in any discernible 'high performance' form (Osterman, 1994; see also Lawler, Mohrman, & Ledford, 1992; Gephart, 1995). One national survey (National Center on the Educational Quality of the Workforce, 1995) concluded that:

> Despite the considerable attention given to new modes of work organization, the use of high-performance work systems among employees still remains the exception rather than the rule. Only one-quarter of establishments reported using any bench-marking programs to compare practices and performances with other organizations, and only 37 percent reported that they had adopted a formal Total Quality Management (TQM) program. Very few workers engage in practices that have become the hallmarks of high-performance work: only 12 percent of non-managerial workers participate in self-managed teams, and only 17 percent participate in job rotation. (p. 3)

There does appear to be a significant relationship between extensive adoption of any of these 'flexible' work practices and the percentage of core employees who receive (company-identified) formal off-the-job training (Osterman, 1994, pp. 182–187). But such formal training is only the tip of the learning iceberg among workers. The massive extent of work-related learning now occurring on and off the job is historically unprecedented.[14] The actual uses of much of this learning at work remains highly problematic even in the small number of high performance firms.

Whether the new participatory model is called TQM, ISO 9000+ or re-engineering, there has generally been little recombining of technical skills and much emphasis on workers sharing their existing production knowledge for more efficient production, ultimately leading to leaner production systems and less workers performing production tasks. From the vantage point of most North American workers, the vast majority of work organizations, including most high performance ones, actually continue to operate on principles of hierarchical control of technical design and planning knowledge as well as strategic investment and management decisions by small numbers of executives and experts. There is a strictly limited capacity to plan or design the technical division of labour by most subordinates just as in older mass production forms. As means to encourage greater allegiance and productivity, there may be flatter hierarchies, increasing incorporation of subordinate workers into consultation processes such as work teams and quality circles, and broader access to computer-based information systems in a minority of work organizations. But, while lower levels of management and supervisory positions may be eliminated in this process, the surveillance and constraint over most workers' worksite practices has often increased rather than decreased through the centrally controlled manner in which microelectronic technologies usually have been introduced (Parker & Slaughter, 1994). Over half of all non-managerial employees now participate in regular meetings to discuss work-related problems (National Center on the Educational Quality of the Workforce, 1995, p. 3). But another recent national survey of worker representation and participation finds that, although the majority of workers feel it is important for them to have a lot of influence on decisions about such matters as scheduling, compensation, training, safety, technology use and work goals, only about a quarter report that they have a lot of involvement; most of those who said they wanted more actual involvement also said they would be unlikely to get it (cited in Gephart, 1995, pp. 43–44).

An estimate of trends in workers' perceptions of their extent of participation in workplace decision-making is provided by our Ontario survey series, which regularly asked employees about their extent of involvement in planning and supervisory roles in their jobs between 1980 and 1992.[15] Managers, professionals, semi-professionals and supervisory employees perceived little change in their degree of authority during this period. The vast majority of managers have continued to see themselves in controlling roles, while nearly all supervisors also identify themselves in terms of their control of subordinates. Smaller majorities of professional and semi-professional employees continue to consider their jobs in terms of combinations of a significant design role and supervisory leadership of other workers. The most notable changes have been in service and industrial workers' increasing sense of their involvement in design and supervisory roles. The proportions of workers who feel they are closely supervised by superiors have fallen by about half over this period, while those who feel they have a significant design or team leading role has roughly doubled. Sceptical researchers have rightly identified definite limits to the 'responsible autonomy' of workers in relation to managerial prerogatives (Friedman, 1977) and accurately characterized some worker participation schemes as sophisticated means to enhance management control – basically 'democratic Taylorism' (Adler, 1993). Nevertheless, these workers' shifting perceptions are probably related to actual increases in consultative workplace practices and consequent incremental gains in popular support for notions of workplace democracy. While the technical skills of workers may continue to be significantly underutilized in their jobs, they are increasingly being consulted about the deployment of those technical skills that they are permitted to use.

Looking beyond the North American context, there are important differences among the advanced industrial economies in the predominant models of social organization of the workplace, particularly in terms of their recognition and effective integration of workers' skills and knowledge. One of the sharpest analyses of these differences is William Lazonick's (1991) comparison of the business organization structures and strategies that have prevailed in U.S. 'managerial capitalism,' in contrast to the previously dominant 'proprietary capitalism' of the United Kingdom and the emergent 'collective capitalism' of Japan. In simple terms, leading Japanese companies have managed to integrate shop floor operatives, as well as the line and staff specialists in the middle and the managerial generalists at the top of the enterprise, into consensual decision-making processes. U.S. companies created 'technostructures' of committed managers and specialists with secure career ladders and discretionary work roles (Galbraith, 1985), but have refused to seriously consider operative employees as members of the same family. The leaders of British firms have traditionally regarded themselves as exclusive guardians of the firm, while leaving formation of specialist standards to the lower echelons and control of work organization on the shop floor. Lazonick (1991) summarizes the consequences of these models for skill utilization in the workplace:

Through the organizational commitments inherent in permanent employment, the skills and efforts of male blue-collar workers have been made integral to the organizational capabilities of their companies, thus enabling the Japanese to take the lead in innovative production systems such as just-in-time inventory control, statistical quality control, and flexible manufacturing. Critical to the functioning of these production systems is the willingness of Japanese managers to leave skills and initiative with workers on the shop floor. Indeed, the recent success of Japanese mass producers in introducing flexible manufacturing systems owes much to the fact that, for decades before the introduction of the new automated technologies, blue-collar workers were granted considerable discretion to monitor and adjust the flow and quality of work on the shop floor. Japanese practice is in marked contrast to the U.S. managerial concern with using technology to take skills and the exercise of initiative *off* the shop floor, a practice which goes back to the late nineteenth century when the success of U.S. mass production was dependent on breaking the power of craft workers and transferring the sole right to plan and coordinate the flow of work ... nor did [Japanese employers] have to resign themselves simply to leaving skills on the shop floor in the hands of autonomous craftsmen, as was the case in Britain. (pp. 42–43)

Lazonick probably exaggerates the extent of utilization of workers' skills in Japan through this more inclusive social division of labour. Certainly there is evidence of substantial underemployment there. 'Lifetime' employment in the leading firms has relied heavily on temporary labour in a wide array of less secure statuses, particularly for women and in smaller firms. Permanent employment provisions are now declining as both official unemployment and use of temporary workers mount (Mullaby, 1994; Odrich, 1997). Moreover, the detailed technical division of labour has remained almost as fragmented and management-controlled as in the U.S. model, even if the divisions have been more flexible. But through an array of integrative institutional structures and strategies, leading Japanese firms were able to increase the social involvement of many workers' skills in job performance (Kamata, 1983).

Scandinavian and some other continental European countries, notably Germany with its co-determination model, have also developed institutional models that have enabled more integrative participation by workers in the production- and knowledge-development decisions of their firms (Maurice, Sellier, & Silvestre, 1996). The stronger union movements in these countries have ensured more equitable sharing of the consequent productivity gains rather than ploughing them back into expanded production, so global market share increases have been less spectacular for European firms than in the Japanese case during the 1970s and 1980s. More generally, such comparative analyses suggest that the extent of skill utilization in the workplace is a function of the social bargains that have been struck and continue to be negotiated between employers and employees rather than any immutable trend. The success of this Japanese model in increasing productivity and the consequent 'Japanese challenge' in established markets of American firms provoked increasing management receptivity to experiment with new forms of industrial relations in the United States, just as the post-World War II reconstruction and the 'American challenge' did previously in Europe (Servan-Schrieber, 1971). While the roots of managerial capitalism run deep in North America, even here shifts to new social divisions of labour that require increased worker input have been underway for some time at levels ranging from business organizational strategies to specific job redesign (Kochan & Useem, 1992). But, as the U.S. surveys cited above indicate, such shifts to greater worker involvement in production decisions appear to have been very gradual and limited to date.

So what effects have these continuities and changes in the technical and social divisions of labour had on the occupational class structure?

THE CHANGING CLASS STRUCTURE: MORE EXPERTS, FEWER WORKERS?

The most explicit prediction made by post-industrial theorists like Bell is that the proportion of expert employees in the class structure is bound to increase rapidly while the proportion of manual workers declines. The first difficulty is determining which jobs count as experts; the second, what class designation to give them. For Bell (1973), 'the major class of the emerging new society is primarily a professional class, based on knowledge rather than property,' with four different 'estates' – the scientific, the technological (applied skills of medicine, economics and medicine), the administrative, and the cultural (artistic and religious) – only loosely associated through their common defence of the idea of learning (p. 374). Classical professionals such as doctors, lawyers and architects, modern professionals such as scientists and engineers, as well as managers with specialized knowledge in any of these areas are widely assumed to be members of this class. But what of the growing numbers of technologists and technicians in these areas? They acquire highly specialized knowledge but are often highly constrained in opportunities to apply it. In support of their central predictions, post-industrial theorists initially claimed these jobs, along with other white-collar service jobs, are part of a 'new middle class' (Friedson, 1973). Conversely, Marxist theorists typically claimed them to be the 'new working class,' technical workers whose specialized knowledge is becoming increasingly strategic to automated production processes (Mallet, 1975). Subsequent conceptual and empirical works from both perspectives have been more likely to recognize complexities and contradictions in the class identity of such jobs (Walker, 1978; Abercrombie & Urry, 1983; Sobel, 1989; Carter, 1985; Crompton, 1993). For my purposes here, technologist/technician jobs will be designated as 'semi-professionals,' rather than arbitrarily conflating them with professionals or definite working class jobs.

Although occupation-based analyses and class analyses are quite closely related, there are important differences. In class analyses, those whose main livelihood comes from ownership of a business are distinguished from those who are hired employees. Someone who is a carpenter by trade might be hired as a skilled industrial wageworker; but another carpenter may own a construction company; yet another might be a foreperson mainly supervising several other carpenters. Similarly, an engineer could be an owner, a manager or a hired professional employee. Studies of job structures based simply on occupational designations may be helpful for identifying the general division of technical skills. But such studies often conflate employers with employees, and also underestimate the number of employees in some occupations who have important authority roles in the workplace (see Wright, 1980). These distinctions are especially significant in relation to rates of increase in the proportions of professional experts in the workforce, given their very small proportions at the beginning of the post-World War II period.

Empirical studies that have attempted to distinguish between the social and technical divisions of labour, including the division between owners of enterprises and wage and salary employees, now provide relevant tests of both post-industrial and Marxist predictions about class trends. Erik Olin Wright, a leading neo-Marxist class theorist, has spearheaded a cross-national series of large-scale surveys to carefully estimate the current class structures of various countries. Based on his own 1980 survey and U.S. census data since 1960, Wright (1997, pp. 91–113) produced his own assessment of the relative efficacy of post-industrial and traditional Marxist theorists' predictions of trends in the distribution of classes. Wright's main findings are consistent with the *direction* of post-industrial theory predictions. The proportion of professional employees is estimated to have almost doubled over this 30-year period, from 3.5 per cent to nearly seven percent of the employed labour force. Conversely, the proportion of workers is found to have declined since 1970, from 59 to 54 per cent; the proportion of skilled workers also declined. Wright (1997) concludes that:

> The specific pattern of sectoral and class shifts for experts and expert managers is consistent with the expectations of those post-industrial theorists who emphasize the increasing importance of knowledge and information in post-industrial economies ... The results ... pose a real challenge to traditional Marxist expectations about the trajectory of development of the class structure of advanced capitalist societies in general and particularly about the process of proletarianization. Contrary to the traditional Marxist expectation, the working class in the United States has declined over the past three decades, and this decline appears, if anything, to be accelerating ... Unless these trends are a temporary detour, it thus appears that the class structure of capitalism continues to become increasingly complex rather than simplified around a single, polarized class antagonism. (pp. 108, 111)

Wright has made major contributions to our understanding of comparative class structures, both through his survey work and his conscientious efforts to adjudicate his own and other class theories with careful reference to empirical data. The main limitations of this particular trend adjudication effort are that it is based partly on imputations from a survey at a single point in 1980 and – like many others – it continues to conflate technical and social divisions of labour in identifying some employee class locations. In particular, respondents' self-reports in this survey about the degree of authority and autonomy they exercise in their jobs has been used as primary criteria to identify managers, supervisors and professional employees. This general practice has been seriously criticised even by some of Wright's collaborators (e.g., Clement and Myles, 1994, pp. 261–266) and the criticisms have provoked several revisions of his class schema. Nevertheless, Wright has continued to use versions of these self-reports to distinguish employees in contradictory class locations from the working class. However, our time series of surveys for Ontario indicate that there are increasingly significant numbers of employees in definitely working-class jobs – as well as a majority of semi-professional employees – who perceive themselves to have meaningful design and supervisory roles. Their assertion of this view does not automatically convert them into either supervisors or professional experts.

Our series of Ontario surveys provide estimates of the Ontario class structure between 1980 and 1996 based on measures of ownership status and the technical and social division of labour, but measures which are not dependent on respondents' self-reports of their workplace authority as Wright's 1980-centred estimates are.[16] The pattern is somewhat different than that found by Wright for the United States. Employers have consistently made up around six or seven per cent of the class structure in both cases, but the self-employed has continued to constitute at least twice as high a proportion of the workforce in Ontario. This reflects a greater persistence of small commodity production in agriculture and other crafts, and is consistent with the later industrialization of Canada than the United States.[17] The smaller proportion of managers in Ontario is also consistent with the fuller development of the managerial capitalist model in the United States, as documented by Lazonick (1991) and others;[18] the proportion of managers may have increased slightly during this period. The proportion of professional employees appears to have remained roughly constant throughout the period, while semi-professionals may have increased somewhat. The most notable change in Ontario seems to have been the rapid decline of supervisors, from 12 per cent to four per cent, in contrast to apparent stability in Wright's U.S. estimates. This is, in fact, a trend predicted by post-industrial theorists as being in correspondence with the rise of professional experts who supervise themselves. But perhaps the most striking finding is that the working class has *not* discernibly decreased. Service worker jobs without supervisory titles and lacking specialized technical knowledge have definitely increased and industrial sector worker jobs have decreased; but both of these components of the working class together continue to comprise nearly half of the class structure. While sampling error cannot be discounted in making such inferences from these Ontario surveys, other census-based Canadian analyses corroborate a gradual decline of supervisory employees over the 1961–86 period and a more substantial growth of semi-professional and managerial than professional employees, as well as the decline of industrial workers and an at least partially offsetting increase of service workers (Myles 1988, p. 343; Clement & Myles, 1994, p. 82).

Leaving aside the larger Canadian petty bourgeoisie and smaller managerial class, the main differences between Wright's U.S. estimates and these Ontario estimates of changes in the class distribution revolve around different measures of the supervisory role. The proportion of employees with official occupational titles of supervisor or foreperson is declining in both Canada and the United States.[19] Unless one is prepared to assume with Wright that the increasing consultation of workers can turn them into lower level members of the professional-managerial structure, the most reasonable conclusions from these findings are: (1) that definite working-class jobs remain around half of the employed workforce in both countries; and (2) that professional jobs may be increasing slowly at the expense of supervisory employees.

Comparative trend analyses of changes in the occupational class distributions using other measures and including additional European countries and Japan (Steven, 1983; Savage et al., 1992) have found similar patterns: continuing working-class majorities and expanding semi-professional and professional–managerial class groups, but no country where professional experts constitute as much as ten per cent of the class structure. Whatever more sensitive and precise subsequent empirical readings determine in this regard, it is at least clear that working-class jobs still occupy around half of the workforce in most advanced private market economies and that, at the current rates of increase of professional experts, they will remain a small minority of the class structure for the foreseeable future. It is also true that there is no discernible current trend toward the proletarianization of the vast majority of the employed workforce into working class jobs within advanced capitalist societies (see Marshall, 1997) – if we discount the growing numbers who cannot get any legitimate paid employment.

There have also been suggestions, based on workers' self-reported training requirements, that skill requirements are becoming more polarized within working class jobs themselves. Myles and Clements' 1982–83 Canadian Class Structure Survey (Myles, 1988, pp. 351–352) found that both blue-collar and white-collar workers' self-reports of required training time for their jobs produced more polarized skill ratings than standard SVP scores; in particular, Myles found that much higher proportions of workers self-reported that their jobs took less than a month to learn than SVP scores indicate. To assess this posited trend and also any other general trends in relations between class positions and skill requirements, we have analysed GED scores by class position, as well as by skilled and other (i.e., semi-skilled and unskilled) industrial and service worker jobs, in the Ontario surveys from 1980 to 1996.[20] The findings, based once more on largely invariant GED ratings done in the 1970s, offer little support for any major skill upgrading in relation to the changing occupational class distribution of the entire Ontario labour force. In particular, compositional changes in managerial, professional and semi-professional class positions have generated no significant skill upgrading during this period. Of course, the GED scores probably provide conservative estimates of actual upgrading because of their very limited capability to read skill changes within specific occupations. With regard to the polarization thesis, the range of GED scores (as estimated by standard deviation measures) has remained quite constant within most class positions. An increasing gap between the mean scores of skilled workers and semi/unskilled workers in the *declining* industrial sector offers some support for skill polarization, but the skill difference appears to be closing between skilled and other workers in the *expanding* service sector. An extensive survey-based cluster analysis of 1973–90 current population distributions of employment and quality of jobs in the United States also found little evidence of declining numbers or decreasing skill requirements in the lowest job clusters corresponding to the class positions of semi/unskilled service and industrial workers (Gittleman & Howell, 1995). So, there is only limited evidence of skill polarization. However, there is much greater evidence of polarization of some other aspects of job quality, especially wage polarization which is addressed in the following section.

Overall, the changing class structure is probably associated with gradually increasing skill requirements for paid work in most advanced private market economies. Daniel Bell's professional class is increasing, but very slowly. Working class jobs with narrow technical task requirements and very limited social authority continue to constitute the numerically predominant class position.

The so-called 'post-industrial era' does not appear to have produced the oft-claimed more interesting and fulfilling paid work for burgeoning numbers of professional experts and other knowledge workers. Certainly the proliferation of information technology has not produced the more pleasurable work for all that advocates like Bell had projected. As Krishan Kumar (1995) concludes his own recent assessment of 'post-industrialism:'

There is no question of the significance of the new information technology in large areas of social and economic life. This does not amount to the establishment of a new principle of society, or the advent of some 'third wave' of social evolution. In most areas, information technology has speeded up processes begun some time ago; it has aided the implementation of certain strategies of management in organizations; it has changed the nature of work for many workers; it has accelerated certain trends in leisure and consumption. But it has not produced a radical shift in the way industrial societies are organized, or in the direction in which they have been moving. The imperatives of profit, power and control seem as predominant now as they have ever been in the history of capitalist industrialism. The difference lies in the greater range and intensity of their applications made possible by the communications revolution; not in any change in the principles themselves. (p. 154)

These trends are much more modest than the visions of a knowledge-based economy initially projected by post-industrial theorists in the early 1960s, and especially modest in comparison with the massive expansion of advanced schooling and adult education.

THE LIMITS OF HUMAN CAPITAL THEORY

The most influential explanation currently on offer to account specifically for education-job relations is *human capital theory*. The core thesis is that peoples' learning capacities are comparable to other natural resources (i.e., factors of production) involved in the capitalist production process; when the resource is effectively exploited the results are profitable both for the enterprise and for society as a whole.[21] From its inception in the United States after World War II, human capital theory tended to equate workers' knowledge levels primarily with their levels of formal schooling, to rely on quantitative indices of amount of schooling in estimating individual economic returns to learning, and to infer that more schooling would lead to higher productivity and macro-economic growth (e.g., Schultz, 1963; Becker, 1964). Throughout the post-1945 expansionary era, the simultaneous increase of school participation rates and earned incomes in advanced industrial market economies lent evident support to both the *individual and aggregate* dimensions of this perspective and encouraged the popular view that more schooling would inevitably lead to greater economic success.

The *individual* level relationship between educational attainment and income has remained strong in relative terms. A representative example is an international survey by the Organisation for Economic Co-operation and Development (OECD 1994b, Table 7.A.1).[22] This survey summarizes the strength and stability of this relationship in most of the G7 countries and Sweden in terms of the greater

103

earnings accruing to those with university degrees in comparison to those with high school diplomas. In all of these countries, university graduates have consistently earned significantly more than high school graduates. Individual investment in higher education has therefore continued to represent a reasonable economic choice as long as the individual economic costs of obtaining it (in terms of tuition fees and deferred income) were not prohibitive.

However, simple earnings ratios do not tell the whole story. As Mishel, Bernstein, and Schmitt (1997, p. 170) summarize for the U.S. case, real wages in constant dollars were lower in the mid-1990s than they were in the early 1970s for all workers except those with advanced degrees.[23] The wages of other college graduates slowly climbed back to early 1970s levels, but those of people without a college degree have continued to fall precipitously. The decline in wages for the non-college workforce may be attributable to many factors, including de-unionization, a shift to low wage industries, a falling minimum wage, and import competition. But, as the data in the prior section indicate, this wage decline is unlikely to be related to the declining technical skill of the U.S. workforce. In any case, it is clear that the main cause of the growing wage gap between U.S. college graduates and less educated workers has been the decline of non-college workers' wages rather than any strong growth in the college wage.

More generally, while school enrolment rates continued to increase since the early 1970s, average incomes have stagnated, unemployment rates have fluctuated upwards and underemployment of highly schooled people has been recognized as a social problem. The applicability of human capital theory's *aggregate* or societal-level 'returns on learning' claims has been thrown into doubt. The belief that more education brings greater societal economic benefit has been a general article of faith in all post-industrial theories and a cornerstone of human capital theories. As noted above, the end of the post-World War II expansionary era in the early 1970s brought serious challenge to this belief. As Mishel, Bernstein and Schmitt (1997, Table B, 25)[24] summarize, real increases in average wages and benefits for the U.S. labour force as a whole virtually ceased during the 1970s, while the average education and skill levels of the workforce continued to increase. Contrary to the precepts of human capital theory, collective investment in education has grown significantly, while compensation growth has stagnated.

During the same period – 1973 to 1995 – the real U.S. gross domestic product rose by nearly 40 per cent, while real hourly wages of non-supervisory workers declined by about 15 per cent; during the 1980s, virtually all of the earnings gains went to the top 20 per cent of the workforce, two-thirds accruing to the top one per cent of earners (Thurow, 1996). Similar trends have been found in Canada (Morisette, 1995). By the mid-1990s, the typical U.S. chief executive officer was making well over 100 times as much as the typical factory worker. This huge wage gap, far larger than in any other advanced industrial economy, had more than doubled since the 1970s (Sklar, 1995, p. 11).[25] But aside from the extraordinary gains of executives, the rising wage differential between college educated and non-college educated employees during the 1980s and 1990s in the U.S has been more the result of declining wages for the many than of increasing salaries for the few.

In this context of stagnant wages and continuing general increases in the education and skill levels of the overall workforce, the association between income and conventional measures of skill such as GED and SVP has been modest and declining. As Gittleman and Howell (1995, pp. 423–427) document for the U.S. case in their 1973–90 analysis of six job quality 'contours,' the majority of 'subordinate primary' contour blue-collar workers who are unionized have been able to protect their wage levels far better than white-collar service workers who have higher cognitive skill requirements in their jobs but who are rarely unionized; the poor, non-union 'secondary' service and blue-collar jobs that remained around 40 per cent of U.S. jobs during the 1980s, and which employed very high proportions of blacks and Hispanics, saw *wage levels and most other aspects of job quality decline while occupants' education levels increased.* Earlier comparative analyses of skill and wage trends during the 1960–85 period found that low-skill, high-wage jobs were declining in the goods industries while jobs with low wages but at least moderate skill levels were increasing in service sectors (Howell & Wolff, 1991). The growing weight of empirical evidence makes it clear that, rather than a 'skill deficit,' most working Americans are now experiencing a 'wage deficit' (Sklar, 1995, p. 28; Mishel & Teixeira, 1991). The most highly educated workforce in the world now works longer for less than do less educated but more unionized workers in other major industrialized countries (OECD, 1994c, pp. 22–23).

Human capital theory clearly needs to be retooled. There have been at least three sorts of retooling efforts which focus, respectively, on stressing the relative individual benefits of schooling, enhancing the quality of schooling, and emphasizing the benefits of lifelong learning.

Adherents to the original human capital thesis have attempted to defend it against critiques that it has failed to take account of changing aggregate-level conditions by focusing quite narrowly on documenting continuing *relative* economic benefits, especially the lower unemployment rates and relatively high earnings of those with higher formal credentials. The declining collective economic rewards for educational investment tends to be regarded as a continuation of only partial compensation through individual incomes and more intangible spin-off benefits for the general enrichment of civil society; so nations that have invested more in schooling are still considered ahead in global competition (Becker, 1993, 1996). Recent sociological perspectives, such as Ulrich Beck's (1992) individualization theorem, that stress the disintegration of class commonalities and the rise of competition as the main mode of human interaction, offer some theoretical support for closer attention to individual training and job choices (see Timmerman, 1995). But the narrowing of the empirical target to relative individual benefits simply ignores the biggest challenge to human capital theory, the evident societal underemployment of credentialed knowledge.

Secondly, some human capital advocates have suggested that declining or unimproving quality of schooling is now the central problem and that by raising standards, starting earlier or providing more privatized or specialized forms, both human capital creation and economic growth can be rejuvenated (Heckman &

Klenow, 1997). Nobody would argue against continuing to try to improve the quality of educational services; but many would disagree that educational quality has in fact declined. Some human capital analysts offer more nuanced relative arguments for school reforms to enhance national productivity and economic competitiveness based on comparative studies of superior student performance in other countries, such as U.S. comparisons with Japan, Taiwan and China (Stevenson & Stigler, 1992). But the general assumption is that the post-industrial/knowledge economy requires a leap in workers' skills and that the schools must perform to higher standards to close the gap. The focus is usually on the skills purportedly needed by 'high performance' firms, and numerous innovative school reforms have been suggested to make the schools more responsive to these needs and thereby close the gap (e.g., Berryman & Bailey, 1992; Marshall & Tucker, 1992; Resnick & Wirt, 1996).

The claim that declining school quality is serving to depreciate human capital is typically made in terms of young people's falling performance levels on standardized tests. Such historical comparisons are often fraught with fallacy-of-composition errors of logic – that is, either average scores of entire current youth cohorts are compared with those of more restricted earlier enrolments, or specific bits of knowledge are used to argue an increasing general ignorance thesis. While most of these claims have now been systematically refuted (see especially Sandia Laboratories, 1993; Berliner & Biddle, 1995, 1996; Mishel et al., 1997, pp. 182–184), they continue to be recycled in evermore selective forms. Of course, the curricula and pedagogies of current educational systems will change, and we can and should continue to try to improve them; raising standards, starting earlier and more relevant curriculum all remain worthy objectives. But rather than bemoaning decline from an idealized past, or becoming fixated on international league tables of current math scores, we should celebrate the fact that much larger and increasing proportions of today's young people are mastering much larger and increasing bodies of school knowledge (see Bracey, 1997). Indeed, the recent purported crisis in adult illiteracy has also found little empirical basis.[26]

In sum, the evidence does not show any cumulative general decline in the quality of education. What it does show is that people of all ages in advanced industrial market economies are increasingly using their learning capacities more effectively through the institutions of organized education to gain greater amounts of knowledge. If the aggregate North American quality of schooling has not been shown to decline inter-generationally, this is a significant achievement in light of the massive increases in the proportion of the population participating and particularly the increasing proportions of non-English speaking entrants into the school system. Blaming the quality of the educational system for the breakdown of the aggregate learning–earning connection is like blaming the producer of any form of labour for employers' failure to utilize it. Do we blame the chef for the patron's failure to finish a well-cooked meal?

Thirdly, some popular revisionist approaches to human capital theory no longer focus on schooling but on 'human capital externalities,' such as lifelong job-related learning among workers (Lucas, 1988; Romer, 1994). The dynamic centre of human capital creation is now seen to reside either in highly concentrated urban zones where 'symbolic analysts' live, work and continually solve, identify and broker production problems (Reich 1991), or in 'learning organizations' which create intellectual capital by facilitating collaborative problem-solving within their workforces (Senge, 1990; Nyhan, 1991). The central empirical claim of human capital theory – that greater learning efforts are closely related to higher earning level – is resuscitated by downplaying schooling and by emphasizing that effective employees must become continual adult learners in an increasingly globally competitive enterprise environment (OECD, 1996c).

The 'learning organization' arguments of human capital revisionists like Reich and Senge, although largely rhetorical to date, begin to draw greater attention to aspects of learning previously ignored or taken for granted by human capital theory's earlier fixation on schooling and credentialed knowledge, namely the informal work-related learning of workers and their cumulative bodies of tacit knowledge. In some sense, we all know that substantial informal learning is essential to master a new job. Most employers rely heavily on informal on-the-job training. However, ethnographic studies and more extensive surveys of work-related learning[27] seriously undermine learning organization revisions of human capital theory, by exposing the lack of sustained relations between continued learning and earning for most workers.

Corporate executives, professional employees and service and industrial workers all now spend about the same amount of time in work-related informal learning.[28] Human capital theory assumes that those who are more highly compensated are exercising greater learning capacities. But these results suggest that, at least in terms of informal learning time, the most poorly paid employees are devoting just as much effort to work-related learning in general as the most highly paid employers. The striking occupational class differences in the extent to which people get to use this acquired knowledge in their actual jobs have also been extensively documented,[29] especially in terms of the discrepancy between the *general work-related* informal learning and *job-specific* unpaid learning of service and industrial workers. The fact is that large and growing numbers of people do substantial amounts of work-related informal learning throughout their working lives. But many either do not have the opportunity to apply this acquired knowledge in their paid workplaces or, if they can apply it informally, to be recognized and rewarded for doing so. The promoters of learning organizations have got it backwards. The challenge is not to facilitate more collaborative learning but to establish fair incentive structures, especially among service and industrial workers, to use and compensate the extensive amount of informal learning that is already occurring.

Growing proportions of people who have invested many years of their lives in acquiring advanced formal educational qualifications are unable to obtain commensurate jobs. The growing proportions of underemployed youths generally continue to try to realize their extensive educational investments in the job market, and even continue to make more such investments. The prospect of losing these investments through not being able to use them in the job market is again increasing (Krahn, 1997). But, more generally, most people find diminishing credibility in human capital advocates' arguments that those with the most formal education are still likely to get good jobs, when they see so few of these to go around.

All of these efforts to repair human capital theory remain in jeopardy because of their failure to account for the growing general gap between peoples' increasing learning efforts and knowledge bases on the one hand, and the diminishing numbers of commensurate jobs to apply their increasing knowledge investments on the other. The large body of accumulating evidence on the massive extent of both people's learning activities and their underemployment represents a major contradiction for human capital theory (see Livingstone, 2004, 2009). Appeals to an immanent knowledge economy have limited credibility for those living in the education–jobs gap. The 'learning for earning' thesis is increasingly reduced to a strategy for relative individual advantage and decreasing marginal returns. Human capital theory appears to have reached its limit as a rationale for increased social investment in education.

CONCLUDING REMARKS

The image of contemporary society inherent in post-industrial/knowledge economy and human capital theories proves illusory. While an aggregate upgrading of the technical skills needed for job performance is gradually occurring, our collective acquisition of work-related knowledge and credentials is far outpacing this incremental shift. Such underemployment is scarcely recognized in knowledge economy and human capital theories, beyond the 'frictional adjustment' that is regarded as natural in market economies. What the cumulative findings of increasing technical skill levels, changing cross-national patterns of social divisions of labour and general class distributions point out is that the relations between knowledge and work are not explicable through simple evolutionary growth models. The organizational structures of the workplace and the strategies used by employers and employees vary quite widely across current industrial market economies. The Japanese model of 'collective capitalism' appears to have been relatively effective in utilizing the working knowledge of operative level workers in lifetime contract conditions within leading firms. This leading edge case clearly illustrates that there is nothing inevitable about development of the technical and social divisions of labour. The employment contract can be modified in various ways to include or exclude the knowledge and skills of the non-owning classes. The North American model of 'managerial capitalism' is generally regarded as being much more exclusionary of the knowledge and skills of operative workers. While such models may well be gross simplifications of actual conditions, the high levels of performance underemployment documented among the North American labour force (Livingstone, 2004, 2009) are consistent with this model.

It is becoming increasingly apparent that the connections between knowledge and work are mediated by the individual and collective negotiating powers of those in different class, gender, race and generational groups. For example, the proportion of the U.S. labour force that is unionized has dropped from a peak of over 35 per cent in 1945 to less than 15 per cent overall and even lower in the private sector by the mid-1990s; the sharpest drop has been since the mid-1970s, demarcated by President Reagan's wholesale firing of striking air controllers in 1981 (Sklar, 1995, pp. 30–32). While productivity and profits recovered to post-World War II highs in the 1990s, the wages of a politically weakened workforce continued to stagnate. The 'downsizing of America' in terms of good jobs and future expectations has reached deeply into the previously secure middle classes (New York Times, 1996; Ehrenreich, 1989; Rubin, 1994). The depth of citizen resentment of these conditions is provoking elected politicians to speak out. In the words of David Boniar, U.S. Congress minority whip prior to the 1996 federal election:

> There's something wrong when the stock market reaches record highs driven by corporate profits that are up 14 percent, while the amount corporations are spending on wages and benefits is falling ... If we can't speak out against the growing chasm between the rich and the rest of America for fear that somebody will accuse us of waging class warfare, then we really are lost in the wilderness. (quoted in Handelman, 1996, p. F4)

The desperate and ultimately successful mid-1997 nationwide walkout of United Parcel Service's workforce of frequently well-educated, largely part-time and poorly paid drivers, loaders and sorters may represent another benchmark in U.S. negotiations over job quality (Herbert, 1997). At least some corporate leaders in North America are now willing to speak publicly about the depth of the economic benefits problem. As Courtney Pratt (1997), then-President of Noranda Metals, declared:

> If the business community doesn't come together to define its social responsibility and then to act on that definition, I fear we will not achieve that better society ... We are increasingly becoming a society of haves and have-nots ... and in our streets the plight of the extreme have-nots is increasingly visible to us all ... [and] profoundly disturbing ... [W]e risk being pulled apart – polarized – at a time when we should be recommitting to each other. (p. 3)

All this is a far cry from the optimistic post-industrial projections of the 1960s, as well as those of many current knowledge economy and human capital theorists. Conflicts of interest between haves and have-nots need to be recognized as a starting point for understanding changes and continuities in the education-jobs gap.

NOTES

[1] It is interesting to note that human capital theory is in accord with the Marxist labour theory of value on this recognition of labour as the primary source of wealth in capitalist society. From eighteenth-century physiocrats who imputed primary value-creating capacity to the land up to our contemporary econometricians, dominant economic theories have tended to diminish the role of

labour in the creation of wealth. The limits of human capital theory, as will be illustrated in this chapter, are its fixation with individual market transactions and blindness to macro-level underemployment. In Marxist terms, human capital theory is preoccupied with *value creation* while ignoring *value realization*. That is, human capital theory insists on the importance of investment in education, the imparting of value to the future labourer, but does not directly address the fact that this embodied value must be harnessed in the production of goods or services by labour power in order for the human capital invested to be realized. It is precisely this failure of value realization that constitutes the education–jobs gap. I am indebted to Wally Seccombe for developing this comparison.

[2] For my own early critique of the 'post-industrial' perspective, Porter's rejoinder and my reply, see Livingstone (1972).

[3] See Stehr (1994) for a recent revisionist overview of post-industrial/knowledge *society* theories which attempts to respond to some critiques and recuperate the concept by formulating an explicitly non-evolutionary version which stresses its theoretical elasticity and transitional character, and with decidedly less emphasis on economic aspects of social relations than its predecessors.

[4] The increasingly extensive pursuit of both formal and informal learning activities in advanced market societies is documented in Livingstone (2004, 2009, 2010).

[5] For discussion of the various dimensions of underemployment and reviews of the relevant empirical research literature, see Livingstone (2004, 2009).

[6] A prominent example of a post-modernist thinker who has self-consciously attempted to offer a macro-level explanation for contemporary social conditions is Francis Fukuyama (1993). For an overview of this genre of contemporary social theories, see Jencks (1989).

[7] In addition to evolutionary explanations, other forms of explanation of social change and continuity that have been common in the social sciences at various times include functionalist, genetic, historicist (e.g., 'great man' theories of history), and inter-group struggle theories. For useful accounts of the varieties of social explanation, see Robert R. Brown (1964) and Christopher Lloyd (1986).

[8] Murphy (1993) has traced the development of the conflation of social and technical divisions of labour and the emergence of technological determinism in classical political economy, with particular attention to the influences of Adam Smith and Karl Marx. Murphy also draws on Aristotle to distinguish natural, customary and stipulated or deliberately designed aspects of divisions of labour.

[9] More recent empirical research substantiating the trends identified in the following discussions may be found in Livingstone (2009, 2010).

[10] The detailed findings were presented in the original published version. The primary sources of the occupation-specific GED scores were Temme (1975) for the United States and Hunter (1986) for Canada.

[11] Again, the detailed findings were presented in the original published version. While each individual job title has been given a whole number rating on both the GED and SVP scales by government analysts, the groupings of thousands of these titles into summary occupational classifications results in average scores, which produce a continuous rather than a simple ordinal scale. The mid-point split procedure groups all scores up to 1.5 as 1, from 1.5 to 2.5 as 2 and so on, with scores over 5.5 up to the maximum of 6 grouped as 6. We have also analysed the same data with a grouping that reduces all scores below any whole number to the lower skill level (e.g., 1.75 becomes 1) and an alternative grouping that raises all scores above any whole number to the higher skill level (e.g., 1.25 becomes 2). The trends in each case are very similar.

[12] Once again, the detailed findings were presented in the original published version. Both Eckhaus (1964, Table 3, 185) and Berg (1970, Table III-1, 46) apparently used median scores to produce their estimates of the distributions of GED skill levels in the U.S. labour force. Eckhaus used an earlier seven-point scale, which I have grouped downward for equivalence with the six-point scale that has been used since the 1950s. Eckhaus also produced estimates for 1950 using the seven-point

scale. When they are regrouped downward, his 1950 estimates are fairly similar to those of Berg, but Berg's estimates are used here because they rely on the now standard six point scale.

[13] Detailed findings were presented in the original published version.

[14] See chapters two and three in Livingstone (2004), as well as Livingstone (2009, 2010).

[15] Detailed findings were presented in the original published version.

[16] Detailed findings were presented in the original published version.

[17] For more extensive accounts of historical and current trends in the class structures of the United States and Canada, see, for example, for the United States, Szymanski (1983), Kerbo (1983), Wright (1997); for Canada, see: Ornstein (1983), Clement (1988), Livingstone & Mangan (1996).

[18] Clement and Myles' (1994, pp. 63–90) analysis confirms the stronger managerialist tendency of the U.S. class structure in comparison with Sweden, Norway and Finland with regard to the regulation of labour. They find a more mixed mode in Canada, with the largely American branch plant goods producing sectors having a similar proportion of employees with managerial authority to the United States, while Canadian government and service sectors are closer to the Nordic model of less managers and greater worker consultation. It should be noted, however, that these comparative analyses are based primarily on survey respondents' self-reports, all of which likely provide overestimates of many respondents' actual managerial authority.

[19] Special tabulations of 1986 and 1991 Canada census as well as secondary analysis of the 1972–94 NORC U.S. data set (Davis and Smith, 1994).

[20] Detailed findings were presented in the original published version.

[21] As in mainstream economics generally, human capital theory has been largely indifferent to negative effects of resource exploitation.

[22] Detailed findings were presented in the original published version.

[23] Detailed findings were presented in the original published version.

[24] Detailed findings were presented in the original published version.

[25] According to the OECD (1996c), CEO:factory worker wage ratios for some relevant countries were as follows: United States 120; Canada 36; United Kingdom 33; Germany 21; Japan 16.

[26] See chapter one in Livingstone (2004).

[27] See chapter one in Livingstone (2004) as well as Livingstone and Sawchuk (2004).

[28] See chapter two in Livingstone (2004).

[29] See chapter one in Livingstone (2004).

REFERENCES

Abercrombie, N. & Urry, J. (1983). *Capital, labour and the middle classes: Capital, labour and the middle classes*. Controversies in Sociology, 15. London: George Allen & Unwin.

Adler, P. (1993). The 'learning bureaucracy:' New United Motor Manufacturing, Inc. *Research in Organizational Behavior, 15*, 111–194.

Aronowitz, S. (1973). *False promises: The shaping of American working class consciousness*. New York: McGraw-Hill.

Becker, G. (1964). *Human capital: A theoretical and empirical analysis, with special reference to education*. New York: National Bureau of Economic Research.

Beck, U. (1992). *Risk society: Towards a new modernity*. London: Sage.

Becker, G. (1993). *Human capital* (3rd ed.). Chicago: University of Chicago Press.

Becker, G. (1996, March 11). Human capital: One investment where America is way ahead. *Business Week*.

Beirne, M. & Ramsay, H. (Eds.). (1992). *Information technology and workplace democracy*. London: Routledge.

Bell, D. (1964). The post-industrial society. In Ginzberg, E. (Ed.), *Technology and social change* (pp. 44–59). New York: Columbia University Press.

Bell, D. (1973). *The coming of post-industrial society*. New York: Basic Books.

Berg, I. (1970). *Education and jobs: The Great Training Robbery*. New York: Praeger.

Berggren, C. (1992). *Alternatives to lean production: Work and organization in the Swedish auto industry*. Ithaca, NY: ILR Press.

Berggren, C. (1994, Winter). NUMMI vs. Uddevala. *Sloan Management Review*, 35(2), 37–45.

Berryman, S.E. & Bailey, T.R. (1992). *The double helix of education and the economy*. New York: Institution on Education and the Economy.

Berliner, D. & Biddle, B. (1995). *The manufactured crisis: Myths, fraud, and the attack on America's schools*. Reading, MA: Addison-Wesley.

Berliner, D. & Biddle, B. (1996, February). Making molehills out of molehills: Reply to Lawrence Stedman's review of *The manufactured crisis*. *Education Policy Analysis Archives*, 4(3).

Betcherman, G. (1994). *The Canadian workplace in transition*. Kingston, ON: Industrial Relations Centre, Queen's University.

Bracey, G. (1997). *The truth about Americas' schools: The Bracey Reports, 1991–97*. Bloomington, IN: Phi Delta Kappan Educational Foundation.

Braverman, H. (1974). *Labor and monopoly capital: The degradation of work in the twentieth century*. New York: Monthly Review.

Brown, R.R. (1964). *Explanation in social science*. Chicago: Aldine.

Brown, C., Reich, M., & Stern, D. (1990). *Skill and security and evolving employment systems: Observations from case studies*. Berkeley & Los Angeles: University of California Press.

Cappelli, P. (1993). Are skill requirements rising? Evidence from production and clerical jobs. *Industrial and Labor Relations Review*, 46(3), 515–530.

Carter, R. (1985). *Capitalism, class conflict and the new middle class*. London: Routledge & Kegan Paul.

Clement, W. (1988). *The challenge of class analysis*. Ottawa: Carleton University Press.

Clement, W. & J. Myles. (1994). *Relations of ruling: Class and gender in postindustrial societies*. Montreal: McGill-Queen's University Press.

Crompton, R. (1993). Class and stratification: An introduction to current debates. Oxford: Polity.

Davis, J.A. & Smith, T.W. (1994). *General Social Surveys 1972–1994*. Chicago: National Opinion Research Center.

Dawson, P. & Webb, J. (1989, June). New production arrangements: The totally flexible cage? *Work, Employment and Society*, 3(2), 221–238.

Derber, C., Schwartz, W., & Magrass, Y. (1990). *Power in the highest degree: Professionals and the rise of a new mandarin order*. New York: Oxford University Press.

Drucker, P. (1954). *The practice of management*. New York: Harper.

Eckaus, R.S. (1964). Economic criteria for education and training. *Review of Economics and Statistics*, 46(1), 181–190.

Ehrenreich, B. (1989). *Fear of falling: The inner life of the middle class*. New York: Pantheon.

Fine, S.A. (1968). The use of the dictionary of occupational titles as a source of estimates of education and training requirements. *Journal of Human Resources*, 3(3), 363–375.

Friedman, A. (1977). *Industry and labour: Class struggle at work and monopoly capitalism*. London: Macmillan.

Friedson, E. (1973). Professionalization and the organization of middle-class labour in post-industrial society. In Holmes, P. (Ed.), *Professionalization and social change* (pp. 47–59). Keele: University of Kent.

Fukuyama, F. (1993). *The end of history and the last man*. New York: Maxwell.

Galbraith, J.K. (1985). *The new industrial state* (4th ed.). New York: Mentor.

Gephart, M.A. (1995). The road to high performance. *Training and Development*, 49(6), 30–44.

Gittleman, M.B. & Howell, D.R. (1995). Changes in the structure and quality of jobs in the United States: Effects by race and gender, 1973–1990. *Industrial and Labor Relations Review*, 48(3), 420–440.

Handelman, S. (1996, April 6). The downsizing of America: Economic insecurity fuels class warfare. *Ottawa Citizen*.

Harris, L. (1991, September). *An assessment of American education: The view of employers, higher educators, recent students and their parents.* New York: Lou Harris & Associates Information Services.

Heckman, J. & Klenow, P. (1997, October). *Is there underinvestment in human capital?* Unpublished paper. Chicago, Center for Social Program Evaluation, University of Chicago.

Herbert, B. (1997, August 12). A workers' rebellion. *Globe and Mail*, B2.

Horowitz, M. & I. Herrnstadt. (1966). Changes in skill requirements of occupations in selected industries. In National Commission on Technology, Automation and Economic Progress (Ed.), *Technology and the American economy* (Vol 2: Appendix) (pp. 223–287). Washington, DC: Government Printing Office.

Howell, D.R. & Wolff, E.N. (1991). *Trends in the growth and distribution of skills in the U.S. workplace, 1960–1985.* Industrial and Labor Relations Review, *44*(3), 486–502.

Hunter, A. (1988). Formal education and initial employment: Unravelling the relationships between schooling and skills over time. *American Sociological Review*, *53*(5), 753–765.

Jencks, C. (1989). *What is post-modernism?* (3rd ed.). London: Academy Editions.

Kamata, S. (1983). *Japan in the passing lane: An insider's account of life in a Japanese auto factory.* Boston: George Allen & Unwin.

Kerbo, H.R. (1983). *Social stratification and inequality: Class conflict in the United States.* New York: McGraw-Hill.

Kochan, T.A. & Useem, M. (Eds.). (1992). *Transforming organizations.* New York: Oxford University Press.

Krahn, H. (1997). On the permanence of human capital: Use it or lose it. *Policy Options*, *18*(6), 17–21.

Kumar, K. (1995). *From post-industrial to post-modern society: New theories of the contemporary world.* Oxford: Blackwell.

Latouche, S. (1993). *In the wake of the affluent society: An exploration of post-development.* London: Zed Books.

Lawler, E., Mohrman, S., & Ledford, G. (1992). *Employee involvement and Total Quality Management: Practices and results in Fortune 1000 Companies.* San Francisco: Jossey-Bass.

Lazonick, W. (1991). *Business organization and the myth of the market economy.* New York: Cambridge University Press.

Levin, H., Rumberger, R., & Finnan, C. (1990). *Escalating skill requirements or different skill requirements?* Conference on Changing Occupational Skill Requirements: Gathering and Assessing the Evidence. Brown University, June 5–6.

Livingstone, D.W. (1972). Inventing the future: Anti-historicist reflections on Towards 2000. *Interchange*, *3*(4), 111–123.

Livingstone, D.W. (1983). *Class, ideologies and educational futures.* London: Falmer.

Livingstone, D.W. (1996). *Steel work: Recasting the core workforce at Hilton Works, 1981–96.* Final report of the Workplace Change Section of the Steelworker Families Project. Toronto: Department of Sociology and Equity Studies in Education, Ontario Institute for Studies in Education.

Livingstone, D.W. (1997). Computer literacy and the 'knowledge economy' and information control: Micro myths and macro choices. In Moll, M. (Ed.), *Tech high: Globalization and the future of Canadian education* (pp. 99–116). Ottawa: Canadian Centre for Policy Alternatives.

Livingstone, D.W. (2004). *The education-jobs gap: Underemployment or economic democracy.* Aurora, ON: Garamond.

Livingstone, D.W. (Ed.) (2009). *Education and jobs: Exploring the gaps.* Toronto: University of Toronto Press.

Livingstone, D.W. (Ed.) (2010). *Lifelong learning in paid and unpaid work.* London: Routledge.

Livingstone, D.W., Hart, D., & Davie, L.E. (1985). *Public attitudes toward education in Ontario: Fifth OISE survey.* Toronto: OISE Press.

Livingstone, D.W. & Mangan, M. (Eds.). 1996. *Recast dreams: Class and gender consciousness in Steeltown.* Toronto: Garamond.

Livingstone, D.W. & Sawchuk, P. (2004). *Hidden knowledge: Organized labour in the information age.* Aurora, ON: Garamond.

Lloyd, C. (1986). *Explanation in social history.* New York: Blackwell.

Lowe, G. (1996, March 31). *The use of computers in the Canadian workplace.* Paper prepared for Information Technology Innovation, Industry Canada.

Lucas, R.E. (1988). On the mechanics of economic development. *Journal of Monetary Economics, 22,* 3–42.

Mallet, S. (1975). *The new working class.* Nottingham: Spokesman.

Marshall, G. (1997). *Repositioning class: Social inequality in industrial societies.* London: Sage.

Marshall, R. & Tucker, M. (1994). *Thinking for a living: Education and the wealth of nations.* New York: Basic Books.

Maurice, M., Sellier, F., & Silvestre, J. (1986). *The social foundations of industrial power.* Cambridge: MIT Press.

Mishel, L. & Teixeira, R. (1991). *The myth of the coming labor shortage: Jobs, skills, and incomes of America's workforce 2000.* Washington, DC: Economic Policy Institute.

Mishel, L., Bernstein, J. & Schmitt, J. (1997). *The state of working America: 1996–1997.* Armonk: M.E. Sharpe.

Menzies, H. (1996). *Whose Brave New World? The information highway and the New Economy.* Toronto: Between the Lines.

Morissette, R., Myles, J., & Picot, G. (1993). *What is happening to earnings inequality in Canada?* Analytical Studies Branch: Research Paper Series, 60. Ottawa: Statistics Canada.

Mullaby, S. (1994, July 9). A survey on Japan. *Economist, 332,* 3–18.

Murphy, J.B. (1993). *The moral economy of labour: Aristotelian themes in economic theory.* New Haven: Yale University Press.

Myles, J. (1988). The expanding middle: Some Canadian evidence on the deskilling debate. *Canadian Review of Sociology and Anthropology, 25,* 335–264.

National Center on Education and the Economy (NCEE). (1990). *America's choice: High skills or low wages.* Washington, DC: NCEE.

National Center on the Educational Quality of the Workforce (NCEQW). (1995). *First findings from the EQW National Employer Survey.* Philadelphia: NCEQW.

New York Times. (1996). *The downsizing of America.* New York: Random House.

Nisbet, R. (1970). *Social change and history: Aspects of the Western theory of development.* New York: Oxford University Press.

Nyhan, B. (1991). *Developing people's ability to learn: A European perspective on self-learning competency and technological change.* Brussels: European Interuniversity Press.

Odrich, B. (1997). *Japan in the 1990s: Facing higher unemployment in Japan.* Retrieved from www.nkk.co.jp/nkknews/36-6/japan.htm.

Organisation for Economic Co-operation and Development (OECD). (1994a). *The OECD job study: Facts, analysis, strategies.* Paris: OECD.

Organisation for Economic Co-operation and Development (OECD). (1994b). *The OECD jobs study: Evidence and explanations.* Part II: The adjustment potential of the labour market. Paris: OECD.

Organisation for Economic Co-operation and Development (OECD). (1994c). *OECD societies in transition: The future of work and leisure.* Paris: OECD.

Ornstein, M.D. (1983). The development of class in Canada. In Grayson, J.P. (Ed.), *Introduction to sociology: An alternate approach* (pp. 216–259). Toronto: Gage.

Osterman, P. (1994, January). How common is workplace reform and who adopts it? *Industrial and Labor Relations Review, 47*(2), 173–188.

O'Toole, J. (1977). *Work, learning, and the American future.* San Francisco: Jossey-Bass.

Parenti, M. (1996). *Dirty truths.* San Francisco: City Lights.

Parker, M. & Slaughter, J. (1994). *Working smart: A union guide to participation programs and reengineering.* Detroit: Labor Notes.

Perkins, H. (1996). *The third revolution: Professional elites and the modern world.* London: Routledge.

Porter, J. (1971). *The vertical mosaic*. Toronto: University of Toronto Press.

Pratt, C. (1997, September 29). Business accountability: Shareholders, stakeholders or society? Address to the Canadian Club of Toronto.

Reich, R. (1991). *The work of nations: Preparing ourselves for 21st century capitalism*. New York: Vintage.

Resnick, L.B. & Wirt, J.G. (Eds.). (1996). *Linking school and work: Roles for standards and assessment*. San Francisco: Jossey-Bass.

Richta, R. (1969). *Civilization at the crossroads: Social and human implications of the scientific and technological revolution* (Slingova, M., Trans.). White Plains, NY: International Arts and Sciences Press.

Rubin, L. (1994). *Families on the fault line: America's working class speaks about the family, the economy, race, and ethnicity*. New York: Harper Collins.

Sandia Laboratories. (1993). Perspectives on education in America. *Journal of Educational Research*, *86*(5), 259–310.

Savage, M., Barlow, J., Dickens, P., & Fielding, T. (1992). *Property, bureaucracy and culture: Middle-class formation in contemporary Britain*. London: Routledge.

Schultz, T.W. (1963). *The economic value of education*. New York: Columbia University Press.

Senge, P. (1990). *The fifth discipline: The art and practice of the learning organization*. New York: Doubleday.

Servan-Schreiber, J.J. (1971). *The American challenge*. New York: Avon.

Sklar, H. (1995). *Jobs, income, and work: Ruinous trends, urgent alternatives*. Philadelphia: Community Relations Division, American Friends Service Committee.

Smith, A. (1982 [1776]). *The wealth of nations* (Books 1–3). Skinner, A. (Ed.). New York: Penguin.

Smith, V. (1994). Braverman's legacy: The labor process tradition at 20. *Work and Occupations*, *21*(4), 403–442.

Sobel, R. (1989). *The white collar working class: From structure to politics*. New York: Praeger.

Sorokin, P. (1937–1941). *Social and cultural dynamics: A study of change in major systems of art, truth, ethics, law and social relationships* (4 vols.). Boston: Porter Sargent.

Spenner, K. (1983, December). Deciphering Prometheus: Temporal change in the skill level of work. *American Sociological Review*, *48*(6), 824–837.

Stehr, N. (1994). *Knowledge societies*. London: Sage

Steven, R. (1983). *Classes in contemporary Japan*. Cambridge: Cambridge University Press.

Stevenson, H.W. & Stigler, J.W. (1987). *The learning gap: Why our schools are failing and what we can learn from Japanese and Chinese education*. New York: Touchstone.

Syzmanski, A. (1983). *Class structure: A critical perspective*. New York: Praeger.

Temme, L. (1975). *Occupation: Meanings and measures*. Washington, DC: Bureau of Social Science Research.

Thurow, L. (1974). Measuring the economic benefits of education. In Gordon, M. (Ed.), *Higher education and the labor market* (pp. 373–418). New York: McGraw-Hill.

Timmermann, D. (1995). Human capital theory and the individualization theorem. In Neubauer, G. & Hurrelmann, K. (Eds.), *Individualization in childhood and adolescence* (pp. 223–245). Berlin: Walter de Gruyter.

Touraine, T. (1969). *The post-industrial society: Tomorrow's social history: Classes, conflicts and culture in the programmed society*. New York: Random House.

US Department of Labor. (1993). *High performance work practices and firm performance*. Chicago: US Department of Labor.

Walker, P. (Ed.). (1978). *Between labour and capital*. Montreal: Black Rose.

Wood, S. (Ed.). (1989). *The transformation of work: Skill, flexibility and the labour process*. London: Unwin Hyman.

World Bank. (1997). *World development report: The state in a changing world*. Oxford: Oxford University Press.

Wright, E.O. (1997). *Class counts: Comparative studies in class analysis.* Cambridge: Cambridge University Press.
Wright, E.O. (1980). Class and occupation. *Theory and Society, 9*(1), 177–214.

PHILLIP BROWN & HUGH LAUDER

GLOBALIZATION, KNOWLEDGE, AND THE MYTH OF THE MAGNET ECONOMY

INTRODUCTION: THE RISE OF THE MAGNET ECONOMY

The dominant view today is that we have entered a global knowledge economy, driven by the application of new technologies and collapsing barriers to international trade and investment, accelerating the evolutionary path from a low- to a high-skills economy. Becker (2002) has depicted an 'age of human capital,' where the prosperity of individuals and nations rests on the skills, knowledge and enterprise of all rather than the elite few that drove industrial capitalism in the twentieth century. This view is reflected in the central role of education in national economic and social policy. Not only is education seen to hold the key to a competitive economy, but it is also seen to be the foundation of social justice and social cohesion:

> Our future success depends upon mobilizing even more effectively the imagination, creativity, skills and talents of all our people. And it depends on using that knowledge and understanding to build economic strength and social harmony. (Department for Education and Skills, 2003, p. 2)

This view echoes the prophets of the post-industrial economy (Bell, 1973; Drucker, 1993). Bell predicted that the growing importance of 'knowledge' work, reflected in the historical shift from blue-collar to white-collar work, would significantly raise the demand for educated workers, who would enjoy greater autonomy in their work. Drucker (1993) argued that we have entered a new stage of post-capitalist development, one in which it is no longer ownership of capital that generates wealth creation, but rather the application of knowledge. This he argued has led to a power shift from the owners and managers of capital to 'knowledge workers,' thereby marking a new stage of capitalist development. In these terms, the prosperity of individuals, companies and nations has come to depend on human and intellectual capital rather than on issues of ownership that defined Marxist accounts of the capitalist system (e.g., Braverman, 1974).

This evolutionary model of an inexorable shift from physical to mental labour is not limited to the changing relationship between education and the occupational structure within specific societies. It is extended to include the relationship between nation-states. The rise of the global knowledge-based economy is believed to remove much of the source of conflict and strife between nations. Trade

D.W. Livingstone and D. Guile (eds.), The Knowledge Economy and Lifelong Learning:
A Critical Reader, 117–146.

liberalization is presented as a 'win–win' opportunity for both developing and developed nations.[1] The territorial disputes that drove nations to war in pursuit of land and material wealth become less important in terms of power, privilege and wealth. According to Rosecrance:

> In the past, material forces were dominant in national growth, prestige, and power; now products of the mind take precedence. Nations can transfer most of their material production thousands of miles away, centring their attention on research and development and product design at home. The result is a new and productive partnership between 'head' nations, which design products, and 'body' nations, which manufacture them. (Rosecrance, 1999, p. xi)

This shift from *bloody wars* to *knowledge wars* represents the highest stage in evolutionary development as nations put down their weaponry to concentrate on the competition for ideas, skills and knowledge that contribute to economic advantage. This represents a logical extension of muscle to mental power, given that 'it is knowledge, not cheap labour; symbols, not raw materials, that embody and add value' (Toffler, 1990, p. 82).

These new rules of wealth creation rest on 'out-smarting' economic rivals. Schools, colleges, universities, think tanks, design centres and research laboratories are now on the front line in the search for competitive advantage. This is reflected in current attempts to develop comparative measures of academic performance by organizations such as the Organisation for Economic Co-operation and Development (OECD) in their PISA studies and by the International Education Association (IEA). And as 'standards of organizational performance have gone global,' the quality of a nation's human resources are judged on relative rather than absolute criteria (Carnevale & Porro, 1994, p. 13). Therefore, it is not only the qualities of individual students that are being assessed, but the quality of national systems of education and training as a whole.[2]

As Gordon Brown (2004), at the time the U.K.'s Chancellor of the Exchequer, has suggested,

> if we are to succeed in a world where offshoring can be an opportunity ... our mission [is] to make the British people the best educated, most skilled, best trained country in the world.

This mobilization of the people to the common 'educational' cause has many of the features of conscription. In short, it is asserted that there is no other source of individual, family or national welfare as nation-states are largely powerless to protect domestic markets from international competition or the strictures imposed on interest rates and public spending by the financial markets. Moreover, state support of uncompetitive businesses will, so the argument goes, hinder economic prosperity as competitiveness is best achieved through open competition within the international arena. Indeed, some view 'national' labour markets as an impediment to the operation of a global market for labour, within which workers are rewarded according to their contribution, based on skills and productivity rather than national political settlements between government, employers and trade unions (Reich, 1991).

There are, therefore, no British, German or American jobs, only British, German or American workers who confront the ultimate judgement of the global marketplace. The problem this poses for workers in the developed economies is that the Fordist settlement of the last century, based on low skills for relatively high wages, is no longer an option as routine production can now be fulfilled in low-wage economies for a fraction of the cost. Therefore, jobs that can deliver a living wage to 'affluent' workers depend on the creation of high-quality goods and services within niche markets that meet the precise needs of customers and clients.

Robert Reich (1991) explained the growth in income polarization in the United States in the 1980s in terms of the relative ability of workers to sell their skills, knowledge and insights in the global job market. He argued that the incomes of the top 20 per cent have pulled away from the rest because of their ability to break free from the constraints of local and national labour markets. The global labour market offers far greater rewards to 'symbolic analysts' or 'knowledge workers' precisely because the market for their services has grown, whereas those workers who remain locked into national or local markets have experienced stagnation or a decline in income.

Reich, amongst others, interpreted rising wage inequalities as proof of both the realities of the global labour market and as evidence of the failure of the existing education system. The reason why income inequalities have grown was not explained as a 'structural' problem – that the proportion of high-skilled, high-waged jobs is limited by the occupational structure – but due instead to the failure of the education system to make a larger proportion of the workforce employable in the global competition for high-skilled, high-waged work. As Reich (1991) suggested:

> Unlike America's old hierarchical and somewhat isolated economy, whose white-collar jobs were necessarily limited in proportion to the number of blue-collar jobs beneath them, the global economy imposes no particular limit upon the number of Americans who can sell symbolic-analytic services worldwide. In principle, all of America's routine production workers could become symbolic analysts and let their old jobs drift overseas to developing nations. (p. 247)

It is believed, therefore, that there is now a global auction for jobs. Low-skilled jobs will be auctioned on price and will tend to migrate to low-waged economies such as those in Asia or Eastern Europe, while high-skilled jobs will continue to attract higher wages. These jobs will be auctioned on 'quality' rather than price, including the skills, knowledge and insights of employees. The main bidders for 'quality' jobs are assumed to be today's leading economies. This offers the potential for countries such as the United Kingdom, France and the United States to become *magnet* economies, attracting a disproportionate share of these high-skilled, high-wage jobs (Brown & Lauder, 2001).

While the politics of the magnet economy have focused on lifting the skills and incomes of indigenous workers, there is also growing emphasis on attracting foreign workers that meet the needs of the national economy (Robertson et al., 2002). In other words, the developed economies are not only in competition for quality jobs but also for the most talented workers. This has been a feature of the competitive strategies of both the United States and Singapore (Alarcon, 1999; Low, 2002). It has also become a more prominent feature of policy in the United Kingdom in an attempt to overcome skill shortages and to redress the tendency for it to be a net exporter of inventors, scientists and entrepreneurs.

The proponents of the magnet economy also assume a transformation in the relationship between education and social justice. In the second half of the twentieth century, the ideology of meritocracy was premised on the idea that a fair and efficient society depended on the creation of a level playing field that would give all within that society the chance to compete on equal terms regardless of social class, gender or ethnicity. Today, it is assumed that the nature of this competition has changed. The occupational structure is no longer restricted, as noted in the above quotation from Reich. The children from wealthy backgrounds no longer have an unfair advantage over children from disadvantaged backgrounds, because of the international character of the labour market. What holds back the children from disadvantaged background is not the fact that those from privileged backgrounds enjoy all the educational advantages, but their lack of credentials, knowledge and skills which prevent them from competing in the global competition for high-skilled, high-wage employment.

Therefore, a 'fair' educational system is no longer one that attempts to create a level playing field but one dedicated to raising the standards of all and facilitating greater access to higher education in order to arm the workforce with the credentials, knowledge and skills that are valued in the global labour market. Hence, competition for the best jobs is not between neighbours but nations. Holding back the most talented or preventing parents from investing in private education is likely to damage national competitiveness, as these are the people most likely to drive the economy. This does not prevent other students fulfilling their aspirations because the same jobs are available to all those with the energy, talent and commitment to develop marketable skills within the global economy.

AN ASSESSMENT

This article will now assess the underlying assumptions of the magnet economy and especially the changing relationship between education, jobs and rewards. We will argue that while there has been a fundamental change in the relationship between education, economy and society it is far removed from the policy rhetoric of the knowledge economy described above. Our account of the social and economic realities of the early twenty-first century will focus on four facets of the dominant policy discourse.

Firstly, we examine the idea that countries such as the United Kingdom and the United States can become high-skilled, high-waged 'magnet' economies, able to resolve problems of labour demand and income inequalities through educational reform. We will argue that this fails to understand how multinational companies are developing human resource strategies that increase the likelihood of a larger proportion of high-skilled jobs being established in relatively low-waged economies. Governments in the developed economies have yet to acknowledge the full consequences of countries such as China and India expanding their educational systems to compete for high-skilled work within key sectors of the global economy or trends towards the 'offshoring' of skilled along with semi-skilled and unskilled jobs.

Secondly, the official policy discourse is driven by a view of human capital that assumes a tightening bond between education, jobs and rewards, with a rising wage dividend for those who invest in higher education.[3] We will argue that the basic premise of the rhetoric concerning human capital – that investments in education and training lead to rising wages – is not a universal law of economic development, but a 'transitional' case where there are no guarantees that the educational system will meet the expectations of students, families or governments.

The global economy cannot keep pace with the individual demand for high-skilled work as access to tertiary education becomes more widespread both within and across countries. The global expansion of tertiary education leads to downward pressure on the incomes of skilled workers in the developed economies along with some upward pressure on those in developing economies. But at the same time there are trends towards 'winner-takes-all' markets (Frank & Cook, 1996) that reveal that people with similar qualifications in the same occupations, organizations and countries experience increasing polarization in earnings and future career prospects.

Thirdly, the anticipated power shift from employers to 'knowledge' workers has not materialized. The view that there will continue to be an exponential increase in the demand for knowledge workers who will be encouraged to use their creative energies to the full is ahistorical. It fails to take account of the tendency for periods of rapid technological innovation to be followed by standardization (Weber, 1945). This is as true for 'knowledge' workers today as it was for craft workers in the fledgling automobile industry at the beginning of the twentieth century. A feature of paid work under capitalism is that the nature of jobs and skills change. There is no credential ladder-to-heaven that, once climbed, leads to guaranteed high status and rewarding work. The competitive pressures created by economic globalization have led companies to limit the discretion of knowledge workers and 'devalue' the contribution of many. It is, therefore, not just a matter of the oversupply of skills that threatens the equation between high skills and high income; where 'knowledge' is routinized, it can be substituted with less skilled and cheaper workers at home or further afield.

Fourthly, it will be argued that the emphasis on individual employability and raising the educational standards of all ignores increasing 'positional' conflict in access to education and tough-entry jobs (Hirsch, 1977; Brown, 2003). As the oversupply of graduates forces many to enter employment that does not utilize their knowledge, skills or creativity, the competition for elite jobs intensifies, leaving employers with problems of how to select between large numbers of highly qualified candidates and how to legitimate their selection decisions (Brown & Hesketh, 2004). It has also led social elites to find new forms of social closure to give them a competitive advantage.

Therefore issues of equality of opportunity have become more rather than less important. But these questions can no longer be restricted to the politics of individual nation-states but have increasingly global ramifications. In sum, this analysis challenges the major tenets of the dominant discourse of education, knowledge and the global economy. To grasp its full implications each of the above points will be discussed in more detail.

A MAGNET ECONOMY OR GLOBAL 'DUTCH' (REVERSE) AUCTION?

From a Western perspective, the idea of the magnet economy offers a comforting picture of a global economy in which low-skill, low-wage work is shipped to developing countries while prosperous Western workers make good incomes through their knowledge and creativity (Reich, 1991). This is based on the assumption that most of the foreign direct investment (FDI) in research, development, design, marketing, legal services and other areas of high-skilled activity will be concentrated in those developed economies at the forefront of the knowledge revolution.

A major weakness of this view is its failure to understand how multinational companies are transforming their corporate strategies to take advantage of the global potential not only to sell products and services but to transform how and where they produce, and this is no longer restricted to locating 'screwdriver' production plants or 'back office' data processing in low-wage economies.

It also fails to understand the skill formation strategies being adopted by countries including China, India and Russia. The comparative advantage of a high-skilled workforce in the developed nations is understood as a comparative disadvantage in less developed economies, and many developing economies are determined to close the skills gap. In China, an official policy statement on employment prospects to 2020 states:

> It is necessary to fully utilize various education resources, strengthen the improvement in human resources quality, direct major efforts to the promotion of quality-oriented education, stress cultivation of practical abilities, and make efforts in improving education quality, so as to train millions of high-calibre workers, thousands of special talents and a large number of outstanding innovative talents for the socialist modernization drive. (People's Republic of China, 2004)

This has led to the rapid expansion in the global supply of high-skilled workers that also has major implications for the future of high-skilled, high-waged work in Western nations. China had six times as many university students as the United Kingdom and almost as many as the United States in 2001. This amounts to 15 per cent of the age cohort. There were even more ambitious plans to increase enrolment to Chinese senior high schools from 27 million in 2000 to 46 million in 2005 (see China Education and Research Network, 2001). The expansion of higher education in India is following a similar path.[4]

While a degree of scepticism is required with respect to the accuracy of these statistics, they show that in six years higher education numbers in China, India and Russia almost doubled, from a combined total of 15.8 to 30 million students. This is almost double the combined total for the United States and the United Kingdom, at 15.7 million. There is already a good supply of highly qualified Indian, Chinese and Russian workers entering the global labour market.

Rather than a magnetic attraction to a specific location, global economic integration has enabled companies to create a new spatial division of labour for high-skilled activities, including research, innovation and product development, as well as for low-skilled, low-waged work. Given the importance attached to knowledge-intensive industries as a source of new high-skilled employment in the developed economies, we will use the electronics industry to expose the problems underlying the idea of the magnet economy.

In the 'take-off' of the electronics industry in the United States during the 1980s, the two major regional areas, Silicon Valley and Route 128, attracted $12 billion in venture capital (Saxenian, 1994). At today's prices that is a considerable sum, if thought of in terms of potential foreign direct investment. Investment of this magnitude can certainly produce high rewards and productivity for those who create intellectual property. However, the nature of globalization in the electronics industry has meant that such investment does not translate into the employment of large numbers of skilled workers concentrated in the West, far less in one country.

In the 1960s and 1970s, companies such as Ford, IBM or Siemens were characterized as 'national champions' as they not only paid taxes that contributed to the public exchequer, but also offered mass employment within the home nation. However, the IBMs and Siemens of the post-war period that controlled all elements of hardware and software production have given way to fragmented horizontal structures across national boundaries that combine speed and flexibility, while offloading corporate risk. Facilitated by the personal computer, the internet and an increasing supply of highly qualified employees in developing countries, these networks extend across the globe, particularly to the Pacific Rim, India and Eastern Europe.

Saxenian (2002) has charted the development of this industry.[5] The story starts with an increasing number of Taiwanese, Indian and Chinese students enrolled in PhD programmes in the United States.[6] During the 1980s, Taiwan sent more doctoral students to the United States than any other country. The first generation of these students tended to stay in the United States, working in the semi-conductor industry before returning home to establish their own businesses. Encouraged by government policies, approximately 6,000 doctoral engineers were returning home each year by the mid-1990s (Saxenian, 2002). The combination of the knowledge and networks established in the United States by the first generation of IT entrepreneurs, coupled with the critical mass of expertise of returnee graduates, enabled Taiwan to capitalize on the possibilities of a horizontally structured industry operating across national borders.

The emergence of the electronics industry in Bangalore in India also demonstrates how less skilled employment in the IT industry was exported from Western economies to enclaves in the developing world (Kobrin, 2000). The education and training of electronic engineers provided the necessary human capital for the electronics industry in Bangalore to take off. But contrary to the view that only lower skilled work would be subject to price competition, the IT industry suggests that this is at best wishful thinking. India's tertiary education system now trains over 67,000 computer science professionals annually and another 200,000 enrol each year in private software training institutions. The cost advantage to companies employing software professionals in India in comparison to the United States has become very sizeable. Indian programmers are around 14 times cheaper than those in the United States. But much of the work of Indians in the past has been at the low end of the market. Saxenian (2000a) has shown that the annual revenue per employee in the Indian software industry was $15–20,000, whereas in Israel and Ireland the corresponding figure was $100,000 per employee. However, wages have risen in Bangalore and there is now concern that, with increasing competition from China, Russia and Romania, amongst others, the industry will price itself out of the market unless it moves into higher value-added production (Yamamoto, 2004). This may be facilitated by the large numbers of Indian entrepreneurs in Silicon Valley, where in 1998 they were running more than 775 technology companies, accounting for $3.6 billion in sales and 16,600 jobs (Saxenian, 2000a).

This example highlights the flip side of the magnet economy. If the latter assumes a virtuous circle of high-skilled and high-waged employment contributing to national prosperity, the converse is that of a global auction. This operates as a Dutch or reverse auction, where unlike at an art or antique auction where the highest bidder wins, in a Dutch auction corporate investors are able to play off nations, communities and workers as bidding spirals downwards and multinational companies win concessions such as cheap rents and tax holidays in exchange for investments in jobs, technology and commercial property (Brown & Lauder, 1997, p. 2).

The policy discourse of the knowledge economy assumes that the competition for high-skilled employment would be fought out between the developed economies as low-skilled, low-waged work would migrate to less developed economies (Reich, 1991). However, a number of less developed countries including India, China and Malaysia are increasingly competing for high-skilled work that could reduce the bargaining power of high-skilled workers in the West. Hence, high-skilled workers in the developed economies may be subject to the same price competition that has to date been limited to those in routine occupations. Consequently, many of the jobs undertaken by university graduates in the United Kingdom and the United States could be done more cheaply elsewhere.

This analysis of the IT industry also shows that even when there is a concentration of technology firms such as in Silicon Valley, the cost of training and labour can be reduced by hiring qualified workers from low-waged economies. In the United States, 55,000 qualified workers from India were granted temporary visas in 1999 (Saxenian, 2000b). Hence, there does appear to be a magnetic effect by which qualified workers in less developed economies are attracted to work in the developed economies. But here it is high-skilled *workers* rather than high-skilled jobs that are being attracted; precisely the opposite effect to that assumed in the official discourse surrounding the magnet economy.

While the importance of 'talent' has been a key component of American capitalism for over a century, in the current economic climate it may reduce the incentives for companies to invest in the training of indigenous workers and lead employers to reduce the cost of indigenous knowledge workers. 'Guest' workers typically do the same jobs for fewer rewards and inferior contracts of employment. Hence, even in areas where there is increased demand for high-skilled workers, there is a growing propensity to import qualified labour rather than invest in the skills of the less qualified and socially disadvantaged.[7]

It might be argued that the electronics industry, although clearly significant, is but one, perhaps atypical, example. However, a characteristic of knowledge-intensive industries is that they do not require large numbers of skilled workers (Keep, 2000). In 2004, the market capitalization of internet company Google was around $30 billion, but it employed just 2,000 people. At the same time eBay had a capitalization of around $54 billion and employed 4,400. In contrast, Tesco, a leading U.K. retail company, had a capitalization similar to Google (£19 billion) but employed 240,000 worldwide.

It is also important not to exaggerate the impact of globalization, as not all knowledge work is structured by industries across the globe. For example, research and development for multinationals tends to remain in the home country of multinationals (Brown et al., 2001), although there is evidence that this has begun to change in some multinational companies.[8] There are a significant number of managers and professionals whose livelihood depends more on the state of domestic rather than global markets, especially those working in the public sector. But this does not undermine our argument that income inequalities and positional conflict cannot be resolved through the creation of a high-skill, high-wage magnet economy.

It might also be claimed that while knowledge-intensive industries do not require vast armies of skilled workers, they have downstream effects in terms of knowledge and wealth that generate new business enterprise and support services. But this does not follow. It is clear, for example, that Bangalore is an enclave and that its success has had a limited 'knock-on' effect for the rest of India (Kobrin, 2000).

Equally, while extolling the virtues of Silicon Valley as the high temple of the knowledge economy, Finegold (1999) recognized that knowledge workers live side by side with:

> a large much lower skilled and lower-paid workforce ... income inequality between these high and low skilled workers appears to be widening in these regions, even more than in the United States as a whole; in Silicon Valley the

125

average earnings of the top 20 per cent of households rose steadily from 1991 to 1997 to over $130,000 while the earnings of the bottom 20 per cent fell 8 per cent to under $35,000. (p. 65)

The contrasting fortunes of employees in Silicon Valley brings into sharp relief Castells's view that the knowledge-based, network economy can link up 'valuable people and activities from all over the world, while switching off from the networks of power and wealth, people and territories dubbed as irrelevant' (Castells, 1998, p. 1).[9] The United Kingdom, along with the United States, is not a high-skilled, high-waged economy, but one in which this accurately reflects the fortunes of a minority of workers who stand alongside an increasingly large proportion of well-qualified but low-waged workers, who in turn stand beside the low skilled and low waged. This analysis suggests that the imperative to stimulate demand for knowledge workers will remain a key policy objective in all the developed economies. However, against a backdrop of mass higher education, the dominant discourse overestimates the extent to which even the most successful nations within the global economy can create mass high-skilled employment (see Hecker, 2003, p. 83; Keep, Mayhew, & Payne, 2006).

Indeed, the emphasis on knowledge workers and labour market flexibility as a means to survival in the global economy only holds true if the supply of relevant skills is limited. Once there is an oversupply, the competition shifts to a global auction based on quality and price. The assumption that skill can provide workers with a shelter from the drive to lower wage costs no longer holds.

The implication of the analysis so far is that the expansion of higher education may lead to the creation of a substantial wastage of talent amongst college and university graduates leading to a greater dispersion in incomes as graduates accept sub-graduate work. It is to the evidence on this question that we now turn.

THE DEATH OF HUMAN CAPITAL?

As we have shown, the idea of the magnet economy is based on the view that we live in an 'age of human capital,' where 'the economic successes of individuals, and also of whole economies, depends on how extensively and effectively people invest in themselves' (Becker, 2002, p. 3). It is assumed that within the knowledge economy wages will rise in line with the academic profile of the workforce. The more people invest in their education and training the more they will earn and the more the economy will prosper through improvements in productivity. The equation high skill equals high income also serves to justify inequalities as people are believed to earn what they are worth, as reflected in their credentials. It also holds out the prospect of widespread prosperity because the only limit to raising incomes is inadequate investment in education and training rather than the economic and social realities of work in the twenty-first century. The political appeal of the rhetoric of human capital is obvious and its consequences are far-reaching. The worldwide expansion of higher education has taken place behind the slogan 'learning is earning.' In the United Kingdom, as elsewhere, the learning dividend has also been used to justify increased fees for university education.

Evidence on rates of return to education is often based on differences in the incomes of university-level graduates and non-graduates. Organisation for Economic Co-operation and Development (OECD, 2002; see also Blöndal et al., 2002, p. 19) figures suggest that the United Kingdom and the United States have larger graduate premiums than other OECD countries, with over double the premium achieved by graduates in countries such as Italy and Japan. These figures[10] also show that the returns to men are greater than those for women in most of the countries surveyed, with the exception of Canada and the Netherlands.

There are a number of problems with this kind of evidence. Firstly, while a university education is on 'average' associated with earning an income higher than that of non-graduates, it is misleading to conclude that this reflects the increasing value of knowledge work rather than a decline in the incomes of those without a university education. Secondly, focusing on the average earnings of graduates may hide growing disparities in graduate incomes, wherein a relatively small number of high earners pull up average earnings. Thirdly, it is misleading to assume that past returns offer an accurate guide to future returns. Finally, we also need to make greater use of trend data rather than relying on snapshots of differences in the incomes of graduates and non-graduates at a specific point in time.[11] Mindful of these problems, Mishel et al. (2003) have examined evidence from the United States that focuses on difference within the college graduate population as well as between graduates and non-graduates. They also presented trend data from 1973 that provide an assessment of whether the value of a college degree has increased over time, as assumed in the rhetoric of the knowledge economy.

Other figures (see Mishel et al., 2003, p. 167) present a different picture to the mantra of 'learning is earning.' Indeed, if the graduate premium were calculated on the economic value of a college degree in 1973 as opposed to its current market value, the 'headline' story of rising graduate returns would look very different. Mishel et al. show that it is only male and female college graduates in the 'higher earner' category that have enjoyed any growth in real income since 1973. In other words, the vast majority of college graduates have received no additional 'premium' on their investments in their human capital compared to college graduates in the 1970s, although they continue to earn more than those without a college education. But even here the picture is equivocal as the high-earning category of those who left high school before going to college was better paid than the median income for college graduates (although the differential has narrowed in recent years). This evidence shows that with the exception of the high-earning graduates, there is a degree of substitution between graduate and non-graduate jobs which manifests itself in many graduates being overqualified (Livingstone, 1998; Pryor & Schaffer, 2000). In this respect, the story in the United States parallels that of the United Kingdom.

In the United Kingdom, Brynin (2002a) compared the social status of fathers' occupations with those of their sons and daughters. He found that the first jobs taken by young people today are often of lower income and status compared to when their fathers first entered the labour market. Equally, while the occupational status of fathers increased over time, this was not the case for their sons or

127

daughters. This research directly challenges one of the core arguments in the post-industrial literature, that as jobs in the manufacturing sector declined, more high-skilled jobs would be created in the service sector.[12]

Brynin's (2002a) macro-findings are supported by a study of key service sectors. Mason (2002) found that around a third of graduates were undertaking non-graduate jobs and that, for many, it was not expected that these jobs would be upgraded. Battu and Sloan (2000), estimating the numbers of overqualified workers, suggest that approximately 40 per cent of graduates are in non-graduate jobs.[13]

The findings of Mishel et al. (2003) also reveal that female college graduates continue to earn less in each of the earning categories than males, but perhaps the most striking difference is the way male and female top earners have raced away from the rest. They now earn over twice as much as the median college graduate of the same sex. This underlines the need to avoid talking about the 'average' college or university graduate, for when it comes to rewards within the job market, some are far more equal than others.[14]

Further evidence of major differences in the rates of return to those with the same level of education is also provided when race as well as gender differences are factored into the equation of high skills equals high wages. The Current Population Census data in the United States show that White men with a Bachelor's degree earn around $10,000 a year more than Black or Hispanic men with the same qualification. The difference between White men and Hispanic females widens to virtually $20,000.[15]

This evidence on the rate of returns to education does not destroy the thesis of the magnet economy, even if it challenges the rhetoric of the human capital model of rising skills and incomes in the evolutionary drive to technological progress. It can still be argued that the widening income inequalities that characterize top-earning college graduates reflect their ability to market themselves within the global labour market. However, if increasing income polarization was a consequence of the neutral operation of the global economy, we should find the same trend in all the advanced economies. Brown et al. (2006, calculations based on OECD labour market statistics) show that this is not the case as the increasing polarization in income is far more pronounced in the United States and to a lesser extent the United Kingdom. Some countries including Japan experienced a narrowing of differentials and in most of the other countries there was little discernible change during this period. It is of course possible that these differences reflect a time lag and other countries will witness a similar increase in wage inequalities in the future. However, the existing evidence points to the fact that there are significant societal differences in the way labour markets, employment and rewards are organized and distributed that shape the relationship between education, jobs and rewards.

This evidence suggests that income inequalities in the United States and United Kingdom cannot be explained by the creation of a global labour market, as Reich and others have suggested, but instead in the way the United States and the United Kingdom have responded to global economic conditions. This response, like the global economy itself, has been shaped by the political dominance in both countries of neo-classical economics that extol the virtue of flexible labour markets and competitive individualism (Kay, 2004). The debate about what is distinctive about the United States and the United Kingdom takes us beyond the confines of this article, but the polarization in income can be explained more convincingly in terms of differences in labour market power rather than returns to skills (although they are not mutually exclusive). Howell (2002), for instance, rejects what he calls the 'unified' theory that explains income inequalities in terms of skills: those with high skills have higher incomes; correspondingly those with low skills have low and falling incomes because they cannot operate with new technologies. Equally, the unified theory asserts that the labour rigidities that are intended to protect jobs, such as those assumed to exist in mainland Europe, create greater unemployment than in the flexible labour markets found in the United States and the United Kingdom. Therefore, the policy solution is to create labour market flexibility and greater educational opportunities for the less skilled. However, Howell's detailed comparative analysis finds little evidence to support this theory and he argues that we need to look at issues of labour market power and political ideology.

A consequence of Howell's (2002) analysis is that income polarization in the United States and the United Kingdom can be seen to enable company executive and senior managers, along with those who worked in the financial markets, to engage in 'wealth extraction' rather than the development of sustainable forms of 'wealth creation' (Lazonick & O'Sullivan, 2000). This largely explains why a study reported by Bound and Johnson (1995) found that in the United States a large part of the increase in the returns to a university degree was due to an increased premium put to use in the business and law fields. The wages of computer specialists and engineers actually fell relative to high school graduates.

Our argument here is that human capital has become a victim of its own success, at least in its influence over government policy. Human capital is itself subject to the laws of diminishing returns. It is losing its capacity as a source of competitive advantage for both individuals and nations because the 'positional' advantage of those with higher education and skills is not only declining domestically (as higher education is expanded) but also globally. Therefore, while much current thinking about the relationship between education, jobs and rewards is based on an evolutionary model of rising skills and incomes, this now looks more like a 'transitional' case limited to the twentieth century, one in which access to higher education was limited to a few. In mass – if not universal – systems of higher education and at a time when vast numbers of highly skilled workers are available in developing economies, the global expansion of tertiary education has outstripped the demand for high-skilled workers, creating downward pressure on the incomes of skilled workers in the developed economies along with some upward pressure on those in emerging economies.

The paradox of human capital is that at a time when human knowledge is being taught, certified and applied on a scale never witnessed previously in human history, the overall value of human 'capital' is likely to decline, apart from the case of leading-edge knowledge that has clear market application. For the few, investments of effort, time and money will continue to be handsomely rewarded, but for the most it will take the form of defensive expenditure; it is a necessary investment to have any chance of getting a decent job. We will return to the issue of positional competition, but our next task is to examine the idea of a power shift from those who owned and controlled the means of production in the twentieth century to the 'knowledge' workers of today.

KNOWLEDGE WITHOUT POWER

The imagery of the knowledge economy centres on a power shift (Bell, 1973; Drucker, 1993) resulting from a fundamental change in the means of wealth creation. As the economy comes to depend on human ingenuity, knowledge and creativity, the most important corporate asset is its intellectual capital (Stewart, 2001). It is argued that this has given 'knowledge' workers greater control and autonomy over the nature and pace of their work. The rhetoric of the knowledge economy assumes that innovation and creativity are enduring features of the new economy but such assumptions are both static and ahistorical. Brint (2001) cautions against such a view:

> Theorists of the knowledge economy have often missed the historical dimension of industrial growth and maturation. Are the insurance or the automobile industries knowledge-intensive? Most of the theorists would likely say they are less-knowledge-intensive than the computer industry. However, both the concept of life insurance and actuarial studies on which contracts were based were intellectual innovations in their time (Clough, 1946). The internal combustion engine was, of course, a marvellous breakthrough in its time. Our sense of the computer software industry as particularly knowledge-intensive reflects the rapid growth and turbulence in the industry and the constantly upgraded products the industry has been producing in recent years (McLauglin, 1999). Many years in the future, we shall see the same standardization in the computer software industry that a previous generation witnessed in the insurance and automobile industries. (p. 116)

Based on these observations, Brint draws out three characteristics of knowledge-centred industries. They are: (1) speed of change is an important factor suggesting that research and development are at a premium in creating a competitive edge; (2) new issues susceptible to expert analysis regularly emerge; (3) the knowledge necessary for operating in service industries is embedded in the providers themselves. But as in goods-producing industries, if services become standardized and commodified, they no longer constitute knowledge-centred industries.

This analysis is helpful because it defines what may be constituted as knowledge-centred industries at any given time. It enables us to distinguish such industries that are likely to be subject to routinization from those that are not. For example, research-based activities in the pharmaceuticals industry are unlikely to be routinized because of the creativity involved, while many activities within the banking industry are (see below). It also helps us to understand why there has not been a 'democratization' of the workplace as knowledge is being managed in ways that stand in stark contrast to the proponents of the knowledge economy.

John Burgoyne has made a useful distinction between 'knowledge work' and 'knowledge worked' (Brown & Hesketh, 2004, p. 55). While companies have an increasing demand for knowledge workers capable of crossing existing knowledge boundaries in the creation of integrated products and services such as mobile phones that double as a camera or MP3 player, most of these higher-level activities can be transformed into occupational activities where the knowledge has been 'worked' in advance, leaving people to apply knowledge captured in computer software, work manuals or written procedures.

This analysis draws attention to the fact that regardless how the economy is characterized, in terms of knowledge, information or post-industrialism, it is based on the principles of capitalism and the profit motive. While innovation and the exploitation of new ideas is a key aspect of today's global economy, it is also driven by the need to standardize knowledge so that it can be rapidly processed and reproduced at lower cost and with greater predictability than when it is in the hands and minds of highly specialized knowledge workers (experts). This drive to standardization, as much as innovation, has become an integral part of the competitive strategy of many multinational companies for the simple reason that it not only offers them greater control over the 'product,' but also enables them to reduce costs by offshoring activities to countries where labour costs are significantly lower. Furthermore, as companies develop people strategies at an international, if not global, level, the integration of activities involves the application of common standards that erode national differences in employment practices. For global companies it is less of a question of 'when in Rome' because 'we are all in Rome!'

Standardization shifts the priority from creativity to control. It enables greater control of the workforce by closely prescribing tasks while reducing its costs.[16] The key distinction here, one that we can adapt from Bernstein (1997), is between strong and weak classification and frames. Strong classification and frames emphasize existing states of knowledge and received problems, whereas weak classification and framing emphasize the importance of ways of knowing, of constructing problems, rather than solving problems with appropriate routines. This enables us to chart changes in the nature of knowledge work such that while it may, initially, have been weakly classified and framed, as standardization is established such that it becomes more strongly classified and framed. As jobs change in this way, we might expect to see workers' autonomy or discretion downgraded or removed while the complexity involved in their routines is maintained or indeed increased.[17]

The distinction between discretion and complexity merits some discussion because it is used in empirical analyses of changes in the demand for skill and it highlights the way university graduates may be used for non-graduate work. It was noted in the previous section that a significant minority of graduates in the United

Kingdom undertake non-graduate work. This has led Brynin (2002b) to suggest that:

> We are, therefore, seeing an increasing demand for graduates but perhaps for work not traditionally at the graduate level. There is no general upgrading of labour but a complex redistribution of skills and their rewards ... We can, therefore, perhaps see the use of graduates not merely as a response to oversupply, nor only as a reaction to the demand for ever rising educational skills, but as a tool in the armoury of methods for redistributing labour and reducing its average costs. (p. 366)

He goes on to hypothesize that graduates are being used to fill the demand for intermediately skilled work because of weaknesses in the supply of intermediately skilled workers.[18] However, graduates may be preferred to intermediately skilled workers because the division of labour has been reconstructed in ways that suit some of the skills that graduates acquire at university. The major influence on this change in the division of labour concerns the process of management de-layering that started in the 1980s. This enabled many middle-management jobs to be stripped out with closer communications between senior managers and workers. What facilitated this process was new technology related to the introduction of the personal computer (Aronowitz & De Fazio, 1994).

In turn, this has meant that many in intermediate positions as well as those in lower positions now have to cope with greater job complexity, and it is on account of this that employers may believe graduates are better able to deal with intermediate positions as compared to non-graduates. But one of the hallmarks of being a graduate in the past was the ability to exercise autonomy in the work undertaken. In order to study for a degree, a high level of autonomy is required. Since employers are not asking these graduates to exercise judgement or discretion regarding key decisions about the job, they do not pay them as much as those undertaking graduate-level work. Hence we would expect to see a widening dispersion in graduate incomes as more graduates come onto the jobs market. The utilization of graduate skills in this attenuated way does give employers greater flexibility at cheaper cost than if they made full use of the skills graduates have to offer.

This analysis is supported by statistical evidence. Felstead et al. (2002) found a significant decline in the level of discretion over job tasks, especially among managers and other professionals. It was also particularly notable in 'Education,' 'Public Administration,' 'Finance,' 'Real Estate,' and 'Business Services.' They concluded their survey of skills in the United Kingdom by suggesting that:

> more skilled jobs typically require higher levels of discretion over job tasks. Despite this, the rise in skills among employees has not been accompanied by a corresponding rise in the control they can exercise over their jobs. Rather there has been a marked decline in task discretion. For example, the proportion of employees reporting a great deal of choice over the way they do their job fell from 52 per cent in 1986 to 39 per cent in 2001. This decline occurred for both men and women. (2002, p. 73)

An everyday example may help to clarify the processes involved. In the 1990s many retail banks in the United Kingdom and the United States divided their market between the mass 'Fordist' segment, in which the majority experienced electronic banking with call centres to address specific problems, while those earning relatively high incomes could be assigned a personal relations manager with whom they dealt face to face. These managers had the discretion to loan a substantial amount unsecured and even more with security. Judgement and experience were required to successfully loan money unsecured. More recently, this form of discretion with all the experience and acquired knowledge that it presupposed has been removed in some of the major clearing banks. Now loans have to be agreed by a 'credit controller.' This 'credit controller' is, in the first instance, a computer program that automatically assesses a loan application according to pre-specified criteria. Only in appealing against the credit controller's judgement, as represented by the computer program, does the manager have a role. But even here there is no indication that their judgement will carry weight. Effectively, the role of the personal relations manager is no more than one of 'front of office' sociability. As one manager put it to us, 'a junior with a ready smile could do my job now.' And, in this particular case, juniors on far lower salaries *are* being introduced to do the job.

The education required to learn a series of routines and to make a limited set of strongly classified and framed judgements is not at the same level as that required of individuals whose work requires creativity and the freedom to work unsupervised for long periods. Hence, it is possible to see why this type of white-collar Fordism does not require high levels of education, although this does not mean that companies will curtail the use of university graduates in the banking sector. University graduates will continue to be valued for their social and communication skills alongside any technical requirements of the job. Their behavioural competence in working with colleagues, customers and clients is more important than the use of creative intellect. The problem is that the jobs on offer are far removed from the expectations harboured by most graduates as they enter the labour market.

One of the basic tenets of the shift from Fordist to post-Fordist forms of work organization (Brown & Lauder, 1997) was that accountability and control of workers would focus on outcomes rather than constant supervision and surveillance. So long as targets were met, how those targets were achieved would be a matter of human creativity and ingenuity. Now, process as well as product can be micro-managed through the use of software programs that monitor e-mails and telephone conversations, along with the use of electronic manuals that prescribe many aspects of the job that can be easily updated to meet changing circumstances. Consequently, the potential for individual discretion and creativity to be exercised can be squeezed out, which is precisely what has happened in the example of the bank manager.

We need to emphasize two points about this argument. Firstly, these control strategies will not be implemented uniformly across the globe. Shoshana Zuboff (1988) demonstrated that the introduction of computer technology could be used to reduce skill, discretion and judgement, or alternatively to complement them. Hunter et al. (2001) have also stressed that how technology and skill are structured within an organization will be key to understanding the wider roles of education and skill in the economy.[19]

There are also some forms of knowledge work that are more susceptible to standardization than others. Work based on expert scientific knowledge, creativity and individual enterprise, especially where it involves highly profitable networks, is likely to escape standardization, but this leaves a large number of professional and managerial workers vulnerable.[20]

Secondly, this discussion of knowledge without power has focused on the modern workplace, but it equally applies to the market situation. A further paradox of the knowledge-driven economy is that the more widespread access to expert knowledge becomes, the less it offers a source of power to define the work context or offer a source of power within the job market.

While there is a tendency to focus on the technical requirements of work, it is important to recognize that the power that derives from individual certification and knowledge will increasingly depend on 'social' considerations. As Mats Alvesson has suggested:

> the ambiguity of knowledge and the work of knowledge-intensive companies means that 'knowledge,' 'expertise' and 'solving problems' to a large degree become matters of belief, impressions and negotiations of meaning. Institutionalized assumptions, expectations, reputations, images, etc. feature strongly in the perception of the products of knowledge-intensive organizations and workers. (2001, p. 863)

The value added associated with many knowledge-intensive industries (i.e., consultancy, financial services) stems from convincing clients that large fees or high prices are legitimate when professional knowledge is utilized. The 'personal' is the product that is being sold as it represents the embodiment of corporate value (Rose, 1999). Management consultants, for instance, not only have to be convincing to colleagues but to clients and customers. They must define and epitomize valued knowledge. This involves standards of appearance, speech, deportment and social confidence that demonstrate that one is in tune with clients, customers and partners, as firms are entrusting the individual with the knowledge claims of the organization. The extent to which this embodiment of the firm matters will obviously depend on the nature of the business, but the more businesses are encouraged to get closer to clients and customers, the more important 'personal' capital will become (Brown & Hesketh, 2004).

The link between the 'branding' of companies as world class, leading edge, upmarket, and so on and the people who work for them furthers our understanding of why for many knowledge is not power. As the numbers entering the job market with higher degrees continue to increase, being good is no longer good enough. Companies with ambitions to 'be the best' also want to be seen to recruit the 'best' talent. This involves companies competing for managers and professions with established 'reputations' within the marketplace and for graduates from universities reputed to be world class.

For those defined as part of this talented elite (Michaels et al., 2001), the rhetoric of the knowledge economy is close to reality, as they are the most likely to enjoy greater levels of discretion within their jobs and a high level of market power should they decide to seek alternative employment. But this is far removed from the realities of the knowledge economy for most.

Employability for most is not an expression of market power but a constant source of economic vulnerability, as they are constantly reminded that there is no such thing as a job for life (Sennett, 1998). Along with a growing recognition of the contrasting fortunes of those with the same formal credentials, this has led to an increasing intensification in the competition for education and jobs that has become global.

STANDARDS OF JUSTICE: GETTING AHEAD IN EDUCATION AND THE LABOUR MARKET

The protagonists of the knowledge economy have focused much of their attention on issues of individual employability. This reflects employer complaints that many of those entering the workforce, including the highly qualified, lack the social and self-management skills that are required. They also assume that the barriers to opportunity that characterized the Fordist era have been lifted and the nature of competition transformed. We have noted that the major issue for policy makers is no longer one of how to equalize the national competition for education and jobs, but rather how to 'outsmart' other nations in a bid to capture a lion's share of high-skilled, high-waged jobs. Issues of inclusion and exclusion are defined, solely, in terms of raising educational standards and extending access to university.

Trends in education, employment and income distribution do not support this view that the historical conflict between justice and efficiency has been resolved, but points to an intensification of the struggle for credentials and tough-entry jobs (Hirsch, 1977; Brown, 2003). The focus on individual employability (supply side) rather than a political commitment to job creation (demand side) is a political sleight of hand that shifts the responsibility for employment firmly onto the shoulders of individuals rather than the state.

While there is no doubt that the technical and social requirements of 'knowledge' work have changed, the increasing focus on a broader range of employability skills such as drive, resilience or interpersonal sensitivity offers employers a convenient way of legitimating their recruitment decisions when large numbers of applicants can no longer be rejected because they lack the appropriate credentials or technical expertise. Any class, ethnic or gender bias in these decisions is extremely difficult for individual candidates to contest, even though they reflect a growing chasm between what is required to get the job as opposed to what is required to do the job (Brown & Hesketh, 2004).[21]

The issue of equality of opportunity in recruitment raises broader concerns about the official emphasis on lifting educational standards rather than on narrowing inequalities in the performance of different classes and social groups. It is not that raising standards is unimportant, but that it cannot provide a solution to the problem of positional conflict. Rather than dampen competitive tensions in education and the labour market, social conflict has intensified in the scramble to secure a competitive advantage. When there are more contestants than jobs, how one stands relative to others becomes important. Positional considerations also become more important when access to higher education is extended at the same time that there is growing differentiation within the same occupation. In the mid- to late-twentieth century, a job title was closely related to job entitlements. Most of those in the same profession or of the same managerial status received similar remuneration packages and career opportunities. Frank and Cook (1996) argue that this is no longer the case, as the fortunes of those in occupations such as law, management, medicine, journalism and academia have significantly diverged; hence the wide disparity in income documented in the previous discussion. This, they suggest, has led to the creation of winner-takes-all markets.[22]

A consequence is increasing competition for the glittering vocational prizes. This not only leads to a major misallocation of human capabilities, but to increasing market congestion that has major repercussions for individuals, families and society. For individuals and families the fundamental problem posed is that while students attempt to raise their game, resulting in higher levels of credential achievement, this does little to improve their relative chances of entering tough-entry colleges, universities or jobs. If everyone adopts the same tactics in the competition for positional advantage, no one secures an advantage. This creates an opportunity trap that is forcing people to spend more time, effort and money trying to access the education, certificates and jobs they want, with few guarantees that their aspirations will be realized (Brown, 2006).[23]

The focus on raising standards rather than equity ignores the fact that some individuals and families are much better placed to mobilize their material, cultural and social assets to increase their chances of winning the competition for elite credentials and jobs. The emphasis on parental choice and market competition within education serves to legitimate, as least in political terms, the huge inequalities in the quality of educational experiences (Lauder et al., 1999).

At the societal level, this congestion has already led to intense conflict amongst the middle classes (Ball, 2003; Power et al., 2003). However, a clear implication of our argument is that access to elite employment, increasingly open to international competition, will be restricted to those transnational and national elites that can gain access to the globally most prestigious universities (Lowe, 2000). To put it provocatively, within the foreseeable future the children from middle-class backgrounds that fail to gain access to these universities will be left to fight over the scraps.

This argument finds support in recent trends within higher education which suggest the emergence of a global hierarchy of 'world class' universities (Wolf, 2002). In such a market, the 'best' students are attracted to the universities with the highest reputations that in turn attract the best academics because they can pay for them.[24]

Consequently, the elite American and European universities are likely to provide the international benchmark for academic excellence for the foreseeable future. And it is the students from those universities that meet such benchmarks that are most likely to succeed in the competition for elite jobs. We know already that these leading universities largely recruit from high-earning families. The richer their background, the more likely students will attend the 'Harvards' and 'Oxfords' of the higher education system (Power et al., 2003), contributing to a pattern of exclusion which is manifest in recent studies of social mobility in both the United Kingdom (Ermisch & Francesconi, 2002; Galindo-Rueda & Vignoles, 2003) and the United States (Perrucci & Wysong, 1999).

Although educational systems retain strong national characteristics, the early steps towards global integration are likely to have a profound impact on the future of positional competition (Marginson, 2004). It is those international elites that have been able to mobilize their wealth and cultural resources in the acquisition of credentials that will benefit most in a global competition for high-skilled jobs.[25] While national elites in countries that have maintained meritocratic rules in an attempt to equalize educational opportunities will increasingly be viewed as holding back their children in the global competition. Consequently, not only will market rules be endorsed by social elites who already play by these rules, but the social elites from other countries such as Germany, France, Sweden and Korea[26] may also break free of the restraints imposed on the wealthy through national rules of meritocratic competition to gain positional advantage for their offspring (Brown, 2000, p. 646).

Faced with these developments, centre-Left governments have avoided one of the most important questions to confront the centre-Left in the early twenty-first century; that is, how to organize the competition for a livelihood in such a way that genuinely equal opportunity is available to all? Avoiding this problem by appeals to the need to raise educational standards for all in the global market offers little insight into how the question of social justice is to be addressed.

CONCLUSION

This chapter has argued that the idea of a magnet economy is the latest version of an evolutionary model of technological, economic and social change in which issues of inequality, opportunity and social conflict are resolved through increasing investment in education and human capital. We have come to a different conclusion.

The research evidence does not support the idea of a rapid increase in the demand for highly skilled workers although there has been a rapid expansion of tertiary education. Indeed, there are increasing numbers of highly educated people in jobs for which they are overqualified. What growth there has been in the demand for skills within the economy has also been uneven across occupations and industries. Equally, most of the changes in skill sets demanded by employers focus on the personal and social context of work rather than on the technical demands of the job. Employers want people with drive, commitment and business awareness.

137

They want new employees who can hit the ground running and who have the social confidence and emotional intelligence to get on with colleagues and customers. They want people who are able to work without close supervision and who are willing to embrace change rather than resist it.

These personal characteristics are associated with higher levels of education regardless of the technicalities of the job. Therefore, the demand for skills within a knowledge-driven economy cannot be understood in a linear way from low to high skills based on a model of technological evolution. It has also been argued that the demand for technical skills may have reached a ceiling under present economic conditions for the reasons we have discussed. There is also evidence of increasing attempts to routinize and standardize knowledge work driven by the global integration of business activities. It also reflects the trend towards business outsourcing and offshoring. Standardization is a necessary precondition for the relocation of increasingly complex work to developing economies that have a ready supply of high-skilled workers willing to work for relatively low wages. The consultancy firm ATKearney have predicted that over 500,000 U.S. jobs in the financial sector (approximately 8 per cent of the workforce in that sector) will be moved offshore by 2008. They also note that until recently, most offshore transfers have entailed back-office functions such as data entry and transaction processing, but that these new transfers will involve 'a wide range or high-end internal functions ... including financial analysis, research, regulatory reporting, accounting, human resources and graphic design' (ATKearney, 2003, p. 1). These transfers are anticipated to reduce annual operating costs, in the United States, by more than $30 billion.

This analysis suggests that the overriding problem confronting governments is not deficiencies in the employability skills of graduates, but problems of demand and skill utilization: there are not enough good-quality jobs available, coupled with the failure of employers to exploit the potential for higher productivity and growth that mass education now offers.

We have also argued that the problem of domestic demand for high skills cannot be resolved through the operation of the global labour market. We reject the win–win scenario as developing nations such as China and India have entered the competition for high-skilled employment that may depress rather than increase the demand for highly skilled workers in the developed economies.

A paradox of the knowledge economy is that 'human capital' is increasingly subject to the laws of diminishing returns as more people gain access to tertiary education both at home and abroad, and knowledge workers in the developed economies are forced to compete with well-educated employees willing to work for much lower incomes in developing economies. Therefore, further investments in human capital will not narrow income inequalities; as Simmel observed at the turn of the twentieth century, a rise in the level of knowledge in a society 'does not mean by any means ... a general levelling, but rather the opposite' (1978, p. 440). There will not be a general levelling of incomes in an upward or downward direction. For the fortunate fifth and especially the very fortunate 5–10 per cent at the apex of occupational pyramids, whether as lawyers, designers, consultants or academics, those defined as outstanding talent are likely to prosper, as market competition has a propensity to exaggerate the rewards of success and the price of failure.

But if globalization cannot resolve longstanding issues of 'who does what' and 'who gets what,' it has contributed to both the intensification of positional conflict and to a transformation in the nature of the competition for a livelihood. Increasing inequalities in occupational rewards and career prospects place a premium on gaining access to internationally recognized schools, colleges and universities. The middle-class families in the United Kingdom and the United States, along with those from elite backgrounds, have abandoned any lingering commitment to 'meritocratic' competitions in education that characterized the 1960s and 1970s. Elite credentials are now an essential commodity that must be fought for through the mobilization of all the financial, cultural and social capital that families can muster in the market for elite education and occupations. And as multinational companies and intergovernmental agencies recruit 'cosmopolitans' rather than 'locals' (in every sense of these terms), social elites from around the world are demanding a level playing field in competition with elites from other countries, which further undermines national policies committed to equality of educational and occupational opportunity (Robertson et al., 2002).

An unintended consequence of the application of human capital ideas to public and economic policy is that it is creating increasing problems in the management of expectations. The developed economies are in danger of creating a heady cocktail of discontent: students and their parents may find that a degree fails to deliver the standard of living they have been led to expect and employers will have too many overqualified and disgruntled employees. This has wider political ramifications. A disillusioned middle class may well flex its political muscles to gain a better deal for family members as they invest increasing amounts of time, effort and money in maintaining the status and standard of living to which they have become accustomed.

In the past, it has been assumed that middle-class youth might turn to the Left (Bowles & Gintis, 1976). A more likely scenario today is that it may lead to pressure towards the national protection of jobs and greater restrictions on the global movement of labour. In the United States, measures have already been taken by some states to ensure that public sector employment is kept within the United States rather than being exported overseas. If we were to forecast the source of political debate and change over the next decade, it would be the disenchantment of the middle class in Western societies with the promises held out for education and labour market opportunities.[27]

Finally, this analysis highlights the need to reframe the issues examined in this article. It calls for the development of a conceptual framework that not only encompasses changes within education, work and the labour market, but also the relationship between the local, national and global. The labour market outcomes described in this article cannot be explained by the national profile of the education system in question. They reflect changes in the production, reordering and reproduction of the global division of educated labour. How individuals, families, companies and nation-states respond to these challenges is in urgent need of 'knowledge' work of the most creative kind.

NOTES

1. See, e.g., www.dti.gov.uk/ministers/speeches/hewitt200904.html.
2. Economists used to treat national economies as hermetically sealed units which limited international comparisons to rates of economic growth. Educational investment was important only in so far that it appeared to correlate to such differences in growth rates. There was little sense of an international labour market within which differences in the quality of education could have a decisive impact on the livelihoods of workers within different countries.
3. Within human capital theory it is permissible for the incomes of highly qualified graduates to fall, but within the policy discourse this is largely ignored because it is assumed that new technologies will lead to a rise in the demand for graduates. Hence what is called the 'skills bias' theory is conflated with human capital arguments leading to the assumption that the more educated will be more productive because they are more able to exploit the potential of technologies (Lauder et al., 2005).
4. The figures on China and India were compiled with the assistance of Gerbrand Tholen. For a broader statistical analysis of these issues, see Brown et al. (2005).
5. See also Saxenian (1994, 2000a, 2000b, 2002).
6. See also Alarcon (1999).
7. This magnet effect is not restricted to the IT industry. There are examples of qualified teachers, doctors and nurses being attracted to countries like the United Kingdom at the same time that indigenous workers are unemployed or in low-skilled employment. However, the causes for increased recruitment in these cases do not lie in the rise of the knowledge-based industries in the first instance, but in the electoral politics related to increased education and health expenditure. However, under General Agreement on Trade and Services (GATS) state workers may be subject to increased overseas competition.
8. Preliminary evidence is from our current project on the global strategies of multinational organizations and the future of skills, funded by the Economic and Social Research Council (Phillip Brown, David Ashton, and Hugh Lauder).
9. The process by which exclusion occurs will not be random; explanations will require theories of hegemony, imperialism and post-colonialism in the context of globalization.
10. The rates of return to tertiary education are calculated by comparing the benefits and costs with those of upper-secondary education. In Italy, reliable data on earnings for women were not available.
11. For an earlier analysis of this kind that draws the key distinction between cross-sectional and longitudinal data, see Levin and Kelly (1997).
12. Time has highlighted two problems with the 'white collar' scenario. Firstly, although the proportion of white-collar workers has increased dramatically, the numbers entering white-collar work are now stable (Mishel et al., 2003). Secondly, there was an expectation that white-collar work would be equated with skills upgrading, but in fact, as Esping-Andersen (1999) has shown, after the first wave of increase in white-collar workers subsequent waves have experienced low-skill, low-income work.
13. Graduate as opposed to non-graduate work can be defined in at least three ways. Workers can be asked whether their jobs use the kinds of skills that qualified them to become graduates; employers can be asked the same type of question; or a system of job classification that defines jobs in relation to educational levels can be used to assess the demand and supply of graduates relative to it. See Felstead et al. (2002), Mason (2002), and Battu and Sloan (2001) respectively for research using these strategies.

14 The within-group inequality in earnings for college graduates is not only far greater than that of the lower skilled, it has also been growing more rapidly, whereas non-graduates experienced a slow or no growth in within-group variance in earnings. See Lemieux (2003).

15 Median annual earnings (US$) by educational attainment, race, and sex, 1999, US Census Bureau, current population survey, March 2000, limited to year-ground, full-time workers aged 25 year and older.

16 This highlights the inherent conflict between 'knowing' as part of the work experience and 'knowledge' as an economic commodity (Scarbrough, 1999, p. 5). In other words, the advent of the knowledge-based economy has not resolved the enduring problem of how to convert the employment potential of knowledgeable and creative individuals into productive activities that contribute to bottom-line profits (Marx, 1976).

17 The utility of Bernstein's distinction is that classification and framing enable us to chart the change in the nature of knowledge work. The distinction between complexity and autonomy is to be found in de Witte and Steijn (2000), while Evetts (2002) emphasizes the accuracy of 'discretion' over that of 'autonomy.'

18 However, we need to distinguish carefully between issues concerning the utilization of skill from those of demand and supply of credentials (Livingstone, 1998). There is a debate about the levels of demand and supply of intermediately skilled workers that has produced conflicting results. While surveys of employers suggest that there are skill shortages for intermediately skilled workers (Mason & Wilson, 2003), surveys of workers (Felstead et al., 2003) suggest that there is an oversupply of the intermediately skilled relative to demand. Mason (2002) has argued that the problem is not one of oversupply but the supply of appropriately skilled workers at this level; hence the need for two-year Foundation rather than three-year degrees. However, surveys of employers are likely to be inaccurate for two reasons. Firstly, they focus on what employers would ideally like, but even this ideal may reflect current ideologies about best practice rather than what actually occurs. For example, Mehralizadeh (1999) has shown that, for a leading car manufacturer in the United Kingdom, while senior management emphasized the importance of process or key skills, workers on the shop floor did not believe they were of significance in practice. Middle managers acknowledged that there had been a major debate about the significance of key skills. There is an additional problem confronting researchers of the knowledge-based economy in that there is often a hiatus between macro-level studies that seek to take into account national level data on, say, the relationship between new technology, work practices and pay on the one hand, and case studies which may often lead to contrary findings on the other (Brown & Campbell, 2002). The problem is that there are not sufficient case studies employing the same methodology and theories to aggregate up to the macro-level. This means, as we have done in this chapter, that we have to rely on quantitative studies of skills to identify the macro-trends with qualitative studies illuminating particular choices and strategies.

19 In looking at graduate jobs, Elias and Purcell (2003) identify new and niche graduate jobs: these include entertainment and sports, hospitality and occupational hygienist professions. They report that on average these types of 'graduate' jobs earn less than what they term modern graduate occupations (e.g. management, IT and the like). The former are an example of what Meyer (1977) described as the creation of professions through education. This leads to a more complex analysis of how occupations are structured than suggested by assuming that demand elicits supply; it is an example of 'demand' being constructed.

20 It could be argued that as the pace of innovation increases so the demand for knowledge workers will not decline because new innovations require loosely classified and framed jobs that give workers a high degree of discretion over problem solving. In other words, our more pessimistic prognosis is unjustified; however, the trends identified here suggest the opposite. A further consideration beyond the remit of this chapter would be to examine the specific factors that have driven many corporations down the road of routinization and cost-cutting. Clearly, economic globalization has a part in this account. One of the major economic forces unleashed by globalization has been an intensification of competition due to the advent of improved information

141

flows through the internet and the speed in which production facilities can be established or closed down. This has intensified competition on price. Buyers can trawl the internet for products, large companies can set up auctions amongst their suppliers and the ease with which factories and offices can be established and closed down around the globe has meant that multinational companies can determine where they will direct their investment based on, amongst other things, the quality and price of labour, as we have seen in the discussion of the magnet economy.

[21] Economists seek to explain selection for elite graduate jobs in rational terms, albeit acknowledging that some of these 'intangible' qualities are hard to measure (see Pryor & Schaffer, 2000; Acemoglu, 2002). In contrast, we are suggesting that recruitment to these elite jobs is based on group conflict presupposed by positional competition (see below).

[22] The notion of a winner-takes-all labour market suggests that globalization can lead to distortions in the rational workings of the labour market, as musicians, authors, consultants, etc. increasingly gain global exposure. Equally, as the labour market for employees, including managers, consultants, accountants and lawyers, extends beyond national borders, those who are able to develop international reputations can leverage greater market power when it comes to negotiating their salaries and benefit packages.

[23] The knock-on effect of a congested graduate market may be downward occupational mobility. In the United States, this appears to have had a significant impact on joblessness among poorly educated men of prime working age (Pryor & Schaffer, 1999), although such an effect is not apparent in the United Kingdom (Battu & Sloane, 2001).

[24] It is important not to overemphasize the shift to a winner-takes-all market for higher education. Room (2000) has, for example, noted that the market for overseas students is segmented: 'International flows of students follow well-defined routes which in many cases are underpinned by traditional linguistic and cultural links between the former imperial powers and their colonial territories' (p. 111). However, we are suggesting that the conditions for the creation of such a market now exist.

[25] These differences in the rules of competition reflect contrasting social priorities. Meritocratic rules, for instance, involve restrictions on the middle classes in the use of their superior market power in the interest of social cohesion or state legitimation.

[26] Korea is an interesting example of a country which until recently prevented its indigenous students from attending international schools in that country which offer qualifications like the International Baccalaureate, enabling students to attend elite universities in the United Kingdom and the United States.

[27] Capitalism, however, has always offered scope for progressive reform just as it has the potential to widen inequalities and undermine social justice. There remain important differences in the way nation-states seek to develop 'high-skilled' strategies and differences in the way employers utilize the skills and capabilities of their workforce. These are crucial issues because, while the aspiration to high-skills economies (Brown et al., 2001) is unlikely to solve the distributional question, high-skilled work is necessary to generate a 'social dividend' that can advantage all in society.

REFERENCES

Acemoglu, D. (2002, March). Technical change, inequality and the labour market. *Journal of Economic Literature, 40*, 7–72.

Alarcon, R. (1999). Recruitment processes among foreign-born engineers and scientists in Silicon Valley. *American Behavioural Scientist, 42*(9), 1381–1397.

Alvesson, M. (2001). Knowledge work: Ambiguity, image and identity. *Human Relations, 54*(7), 863–886.

Aronowitz, S. & De Fazio, W. (1994). *The jobless future: Sci-tech and the dogma of work.* Minneapolis: University of Minnesota Press.

ATKearney. (2003). US financial services firms to move more than 500,000 jobs overseas over the next five years. Retrieved from www.atkearney.com/main.

Ball, S. (2003). *Class strategies and the education market: The middle class and social advantage*. London: RoutledgeFalmer.

Battu, H. & Sloane, P. (2000). Overeducation and crowding out in Britain. In Borghans, L. & De Grip, A. (Eds.), *The overeducated worker? The economics of skill utilization* (pp. 157–174). Cheltenham: Edward Elgar.

Becker, G. (2002). The age of human capital. In Lazear, E.P. (Ed.), *Education in the twenty-first century*. Hoover Institute. Retrieved from www.hoover.org/publications/books/fulltext/ed21st.

Bell, D. (1973). *The coming of post-industrial society: A venture in social forecasting*. New York: Basic Books.

Bernstein, B. (1997). Class and pedagogies: Visible and invisible. In Halsey, A.H., Lauder, H., Brown, P., & Stuart Wells, A. (Eds.), *Education, culture, economy and society* (pp. 59–79). Oxford, Oxford University Press.

Blöndal, S., Field, S., & Girouard, N. (2002). *Investment in human capital through post-compulsory education and training: Selected efficiency and equity aspects*. OECD Economic Department, working papers, 333. Retrieved from www.olis.oecd.org/olis/2002doc.nsf/linkto/eco-wkp.

Bowles, S. & Gintis, H. (1976). *Schooling in capitalist America*. London: Routledge & Kegan Paul.

Braverman, H. (1974). *Labour and monopoly capital: The degradation of work in the twentieth century*. New York: Monthly Review.

Brenner, R. (2002). *The boom and the bubble in the US economy*. London: Verso.

Brint, S. (2001). Professionals and the 'knowledge economy:' Rethinking the theory of post industrial society. *Current Sociology, 49*(4), 101–132.

Brown, C. & Campbell, B. (2002). The impact of technological change on work and wages. *Industrial Relations, 41*(1), 1–33.

Brown, G. (2004, November 9). Gordon Brown's confederation of British industry speech. Retrieved from http://news.ft.com/cms/s/eb4dc42a-3239-11d9-8498-00000e2511c8.html.

Brown, P. (2000). The globalization of positional competition. *Sociology, 34*(4), 633–653.

Brown, P. (2006). The opportunity trap. In Lauder, H., Brown, P., Dillabough, J.-A., & Halsey, A.H. (Eds.), *Education, globalization and social change* (pp. 381–397). Oxford: Oxford University Press.

Brown, P. & Hesketh, A. (2004). *The mismanagement of talent: Employability, competition and careers in the knowledge economy*. Oxford: Oxford University Press.

Brown, P. & Lauder, H. (1997). Education, globalization and economic development. In Halsey, A.H., Lauder, H., Brown, P., & Stuart Wells, A. (Eds.), *Education, culture, economy and society* (pp. 172–192). Oxford: Oxford University Press.

Brown, P. & Lauder, H. (2001). *Capitalism and social progress: The future of society in a global economy*. Basingstoke: Palgrave.

Brown, P., Green, A., & Lauder, H. (2001). *High skills: Globalisation, competitiveness and skill formation*. Oxford: Oxford University Press.

Brown, P., Lauder, H., Ashton, D., & Tholen, G. (2006). Towards a high-skilled, low-waged economy? A review of global trends in education, employment and the labour market. In Porter, S. & Campbell, M. (Eds.), *Skills and economic performance* (pp. 55–90). London: Caspian.

Brynin, M. (2002a). Overqualification in employment. *Work, Employment and Society, 16*(4), 637–654.

Brynin, M. (2002b). Graduate density, gender and employment. *British Journal of Sociology, 55*(3), 363–381.

Carnevale, A.P. & Porro, J.D. (1994). *Quality education: School reform for the new American economy*. Washington, DC: US Department of Education.

Castells, M. (1998). *The end of the millennium. The information age: Economy, society and culture*, vol. 3. Oxford: Blackwell.

China Education and Research Network (2001). *Chinese university students to top 16 million*. Retrieved from www.edu.cn/20010903/200991.shtml.

Department for Education and Skills (2003). *The future of higher education*. White Paper. London: Her Majesty's Stationery Office.

De Witte, M. & Steijn, B. (2000). Automation, job content and underemployment. *Work, Employment and Society, 14*(2), 245–264.

Drucker, P. (1993). *Post-capitalist society.* London: Butterworth/Heinemann.

Elias, P. & Purcell, K. (2003). *Measuring change in the graduate labour market: Researching graduate careers seven years on.* Research report, 1. Warwick Institute for Employment Research and the Employment Studies Research Unit, University of West of England.

Ermisch, J. & Francesconi, M. (2002). *Intergenerational social mobility and assortative mating in Britain.* Discussion paper, 465. Bonn: Institute for the Study of Labour.

Esping-Andersen, G. (1999). *The social foundations of postindustrial economies.* Oxford: Oxford University Press.

Evetts, J. (2002). New directions in state and international professional occupations: Discretionary decision-making and acquired regulation. *Work, Employment and Society, 16*(2), 341–353.

Felstead, A., Gallie, D., & Green, F. (2002). *Work skills in Britain, 1986–2001.* London, Department for Education and Skills.

Felstead, A., Gallie, D., & Green, F. (2003). Job complexity and task discretion: Tracking the direction of skills at work in Britain. In Warhurst, C., Keep, E., & Grugulis, I. (Eds.), *The skills that matter,* (pp. 148–169). Basingstoke: Palgrave.

Finegold, D. (1999). Creating self-sustaining high skill ecosystems. *Oxford Review of Economic Policy, 15*(1), 60–81.

Frank, R.H. & Cook, P.J. (1996). *The winner-take-all society.* New York: Penguin.

Galindo-Rueda, F. & Vignoles, A. (2003, May). *Class ridden or meritocratic? An economic analysis of recent changes in Britain.* Centre for Economics of Education, London School of Economics.

Hecker, D.E. (2001, November). Employment outlook 2000–2010: Occupational employment projections to 2010. *Monthly Labor Review.*

Hirsch, F. (1977). *The social limits to growth.* London: Routledge & Kegan Paul.

Howell, D. (2002). Increasing earnings inequality and unemployment in developed countries: Markets, institutions and the 'unified theory.' *Politics and Society, 30*(2), 1923–1943.

Hunter, L., Bernhardt, A., Hughes, L., & Skuratowicz, E. (2001). It's not just the ATMs: Technology, firm strategies, jobs and earnings in retail banking. *Industrial and Labour Relations Review, 54*(2A), 402–424.

Kay, J. (2004). *The truth about markets.* London: Penguin.

Keep, E. (2000). *Creating a knowledge driven economy: Definitions, challenges and opportunities.* Centre on Skills, Knowledge and Organisational Performance, University of Warwick.

Keep, E., Mayhew, K., & Payne, J. (2006). From skills revolution to productivity miracle: Not as easy as it looks? *Oxford Review of Economic Policy, 22*(4), 539–559.

Kobrin, S. (2000). Development after industrialisation: Poor countries in an electronically integrated global economy. In Hood, N. & Young, S. (Eds.), *The globalisation of multinational enterprise activity and economic development* (pp. 133–149). Basingstoke: Macmillan.

Lauder, H. & Hughes, D. (1999). *Trading in futures: Why markets in education don't work.* Buckingham, Open University Press.

Lauder, H., Egerton, M., & Brown, P. (2005). *A report on graduate earnings: Theory and empirical analysis.* Cardiff, National Assembly of Wales.

Lazonick, W. & O'Sullivan, M. (2000). Maximising shareholder value: A new ideology for corporate governance. *Economy and Society, 29*(1), 13–35.

Lemieux, T. (2003). *Residual wage inequality: A re-examination.* University of British Columbia, CLEER working paper, 2. Retrieved from www.econ.ubc.ca/cleer/papers/cleer002.pdf.

Levin, H.M. & Kelly, C. (1997). Can education do it alone? In Halsey, A.H., Lauder, H., Brown, P., & Wells, A.S. (Eds.), *Education, culture, economy and society* (pp. 240–252). Oxford: Oxford University Press.

Livingstone, D. (1998). *The education–jobs gap: Underemployment or economic democracy.* Boulder, CO: Westview.

Low, L. (2002). Globalization and the political economy of Singapore's policy on foreign talent and high skills. *Journal of Education and Work, 15*(4), 409–426.

Lowe, J. (2000). International examinations, national systems and the global market. *Compare, 29*(3), 317–330.

Marginson, S. (2004). Competition and markets in higher education: A 'glonacal' analysis. *Policy Futures in Education, 2*(2), 175–244.

Marx, K. (1976). *Capital: A critique of political economy,* vol. 1. Harmondsworth: Penguin.

Mason, G. (2002). High skills utilization under mass higher education: Graduate employment in service industries. *Journal of Education and Work, 15*(4), 427–456.

Mason, G. & Wilson, R. (2003). *Employers skill survey, new analyses and lessons learned.* London: National Institute of Economic and Social Research.

Mehralizadeh, Y. (1999). *The relationship between schools and the demands of paid work.* PhD thesis, University of Bath.

Meyer, J. (1977). The effects of education as an institution. *American Journal of Sociology, 83,* 55–77.

Michaels, E., Jones, H.H., & Axelrod, B. (2001). *The war for talent.* Boston: Harvard Business School Press.

Mishel, L., Bernstein, J., & Boushey, H. (2003). *The state of working America 2002–2003.* Ithaca, NY: Cornell University Press.

Organisation for Economic Co-operation and Development (OECD). (2000). *OECD information technology outlook.* Paris: OECD.

Organisation for Economic Co-operation and Development (OECD). (2002). *Education at a glance.* Paris: OECD.

People's Republic of China. (2004, April). *China's employment situation and policies, section VI.* Employment prospects for the early part of the 21st century. White Paper. Beijing. Retrieved from www.china.org.cn/e-white/20040426/6.htm.

Perrucci, R. & Wysong, E. (1999). *The new class society.* Lanham, MD: Rowman & Littlefield.

Power, S., Edwards, T., Whitty, G., & Wigfall, V. (2003). *Education and the middle class.* Buckingham: Open University Press.

Pryor, F. & Schaffer, D. (2000). *Who's not working and why? Employment, cognitive skills, wages and the changing US labour market.* Cambridge: Cambridge University Press.

Reich, R. (1991). *The work of nations.* London: Simon & Schuster.

Robertson, S., Bonal, X., & Dale, R. (2002). GATS and the education service industry. *Comparative Education Review, 46*(4), 472–497.

Room, G. (2000). Globalisation, social policy and international standard setting: The case of higher education credentials. *International Journal of Social Welfare, 9,* 103–119.

Rose, N. (1999). *Governing the soul: The shaping of the private self* (2nd ed.). London: Free Association Press.

Rosecrance, R. (1999). *The rise of the virtual state.* New York: Basic Books.

Saxenian, A. (1994). *Regional advantage, culture and competition in Silicon Valley and Route 128.* Cambridge, MA: Harvard University Press.

Saxenian, A. (2000a). The Bangalore boom: From brain drain to brain circulation? In Kenniston, K. & Kumar, D. (Eds.), *Bridging the digital divide: Lessons from India.* Bangalore: National Institute of Advanced Study.

Saxenian, A. (2000b, May). *Bangalore: The Silicon Valley of East Asia?* Paper presented at the Conference on Indian Economic Prospects, Stanford, CA.

Saxenian, A. (2002). Transnational communities and the evolution of global production networks: The case of Taiwan, China and India. *Industry and Innovation, 9*(3), 183–202.

Scarbrough, H. (1999). Knowledge as work: Conflicts in the management of knowledge workers. *Technology Analysis and Strategic Management, 11*(1), 5–16.

Sennett, R. (1998). *The corrosion of character.* New York: W.W. Norton.

Simmel, G. (1978). *The philosophy of money.* Frisby, D. (Ed.). London: Routledge.

Stewart, T.A. (2001). *The wealth of knowledge.* London: Nicholas Brealey.

Toffler, A. (1990). *Power shift: Knowledge, wealth and violence at the edge of the 21st century*. New York: Bantam.

Weber, M. (1945). *From Max Weber: Essays in sociology*. Gerth. H. & Mills, C.W. (Eds.). London, Routledge.

Wolf, A. (2002). *Does education matter: Myths about education and economic growth*. London, Penguin.

Yamamoto, M. (2004). *Will India price itself out of offshore market?* Retrieved from http://news.com.com/Will+India+price+itself+out+of+offshore+market/2100-10223-5180589.html.

Zuboff, S. (1988). *In the age of the smart machine: The future of work and power*. New York: Basic Books.

PAUL DUGUID

'THE ART OF KNOWING'

Social and Tacit Dimensions of Knowledge and the Limits of the Community of Practice

In the years since its appearance, Lave and Wenger's (1990, 1991) notion of 'community of practice' (hereafter, CoP) has developed a remarkably wide following. Its appeal owes a good deal to the seductive character of *community*, aptly described as a 'warmly persuasive word' (Williams, 1976, p. 66). As Østerlund and Carlile (2005) note, most citations of Lave and Wenger have focused on community and ignored practice. Yet it is practice that makes the CoP, the social locus in which a practice is sustained and reproduced overtime, a distinct type of community[1] *practice* is thus critical to CoP analysis. We should not, however, lose sight of the community. The CoP is inherently and irreducibly a social endeavour.

Inevitably, claims about its inherently social character put CoP theory at odds with individualist approaches to knowledge, found most noticeably in economics, where ideas of something irreducibly social are generally viewed with distaste. Von Hayek (1988) regards *social* as a 'weasel' word. Von Mises suggests that any dissent from economists' methodological individualism 'implies that the behaviour of men is directed by mysterious forces that defy analysis and description' (1962, p. 17). Yet the force of von Mises's argument is itself a little mysterious. There is no logical reason why the rejection of methodological individualism entails mystical forces – though it may entail disagreements with economists. Other economists (Cowan et al., 2000) have detected more mysticism in discussions of 'tacit knowledge.' In an attempt to locate much of the importance of the CoP in the tacit knowledge shared among its members, this chapter advances its case primarily in contrast to economistic claims for the theoretical sufficiency in accounts of human practice of explicit knowledge of individuals. The chapter accepts that both notions – the CoP and the tacit – have been deployed with a fair amount of mysticism. But it argues that both, nonetheless, have residual analytical usefulness and raise important issues about learning that are overlooked by standard economic explanations. Thus, the chapter hopes to show how and where CoP theory can illuminate, while economics perhaps cannot, what Polanyi (1966) calls 'the art of knowing.'

It begins by exploring the tendency within economics to align knowledge with information. It then examines the argument of Cowan et al. (2000) in some detail, questioning their confident substitution of the tacit with the explicit. Having argued

D.W. Livingstone and D. Guile (eds.), The Knowledge Economy and Lifelong Learning: A Critical Reader, 147–162.

that the tacit deserves a place in discussions of knowledge, the article then explores this concept in the context of communities and networks of practice. Finally, it concludes that the features of CoP theory that make it insightful both limit the areas where it can be useful and restrict its compatibility with other theoretical viewpoints.

KNOWLEDGE AND ECONOMISTS

Ideas of the 'information' or 'knowledge' economy have drawn many economists towards epistemological issues. Early pioneers such as von Hayek (1937, 1945), Machlup (1962), and Arrow (1969) are no longer alone. One way knowledge has been made economically manageable has been to reduce it to information. This move burrows through awkward aspects of knowledge in search of some sort of fundamental particle that is economically tractable.[2] Cognitive science and computer science have made parallel moves, concluding that human knowledge and machine information are ultimately one.[3] Perhaps the most confident account of the economic demystification of knowledge comes from Simon, a computer scientist and economist:

All the aspects of knowledge – its creation, its storage, its retrieval, its treatment as property, its role in the functioning of societies and organization – can be (and have been) analyzed with the tools of economics. Knowledge has a price and a cost of production; there are markets for knowledge, with their supply and demand curves, and marginal rates of substitution between one form of knowledge and another. (Simon quoted in Ancori et al., 2000, p. 256n)

If Simon is right, innovation, learning, and knowledge diffusion are no more problematic than the production and distribution of widgets. With the right incentives, knowledge will be produced, articulated, and shared without problem. All that remains is a little work for political economists.

Some economists remain less confident, finding awkward puzzles in the way people deploy knowledge and, to the exasperation of Cowan et al. (2000), continuing to invoke the notion of tacit knowledge. Implicitly asking how can we exchange something that we can't articulate and may not even know we possess, tacit arguments fit uneasily within Simon's paradigm. Cowan et al. attempt to mop up this recalcitrant rearguard and end, at least for economists, this alliance with an economically problematic notion. They believe that the stakes are high:

The concept of the inextricable tacitness of human knowledge forms the basis of arguments ... against ... every construction of rational decision processes as the foundation for modeling and explaining the actions of individual human agents. (Cowan et al., 2000, p. 218)

If the tacit survives as analytically defensible, not only Simon's models of knowledge but also all economic models of human action might be at risk.[4]

The Sceptical Economists

Cowan et al. dub their critique 'the skeptical economists' [hereafter, SEs] guide to "tacit knowledge"' (2000, p. 213). They motivate their discussion around a paradox in arguments for government-subsidized research. On the one hand, they say, subsidy seekers argue that because markets deal poorly with public goods like information, government intervention is necessary. Yet when it is claimed that some nations will free ride on the research subvention of others, the same people (according to the SEs) argue that tacitness makes innovative knowledge 'sticky' and so prevents free riding. Knowledge, the SEs argue, can't be both so 'leaky' that markets fail, and yet so 'sticky' that free riding fails. The source of this incoherence, they claim, lies in this quasi-mystical notion of tacitness. Champions of the tacit are guilty, the SEs argue, of concluding that what they can't see must be inherently invisible. While a group of experienced colleagues may, in Polanyi's (1966) famous phrase, 'know more than [they] can say,' it does not follow that what is left unsaid is fundamentally unsayable. Knowledge workers may lack incentives to overcome the 'substantial marginal cost' of codification, but there is no ontological barrier between tacit and explicit.[5] Scrutiny of this argument is difficult because the SEs do not examine any economists who actually fall foul of this paradox. An earlier version of the chapter (Cowan et al., 1999) pins blame on an odd Anglo-French group, Harry Collins, Michel Callon, and Bruno Latour, and the three make a residual but barely explained appearance in the later chapter. Not only do these three antagonists sit uneasily together, but none is an economist, and none is known for this argument. Another candidate might be the conservative scientist Kealey (Cowan et al., 2000, p. 224n12), who does oppose government-subsidized R&D. He has already suffered a withering critique at the hands of one of the SEs (David, 1997). Curiously, neither Kealey's spurious argument nor David's damning dismissal turn on the tacit. Furthermore, Kealey too – as David (1997) makes abundantly clear – is not an economist. In the absence of named protagonists, the SEs target has many of the characteristics of a straw man.

There are reasons to doubt the force of the SE argument. First, while inveighing against the idea of unarticulable knowledge, the SEs dismiss it from their argument as 'not very interesting' (Cowan et al., 2000, p. 230) and instead discuss articulable knowledge and the conditions of its codification. Thus they beg the central question they purport to raise. Second, while they report Polanyi talking of a *tacit* dimension to knowledge (p. 249, emphasis added), they fail to treat it as dimension, putting tacit and explicit on a continuum ('Our focus has been maintained on ... the dimension along which codification appeared at one extremum and tacitness occupied the other' [p. 249]). Two dimensions and two ends of a continuum are, of course, distinct. Polanyi was arguing that the tacit is not reducible to the explicit. The SE are determined that it should be, hence their translation of dimension into continuum.[6]

Third, while lamenting that the tacit has come loose from 'epistemological moorings' (p. 213), the SEs themselves duck philosophical questions. For instance, they characterize Polanyi's epistemological argument as primarily a theory of perception. Equally, the SEs allude to Ryle's (1949) famous distinction between

149

knowing how and *knowing that*, but do not bother to consult Ryle himself.[7] Ryle, like Polanyi, argues that the two aspects of knowing are complementary, knowing *how* helping to make knowing *that* actionable. They are not, however, substitutable: Accumulation of knowing that does not lead to knowing how. Knowing that, we acquire in the form of explicit, codified information. By contrast, 'we learn *how*,' Ryle argues, 'by practice' (1949, p. 41).

The idea that knowing that does not produce *knowing how* is important. Oakeshott (1967) talks of

> the tacit or implicit component of knowledge, the ingredient which is not merely unspecified in propositions, but which is unspecifiable in propositions. It is the component of knowledge which does not appear in the form of rules and which, therefore, cannot be resolved into information or itemized in the manner characteristic of information. (p. 167)

Such arguments highlight the philosophically problematic recursiveness implicit in the idea that knowledge can be transferred through codification. Codification cannot explain how we come to read new codes. If all we have is the explicit, then a new codebook must either explain itself or require another codebook to do the explaining. The argument is thus trapped between circularity (with codebooks explaining themselves) and an infinite regress (with code-books explaining codebooks). Such explanations must, as Wittgenstein (1958) argues, 'come to an end somewhere' (p. 3e).[8] Ryle points to another, irreducible kind of knowledge or activity that gets us started, that shows us *how* and gives us, in Oakeshott's terms, the necessary 'judgment' to put rules into effect.[9] Indeed, a chain of epistemological arguments stretching back to Socrates and the Meno suggests that codified knowledge, the explicit dimension, rests on an uncodifiable substrate that tells us how to use the code. In Aristotle's words:

> While it is easy to know that honey, wine, hellebore, cautery, and the use of the knife are so, to know how, to whom, and when these should be applied with a view to producing health, is no less an achievement than that of being a physician. (Aristotle, 1908, book 5, part 9)

Explicit knowledge, from this viewpoint, is not a self-sufficient base, but a dependent superstructure. 'Into every act of knowing' Polanyi claims, 'there enters a tacit ... contribution' (1958).

Thus while knowledge may include codified content, to be used it requires the disposition to apply it, which cannot itself, without risk of recursion, be propositional. As Fodor (1968) puts it, knowledge involves not simply [indeed not even necessarily] knowing how the thing is done, but knowing how to do it, and the two are quite distinct. Explaining a joke is quite different from telling a joke. They may both play a part in the world of humour, but they are not equivalent or substitutable.

In their eagerness to dismiss the tacit, the SEs portray it as little more than a fad brought into economics by Nelson and Winter (1982) and rapidly blown out of proportion:

A notion that took its origins in the psychology of visual perception and human motor skills has been wonderfully transmuted, first from an efficient mode of mental storage of knowledge into a putative epistemological category (having to do with the nature of knowledge itself), from there into a phenomenon of inarticulable inter-organizational relationships and finally to the keys to corporate, and perhaps national, competitive advantage! (p. 223)

Rooting Polanyi in the 'psychology of visual perception' ignores his struggle to understand scientific invention, though this is close to the SEs heart. (Polanyi was, of course, himself a gifted chemist.) It also overlooks the immediate appeal of his idea in diverse fields, including linguistics (Chomsky, 1965), physics (Ziman, 1967), philosophy (Fodor, 1968), political science (Oakeshott, 1967), the sociology of economics (Coats, 1967), and economics (Richardson, 1972), the last coming well before Nelson and Winter.[10] All appear to have recognized that Polanyi addressed an absence not so much to do with the stock of knowledge within their field as with the acquisition and appropriate use of that knowledge. Indeed, this multidisciplinary eagerness reflects less the emergence of a new fad than the dwindling of an old one – the time-honoured faith, identified with the enlightenment but going back much further, in explicit, codified knowledge. This faith gave rise to a long pursuit of such things as the universal library and the complete instruction manual.[11] Championing the explicit to the exclusion of the tacit may threaten to take us back, not forward.

A LITTLE LEARNING

Learning throws light on the importance of the tacit for dealing with codified knowledge. It is impossible to specify and hence codify *all* the knowledge involved in even the most elementary practice (as Fodor [1968] points out, this would take us down to the level of firing neurons and beyond). Were it possible, it seems unlikely to be helpful. A brief list of all that is involved in tying a shoelace would overwhelm a learner. Despite the SEs' faith in explication, in instruction as in design there is great value in economy in the sense of leaving as much as possible unsaid (Kreiner, 2001; Brown & Duguid, 1996). But in considering codification, quantity is not the only issue. Quality matters as well, for it is not clear that codified knowledge is equivalent to the tacit knowledge it comes from. The codification of knowledge may be less a matter of translation (though translation itself is rarely innocent) than transformation, whereby the codified no longer serves the purpose of the tacit it replaces.[12] Uncodified knowledge provides background context and warrants for assessing the codified. Background no longer works as background when it is foregrounded.

In learning situations, for example, it is not simply what a mentor or teacher can say, but also what he or she implicitly displays about the particular art, craft, or discipline. As a thought experiment, consider those enormously lucrative textbooks that in one 'new' edition after another introduce economics students to the discipline. Curiously, their authors often continue teaching, many times prescribing, the very textbook into which they have distilled their codified knowledge. If texts can contain the requisite knowledge, as the SEs suggest, then this is surely an odd situation. It might be argued that these teachers deliberately keep some of their knowledge uncodified to give them a double stream of income, one from writing and another from teaching. That situation, economics suggests, would surely act as an incentive for rivals to codify the missing knowledge in an alternative textbook that would find a ready market. Students armed with the complete knowledge in codified form would not have to pay the fees of the expensive universities where the star professors teach – or go to class at all. Yet economists continue to write and teach. One star economist (McCloskey, 1985) suggests why:

> Economics is ... a matter of feeling the applicability of arguments, of seeing analogies ... of knowing when to reason verbally and when mathematically, and of what implicit characterization of the world is most useful for correct economics. ... Problem-solving in economics is the tacit knowledge of the sort Polanyi described. (p. 178)[13]

Indeed, the failings of many teachers can probably be attributed less to their lack of explicit knowledge of a discipline than to their inability to exhibit the underlying practice successfully. For all their disciplinary wisdom, teachers are usually unaware of quite what, from their students' perspective, is on display and of the 'stolen knowledge' (Brown & Duguid, 1995) their students carry away.

The idea that knowledge people reveal in action complements what they reveal in precepts is again an old one. It penetrates the false dichotomy that opens the *Meno*: 'Can you tell me, Socrates, whether virtue is acquired by teaching or by practice?' (Plato, 1953). It also helps explain the power of apprenticeship and why apprenticeship is not merely the preferred method of 'manual' trades, but also of the higher reaches of academic disciplines. Polanyi noticed this about his own discipline:

> The large amounts of time spent by students of chemistry, biology and medicine in their practical courses shows how greatly these sciences rely on the transmission of skills and connoisseurship from master to apprentice. It offers an impressive demonstration of the extent to which the art of knowing has remained unspecifiable at the very heart of science. (Polanyi, 1958, p. 55)

Hayek reports something very similar about his discipline:

> We need to remember only how much we have to learn in any occupation after we have completed our theoretical training, how big a part of our working life we spend learning particular jobs ... Even economists who regard themselves as definitely above the crude materialist fallacies ... commit the same mistake ... toward the acquisition of such practical knowledge ... the reproach of irrationality. (von Hayek, 1945, p. 522)

But the political scientist Oakeshott perhaps best sums up the process:

> And if you were to ask me the circumstances in which patience, accuracy, economy, elegance and style first dawned upon me, [they came from] a

Sergeant gymnastics instructor … not on account of anything he ever said, but because he was a man of patience, accuracy, economy, elegance, and style. (Oakeshott, 1967, p. 176)

Oakeshott reflects Ryle's (1949) argument that to do something patiently, accurately, economically, elegantly, or stylishly does not involve two processes – an act and a 'mental' monitoring, each of which can be specified in a set of rules. (In organizational literature, Weick, Sutcliffe, & Obstfeld's [1999] notion of 'mindfulness' echoes Ryle's insight.[14]) Further, Oakeshott emphasizes that transferring knowledge, particularly to newcomers, involves more than transferring codified knowledge. Declarative statements are always underconstrained – usefully so, if our argument holds that voluminous explicit information is more likely to increase uncertainty than reduce it. Suffering from problems of self-referentiality, no text is able to determine the principles of its own interpretation. Or, to put it another way, all are open to multiple interpretations. Approaching a text as sincere or ironic yields two diametrically opposed interpretations of its meaning (a problem that famously landed Daniel Defoe in the stocks). A tacit understanding of the ground rules for interpretation thus plays a role in grounding a particular interpretation of a text – a facet of interpretation that originates outside the text to be interpreted.

INTERPRETIVE COMMUNITIES

Which interpretation is seen as appropriate depends not on the text, but on the nature of the community making the interpretation (Fish, 1994). As Arrow (1974) and Leonard and Sensiper (1998) point out, the same knowledge is used in quite different ways in different occupational communities, much as the Bible finds radically different interpretations among different sects. Consequently, as teachers induct students into their discipline, they spend a great deal of time showing students how to read, for this is not simply a matter of learning to decode a text in the abstract, but of learning to decode from the perspective of that discipline (which is why we should not be too hard on those economists who teach from their textbooks).[15] The knowing *how* that is involved, CoP theory suggests, is the product of communities of practice.

The Community of Practice

Talk of learning, apprenticeship, and communities helps to bring discussion back to the CoP. This, as noted, was introduced as a theory of learning, drawing much of its evidence from studies of apprenticeship (Lave & Wenger, 1991). Within a CoP, knowledge is instantiated dynamically in what Giddens calls knowledgeability, including 'all the things which actors know tacitly about how to "go on" in the context of social life without being able to give them direct discursive expression' (1984, p. xxiii). Membership in the CoP offers form and context as well as content to aspiring practitioners, who need to not just acquire the explicit knowledge of the community, but also the identity of a community member.[16]

Thus, learning in the sense of becoming a practitioner – which includes acquiring not only codebooks but the ability to decode them appropriately – can usefully be thought of as learning *to be* and contrasted to what Bruner (1996) calls 'learning *about*.'[17] The former requires knowing *how*, the art of practice, much of which lies tacit in a CoP. Learning *about* only requires the accumulation of knowing *that*, which confers the ability to talk a good game, but not necessarily to play one. Transforming knowing *how* into knowing *that*, the tacit into its nearest explicit equivalent, is likely to transform learning from learning *to be* into learning *about*. The CoP's knowledge, in tacit or explicit form, may be distributed across the collective and their shared artefacts rather than held by or divisible among individuals (Hutchins, 1995). Within the CoP, the knowing *how* of the community, not merely of an individual, is on display.

Networks of Practice

Because tacit knowledge is displayed or exemplified, not transmitted, in most circumstances a CoP is likely to involve face-to-face interaction.[18] Of course, not all practice is local. In many areas, the practice is shared widely among practitioners, most of whom will never come into contact with one another. The *network of practice* (NoP) designates the collective of all practitioners of a particular practice. For example, Knorr Cetina's (1999) 'epistemic culture' of high-energy physicists constitutes a global NoP that has within it multiple local CoPs. Though practice is not co-ordinated within a NoP as it is in a CoP, common practices and common tools allow distant members to exchange global know *that* and to re-embed it (Giddens, 1990) in effective, coherent ways through the mediation of their locally acquired knowing *how*.[19] Consequently, where practice precedes it, explicit knowledge may appear to have global reach (or to be 'leaky'). Where it does not, the same knowledge may appear remarkably parochial (or to be 'sticky').

The central distinction between the CoP and the NoP turns on the control and co-ordination of the reproduction of a group and its practice. Newcomers enter the network through a local community. You become an economist by entering an economics department in Chicago, or Berkeley, or Columbia – a route that may mark you for life, in part because the tacit knowledge of the local community profoundly shapes your identity and its trajectory.

EPISTEMIC AND ETHICAL DIMENSIONS OF PRACTICE

Economistic explanations of knowledge diffusion focus on the codification of knowledge (Cohendet & Steinmueller, 2000), access to information (Mokyr, 2002), reduction of transaction costs (Williamson, 1981), and specification and protection of private interests (Coase, 1988; North, 1981). The practice perspective modifies these assumptions along two distinct dimensions. On the one hand, there are difficulties around what knowledge people *can* meaningfully share. Such involuntary barriers to sharing might be thought of as epistemic entailments of practice. On the other, there are also difficulties concerning what people *will* share – not everything has its price. Local communities and even disaggregated networks of practice may simply not want to share, or they may want to hide what they know. These voluntary constraints on sharing can be thought of as the ethical entailments of practice. These entailments distinguish the 'can/can't' of knowledge flow from the 'will/won't.' The tacit dimension of a practice's knowledge – knowing *how*'s shaping of propriety, rather than know *that*'s suitability as property – profoundly affects these entailments. Knowledge, that is, may stick or flow for epistemic and ethical rather than just economic reasons.

Epistemic Entailments: Can/Can't

Divisions of labour lead to von Hayek's (1945) divisions of knowledge, which create distinct epistemic cultures. Within such cultures, explicit knowledge can travel and remain actionable; between them, it usually cannot without difficulty. Economists generally acknowledge epistemic barriers between large cultural groups, between, for example, Europe and Asia. They seem less willing to consider them on a smaller scale, yet barriers seem to occur at the level of the CoP. Within CoPs or NoPs the potential for flow is high. Shared knowing *how*, produced by shared practice, creates the possibility of productive sharing of knowing *that*. But when the practice and knowing how of two communities are different, epistemic barriers develop and productively sharing knowing that becomes much more challenging – even when the different practices lie together within an organization (Bechky, 2003; Carlile, 2002).[20] Explication or codification does not solve the problem.[21]

Ethical Commitments: Will/Won't

Arguments like Simon's (described earlier) or Teece's (1986) about 'regimes of appropriation' assume that financial incentives will prevent those who have competitive knowledge from sharing it with those outside the regime. Yet people will sometimes share what self-interest predicts they hold secret, and conversely will not share, despite encouragements, when it expects them to reveal. Whether they will or won't share may be determined by the ethical considerations reflecting a community's standards of propriety.

The idea that practice develops community standards that rise above self-interest is an old one. Marx and Engels argued that those among whom labour is divided develop a 'communal interest' (1978, p. 53). Durkheim (1960) argued that 'the division of labour becomes a predominant source of social solidarity at the same time it becomes the foundation of the moral order' (p. 333). More recently, MacIntyre has argued that 'the self has to find its moral identity in and through its membership of communities' (1981, p. 205).[22] Thompson (1971), following Marx, suggests that such social groups will resist, in the name of their moral interests, appeals to their economic interests.[23] In all, if we want to understand individuals' capacities and motives for sharing knowledge, we need to look not just at the knowledge, but at the communities in which their knowing *how* was shaped.

CONCLUSION: PARADOX RESOLVED?

Though the route has been a long one, we might now be in a position to resolve the paradox that motivated the SEs' critique without needing to reject the tacit all together. To understand the distribution of knowledge, we should not look at knowledge à la Simon, as if it were a widget whose production and consumption could be modelled without reference to producers or consumers. Knowing *that*, as explicit, codified propositions, probably can be modelled this way. But it cannot usefully be isolated from the knowing *how* that makes it actionable.

For the SEs, economic arguments about knowledge appear incoherent when, on the one hand, protagonists claim that knowledge causes markets to fail because it is a public good, yet on the other, the same protagonists apparently maintain that knowledge production merits subsidy and resists free riders because knowledge is not a public good. In short, knowledge appears to be both 'leaky' (Liebeskind, 1996) and 'sticky' (von Hippel, 1994). The argument, however, focuses on knowledge independent of knowers and the situation in which knowledge is used. It is different knowers and their knowing *how* that turn the same knowledge from sticky to leaky. The ability to read gives any competent users of a language access to knowledge codified in that language. But access to that explicit knowledge does not confer the ability to put it into appropriate use. Tacit knowledge, which confers that ability, is, by contrast with the explicit and codified, remarkably sticky.

Knowledge paradoxes arise, then, by confusing the dimensions of knowledge or by assuming that we can substitute one for the other without problems. Nowhere, perhaps, is this more evident than in the endless problems of 'best practice' diffusion. On the one hand, theorists of 'best practice' put their finger on the essential point: Practice is critical. On the other, they regularly attempt to move a best practice from one community to another by codifying and circulating the explicit knowledge. What, of course, is truly critical is the knowing *how* embedded in the practice and wrapped around with ethical and epistemic commitments. Without these – and these are admittedly very hard to transfer – the explicit is worth relatively little. Many have tried to imitate the form of Toyota's production methods; few have managed to replicate the quality of its practice.

Codification is remarkably powerful, but its power is only released through the corresponding knowing *how*, which explains *how* we get to know and learn to do. Because it is not so economically tractable, the SEs try to dismiss this knowing how as readily substitutable by the more compliant knowing *that*. The argument leads them, this chapter argues, to attend to what people can say but to overlook what they can do; to be able to describe what people know, but not account for how they come to know; to be able in theory to quantify a person's knowledge, but not to assess its quality. In making their case, the SEs have mapped a very important part of the terrain of knowledge (see Cowan et al., 2000, Fig. 2), but not all. In particular, they have failed to show how we get access to the terrain and what we can do when we get there.

This argument attempts to reveal limits in some economist's accounts of knowledge. At the same time, it exposes limits to CoP analysis, which has occasionally been stretched well beyond its capacity. By emphasizing how CoP theory differs from more individualist social sciences, the argument also intimates limits to the theory's compatibility. To recap, the argument proposes a theory of knowledge acquisition rooted not in the epistemological stocks of individual heads, but in the flow of practice within communities. Communities, it holds, have emergent properties that, while they are no doubt the outcome of individual actions, amount to more than the sum of those actions and more than the amortization of transaction costs. If this is right, then CoP theories may not fit well with approaches to work and knowledge that, at least on the surface, appear congenial.

For example, Cohen and Prusak (2001) highlight similarities between CoP and social capital (SC) theories. Social capital theories draw attention to networks of individuals that help to embed economic interactions in social relations (Polanyi, 1957; Granovetter, 1973, 1985). Through social exchanges, people build webs of trust (Fukuyama, 1995; Putnam, 1993, 2000), obligation, reputation, expectations, and norms (Coleman, 1988). In these webs, SC theory suggests, people are willing and able to share knowledge and co-ordinate action. Most CoP theorists would go along with these claims, but some would pause at the word 'able.' That is, CoP analysis accepts the importance of social capital networks to understanding why people will and will not share. But it makes a distinction between people's willingness to share and their ability to share, suggesting that people have to engage in similar or shared practices to be able to share knowledge about those practices. Thus, where SC theory points to unseen links, CoP theory points to unseen boundaries – boundaries shaped by practice – that divide knowledge networks from one another. These boundaries may prevent communication despite all the obligations of good will and social capital that connect them or, indeed, all the incentives of financial capital that may entice them. Indeed, while advancing the *social*, a good deal of SC theory has nonetheless remained fairly close to its roots in economics (residual in that word *capital*).[24] This has a couple of implications. First, SC theorists' focus on 'rational actors' (Coleman, 1988) portrays social groups as little more than 'combinations' of individuals (Nahapiet & Ghoshal, 1996). So while SC analysis encompasses a broad array of social groups, including such things as firms, bowling leagues, housing organizations, and families, the CoP perspective, by contrast, limits itself to communities and networks where practice is co-ordinated or at least shared. Second, while some SC theorists, again like economists, view the sharing of knowledge as little more than the exchange of 'information that facilitates action' (Coleman, 1988, p. 104) between individuals, and as primarily determined by ties, strong or weak, and good will, CoP theory suggests the challenge of communication is more complex. SC focuses primarily on the circulation of knowledge promoted by what is here called the ethical commitment of the people involved. But, from the point of view of CoP theory, it overlooks the corresponding epistemic commitment. If that too is not shared – as it is among CoPs and NoPs, but not necessarily among SC networks – then in the end no amount of bowling together will bring about shared, actionable knowledge.

These distinctions are not made to vaunt the superiority or even hegemony of CoP theories over rivals. CoP theory, as has already been suggested, only addresses certain topics involving quite special types of community and networks. SC is much broader and economics, of course, broader still. Indeed, this essay deliberately seeks to restrict the application of CoP theory, pointing instead to other theories that are less limited and more adaptable. It is hoped, however, that the edges of CoP theory thus narrowed will provide a sharper analytical tool that can tell us more about the 'art of knowing.'

NOTES

1. It is this sustenance and reproduction of practice through the opposing demands of continuity and displacement that gives CoPs their interdependent tension and dynamism. Nonetheless, the notion has repeatedly been applied to transient, cross-functional teams and miscellaneous work groups. See, for example, Nonaka (1994).

2. Hables Grey (2002) portrays information as a fundamental particle. The commonplace notion that there is an ascendancy from data through information to knowledge appears regularly in the economics literature (Ancori et al. 2000). Tuomi (2000) exposes flaws in the argument.

3. Shannon and Weaver (1964) note that the technical sense of communication is indifferent to meaning. The technical notion suggests that information reduces uncertainty; many who have to deal with the 'tsunami of information' in the current 'flux' (Steinmueller, 2000, p. 373) understandably assume the opposite. Applying the technical notion to human practice assumes that humans are Turing machines, a complex claim that needs to be argued rather than assumed (Floridi, 1999).

4. While this article does attempt to defend the tacit from this attack, I am more sceptical than the SEs and do not hold that such a defence threatens the foundations of economics.

5. The paradox – though not its political implications – is suggested in Winter (1987) and addressed directly in Brown and Duguid (2000, 2001). Intriguingly, Polanyi, the indirect target of the SEs, was very interested in the political issues. See Polanyi (1944).

6. The economic historian Mokyr (2002) clearly recognizes the dimensional, irreducible character of tacit knowledge ('Tacit knowledge and formal or verbal knowledge should not be thought of as substitutes but as complements,' p. 73).

7. Ryle is often misread, perhaps most egregiously by Nonaka (1994) and Nonaka and Takeuchi (1995).

8. See also Wittgenstein (1958, pp. 19e, 29e, 40e).

9. The SEs concede that 'Successfully reading the code ... may involve prior acquisition of considerable specialized knowledge (quite possibly including knowledge not written down anywhere)' (2000, p. 225). They give no explanation, however, of how such acquisition occurs. (See also pp. 232n18, 233).

10. Richardson (1972), who discussed the terrain between market and hierarchy early and with insight, notes, 'Technology cannot always be transferred simply by selling the right to use a process. It is rarely reducible to mere information to be passed on but consists also of experience and skills. In terms of Professor Ryle's celebrated distinction, much of it is "knowledge how" rather than "knowledge that"' (p. 895).

11. Diderot and D'Alembert's encyclopaedia is the cynosure of enlightenment codification, but such things as Moxon's 'exercises' (1693) offer earlier examples. See also Davis (1975). For early belief

in a universal library and its rebirth in the digital age, see O'Donnell (1998). Philosophically, logical positivism perhaps marked the end of this confidence in the exclusive character of explicit knowledge, though clearly it lives on in economics.

[12] The multiple terms Nonaka (1994) uses to try to encompass the process of translation hint at some of the problems inherent in the notion. As well as translating and transforming, these include *externalizing, converting, interacting, interchanging, articulating, merging, shifting, entangling, resolving, transferring, harmonizing, crystallizing.*

[13] Endorsing Ryle's notion that these things come with practice, McCloskey ends by admonishing students with a very old joke situated insightfully for a new domain: 'How do you get to the Council of Economic Advisors? ... Practice, practice' (McCloskey, 1985, p. 178).

[14] Ryle's argument raises some questions about Argyris and Schön's (1978) notion of 'second loop learning.' See also Giddens's (1984) Rylean discussion of reflexive monitoring, which concludes, 'Understanding is not a mental process accompanying the solving of a puzzle ... It is simply being able to apply the formula in the right context' (p. 20). Polanyi, it needs to be noted, did not agree with Ryle on this point. See Polanyi (1958), p. 372.

[15] David's (1997) critique of Kealey, for example, rightly scolds Kealey, a biochemist, for failing to read economics literature as an economist would.

[16] While 'identity' can seem unpleasantly 'soft' and far distant from hard-headed economic analysis, its importance is stressed in Kogut and Zander's (1996) influential essay.

[17] Compare Aristotle's comment, cited earlier, that knowing when and how to apply treatment is 'no less an achievement than that of *being* a physician' (emphasis added).

[18] See Giddens (1984) and in particular his use of Garfinkel's theory of 'facework.' See also Orlikowski (1992, 2002). (Orlikowski has been centrally instrumental in introducing Giddens' work to organizational studies and this article is particularly indebted to her.)

[19] The looseness of co-ordination within a NoP allows for innovation through epistemic speciation.

[20] Alternative means to bring two different communities into alignment though not necessarily understanding include routines (Nelson & Winter, 1982), boundary objects (Star & Greisemer, 1989), and the price mechanism (von Hayek, 1945).

[21] Whitehead's joke about *Principia Mathematica* – he claimed to understand every word but not one of the sentences – suggests the limits of codification.

[22] As both are cited in this article, it should be noted that Giddens rejects MacIntyre's view of moral order.

[23] Thompson shows how across the eighteenth century, English people used the moral economy to defend their customary rights from the encroachment of the market economy. 'Open source' software offers intriguing modern parallels (Bollier, 2004).

[24] Coleman (1988) is quite explicit. His aim is 'to import the economist's principle of rational action for use in the analysis of social systems proper ... the concept of social capital is a tool to aid in this' (p. 97).

REFERENCES

Ancori, B., Bureth, A., & Cohendet, P. (2000). The economics of knowledge: The debate about codification and tacit knowledge. *Industrial and Corporate Change, 9*(2), 255–287.

Argyris, C. & Schön, D. (1978). *Organizational learning: A theory of action perspective.* Reading, MA: Addison-Wesley.

Aristotle. (1908). *The Nicomachean ethics* (Ross, W., Trans.). Oxford: Clarendon Press.

Arrow, K.J. (1969). Classificatory notes on the production and transmission of technological knowledge. *American Economic Review, 59*(2), 29–35.

Arrow, K.J. (1974). *The limits of organization.* New York: W.W. Norton.

Bechky, B.A. (2003). Sharing meaning across occupational communities: The transformation of understanding on a production floor. *Organization Science, 14*(3), 312–330.

Bollier, D. (2004, March 29). Who owns the sky? Reviving the commons. *These Times.* Retrieved from www.inthesetimes.com/article/710/who_owns_the_sky.

Brown, J. & Duguid, P. (1995). Stolen knowledge. *Educational Technology, 33*(3), 10–15.

Brown, J. & Duguid, P. (1996). Keeping it simple. In T. Winograd (Ed.), *Exploring software design* (pp. 129–145). Menlo Park, CA: Addison-Wesley.

Brown, J. & Duguid, P. (2000). *The social life of information.* Boston: Cambridge University Press.

Brown, J. & Duguid, P. (2001). Knowledge and organization: A social-practice perspective. *Organization Science, 12*(2), 198–213.

Bruner, J. (1996). *The culture of education.* Cambridge, MA: Harvard University Press.

Carlile, P.R. (2002). A pragmatic view of knowledge and boundaries: Boundary objects in new product development. *Organization Science, 13*(4), 442–455.

Chomsky, N. (1965). *Aspects of the theory of syntax.* Cambridge, MA: MIT Press.

Coase, R.H. (1988). *The firm, the market, and the law.* Chicago: University of Chicago Press.

Coats, A.W. (1967, October). Sociological aspects of British economic thought (ca. 1880–1930). *Journal of Political Economy, 75,* 706–729.

Cohen, D. & Prusak, L. (2001). *In good company: How social capital makes organizations work.* Boston: Harvard Business School Press.

Cohendet, P. & Steinmueller, W.E. (2000). The codification of knowledge: A conceptual and empirical exploration. *Industrial and Corporate Change, 92*(2), 195–209.

Coleman, J.S. (1998). Social capital and the creation of human capital. *American Journal of Sociology, 94,* 95–120.

Cowan, R., David, P.A., & Foray, D. (1999). The explicit economics of knowledge codification and tacitness. Paper prepared for the EC TSER 3rd TPIK Workshop, Strasbourg. Retrieved from http://econpapers.hhs.se/paper/wopstanec/99027.htm.

Cowan, R., David, P.A., & Foray, D. (2000). The explicit economics of knowledge codification and tacitness. *Industrial and Corporate Change, 9*(2), 211–253.

David, P.A. (1997). From market magic to calypso science policy: Review of Terence Kealey's *The economic laws of scientific research. Research Policy, 26*(2), 229–255.

Davis. N.Z. (1975). Printing and the people. In *Society and culture in early modern France* (pp. 189–226). Stanford, CA: Stanford University Press.

Durkheim, E. (1960). *The division of labor in society* (Simpson, G., Trans.). Glencoe, IL: Free Press.

Fish, S. (1994). *Is there a text in this class? The authority of interpretive communities.* Cambridge, MA: Harvard University Press.

Floridi, L. (1999). *Philosophy and computing: An introduction.* London: Routledge.

Fodor, J. (1968). The appeal to tacit knowledge in psychological explanation. *Journal of Philosophy, 65*(20), 627–640.

Fukuyama, F. (1995). *Trust: The social virtues and the creation of prosperity.* New York: Free Press.

Giddens, A. (1984). *The constitution of society: Outline of the theory of structuration.* Berkeley & Los Angeles: University of California Press.

Giddens, A. (1990). *The consequences of modernity: The Raymond Fred West memorial lectures.* Stanford, CA: Stanford University Press.

Granovetter, M. (1973). The strength of weak ties. *American Journal of Sociology, 78*(6), 1360–1380.

Granovetter, M. (1985). Economic action and social structure: The problem of embeddedness. *American Journal of Sociology, 91*(3), 481–510.

Hables Grey, C. (2002). The political implications of information theory, digital divide, culture and human-computer interface design and the revolution in military affairs. Paper presented at the SSRC Summer Institute, Information Technology and Social Research: Setting the Agenda, Columbia University, New York.

Hutchins, E. (1995). *Cognition in the wild.* Cambridge, MA: MIT Press.

Knorr Cetina, K. (1999). *Epistemic cultures: How the sciences make knowledge.* Cambridge, MA: Harvard University Press.

Kogut, B. & Zander, U. (1996). What do firms do? Coordination, identity, and learning. *Organization Science*, 7(5), 502–518.

Kreiner, K. (2001). *The ambiguity of sharing: Knowledge management in the context of new product development*. IOA Working Paper. Copenhagen: Copenhagen Business School.

Lave, J. & Wenger, E. (1990, February). *Situated learning: Legitimate peripheral participation*. IRL Report IRL90-0013. Palo Alto, CA: Institute for Research on Learning.

Lave, J. & Wenger, E. (1991). *Situated learning: Legitimate peripheral participation*. New York: Cambridge University Press.

Leonard, D. & Sensiper, S. (1998). The role of tacit knowledge in group innovation. *California Management Review*, 40(3), 112–132.

Liebeskind, J.P. (1996). Knowledge, strategy, and the theory of the firm. *Strategic Management Journal*, 17, 93–107.

Machlup, F. (1962). *The production and distribution of knowledge in the United States*. Princeton NJ: Princeton University Press.

MacIntyre, A. (1981). *After virtue: A study in moral theory*. Notre Dame, IN: University of Notre Dame Press.

Marx, K. & Engels, F. (1978). *The German ideology: Part one*. New York: International.

McCloskey, D.N. (1985). *The rhetoric of economics*. Madison: University of Wisconsin Press.

Mokyr, J. (2002). *The gifts of Athena: Historical origins of the knowledge economy*. Princeton, NJ: Princeton University Press.

Moxon, J. (1693). *Mechanick exercises, or the doctrine of handy-works*. London: J. Moxon.

Nahapiet, J. & Ghoshal, S. (1996). Social capital, intellectual capital, and the organizational advantage. *Academy of Management Review*, 23(2), 242–268.

Nelson, R. & Winter, S.G. (1982). *An evolutionary theory of economic change*. Cambridge, MA: Belknap.

Nonaka, I. (1994). A dynamic theory of organizational knowledge creation. *Organization Science*, 5(1), 14–37.

Nonaka, I. & Takeuchi, H. (1995). *The knowledge-creating company: How Japanese companies create the dynamics of innovation*. New York: Oxford University Press.

North, D.C. (1981). *Structure and change in economic history*. New York: W.W. Norton.

Oakeshott, M. (1967). Learning and teaching. In Peters, R.S. (Ed.), *The concept of education* (pp. 156–177). London: Routledge & Kegan Paul.

Orlikowski, W.J. (1992). The duality of technology: Rethinking the concept of technology in organization. *Organization Science*, 3(3), 398–427.

Orlikowski, W.J. (2002). Knowing in practice: Enacting a collective capability in distributed organizing. *Organization Science*, 13(3), 249–273.

Østerlund, C. & Carlile, P. (2005). Relations in practice: Sorting through practice theories on knowledge sharing in complex organizations. *Information Society*, 21, 91–107.

Plato. (1953). *Dialogues* (Jowett, B., Trans.). Oxford: Clarendon Press.

Polanyi, K. (1957). *The great transformation: The political and economic origins of our time*. New York: Bacon.

Polanyi, M. (1944, Summer). Patent reform. *Review of Economic Studies*, 61–76.

Polanyi, M. (1958). *Personal knowledge*. London: Routledge & Kegan Paul.

Polanyi, M. (1966). *The tacit dimension*. Garden City, NY: Doubleday.

Putnam, R.D. (1993). *Making democracy work: Civic traditions in modern Italy*. Princeton, NJ: Princeton University Press.

Putnam, R.D. (2000). *Bowling alone: The collapse and revival of American community*. New York: Simon & Schuster.

Richardson, G.B. (1972). The organisation of industry. *Economics Journal*, 82(327), 883–896.

Ryle, G. (1949). *The concept of mind*. London: Hutchinson.

Shannon, C. & Weaver, W. (1964). *The mathematical theory of communication*. Urbana, IL: University of Illinois Press.

161

Star, S.L. & James, R.G. (1989). Institutional ecology, 'translations' and boundary objects: Amateurs and professionals in Berkeley's Museum of Vertebrate Zoology, 1907–39. *Social Studies of Science*, *19*, 387–420.

Steinmueller, W.E. (2000). Will new information and communication technologies improve the 'codification' of knowledge? *Industrial and Corporate Change*, *9*(2), 361–376.

Teece, D.J. (1986). Profiting from technological innovation: Implications for integration, collaboration, licensing, and public policy. *Research Policy*, *15*, 285–305.

Thompson, E.P. (1971). The moral economy of the English crowd in the eighteenth century. *Past and Present*, *50*, 76–136.

Tuomi, I. (2000). Data is more than knowledge: Implications of the reversed knowledge hierarchy for knowledge management and organizational memory. *Journal of Management Information Systems*, *16*(3), 103–118.

von Hayek, F.A. (1937). Economics and knowledge. *Economica*, *4*(13), 33–54.

von Hayek, F.A. (1945). The use of knowledge in society. *American Economic Review*, *35*, 519–530.

von Hayek, F.A. (1988). *The fatal conceit: The errors of socialism*. Chicago: University of Chicago Press.

von Hippel, E. (1994). Sticky information and the locus of problem solving: Implications for innovation. *Management Science*, *40*(4), 429–439.

von Mises, L. (1962). *The ultimate foundation of economic science: An essay on method*. Princeton, NJ: Van Nostrand.

Weick, K.E., Sutcliffe, K.M., & Obstfeld, D. (1999). Organizing for high reliability: Processes of collective mindfulness. *Research in Organizational Behavior*, *21*, 81–123.

Williams, R. (1976). *Keywords: A vocabulary of culture and society*. New York: Oxford University Press.

Winter, S.G. (1987). Knowledge and competence as strategic assets. In Teece, D. (Ed.), *The competitive challenge: Strategies for industrial renewal* (pp. 159–184). Cambridge, MA: Ballinger.

Wittgenstein, L. (1958). *Philosophical investigations* (Anscombe, G.E.M., Trans.). Oxford: Basil Blackwell and Mott.

Ziman, J.M. (1967). *Public knowledge: An essay concerning the social dimension of science*. Cambridge: Cambridge University Press.

PETER KENNEDY

THE KNOWLEDGE ECONOMY

Education, Work, and the Struggle to (Re-)Regulate the Distinction
between 'Necessary' and 'Free' Labour Time

INTRODUCTION: DEFINING THE KNOWLEDGE ECONOMY

Exactly how one defines the 'knowledge economy' has been a hotly debated topic. To begin with, there is a lack of clarity about what 'knowledge' is when referring to the 'knowledge economy, with narrow definitions (technical and scientific) dominating the literature over broader definitions (ranging from social skills to spirituality) (Rooney, Hearn, & Ninan, 2005). Definitions of the 'knowledge economy' have tended to fall back on equally ambiguous concepts such as 'the new economy,' 'information society,' and so on, making the enterprise circular rather than cumulative. For Brinkley, 'the weakness or even complete absence, of definition' makes 'the notion of "knowledge economy" rhetorical rather than analytically useful' (Brinkley, 2006, p. 3). However, as the knowledge economy comes laden with ideological connotations, it is not surprising that the rhetorical baggage accompanying definitions are, for some, part of the attraction. Definitional confusion can offer rhetorical convenience in helping to conceal as much as it reveals about capitalist social relations. In other words, pulled clear of the political economy of capitalist exploitation, the language of the 'knowledge economy' is free to wax lyrical about 'fundamental' changes in technology and occupations, which usher in 'creative industries' that combine 'new general purpose technologies ... with intellectual and knowledge assets – the "intangibles" of research, design, development, creativity, education, science, brand equity and human capital – to transform our economy' (Work Foundation, 2008, p. 9). Ambiguous, yet seductive too! In effect, everything from financial services, management consultancies, production and consumption of music CDs, DVD games and movies, books of fiction, PC software, digitalized TV, broadband and educational products, et cetera, are drawn together under the rubric of the 'knowledge economy' and measured in terms of value and employment. For example, we are informed that in the United Kingdom these 'creative industries' now account for £1 in every £10 GDP and employ up to two million people; financial services, including management consultancies and accountancy firms, now employ over one million people and account for over 9 per cent of GDP (HM Treasury 2005: 14); that 'employment in service sector jobs' – the sector said to be at the heart of the knowledge economy – had increased from '61 per cent of all jobs in 1978 to 82 per cent in 2005' (National Statistics, 2006); that 'Between 1995

D.W. Livingstone and D. Guile (eds.), The Knowledge Economy and Lifelong Learning:
A Critical Reader, 163–183.

and 2005 exports of these services grew by over 100 per cent in current terms compared with just over 50 per cent for more traditional service exports such as transport and travel' (Brinkley, 2006, p. 9); and that the knowledge economy is an international phenomenon, with up to 30 per cent of the future 'working population ... working directly in the production and diffusion of knowledge' (European Communities, 2004, p. 19). While these trends may be accurate, whether they constitute something called 'the knowledge economy' signifying an axial transformation in modern capitalist society is debatable.

And yet this is the working supposition of commentators. For some, the transformation is so profound that 'knowledge work' now usurps 'physical' or 'material' labour power in the creation of surplus value, forming a separate category of work from 'material' labour (Rikowsky, 2003). According to this view, the principal stimulus for surplus value in the knowledge economy is argued to be *knowledge and intellect* – regardless of whether it comes from the head of individuals, research labs or science communities – rather than good old-fashioned labour power. This is also the opinion of many who are part of the global capitalist elite. For example, while perhaps not intentionally applying the same concept of surplus value as Marxists do, Alan Greenspan, the former chairperson of the US Federal Reserve, embraces such a view when reflecting how,

> Over the past half-century, the increase in the value of raw materials has accounted for only a fraction of the overall growth of US gross domestic product. The rest of that growth reflects the embodiment of ideas in products and services that consumer's value. (Greenspan, 2003)

Indeed, the more general idea that 'The fuel that has driven the knowledge economy of today rests on a profound structural shift in consumer, collective, and business demand towards high value added, knowledge intensive goods and services' (Brinkley, 2008) has reached the status of orthodoxy among some academic and political communities. The symbiotic relation between technical and aesthetic assets in the production and design of commodities may have been dramatically highlighted by the marketing expertise of, for example, the Apple Corporation, However, the symbiosis is hardly new as the branding and marketing of cars by the likes of Ford Motors over the course of the twentieth century reveals.

Moreover, the belief that something radical is occurring gains apparent support from the dramatic rise in numbers entering post-compulsory education in Western economies, especially against the backdrop of a blurring of boundaries between youth and post-compulsory education systems. In global terms, according to the Centre on Democracy, Development, and Rule of Law (CDDRL), numbers in post-compulsory education have risen dramatically since 1960 (average of 40 for every 10,000 of the population), compared to 2000 (an average of 300 for every 10,000 of the population). If we take Western economies alone the figures are 50 per 10,000 for 1960 accelerating to 350 per 10,000 for the year 2000 (CDDRL, 2005, pp. 60–61). 'Globally, the percentage of the age cohort enrolled in tertiary education has grown from 19% in 2000 to 26% in 2007' (UNESCO, 2009, p. iv). This has led some to the observation that there are:

three dominant features of higher educational expansion in the modern period, which any explanation must address. First, the expansion vastly outruns changes in any plausible national-level independent variable, such as population or economic development levels. Second, the expansion is surprisingly homogeneous across radically varying national societies. And third, the expansion is dramatically concentrated in a particular time period. In short, the expansion of higher education has the quality of a single global 'event' or sea change occurring in the decades following World War II. (CDDRL, 2005, p. 13)

Taking the United Kingdom as a country-specific example confirms the hype: For three decades after 1945, the boundaries of education were, relatively speaking, clearly defined, both internally between different levels and also between education and wage labour. You were generally schooled from five to 16 years old and then either you entered wage labour immediately or you enrolled in post-compulsory education – technical (engineering and craft skills), further (post-16 pre-degree level vocational, arts, humanities) or higher (undergraduate and postgraduate). Today in the United Kingdom one can no longer speak of a *post*-compulsory phase of education; nor can one speak any longer of a relatively distinct boundary between technical, further or higher education, or between education and employment. Education policy has shifted away from the five to 16 years age limit towards a 14–19 years-of-age 'continuum,' which has effectively wiped out any lingering notion that education is an *option* after the age of sixteen. Moreover, policy changes have travelled a long way towards making education semi-compulsory up to and beyond the age of 19, through a range of initiatives including the effective merging of welfare to work (as with the Labour government's New Deal employment). The U.K. government has invested an enormous amount of time and resources into transforming the post-social democratic education landscape. Numbers of students entering further education (FE) and higher education (HE) more than doubled, from 2.2 to 4.7 million and from 1.1 to 2.4 million, respectively, in the decade between 1990–91 and 2002–03 (Economic and Social Research Council, 2006). By 2003, participation rates in HE alone stood at 44 per cent in England, 47 per cent in Northern Ireland, and 52 per cent in Scotland (Economic and Social Research Council, 2006). Moreover, three-quarters of the working population in Scotland are involved in education, euphemistically entitled 'lifelong learning,' whether at work or through distance learning and on the basis of 'learning contracts/accounts' (Scottish Executive, 2005). The institutions of education have also expanded. By 2006 there were 89 universities, a further 60 related HE institutions and 465 FE colleges employing 78,000 full-time HE academic staff and 59,000 full-time FE academic staff, respectively (Department for Education and Skills, 2004).

The emergence of a 'knowledge economy' and an expanding post-compulsory education sector may foster acceptance of the idea that knowledge can be separated from labour power as the source of surplus value. However, the idea does not hold much weight from the standpoint of Marxism, which argues that 'knowledge' cannot create value in isolation; it can only do so as part of the totality of the living labour power of which it is a part and which continues to remain subject to valorization within the circuit of capital. Surplus value cannot be plucked from ideas and intellect per se. While ideas and knowledge, separate from the more traditional notions of living labour power, may be worthy and use-valuable, this does not equate with ideas being the source of surplus value in and of themselves. We have only to reflect on how various Western economies have at one time or another come under scrutiny for falling behind Asian competitors because they have not sought to 'capitalize' on original conception; this is an indication at a very superficial level that creating value is distinct from the knowledge and intellect residing in either the heads of individual entrepreneurs, R&D departments, and/or science and research institutions, no matter how worthy or valuable they may be from a social point of view. Indeed, in the case of the United Kingdom, the argument from the government has always been that unless one converts ideas into action, then they are either frittered away or else some other economy/organization will make use of them as a source of competitive advantage (Department for Education and Skills, 2004).

It is, for example, commonplace to find current-day U.K. government-orchestrated concerns about information technology (IT) following the fate of the motorcycle and car industry in the 1970s due to South-East Asian economies winning out in the competition to 'capitalize' on new ideas and innovations – concerns which indicate the centrality of putting knowledge and ideas into practice in production processes. Such long-running concerns about 'marketing' ideas and knowledge are suggestive for confirming that value is what is created only if and when those ideas and innovations are put into production and consumption to be marketed for profit. For this to happen, as we argue below, ideas and innovations must enter the circuit of capital as *forms* of capital and be worked on and processed into *commodities* by living labour power.

The aim of this chapter is threefold: first, it defends the Marxist argument that the knowledge economy remains part and parcel of the valorization of labour power and so of exploitation of the working class. Second, it argues that the hidden secret of an expanding knowledge economy is to be found in the expanding domain of social labour vis-à-vis value-creating labour. Third, it argues that the hidden secret of mass post-compulsory education is founded on the necessary recalibrations of free and necessary labour time, which manifests in response to the expanding domain of social labour vis-à-vis value-creating labour.

THE KNOWLEDGE ECONOMY AND VALORIZATION

The idea that an emerging 'knowledge economy' can divorce itself from the political economy of conflict between labour and capital cannot be sustained. For Marxists, knowledge and ideas are part and parcel of the capitalist system and the categories of political economy that develop out of it. Knowledge has a 'constant' socio-economic value as part of *constant capital* (the product of past social labour power, the value of which is already determined by the socially necessary labour time taken to produce and sustain science and research communities and the labour power of individuals involved). However, if knowledge and so labour power lie outside of the market (if ideas are generated by the self-employed, or public sector bodies outside of the market, for example), then they do not impart extra value, but are part of capitalist overheads (which is simply another way of saying that they are part of constant capital). Only the labour power that subsequently works on and processes these ideas into mass commodities can generate surplus value (from which profit is derived). On the other hand, if 'knowledge workers' operate in the realm of *variable* capital, if, that is, they are employed by corporations (for example, employed by a large multinational in the music industry like EMI) and so are already within the circuit of capital, then the collective labour power of 'knowledge workers' *plays a part* in generating surplus value. Such knowledge workers may be more highly paid than those workers involved in either mass producing music products or the routine processing of data; however, their role in surplus value generation is not distinctly different from the pool of labour power employed by EMI to create the commodities of, in this case, the music and entertainment industry: their labour power is exploited as part of the general social labour power employed.

In the circuit of capital, where M = money, CC = constant capital, LP = labour power, P/V = production/valorization and C' = commodities embodying surplus value and M' is the monetary expression of surplus value, the inference is that value flows from every point in the circuit, but there is only one source of added or surplus value:

$$M - CC/LP - P/V - C' - M'$$

The logic implicit to this circuit is that in cases where knowledge and innovation work occurs *outside* of the private sector, it takes the form of CC, the value of which is determined by the socially necessary labour time taken to produce the science/research resources at the innovation/design phase, plus the value of the skilled labour power of knowledge workers engaged in the latter. Here knowledge workers play no part in the creation of surplus value, but pass on value to the finished commodity. In cases where knowledge and innovation work takes place *within* the circuit (undertaken directly by private firms), then the skilled labour power component takes the direct form of LP and so forms part of the living labour power from which surplus value is derived in P/V.

Knowledge, so called, is fundamental in raising the productive powers of labour. For example, with the creation and application of new computer-aided designs and software products and assembly lines producing commodities from Fords to football boots, can achieve greater flexibility in the use to which labour power is put in creating surplus value. To take another example, 'knowledge-rich' innovations such as on-line banking can ease the flow of credit and so can help to speed up the circuit of capital and, thereby facilitating value creation this way. Moreover, knowledge and innovation can provide competitive advantage for organizations and so the possibility to expand their market share, while powers of copyright and market status can ensure that a large part of the surplus value produced finds its way back to an elite of knowledge workers, managers, and capitalists, hence giving the impression that it is the latter that creates value.

The essential point here is that knowledge alone cannot create surplus value. The substance of value is abstract labour, the origins of which lie *within* the circuit of capital based on the exploitation of the collective labour power of workers involved in the industries concerned. In this respect, the value-creating potential of, for example, the IT industries rests fundamentally on the mass of unskilled labour power sourced globally, even though most of the value gets redistributed to capitalists, management and knowledge elites; in fact, this re- distributive process may give the illusion that the origin of most of the value creation lies with the latter and not the former, but this is precisely what Marx refers to as commodity fetishism: the process whereby value appears to be generated by things (and thought) distinct from living labour power (Marx, 1976, Ch. 1).

The argument that knowledge workers are distinct because, among other characteristics, they own their own means of production – the knowledge in their head – and are involved in highly complex team tasks, requiring a degree of self-governing autonomy not experienced by workers in the 'old economy,' is usually offered in support of the 'knowledge economy.' There are two main rejoinders: Firstly, while workers enjoy very different circumstances in their work place, it is hard even to conceptualize how knowledge work can ever be separated from physical work in the manner claimed by adherents to this perspective. Knowledge work is part of living labour power and what is described as 'the knowledge economy' is based on the interrelation of manual/mental, or tangible/intangible labour power, which is to say based on the same foundations as industrial capitalism. Moreover, engineering, accountancy, management consultancy and law firms, and other occupations who fall under the definition of 'knowledge work' produce surplus value as part of the wider productive powers of living labour power valorized by capital (Lowendahl et al., 2001). This echoes Marx's references to the all-round productive powers of labour, which embrace thinking and doing and how these become embedded in science, research and technology. Science, research and technology (inclusive of 'knowledge work') *combine* to increase the productive powers of labour, viewed as human activity in its widest sense (Lowendahl et al., 2001). In point of fact, for Marx, it is the indeterminacy of human activity as both the source of surplus labour/value and resistance to the valorization process which tends to reduce human labour to an abstraction (Marx, 1963, p. 46).

Secondly, there is nothing new in knowledge work and its centrality to capitalism. Knowledge workers in civil engineering, designing, architecture, teaching, management, and countless other professional practices were just as fundamental to early twentieth-century industrial capitalism as they are to modern forms of capitalist organization. What is new, as has been noted, is that more and more employment is undertaken in those sectors labelled 'knowledge industries.' However, such developments offer no basis for positing a divide between knowledge workers and labour; in fact, what characterizes modern organization is the increasingly social and seamless division of the labour process, in which, as one author puts it, 'knowledge develops through mutual engagement, joint enterprise and a shared repertoire. The understanding is thus picturing knowledge as a heterogeneous assemblage of tangible and non-tangible elements and as something strongly contextual' (Koch, 2004).

Moreover, the knowledge economy is actually hard to discern from the welter of job degradation we find in late capitalist society. The actual content of work performed by knowledge workers can be varied and rewarding, but can quite often bear a different reality to the status assumed by occupational labels. For example, the knowledge-handling involved in teaching and the servicing work carried out by professionals as diverse as social workers and accountants can become just as routine, codified and subject to technological controls as production line labour (Darr & Warhurst, 2008). Indeed, it has been suggested that knowledge work may not be so 'dissimilar from administrative occupations that have existed for most of the twentieth century' and so are 'not ... particularly distinctive' (Fleming et al., 2004, p. 738).

This 'gap' between actual work *content and occupational* status has a bearing on education too. The capitalist economy, driven by the exploitation of labour power and the necessity to compete for markets, sets its own internal barriers to the development of a highly skilled mass of knowledge workers, particularly on the scale necessary to establishing its functional fit with the expanding education industry. While some authors wax lyrical about the centrality of the development of skilled and autonomous human capital to the knowledge economy, it is also the case that deskilling and temporary low-skill employment contracts remain a core feature of 'knowledge work.' As one article points out, while

Permanent employment ... has been declining in the past two decades ... there has been a steady expansion of various forms of contingent work ... Employees (except for key personnel) become interchangeable, disposable, recallable, and transferable. (Szabó & Négyesi, 2005)

In point of fact, and contrary to the rosy view of an education system feeding the growing demands of the knowledge economy, there is strong evidence that the expansion of education is increasingly dysfunctional for the capitalist economy in the United Kingdom (Keep & Mayhew, 1999). It would appear that a growing service economy has led to the *relative degradation* of employed work that is out of fit with a burgeoning further and higher education industry. Most service sector employment growth is in low grade and poorly paid occupations in the health care, hospitality, cleaning, fast food, catering, and retail sectors (Thompson et al., 2001). Moreover the change towards the degradation of labour/low skill composition of work is structural rather than contingent. The Trades Union Congress (TUC) and academic researchers seem to concur that expanding further education and higher education cannot itself do much to generate the necessary demand for a skilled workforce from capitalists who are deeply embedded in 'product market strategies, service standards, work organization and job design, that make the issue appear to them as over-qualification' (TUC, 2006) in the context of a 'low-skill/low specification equilibrium' political economy (Finegold & Soskice, 1988; see also Payne, 2008).

Of course the sliding scale between skilled and non-skilled is not solely amenable to external technical measures, but is socially constructed through embedding in the contradictory relations of capitalism, between workers and managers, set within the primary contradiction between production for use and production for exchange value and profit. In this respect, what is recognized as skill by managers may be based on 'saturating' the work involved with technical competencies until it is more firmly under the controlling influence of management, while what is non-skilled may merely signify management's current failure to 'capture' and formalize labour power and worker organizations' current failure to capitalize on the *tacit* knowledge of workers (Sawchuk, 2006). The current stand-off between research outputs erring towards the prognosis of either deskilling or skilling (Aneesh, 2001) might well be explained by the fact that deskilling and the counter-tendency toward skilling are *inherent features* of the conflicting and contradictory nature of capitalism in the pursuit of worker control, worker autonomy and profitability. If anything, the trend over recent years is towards decimating secure middle-class jobs and eroding the content of the work itself, alongside the already burgeoning insecure employment as firms 'downsize,' 'right size' and 'rationalize' their workforce in the face of global pressures (Bauman, 1998; Giddens & Hutton, 2000). As Darr and Warhurst (2008) reflect, the overall unintended consequences are that:

> There are now more graduates than graduate jobs available. Graduates then cascade down into jobs previously not requiring degree-level education. Able to do so, firms respond by raising the entry tariff requirements to these jobs to the possession of a degree without necessarily changing the nature of the job. Analysing United Kingdom data, Purcell et al. ... highlight the growing number of previously non-graduate jobs that are now being infiltrated by graduates; so much so that it is better now to talk of 'the jobs that graduates do' rather than graduate jobs. (p. 30)

In summary, one can readily acknowledge that there are no simple deskilling trends. However, such acknowledgments should not obscure the fact that the contemporary dynamics of the capitalist economy do not appear to generate the skill requirements to substantiate the rise of a distinct elite of intellectual labour. Indeed, the argument so far can be boiled down to two counter-claims against claims that the knowledge economy is something distinct and indeed progressive: first, that the knowledge economy and knowledge work are part and parcel of capitalism and the exploitation of labour power; second, that modern-day capitalism is beset by very traditional contradictory processes of skill formation and job degradation that are out of 'fit' with claims of a burgeoning market for highly skilled knowledge workers. However, this still leaves us bereft of an understanding of why there is such a great deal of attention on the 'knowledge economy' and of the relationship between the knowledge economy and the expanding domain of knowledge production in the formal education system.

The second part of this chapter will address these issues. It does so by making labour power – the logic of labour – and not capital the active subject. The next section argues that the knowledge economy and its associated emphasis on ideas and intangible activities is part of what Hardt and Negri term immaterial labour power, an aspect of socialized labour that has the potential to defy valorization. In other words, the knowledge economy signifies the declining rule of value relations as the bedrock for productive activity. To get to the point where we can debate this, the section first situates the above discussion within the broader context of a neo-liberalism based on what Harvey terms 'the political economy of "primitive accumulation,"' or 'accumulation by dispossession' (Harvey, 2003) and the hegemony of finance capital. A subsequent section, again in discussing the 'logic of labour,' shifts attention to the contradiction between 'necessary' and 'free' labour that is implied by immaterial labour power. It will be argued that in *general* terms, the development of the productive powers of labour offer favourable material conditions for the relative expansion of free labour. However, because this productive power and this contradiction between 'necessary' and 'free' is expressed through the capital and labour relation (i.e., antagonism), then the very nature and scope of what is 'necessary' and what is 'free' labour becomes largely embedded in, defined by, this antagonism. To develop this point, the chapter will return to the trends in post-compulsory education and the knowledge economy outlined above to provide the focus for arguing that, as a moving contradictory force, the capital–labour relation transforms 'necessary' to 'unnecessary' and 'free' to '(un-) free' labour, often making the struggle for 'necessary' and 'free' labour, from the vantage point of social labour, more latent than actual. Of course, whether latent or actual, the power of social labour is the source of the capitalist system's declining power to transform labour power into surplus value under profitable conditions and the more this continues the more powerful will become the 'logic of labour' in determining what is and what is not 'necessary' and 'free' labour.

KNOWLEDGE, ECONOMY, AND SOCIAL LABOUR

For Harvey (2003), neo-liberalism represents the political economy of 'primitive accumulation.' With Marx, primitive accumulation referred specifically to the accumulation of exploitable labour power through the enclosure movement, state laws on vagrancy and forcing labour into the capitalist factories emerging in town and cities thrown up in the heat (and blood) of the capitalist agricultural and industrial revolutions. For Harvey, the concept of primitive accumulation can be broadened out to include any resource that is 'external' to the laws of capital accumulation within contemporary capitalism. For example, the stripping of public assets back into the realms of capital and the new forms of *flexploitation* of labour power, driven more intensely by the erosion of collective labour resistance, provides a platform in the short term for absorbing capital surpluses, while it also soaks up surplus labour into more poorly paid and insecure jobs and/or makes this surplus less of a financial burden (due to the declining value of welfare payments), or else invisible as workfare discipline forces the unemployed off the official radar.

In the United States, this form of political economy has reached its apex; the United Kingdom is not so far behind, with Europe being gradually pulled under its orbit. This context has allowed global capital 'operating through the public and private pension funds of the US, the UK, the Netherlands, Canada, Australia and Japan [to] ensure the level of ownership in virtually all publicly quoted companies in the world is large enough to permit the effective involvement of owners in the governance of those corporations' (Monks, 2001, p. 5); a governance which injects short term gains in shareholder value through rationalization, merger and acquisition, as much as investment (Littler & Innes, 2003).

Harvey is not by any means alone in noting the hyper-exploitative and crisis-ridden nature of neo-liberalism and how it is connected to a resurgent imperialism. Such a view is common currency in both Marxist and non-Marxist accounts of the global economy. However, Harvey's crucial insight is the idea that the logic of capital is not only fragile but is premised for survival on an ongoing and far-from-decisive taking back into value relations of what had (and in some cases still remains) 'outside' of capitalism (or put another way, 'inside' the spaces of resistance that capital has either had to cede or still finds difficult to colonize), from commonly held land, the welfare state and social wages to the tacit knowledge labour retains for itself. However, Harvey's insights are limited by the capital logic approach he takes, in which sooner or later accumulation by dispossession closes off spaces of resistance, only for them to open up on new fronts, to eventually be closed off again. Therefore, the insight that capital is fragile and always in struggle to command labour power is frittered away within an eventually endless process of accumulation by dispossession. As De Angelis argues, however, the 'outside' is continually being created and recreated in struggle. The 'value practices' of capital to subordinate other values to those of the market and the circuit of capital are in struggle with movements deriving 'value practices based on other measures of dignity, freedom and commons' on the 'frontline of social reproduction' (De Angelis, 2007).

In this respect, there is a need to emphasis the logic of labour as well as the logic of capital. Hardt and Negri (2000) assist us in doing this by providing a basis for situating the knowledge economy within broader transitions in the value relation characteristic of late capitalism. They offer a paradigm of thinking in which value relations are no longer permanent and they provide the intellectual space to consider value relations in transition. As mentioned earlier, it is fundamental to the assumption that value relations can develop and take transitional forms that the transition simultaneously harbour positives and negatives for capital. In this respect, the transition in value relations offers scope for increasing exploitation of labour power and simultaneously the space for the growing social power of labour to set limits to accumulation, limits that also point beyond capitalism. The paradigm shift means that within Marxism there needs to be an acceptance of the 'logic of labour power' as well as the 'logic of capital.' As I now go on to explain, placing the 'logic of labour' to the fore opens up a more dialectical approach to understanding the knowledge economy, and with it the possibility of explaining transitory forms of capitalism that capital finds increasingly difficult to control.

Hardt and Negri (2000) argue that capital accumulation pivots increasingly on immaterial labour power, or the general social power of labour that both capital and individuals draw from directly. The concept of immaterial labour refers to the sort of labour engaged in by knowledge work identified earlier. However, for Hardt and Negri such labour holds a deeper significance as the power set in motion by general social labour with the potential to transcend the current division of labour between constant capital and living labour power. The emergence of immaterial labour power offers the potential basis for communities and collectives to confront capitalist values and offer alternative forms of living and producing. Moreover, immaterial labour power – labour power upon which late capitalism now depends – is affective labour of care, personal relations, and communal networks, in which case capital develops its opposite: from the control of labour power as abstract atomized labour power to socially networked labour power. The key point is that the relations and networks that bring labour together are central to surplus value generation, yet their deepening and development offer a basis for labour's direct social co-operation, which may potentially transcend sectoral boundaries. The development of a social enterprise or third sector and growth of the knowledge or information commons are two examples. Labour activity stretches the boundaries of 'public' and 'private' into a 'third sector' (charities, social enterprises and informal social organizations), motivated by social values, are not-for-profit and attempt to maintain relative independence from the state. In the United Kingdom, the third sector has a labour force of 870,000 and an income of £116 billion (Cabinet Office, U.K., 2009, p. 1). The fact that in recent decades this sector has grown at the same time as it has been subject to commodification and state support (Williams, 2005, p. 219) is testimony to the struggle being waged over the nature of social labour power underpinning the third sector economy. Meanwhile, the development of the internet has spurred the struggle to defy and reconstitute mechanisms of capitalist enclosure of ownership rights over intellectual labour and knowledge flows (Stiglitz, 1999), while attempts to open up to the commons have been met by resistance and attempts to re-harness the same within the commodity form and so valorization (Fuch, 2010).

In this respect, capital is both powerful and fragile because the more intense forms of exploitation described by Harvey as primitive accumulation are *also* based on areas of accumulation that threaten to transcend capitalism, or, at the very least, threaten the basis of production for value. As Marx argued in *Capital*, the tendency in capitalism is for capital to drive beyond its own measure of value due to the relative displacement of capital for living labour power, the source of surplus value. This same tendency is elaborated on by Hardt and Negri as the stage of immaterial labour power, the substance of which is the setting in motion of the general social power of labour and so setting in motion a bio-politics from below that threatens the basis of capitalist value relations. What we now conceive in terms of the knowledge economy heralds not only the promise for exploiting ideas for capital, but more crucially the development of social production so porous that it transcends the narrower foundations of valorization for capital.

Hardt and Negri refer to various anti-capitalist groups as a force for change – part of a 'multitude,' differentiated by the issues they prioritize (class struggle, environment, gender, race) and by the social group(s) they aspire to or to represent. However, it ought to be stressed that their argument concerning the fragility of capitalism and power of labour does not presuppose that all of these disparate groups either are or will in the near future unite to provide a power as great as that of capital. There is, of course, the possibility of unity, but what leads to the fragility of capitalism for these authors is something *related to anti-capitalist groups: something they are manifestations of* and something they also *power forward*. This something has two related components. On the one hand, capital finds it increasingly difficult to absorb surplus labour. Both the proportion of labour acting as reserve army of labour and labour that has become separated from the labour market increase, and so become increasingly separated from capital. Relative to the enormous amount of capital set in motion, labour power, the source of surplus value, becomes increasingly displaced and placed 'outside' capital. On the other hand, the origin of the value created by labour power that is employed by capital is both difficult to locate (which labour power is 'productive' and which is 'unproductive?') and to control because it is the product of the *general social power of labour*. Moreover, the labour power employed by capital is increasingly a source of labour power, set in motion to increase surplus value that deepens, develops and networks this general social power of labour.

These two components are developing tendencies which, taken together, are the *ontological basis* for the fragility of capitalism outlined by Hardt and Negri. At a minimum level they negatively impact on the work ethic related to wage labour, provide a basis in the spaces of resistance they open up for the multitude of anti-capitalist struggles, and so generate the *possibility* that they may form unities of greater political strength. At the optimum level this calls into question the rule of capital per se and raises the power of people to collectively control their own lives beyond capitalism. I think Hardt's and Negri's point is that society hovers somewhere unstably between the minimum and maximum; a situation in which raising profits and maintaining control over the social power of labour often collide, the one (profit maximizing) diluting the effects of the other (control). Arguably (as I will elaborate in the next section), it is this unstable situation that provides the context for recent developments and links between the economy and education.

Of course, Hardt and Negri have been criticized by Marxists for moving away from Marx's central categories of political economy and the centrality of class struggle, and for glossing over the real divisions between high and low status workers in the service sector and focusing on the 'first world,' when the majority of the world's workforce work in agriculture and industry are experiencing super-exploitation. Moreover, critics do not think much of Hardt's and Negri's use of post-structuralist language, especially terminology like 'bio-power,' or their tendency to adapt to business management rhetoric concerning immaterial labour in the new economy and the confusion between this and 'the multitude' (Callinicos, 2001; Thompson, 2005).

However, these critics also tend to accept capital on its own terms as a never-ending narrative of capitalist accumulation, worker control and resistance, followed by new methods and techniques of accumulation and exploitation, from Fordism to post-Fordism and regulated capitalism to neo-liberalism ad infinitum. These terms offer little or no space for understanding fundamental changes occurring in late capitalism. And, while one might agree with criticisms made of Hardt and Negri (which amount to arguing that they have increasingly tended to displace a Marxist critical political economy of capitalism for post-structural sociology as the theoretical core for analysing contemporary society), it might also be noted that at least Hardt and Negri attempt to keep in focus the principle on which Marx's critique stood, namely, to investigate not only the origins and ascendancy of a mode of production *but also the conditions of its transition and supersession.*

Therefore, limitations aside, from a Marxist perspective the salience of their approach is to highlight labour as an active change agent in struggle against capital, while the saliency of their analysis of immaterial labour would seem to be the insight that, whether or not you work in agriculture, industry or services, you are drawn (no matter how unevenly) into a dense web of global interconnections due to advances in IT, and that this redefines each of the industries, combining what is also uneven and drawing labour together as a social force with the *potential* to transform capitalism.

Wright (2005), in providing a detailed and valuable critique of Hardt and Negri, also identifies what is profound in their argument about modern day capitalism. He reflects how for Hardt and Negri the 'logic of capital is no longer functional to development, but is simply command for its own reproduction,' and so increasingly adrift from labour value as its measure, when the reality is that 'Capital is obliged by its very nature, and for as long as we are stuck with it, to pose "labour time" ... as sole measure and source of wealth' (p. 19). Wright quite correctly sees a contradiction here. But capital *is* contradictory and surely this is Hardt's and Negri's point: capital *is*, on the one hand, obliged by its very nature to pose labour time as the sole measure of value; however, in developing the social power of labour, capital *also*, on the other hand, poses alternative forms of living, which it then is called upon to discipline and control and seek to re-harness to capital.

Here, Hardt and Negri draw implicit attention to a central aspect of Marx and Engel's critique of capital and its inherent transitional properties. Marx and Engels characterized socialism as relations of *direct association.* Marx and Engels were also very clear that labour is already social in an ascendant capitalism too, but indirectly so, through the practice of commodity fetishism, or the power of money capital as the essential mediating and alien social force. The point is that transitional capitalism, signified as the 'knowledge economy,' implies this fetish is losing social power under the logic of direct forms of social labour. If one were to use Marxist terminology re: Hardt and Negri, then what is being argued is that capitalism is at a stage where the primary wellsprings of surplus value are increasingly forms of labour engaged in direct association, albeit alienated within capitalism. In other words, the core area of accumulation in late capitalism necessitates development of forms of *direct association in labour activity*, the very forms that threaten to subvert the capitalist system and its powers of control over labour.

In summary, discourses about the 'knowledge economy' are manifestation of deeper concerns regarding broader transitions within, and potentially beyond, capitalist relations, at the heart of which is the development of forms of social labour that increasingly tend to escape capitalist measurement, making both control over labour and surplus value increasingly difficult. Moreover, as we now move on to consider, this capacity to escape measurement in terms of value occurs in the context of the general displacement of labour for capital, which is manifest in capitalist development. Indeed, the role of an expanding compulsory education industry can be understood in terms of the latter.

SURPLUS LABOUR AND THE STRUGGLE OVER NECESSARY AND FREE LABOUR TIME

This section recognizes that post-compulsory education remains functional to the requirements of the capitalist economy. However, the main argument is that the expanding post-compulsory education system occurs against the backdrop of the developing gap between a reserve army of labour for capital and a population surplus to capital, which compounds the contradiction between necessary and free labour time: post-compulsory education, among other changes, is one attempt to resolve the irresolvable.

For Marxism, the long-term tendency is for living labour power (variable capital) to decline relative to capital (constant capital) in the production of commodities. Marx described how developments in the working population are the outcome of two contradictory tendencies that employment policy must ultimately manage. The first tendency is for a long-term demand for labour power to decline relative to the increase in capital, which is punctuated in the short term by the expansion of labour into new markets and industries. As Marx suggests, 'Since the demand for labour is determined not by the amount of capital as a whole, but by its variable constituent alone, then demand falls progressively with the increase in the total capital ... instead of rising in proportion to it' (Marx, 1963, p. 590). The second tendency is for the economy to lurch through a process of long-term booms and slumps punctuated by short-term business-cycle oscillations. For Marx, while the first tendency compels the need for labour mobility and provides the basis for the development of a labour force surplus to capital, the second tendency makes this surplus a necessary prerequisite of capital accumulation in order to serve as a reserve army of labour. For, as Marx suggests, 'It is capitalistic accumulation itself that constantly produces, and produces in the direct ratio of its own energy and extent, a relatively redundant population of labourers ... for the average needs of the self-expansion of capital' (Marx, 1963, p. 590).

The trend is not uniform, but dialectical. For one thing the displacement of labour power from one industry can be absorbed and usually extended by, for example, the extension of labour power into new or developing industries. There could, for example, be a significant accumulation of capital based entirely on labour-intensive building equipment or mining equipment, et cetera. However, contemporary forms of accumulation in the West – as indicated by the relative displacement of labour from first agriculture and now, increasingly, services (e.g., the rationalization of labour in the banking sector) – are dominated by capital-intensive growth (European Community, 2001). This is no surprise, since the key to increased surplus value on the basis of an upward movement in profit rates is making labour power more productive by increasing the use of technology and science in the form of constant capital. This makes the displacement of variable capital for constant capital a tendency inherent in the nature of the capital-labour relation, and a foundation for the development of a surplus population that can and does outpace the function of reserve army of labour *for capital* (Rosdolsky, 1977). The welfare state and expansion of the public sector has absorbed much of this surplus labour, concealing the tension between the reserve army for capital and labour surplus to capital. More recently, however, as intimated above in the discussion of Harvey's analysis of the capitalist state and primitive accumulation, the state has been attempting to cut back employment, either directly or indirectly through privatization and deregulation of public sector provision of services. The decline of trade union power has also made it easier for capital to cut back on jobs while using its power over labour to revitalize a reserve army from workers it retains, through increasing working hours, intensification of work and a portfolio of 'flexible working' practices.

All of the above created a widening gap between a reserve army for capital and a population surplus to capital requirements – in the economic upswing, which lasted until the financial crash in 2008. The present political and economic climate of escalating unemployment and crisis for capital has only served to more clearly expose this gap (Byrne, 1999). The developing contradiction between surplus population and reserve army requires the capitalist state to pursue a social and economic policy that is able to facilitate the conditions for the recommodification of labour power, while also providing policy mechanisms which act to discipline/manage a population surplus to capital. *All of this provides the material basis for a political project to develop around the tendency to transform free time for and against Capital.* In the normal functioning of capitalism, disposable labour time is managed by reconverting it into surplus labour (value), which means the surplus labour is reabsorbed along with further capital expansion, or else 'surplus labour' is, as Marx argues, converted into 'free time, for a few,' the ruling class. In this sense, for Marx, the developing category of disposable labour time relative to necessary labour time maintains an *antithetical existence* under capitalism. However, Marx (1973) also emphasized that the mass of workers are drawn to the struggle to end this *antithetical existence* of disposable labour time so as to transform it until it is 'measured by the needs of the social individual, and the development of the power of social production,' to be 'calculated for the wealth of all' (p. 708). Under present conditions, where surplus labour grows at a faster rate than any functions it may have as a reserve army of labour for capital, then the issue of managing and so sustaining the antithetical existence of disposable time becomes more crucial to the survival of the capitalist system. Indeed, the modern capitalist state has manoeuvred to manage surplus labour in a number of disparate and mostly ad-hoc ways.

The inexorable rise in the rate of the prison population has been one consequence: it is estimated that in 1993 the total prison population in England and Wales was 41,600 (BBC, 2006), but by 2011 it had more than doubled to 86,654 (*Morning Star*, 2011). As pressure on the resources of the prison and justice systems mount, so too has the barrack-style 'lockdown' mentality has spread into the community. For example, the 1998 Crime and Disorder Act should be interpreted as part of a raft of policies that have shifted emphasis from youth justice to the criminalization of 'problem' families (Muncie, 1999, p. 153), 'corralled in housing estates and neighbourhoods which take on ever more characteristics of the most impoverished regions of the world' (Jones & Novak, 1999, p. 102).

However, perhaps the most prominent policy to contain and manage surplus labour and sustain control over 'free time' has been to expand training and education. In this respect, from the mid-1980s, governments of all shades have made a concerted effort to develop a workfare state that increases labour-market attachment. In the United Kingdom alone, the introduction of Training and Enterprise Councils (TECs) in 1990, the 1986 Restart Programme, the 1989 Social Security Act, the 1995 Job Seekers Act, the 1996 Right to Work Act, and the post-1998 New Deal/Welfare to Work programmes have all worked towards increasing the reserve army of labour and maintaining labour-market discipline. It is against this background that one has the expanding jurisdiction of post-compulsory education, which plays an increasingly important ideological role in sustaining the *antithetical existence of disposable labour time*. The stakes are high: the struggle to end the *antithetical existence of disposable labour time* not only seeks to transform disposable time towards the needs of the all-round individual, but also holds out the possibility of the qualitative transformation of the realm of necessary labour. Necessary labour will lose its one-sided nature (as something we, by and large, tend to shirk) and become an arena in which one can more easily develop one's productive powers and capacities. *Therefore, the struggle over the form of disposable labour time transforms not only the realm of freedom from necessary labour, but also the way necessary labour is conceived and carried out.* The struggle, which capital must find new ways of resisting, is for a society in which the measure of wealth is no longer surplus labour (creating value), but rather the increase in disposable labour time, 'time for the full development of the individual' (Marx, 1973, p. 708).

It is within this political economy that one can situate the expansion of post-compulsory education and lifelong learning regimes. In particular, the rationale for expanding post-compulsory education is defined increasingly in terms of its mediating role in harnessing social need to value production; which is to say, is defined increasingly in terms of *inculcating* forms of commodity fetishism within the cliental – students. Such a context can perhaps further illuminate the current mantra, in which students are not so much educated as caught within a discursive web 'positioning' them as future employees or sellers of labour power, and educators are regarded as 'producers' of practical and work-relevant knowledge, the 'trainers,' of the next generation of 'productive workers.' In an era of declining capital, the intent is just as much ideological as a function of the technical requirements of capitalism for trained workers.

Payne, for example, has drawn attention to the way in which the meaning of 'skill' as the mainstay of learning within an expanding post-compulsory education has been hollowed out to encompass personal habits and social etiquette. Payne suggested that, along with the expansion of the service sector, skill has become something of a free-floating metaphor, escaping the usual definitions surrounding technical knowledge to encompass anything and everything from 'communication skills' to good dress sense and a positive attitude to the 'work ethic.' According to Payne (2000, p. 361), current definitions of 'skill' operative within post-compulsory education have expanded almost beyond meaning to include a range of 'soft,' 'generic,' 'transferable,' 'social' and 'interactionist' skills, basically indefinable and frequently indistinguishable from personal characteristics, behaviours and attitudes, all of which would rarely have been conceived of as skills in the past. Indeed, the free-floating nature of the meaning of skills and training has proved to be fertile ground for the discourse of *vocationalism*, which has served as a vehicle towards colonizing post-compulsory education with the language and practice of the market and commodification. The latter then dovetails with workfare regimes. This *vocational discourse* is clearly evident throughout the post-compulsory education industry. Befitting the attempt to harness and control the forms of disposable labour time, the discourse draws on the narrative of 'preparation for work' and the imbibing of specific and generic work-related 'skills and competencies,' in the context of a crisis-ridden capitalist system that can provide, for many, at most a revolving door into a mixture of poor work, low-level education, and welfare. In other words, education is increasingly reduced to a commodity, a reduction that is becoming more all-embracing, but in a manner in which the use value of the commodity labour power *for* capital becomes highly variable and unstable because the primary attempt is to bolster a declining objective basis for commodity fetishism and not so much to expand accumulation.

CONCLUSION

This chapter has been principally concerned with providing a Marxist critique of the knowledge economy literature. It has argued that the knowledge economy remains inherent to capitalist exploitation of labour, but more crucially that it should be understood as part of the value relation in transition, with a focus upon the logic of labour power and the increasing difficulties of capitalism in containing the power of social labour within the fragile bounds of late capitalism. In this concluding section, the chapter contends that one response by capital, among others, has been to atomize labour power through a burgeoning post-compulsory education system, which acts as a surplus labour repository, alongside its economic and ideological roles. Under conditions of late capitalism the economic function of education remains crucial, but a fundamental reason why post-compulsory education is expanding is due to the supporting role it provides in regulating free time as surplus labour to be controlled and manipulated *within* capitalism.

While the economic function of education remains crucial to the capitalist political economy, ideological reproduction has become central to present developments described above in which the objective conditions of commodity fetishism have become weakened, leaving the capitalist system also requiring an extension of subjective means of commodity fetishism. Specifically, the degree of importance given to ideological reproduction in the articulation of cultural, social and ideological reproductive functions of education depends on the relative strength of commodity fetishism as an active and internal form of economic and moral control over labour. The greater socialization of labour through forms alien to money (and so abstract labour) – through, for example, immaterial or affective labour networks – implies that what is central to capitalism – commodity fetishism and so the dominance of value over use value – becomes increasingly dysfunctional and, as long as capitalism continues to exist, becomes the focus of attempted partial reforms or replacements. In such a transitory period, institutions, which within an ascendant capitalism served specific functions, no longer have exactly the same function. The delineation of their plurality of functions becomes both blurred and increasingly contradictory in terms of their original underlying objectives.

In this respect, institutions such as education must increasingly find their rationale in the act of imposing an external mediation between value and use value (and therefore reproductive labour) and in this sense must devise their rationale increasingly in terms of regulating or bolstering relations of commodity fetishism. For example, education, which has both an economic and ideological role to play, is particularly sensitive to the blurring of its previous reproductive functions and the mediating roles it takes on within late capitalism vis-à-vis the maintenance of social order. Not only is the expansion of post-compulsory education understandable in this context, so too is the increasing role that ideological reproduction plays in this expansion. In particular, the rationale for expanding post-compulsory education is defined increasingly in terms of its mediating role in harnessing social need to value production; which is to say, is defined increasingly in terms of *inculcating* forms of commodity fetishism within their clientele – students. The special attention given to 'employability,' work experience as fundamental attributes of the learning experience in higher education, is testimony to the centrality of market sentiments. So too is the increasing focus on pricing degrees, courses, and units of study along a continuum defined by the assumed future economic capital students can cash in. The present U.K. government's introduction of fees for degrees paid back as a debt related to future students earning power is very much ideological in nature. Many students will earn below the amount triggering debt repayment and so the degree will be effectively free.

However, the crucial point is that, ideologically, the framework within which choices are made concerning which degree to take and value is that given by the market place in general and the labour market in particular. In all these ways, education as a social need is harnessed to the logic and the sentiments of the capitalist economy.

The strong ideological component sustaining the expansion of higher education is never more exposed than by the language of 'employability.' Far from guaranteeing the movement from education to employment, 'employability' implies one's permanent state of readiness, both physically and mentally, to be employed and, if not employed, to be in a permanent state of employment readiness. In this respect, higher education's ideological reproductive role is also to marshal disposable labour time, and by so doing draw off working-class resistance to the *antithetical existence of disposable labour time*. The stakes are high because the struggle to end the antithetical existence of disposable labour time not only seeks to transform disposable time towards the needs of the all-round individual, but also holds out the possibility of the qualitative transformation of the realm of necessary labour. The ongoing struggle to categorize human activity as *variable capital* colours the general disposition towards necessary labour as something we, by and large, tend to shirk. Hence the qualitative transformation of necessary labour implied by the struggle to end the antithetical existence of disposable labour time, means human activity will lose its one-sided nature and become an arena in which one can more easily develop one's productive powers and capacities. Therefore, the struggle over the form of disposable labour time transforms not only the realm of freedom from necessary labour, but also the way necessary labour is conceived and carried out. Higher education spatially and ideologically performs the service of marshalling this disposable labour time and assists in directing human activity within the category of variable capital. The struggle, which capital must find new ways of resisting, is for a society in which the measure of wealth is no longer surplus labour (creating value), but rather the increase in disposable labour time, 'time for the full development of the individual' (Marx, 1973). In this respect, it is no accident that the rhetoric of education and lifelong learning draws on such notions as the 'developed individual.' But it does so not from the point of view of individual liberation, but from that of the value relation as part of the ideological struggle to avoid the possibilities inherent in disposable/free labour time and the limits imposed on such possibilities by the capitalist system. In other words, the expanding education industry certainly has an economic function to develop the level of skills necessary for capital accumulation, but it also functions increasingly as a barracks for surplus and underemployed labour power, harnessing and colonizing the implied free time towards the values of a capitalist system and away from the attraction of non-capitalist sentiments or pathways that may point beyond capitalist relations.

REFERENCES

Aneesh, A. (2001). Skill saturation: Rationalization and post-industrial work. *Theory and Society, 30*(3), 363–396.

Bauman, Z. (1998). *Work, consumerism and the new poor*. Philadelphia: Open University Press.

BBC On-line. (2006). Average prison population per region. Retrieved from http://news.bbc.co.uk/1/shared/spl/hi/pop_ups/06/uk_prisons_in_the_uk/html/1.stm.

Brinkley, I. (2006). *Defining the knowledge economy*. London: Work Foundation. Retrieved from www.flacso.edu.mx/openseminar/downloads/brinkley_S3.pdf.

Brinkley, I. (2008). *The knowledge economy: How knowledge is reshaping the economic life of nations*. Work Foundation. Retrieved from www.theworkfoundation.com/research/publications/publicationdetail.aspx?oItemId=41&parentPageID=103&PubType.

Byrne, D. (1999). *Social exclusion*. Buckingham: Open University Press.

Cabinet Office, UK. (2009, July). *Key facts on the third sector*. Retrieved from webarchive.nationalarchives.gov.uk/+/http://www.cabinetoffice.gov.uk/media/231495/factoids.pdf.

Callinicos, A. (2001, Autumn). Tony Negri in perspective. *International Socialism*, 33–61.

Centre on Democracy, Development, and the Rule of Law (CDDRL). (2005, January). The world-wide expansion of higher education. *Stanford Institute on International Studies, 32*.

CSR Europe. (2001). *Lifelong learning at the heart of an entrepreneurial and inclusive Europe*. Business Input to the European Commission Consultation on Lifelong Learning. Retrieved from www.csreurope.org/uploadstore/cms/docs/CSRE_Pub_lifelonglearning_report.pdf.

Darr, A. & Warhurst, C. (2008). Assumptions, assertions and the need for evidence: Debugging debates about knowledge workers. *Current Sociology, 56*(1), 25–45.

De Angelis, M. (2007). The beginning of history: Value struggles and global capital. London: Pluto.

Department for Education and Skills (DfES). (2004). *Statistics of education: Education and training statistics for the UK*. Retrieved from www.dfes.gov.uk/rsgateway.

Economic and Social Research Council (ESRC). (2003). *ESRC society today*. Retrieved from www.esrcsocietytoday.ac.uk/ESRCInfoCentre/facts/UK/index14.aspx?ComponentId=7039&SourcePageId=14975.

European Communities (EC). (2004). *Facing the challenge*. Luxembourg: Office for Official Publications of the European Communities.

Finegold, D. & Soskice, D. (1988). The failure of training in Britain: Analysis and Prescription. *Oxford Review of Economic Policy, 4*(3), 21–53.

Fleming, P., Harvey, B., & Sewell, G. (2004). A little knowledge is a dangerous thing: Getting below the surface of the growth of 'knowledge work' in Australia. *Work, Employment and Society, 18*(4), 725–747.

Fuch, C. (2010). Labour and information capitalism on the internet. *Information Society, 26*(3), 179–196.

Giddens, A. & Hutton, W. (2000). *On the edge: Living with global capitalism*. London: Cape.

Greenspan, A. (2003). *Financial markets*. Conference of the Federal Reserve Bank of Atlanta, Sea Island, Georgia. Retrieved from www.federalreserve.gov/BoardDocs/speeches/2003/20030404/default.htm.

Hardt, M. & Negri, A. (2000). *Empire*. Cambridge, MA: Harvard University Press.

Harvey, D. (2003). *The new imperialism*. Oxford: Oxford University Press.

HM Treasury. (2005). *The UK financial services sector: Rising to the challenges and opportunities of globalisation*. London: HM Treasury. Retrieved from www.guidance-research.org/future-trends/banking/links.

Keep, E. & Mayhew, K. (1999). The assessment: Knowledge, skills and competitiveness. *Oxford Review of Education Policy, 15*(1), 1–15.

Koch, C. (2004). The tyranny of projects: Teamworking, knowledge production and management in consulting engineering. *Economic and Industrial Democracy, 25*(2), 277–300.

Littler, C.R. & Innes, P. (2003). Downsizing and de-knowledging the firm. *Work, Employment and Society, 17*(1), 73–100.

Lowendahl, B., Revang, Ø., & Fosstenløkken, S. (2001). Knowledge and value creation in professional service firms: A framework for analysis. *Human Relations, 54*(7), 911–931.

Marx, K. (1963). *Theories of surplus value* (Vol. 1). Progress: Moscow.

Marx, K. (1973). *Grundrisse.* Harmondsworth: Pelican.

Marx, K. (1976). *Capital* (Vol. 1). London: Penguin.

Monks, R. (2001). *The new global investors.* Chichester: Capstone.

Morning Star. (2011). Britain's jail population hits new high. Retrieved from www.morningstaronline.co.uk/news/content/view/full/108494.

National Statistics. (2006). *The labour market in the wider economy.* Retrieved from www.statistics.gov.uk/cci/nugget.asp?id=1423.

Payne, J. (2000). The unbearable lightness of skill: The changing meaning of skill in UK policy discourses and some implications for education and training. *Journal of Education Policy, 15*(3), 353–369.

Payne, J. (2008). Skills in context: What can the UK learn from Australia's skill ecosystem projects? *Policy and Politics, 36*(3), 307–323.

Rikowsky, R. (2003). Value – The life blood of capitalism: Knowledge is the current key. *Policy Futures in Education, 1*(1), 160–178.

Rooney, D., Hearn, G., & Ninan, A. (2005). *Handbook of the knowledge economy.* Cheltenham: Edward Elgar.

Sawchuk, P.H. (2006). Use-value and the re-thinking of skills, learning and the labour process. *Journal of Industrial Relations, 48*(5), 593–617.

Scottish Executive. (2005). *Participation education in lifelong learning.* Retrieved from www.scotland.gov.uk/Publications/2005/12/01155233/52345.

Stiglitz, J. (1999). Knowledge as a global public good. In Kaul, I, Grunberg, I., and Stern, M.A. (Eds.), *Global public goods: International cooperation in the 21st century.* United Nations Development Programme. New York: Oxford University Press. Retrieved from www.undp.org/globalpublicgoods/TheBook/globalpublicgoods.pdf#page=346.

Szabó, K. & Négyesi, A. (2005) The spread of contingent work in the knowledge-based economy. *Human Resource Development Review, 4*(1), 63–85.

Thompson, P. (2005, Summer). Foundations of empire: A critique of Hardt and Negri. *Capital and Class, 86,* 73–98.

Thompson, P., Warhurst, C., & Callahan, G. (2001). Ignorant theory and knowledgeable workers: Interrogating the connections between knowledge, skills and services. *Journal of Management Studies, 38*(7), 923–942.

Trades Union Congress (TUC). (2006). *Submission to the Leitch Review of Skills.* Retrieved from www.tuc.org.uk/skills/tuc-10183-f0.cfm#tuc-10183-2.

UNESCO. (2009). *Trends in global higher education: Tracking an academic revolution.* Retrieved from http://unesdoc.unesco.org/images/0018/001831/183168e.pdf.

Work Foundation. (2008). *The knowledge economy: How knowledge is reshaping the economic life of nations.* Retrieved from www.theworkfoundation.com/research/publications/publicationdetail.aspx?oItemId=41&parentPagel.

Williams, C. (2005). A commodified world? Mapping the limits of capitalism. London: Zed Books.

Wright, S. (2005, August). *Reality check: Are we living in an immaterial world?* Retrieved from www.metamute.org/en/node/5594.

SECTION TWO: SPECIFIC CHALLENGES

SECTION TWO

Specific Challenges

INTRODUCTION

Much of the discussion about the role of knowledge in the economy focuses, as many contributors to Section 1 indicated, on either the contribution of research-based knowledge to economic productivity or firms' demand for people with higher levels of knowledge (as represented by qualifications). The problem with both of these approaches is that if we use quantitative evidence about the use of research-based knowledge and so-called knowledge workers as the primary indicators to discuss the argument about knowledge economies/societies, then we miss an important dimension of such societies and economies. Specifically, we overlook that both presuppose the existence of knowledge culture and practices in economic activity and that such cultures and practices are, in principle, an integral part of all sectors in the economy.

The aim of Section 2 is therefore to consider the diverse and often new ways in which different occupations use the forms of disciplinary knowledge they were introduced to during their professional and/or vocational formation, in conjunction with the knowledge developed from participating in workplace practice, to sustain and/or develop products and services as well as occupational expertise and identity. There is, however, something very different about the contributions to this section compared with other edited collections on 'learning at work' or 'learning in knowledge economies.' All the contributors recognize, albeit from different perspectives, that the ways in which people use knowledge and learn by working alongside other people are mediated by the work/technological designs (that are dropped into workers' lives) as well as by the elements of occupational culture and knowledge, real and imagined, inherited from the past.

To strike this balance between context and practice, the contributors have drawn on a wide variety of concepts, from theoretical perspectives such as cultural historical activity theory, labour process theory, symbolic interaction, science studies, social semiotics, and from different methods, for example, participant observation, life histories based on interviews, surveys, and so on. This has enabled them to continue not only to explore the contextual and relational conception of knowledge advanced by the contributors to Section One, but also to show how the same conception applies to learning.

Fuller, Unwin, Felstead, Jewson, and Kakavelakis, the first contributors to Section Two, use a combination of ideas from the sociology of work and learning theory to demonstrate that contemporary workplaces in industries such as food processing, retail sales, and software engineering give rise to many different forms of knowledge creation and use, and, as a consequence, to different forms of learning and pedagogical approaches. The authors build on Fuller and Unwin's

D.W. Livingstone and D. Guile (eds.), The Knowledge Economy and Lifelong Learning:
A Critical Reader, 187–190.
© 2012 *Sense Publishers. All rights reserved.*

work that demonstrated that organizations differ in the way they create and manage themselves as learning environments. Those organizations conceptualised as 'expansive,' in the sense that their employees experience diverse forms of participation in forms of occupational knowledge and skill, foster more creative forms of learning at work. Fuller et al. reveal how the organization of work and the opportunity to participate in a wide variety of work practices can facilitate learning and knowledge creation for all types of employees and/or parts of an organization. They conclude with observations for policy and methodology. In the case of the former, they maintain that empirically-grounded case studies are vital if policies are to be devised to support the interplay between learning and knowledge creation in workplaces. In the case of the latter, they affirm the importance of researching the productive systems that underpin research sites.

Nerland's paper offers a contrasting, but complementary, perspective. She starts with the recognition that professions' knowledge domains comprise theoretical as well as experience-based knowledge that spans the education–work divide, and that professions form cultures that handle knowledge and constitute processes of learning and identity formation in distinct ways. Nerland supplements these ideas with the concept of 'knowledge cultures' to encapsulate profession-specific modes of thinking and acting. Using the knowledge cultures of computer engineering and school teaching, Nerland examines the ways in which the interplay between profession-specific practices and organizational contexts are responsible for organizing knowledge and framing opportunities for participation in knowledge-creating activities, constructing the learning individual in specific ways, and presenting different kinds of opportunities and demands to individuals for continuous learning in working life.

Drawing on concepts from symbolic interaction and science studies and using participant observation, Bechky reveals the way in which occupational jurisdictions, which manifest themselves after professionals have been enculturated into knowledge culture and practices, are enacted within organizations. Bechky suggests, like Nerland, that in order to gain insight about the interactional process by which these struggles happen within organizations, it is helpful to examine occupational communities' use of organizational artifacts. She describes the ways in which two artifacts – engineering drawings and machines – mediate the relations of engineers, technicians, and assemblers in a manufacturing firm, and how members of these different occupations use artifacts to solve problems that cut across occupational boundaries. In doing so, Bechky adds another dimension to Fuller et al.'s argument that learning and knowledge creation can occur, in principle, for all types of employees and/or parts of an organization, by showing that authority over these objects can reinforce *or* redistribute task area boundaries – and, moreover, by symbolizing the work of occupational groups, the objects also represent and strengthen beliefs about the legitimacy of a group's work.

Bakker and colleagues continue Bechky's argument that in order to understand the ways in which members of different occupational communities use knowledge in workplaces, it is necessary to study interactional processes. Using data gathered from a large biscuit manufacturing and packaging company, they reveal that companies are taking part in process improvement programmes that bring about a growing need for employees, at different levels, to interpret and act on data representations. Their focus on semiotic mediation within activity systems enables them to identify two sets of related 'techno-mathematical literacies,' that is, two sets of functional mathematical knowledge mediated by tools and grounded in the context of specific work situations. The first set concerns some invisible aspects rendered visible through the production of mathematical signs; the second set concerns developing meanings for action from an interpretation of these signs. Bakker and colleagues argue that the increasing role that mathematical signs play in the workplace raises new questions for the design and delivery of mathematics in educational institutions, as well as for programmes to support learning and development in workplaces.

In his chapter, Sawchuk draws attention to the all-too-often hidden political economic dimension of working and learning in knowledge economies. He argues that in advanced capitalism it is important for researchers to pay attention to the ways that the details of everyday occupational life and learning represent an important arena of political economic struggle. Sawchuk pursues this general claim through synthesizing ideas from labour process and cultural historical activity theory to identify two major trajectories of occupational learning within activity involving the production of welfare work. The two trajectories identified are the ways in which welfare workers: (a) learn and re-learn operational expertise as working conditions change; and (b) learn how to engage in occupational accommodation by constructing, re-inheriting, and maintaining alternative orientations to their work than the orientations now expected of welfare workers. This allows him like Fuller et al., to offer a wide-angled account of the working/learning process and thereby to capture the interplay between the development/re-development of skill, identity, and emotional engrossment at work.

The chapter by Guile offers a complementary, but slightly different, perspective a similar yet different angle to the above contributors on the issue of working and learning. Like them, he focuses on the interplay between working and learning and, in doing so, highlights the way in which the process of participation in occupational cultures and practices contributes to the development of vocational expertise and identity. Where Guile differs is that he first addresses the distinctive form these issues take in 'external labour markets' (i.e., contract-based/freelance employment). Guile demonstrates that in the creative and cultural sector widely presumed to be central to knowledge economies, it is vital for young people to learn to supplement traditional vocational expertise with entrepreneurial expertise and social capital if they are to survive in these labour markets. This form of knowledge he refers to as 'Moebius-strip expertise.' Second, and in light of this, Guile maintains that policy makers will have to consider how educational policies can support the development of the aforementioned form of expertise and capital.

Starting with discussions about the 'learning economy' and the 'learning society,' Casey points out that although these notions originally fuelled ideas about promoting education, training, and learning in contemporary organizations and workplaces, this debate has fallen by the wayside and an economic perspective now prevails, one that places emphasis on constructing 'learning organizations' and on 'human resource learning in service of organizational strategies for innovation and competitive advantage in economic activities.' Casey, like Fuller et al. and Sawchuk, is concerned that these economic and managerial models scarcely attend to the human subjectivity of the learner–worker and the worker's diverse learning interests. She argues that the prevailing focus on techno-economic imperatives and managerial elite interests in organizations currently circumscribe and delimit learning in production organizations. Casey proposes instead a more comprehensive approach to learning in organizations. She maintains that to attend explicitly to the needs and interests of workers as learning persons might generate not only improved work practices but also might regenerate links between lifelong learning, societal democratic citizenship, and civilized organizations.

The section ends with a salutary reminder from Young about the importance of disciplinary 'knowledge' to education in general, let alone education for a knowledge economy/society, given the hollowing out of what is meant by knowledge in the transnational policy literature (e.g., of the OECD and the World Bank) and in the perspectives of some researchers. Young argues for the re-assertion of what he refers to as the 'voice of knowledge' as a distinctive factor shaping educational policy; otherwise, he claims that our highly problematic bequest to future generations could be that we fail to indicate which explicit knowledge should be 'transmitted' to the next generation. Moreover, Young echoes our observations in the Introduction that although this potential heritage lacks the global visibility of the debate about environmental crises and forms of sustainable economic life, arguably addressing the 'heritage' issue is fundamental to whether we are able to address the latter crises. In making this point, Young leaves us with the challenge of stating and justifying why knowledge is important for societies and individuals, what types of knowledge are important, what their relation is to one another, and when and how they should be learnt.

The contributors to this section, apart from Young, shed light on the contrasting ways in which people are positioned by what Kennedy referred to in Section One as the 'logic of capital' and position themselves through the 'logic of their labour' to learn to use and develop knowledge in order to both resist and engage creatively with work activities and, in the process, develop their vocational practice and identity. In parallel, Young raises the point of what knowledge should be available to people in educational institutions in order to address not only pressing educational questions and issues, but also environmental and political ones as well.

In revealing the contradictory dynamics of the uses of knowledge in the creation of knowledge economies and societies, the contributors to this section draw attention to the actual interplay between work and learning in an array of current workplaces. Collectively, their contributions highlight the partiality and limitations of the 'economic imaginary' conception of the knowledge-based economy, and demonstrate the crucial role of the agency of labour in humanizing working practice. The implication of the latter issue is pursued in the book's concluding chapter.

ALISON FULLER, LORNA UNWIN, ALAN FELSTEAD, NICK
JEWSON, & KONSTANTINOS KAKAVELAKIS

CREATING AND USING KNOWLEDGE

An Analysis of the Differentiated Nature of
Workplace Learning Environments

INTRODUCTION

This chapter argues that the productive systems of contemporary workplaces give rise to many different forms of knowledge creation and use, and, as a consequence, to different forms of learning and pedagogical approaches. Some of these approaches are utilized to the benefit of the organization and employees (though not, necessarily, in a reciprocal manner), but others are buried within everyday workplace activity (see Billett, 2001).

The chapter draws on evidence from research in public and private sector organizations in the United Kingdom,[1] and uses data from three case study sectors (food processing, retail, and software engineering) to illustrate its arguments. It also draws on previous research in the steel and metals sector, from which Fuller and Unwin (2003, 2004) argued that organizations differ in the ways they create and manage themselves as learning environments. In that study, Fuller and Unwin used a range of data collection methods (including interviews, observations, and weekly learning logs) to investigate learning and workforce development in diverse organizational contexts. The evidence underpinned the development of a conceptual framework which identified a range of pedagogical and organizational factors, each locatable on what was termed the expansive–restrictive continuum. The research concluded that expansive rather than restrictive environments fostered learning at work and the integration of personal and organizational development. It was noted too that individuals differed in the extent to which they engaged in learning. Their responses to opportunities were shaped, at least to some degree, by their personal backgrounds, prior educational experiences, and aspirations, which were referred to as their 'learning territory' (Fuller & Unwin, 2004; see also Evans et al., 2006). It was also recognized that organizations might adopt more restrictive approaches to workforce development as a deliberate strategy for supporting models of work organization which were based on limiting the learning of at least some groups of employees. Table One represents Fuller and Unwin's initial (rather than an exhaustive) attempt to suggest the range of factors (pedagogical, organizational, and cultural) that contribute to approaches to

D.W. Livingstone and D. Guile (eds.), The Knowledge Economy and Lifelong Learning:
A Critical Reader, 191–206.

workforce development and the creation of learning environments, and to put them into a single conceptual framework.

Table 1. Expansive-restrictive continuum

Approaches to workforce development

Expansive	Restrictive
Participation in multiple communities of practice inside and outside the workplace	Restricted participation in multiple communities of practice
Primary community of practice has shared 'participative memory: cultural inheritance of workforce development	Primary community of practice has little or no 'participative memory: no or little tradition of apprenticeship
Breadth of learning opportunities fostered by availability of cross-company/setting experiences	Narrowness of learning opportunities, opportunities restricted in terms of tasks/knowledge/location
Access to range of qualifications including knowledge-based VQ	Little or no access to qualifications
Planned time off-the-job including for knowledge-based courses, and for reflection	Virtually all on-the-job: limited opportunities for reflection
Gradual transition to full, rounded participation	Fast – transition as quick as possible
Vision of workplace learning: progression for career	Vision of workplace learning: static for job
Organizational recognition of, and support for employees as learners	Lack of organizational recognition of, and support for employees as learners
Workforce development vehicle for aligning the goals of individual development and organizational capability	Workforce development used to restrict individual capability to organizational need
Workforce development fosters opportunities to extend identity through boundary crossing	Workforce development limits opportunities to extend identity: little boundary crossing experienced
Reification of 'workplace curriculum' highly developed (e.g., through documents, symbols, language, tools) and accessible to newcomers/apprentices	Limited reification of 'workplace curriculum' patchy access to reificatory aspects of practice
[Substantive] Skills are widely distributed throughout the organization	[Substantive] Skills are located in particular parts of organization
Knowledge and skills (including technical) of whole workforce developed and valued	Knowledge and skills of key workers/groups developed and valued
Managers as facilitators of workforce and individual development	Managers as controllers of workforce and individual development
Multi-dimensional view of expertise	Uni-dimensional top-down view of expertise

Source: Fuller & Unwin, 2004.

In the current project, we are attempting to probe more deeply into the framework's characteristics in order to connect the role of learning with the ways in which work is organized together with the ways in which performance is conceived and measured.

Our research indicates the need for a sharp focus on the dynamic context in which workplace learning takes place, including wider regulatory, sectoral, and organizational characteristics (see Unwin et al. 2007). It is also showing that where people are positioned in the political economy of the workplace affects not only the types of learning in which they engage and the types of knowledge they can acquire, but the extent to and manner in which their learning and knowledge are recognized. As a result, we are trying to understand the nature of the productive systems (Wilkinson, 2002) operating within organizations to understand the underlying phenomena that drive (or impede) learning and the creation, refinement and management of knowledge (Felstead et al., 2006). As such, we are using the image of the Russian nesting doll to capture the multi-layered nature of contemporary organizations and sectors (see Unwin et al., 2007).

The paper is structured in two main sections. The first outlines ways of conceptualizing knowledge and their relevance to exploring who learns what at work. The second uses the case study examples to (re-) examine the concept and role of knowledge(s) and knowing, as applied to contrasting workplaces and workforces. The paper concludes by arguing that developing empirically and contextually grounded understandings of 'knowing' in the workplace can contribute to theoretical debates about types of knowledge as well as providing a basis for critiquing assumptions about knowledge and skills of employees at different levels, with diverse job roles and from various sectors.

UNLOCKING THE NATURE OF KNOWLEDGE AT WORK

Survey evidence has revealed the uneven distribution of learning opportunities across U.K. workplaces (see Felstead et al., 2005). Research has also questioned the access that employees have to learning opportunities given that (global) economic drivers are underpinning employers' attempts to 'sweat' more productivity from their human resources (see Fenwick, 2000; Lloyd & Payne, 2004). Employees in weak labour market positions are likely to have limited job roles and little access to training and career development, and to work within what Fuller and Unwin (2004) have elsewhere called 'restrictive' workplace learning environments. In contrast, others suggest that the emergence of the 'new economy,' high performance, and employee involvement practices (see, inter alia, Whitfield, 2000; Ashton & Sung, 2002) can give rise to more 'learning intensive' workplaces (Skule, 2004). The inclusion of diverse sectoral, organizational, and individual participants in our study is enabling us to investigate the empirical reality of competing perspectives.

Our recent survey work (Felstead et al., 2005) has enabled us to make connections between informal and formal sources of learning and their perceived helpfulness (in terms of doing the job better) to groups at different occupational levels. The findings confirmed that those at the top had the greatest access to courses and qualifications (Felstead et al., 2000), but also revealed that employees at all levels perceived that learning through 'everyday' productive activity at work is the most helpful for doing the job. However, those at the higher end of the occupational hierarchy were more likely to perceive their participation in formal sources of learning as useful. This implies that there is a relationship between the context and characteristics of work settings, the opportunities to learn to which they give rise, and the types of knowledge resources needed for workers to do their jobs effectively. To examine this further, we are looking closely at what constitutes the nature of knowledge in use and in context.

Conceptions of knowledge tend to relate to whether an individual or social perspective is taken (Eraut, 2004). Sfard (1998) has used the metaphor of 'learning as acquisition,' whereby individuals acquire and store context-independent knowledge products in the 'stock room' of their minds (Beckett & Hager, 2002). In contrast, Sfard (1998) used the 'learning as participation' metaphor to capture the social perspective which regards knowledge (and knowing) as being embedded in and created through participation in the social relations which constitute practice (Lave & Wenger, 1991). The idea that knowledge is constructed is consistent with an emphasis on 'knowing' as an active concept (Blackler, 1995).

The 'sociality of knowledge' (Muller, 2000) originates in the idea that (all) knowledge is social, because it is constructed through the social relations operating in particular socio-economic and cultural contexts. 'Social constructivism' represents one form of the sociality of knowledge, 'social realism' another (Young, 2004). From the social constructivist perspective, scientific, disciplinary knowledge can be seen to have high currency, because it is created by high status groups; is acquired through participation in high status settings (such as universities); and because it, or its symbols (certificates), can be exchanged for high status positions in the socio-economic pecking order. Its strong currency is based on its social construction and not on any putative objectivity or efficacy that makes it intrinsically superior to other forms of knowledge (Young, 2004).

However, as Young (2004) argues, the social constructivist approach does not help differentiate the extent to which some types of knowledge are more situated than others. For those seeking to understand what people learn at work, why and how, this perspective has limitations as it tends to foreclose analysis of the different types and sources of knowledge on which different groups in different settings might be drawing. The social realist approach, however, allows that there are different types and sources of knowledge and that some are more situated than others (Young, 2004).

Fuller and Unwin (2003, 2004) showed, for example, how engineering apprentices who had opportunities to participate in a broad range of activities, including the acquisition of theoretical concepts, both on and off-the-job, were in a stronger position to progress within and between firms than those who only had access to on-the-job learning experiences. Put another way, these young people had been given the chance to participate fully in the various parts of the productive system.

194

Eraut (2004) identifies two broad types of knowledge: cultural and personal. He links the former to the social perspective and the latter to the individual perspective. Whilst Eraut acknowledges that both perspectives are important, evidence from our case studies is causing us to question his separation of the social and individual. Our research is suggesting that an (ontological) approach which conceives the personal and collective as mutually constitutive is more fruitful and in keeping with our 'Russian doll' metaphor. The importance of Eraut's analysis is that he reminds us to take account of what employees bring to the workplace from their past experience and that aspects of both cultural and personal knowledge can be 'codified' or 'non-codified.'

The territory covered by non-codified knowledge is broad and varied and needs to be uncovered and elaborated to illuminate the nature of knowing in the workplace. There is a tendency to bracket non-codified cultural and personal knowledge with the notion of tacit knowledge, that which is taken for granted and hard to articulate. Researching the tacit certainly constitutes a methodological challenge, but the evidence being generated in our project is suggesting that whilst there may be some areas of workers' knowledge which are hard to uncover, respondents are often able to articulate a good deal about what they and others need to know in order to do their jobs.

Boreham et al.'s (2002) concept of work process knowledge through which employees gain a more holistic understanding of the production process is relevant here. Workplaces organized along Taylorist lines limit workers' learning to gaining the knowledge they need to perform specific and narrow tasks whereas more flexible, less hierarchical models of work organization, associated with the use of information and communication technologies, encourage employee involvement through team working, employee discretion, and wider knowledge distribution.

Our project is analysing a range of work environments (productive systems) to surface the nature of their social and technical relations, to identify who is involved, and in what ways they cope with continuity, disruption, and change. In addition, the tools and artefacts which mediate organizational activity provide an important lens on how knowledge is actively constructed, distributed and created.

ILLUSTRATING WHO LEARNS WHAT AT WORK

In this section, we draw on transcribed interviews (with employees at all levels) and field notes taken during observation in the workplace in three companies in the food processing, retailing, and software engineering sectors.

Company A: Food Processing

Company A is part of the pre-packed sandwich making industry, which is worth approximately £3 billion to the UK economy. It was founded ten years ago by two friends and currently employees 30 people in the English East Midlands. It now operates as a limited company, with the founders employed as joint managing directors (MDs), and produces around 25,000 sandwiches a week for neighbourhood shops and garage forecourts. Most employees are employed as either sandwich makers/assemblers (17) or van drivers (9).

The main challenge for the MDs is how to take the business forward in terms of, expansion, capital investment in automated machinery, and bringing in specialist personnel. The data reveal the extent and nature of the cultural and personal knowledge being applied in this workplace context and the essential role this is playing in day-to-day decision-making and activities. In the following extract, one MD reflects on the possible advantages of employing an experienced production manager in order to give him more time to develop the business:

> The time I'm there sticking labels on, etc., sort of doing the quality control at the end of the line, I just think to myself 'what else could I be doing with my time in terms of perhaps getting new business, looking at new markets, looking at new product lines' etc., etc., etc.

The MDs 'know' that their management style is critical to the success of the business. It is characterized by: (a) a highly hands-on approach – they can and often do perform all the workplace tasks; and (b) an approachable and friendly relationship with staff. Below, a van driver refers to the importance of daily interaction and information exchange between van drivers and managers. This takes the form of knowledge sharing, swapping experiences and ideas, and, importantly, having their suggestions acted upon:

> Everyday we come in and talk. Can I have five minutes with you? Yeah, no problem. They've [managers] always got time for you ... they will listen to you. One day you go in and there haven't been many salads today ... next day ... all your trays are full salads.

The MD's observations reveal the simultaneous use of cultural knowledge about business (e.g., the relationship between capital and labour, product-market, and quality) and what Eraut calls, 'everyday knowledge of people and situations' (2004, p. 202). Their evidence highlights the challenge of reconciling strategic issues relating to the long-term development of a small business with day-to-day workload demands:

- Working out the most efficient route;
- Knowing what types and prices of sandwiches sell to what type of outlet, in what type of location;
- Collating (in 'the book') and communicating 'field intelligence' (e.g., on sales, customer performance, waste) to managers to enable changes in production;
- Knowing how to vary prices on particular products to optimize sales;
- Seeking and securing new customers and maintaining good relations;
- Applying aesthetic knowledge to present products on outlet shelves to maximize sales; and
- Calculating and collecting the correct amount of money owed by customers.

The following quotation illustrates the van drivers' centrality to organizational performance, and how the different sorts of knowledge they possess are embedded in the social relations of production:

196

It's down to us [van drivers] at the end of the day. He's [MD] blind. We're like his eyes. We have to go out there and we come back with information. Can you change this, can you change that and come back to [MD] and he makes them [sandwiches]. That's how it is.

The evidence from Company A indicates the situated and contextualized nature of the knowledge created and distributed across the social relations which constitute this organization. This is not to say that less context-dependent knowledge is absent from the workplace. Issues relating to environmental health are critical to a food processing and handling business. If the company were subject to a complaint about the safety of its products, it would have to be able to demonstrate 'due diligence' in relation to such matters. Therefore, products are sent to a laboratory for testing to establish their 'safe' shelf life and the appropriate use by date. Some employees have developed significant codified (scientific) knowledge in this area.

The key findings from this case study relate to the significant level of discretion associated with the van driver role and the involvement of the MDs in production. This permits intensive development of what is manifested as tacit knowledge, but which may actually consist of a variety of knowledge types. It is not clear to us that Eraut's distinction between 'personal' and 'cultural' is sufficient to capture the type of collective, co-constructed knowledge creation and ability to make 'hot decisions' (Beckett & Hager, 2002) embedded in the performance of both managers and van drivers. In particular, the context of activity means that collective knowledge(s) are being employed and created through dynamic interaction between colleagues *and* customers. Customers as well as differently positioned workers are part of the network of social relations that characterize this productive system. The van drivers have an inter-dependent peer relationship with their managers, one that enables new knowledge to be co-constructed. This relationship, however, is invisible in structural terms in that the business' organizational chart depicts a typical status hierarchy in which the van drivers are subordinate. The example here contrasts with Eraut et al.'s (2004) case studies of professional sectors where organizations are more likely to be based on knowledge hierarchies. In such settings, managers can be presumed to be capable of providing support and mentoring (and teaching) to those at the preliminary stages in their professional careers and where there is shared recognition that that the novice–expert dimension is an integral aspect of the employee–manager relationship. Whilst the Eraut model is helpful for describing and explaining professional situations, the extent of its generalizability to other groups and settings is questionable.

The concept of work process knowledge is of some help in understanding the food processing case, but our case study is different to Boreham et al.'s (2002) examples of organizations that have introduced new flexible forms of working (often facilitated by ICT). The approach to work organization adopted by Company A is characteristic of the sectoral context and the size of the firm rather than any historical break with past ways of working. It represents a category of company that encourages high levels of employee involvement due to the everyday struggle to improve and survive.

197

Company B: Retail – Supermarket

Company B runs a nationwide chain of supermarkets, employing over 50,000 staff and with a turnover of more than £4 billion. For the purposes of our research, we have conducted interviews with personnel at all levels in two similarly sized stores, as well as with the area manager who has overall responsibility for several outlets. Each store has a manager, several department managers and supervisors, and 'shop floor operatives.'

New technology, such as electronic point of sale systems, has facilitated the centralization of the buying, stock control, and marketing/presentation functions. This has limited the extent to which individual stores can plan their own stock profiles and the way in which their stock is presented to customers. Stock store management (SSM) is implemented via a device called a 'symbol gun,' which is used to check that the physical stock available on the shelves accords with what 'the computer' states the store should have; to collate data on availability; and to write off stock. In terms of actor network theory (Law 1994; Mutch 2002), which conceives networks as consisting of human and non-human elements, the symbol gun can be seen as an important 'member' of the social relations of production in this firm. One store manager observed:

> These little guns obviously are controlling ... obviously, we're putting all the information in to that which takes it to the computers, so I mean without these in this store, we wouldn't know what our stock levels were and we'd be in a bit of a mess, we do rely on those.

Generally, departments with fresh produce have more discretion over stock ordering than those such as grocery which have a relatively long shelf life. Dairy and meat are seen as particularly critical sections for store performance because they combine relatively high turnover with the risk of high wastage if the ordering levels are inaccurate. It is the departmental manager's responsibility to maintain the integrity of stock levels (i.e., to ensure that the physical and computer stock levels match). Knowledge of local conditions and patterns of demand can have a significant impact on departmental and store performance, and this leads to a tension over how much discretion to give departmental managers to alter their centrally determined stock levels. Offering more discretion can lead to positive pay-offs, when the manager's reading of local demand proves accurate, or be negative when the store is left with high levels of spoiled produce. We concentrate here, therefore, on what departmental managers need to know, focusing in particular on an account provided by one dairy and meat manager.

The first quotation confirms that the degree of discretion accorded to department managers differs according to the fragility of the produce and how they use their cultural and personal knowledge to alter what the system suggests should be ordered:

> What you had is grocery where they can't amend very much, but on dairy [I] mean fresh [food], you can amend everything, so you change it as much as you want. And the system, I don't know why, but it tends to order, say, too

much and you just know from knowledge yourself, you sort of look at it, you get a sort of record in your own head. (dairy and meat department manager)

The manager also explained that the computerized ordering system has the capacity to learn: 'Say we've got one product, say it's ordering five cases, I think that's not going to sell, I'll take one, the system sort of resets itself every time you do that.' There is, therefore, inter-dependency between the computer and employee, with both influencing each other's behaviour.

The performance of the department is assessed on three indicators: sales, availability, and waste. Optimum success is achieved when the most profitable balance between the three is reached, as the dairy and meat manager explained:

It's hard to get [to hit targets on all 3 indicators at the same time], you can normally get one without the other, get brilliant waste, cos you've cut back a lot and you haven't got the sales there. To get sales you need to spend more money, which goes ... more waste, but if you want to meet your waste, you've got to try and get a happy medium, which is very difficult. Availability comes with getting sales and waste ...

This respondent spoke about the importance of experience in enabling people to achieve their targets and also about the need to 'be in rhythm' with patterns of demand. He said, 'When you come back off two weeks holiday say ... what you think is right is no longer right to what it was when you left.'

Department managers are also responsible for employees in their 'teams.' The dairy and meat manager explained what he needs to know in order to manage people effectively:

... being able to be a friend but yet be a boss, step away when you need to and yeah just like casual and friendly. You need to be able to separate them too if you need to, if you're too nice all the time you'll get nowhere, always be fair.

His approach to people management has been strongly influenced by the style promoted by the store manager, who is an avid reader of populist management texts such as Blanchard and Johnson's *One minute manager* (1981). Such books focus on the idea that 'your people are your most important asset' and on ways of motivating and empowering them. The store manager makes this literature available to his management team as required reading. This provides an example of codified cultural knowledge that goes beyond the expected organizational documentation available in a supermarket.

Whilst the technology in both case study stores is the same, the way in which it is used and perceived is influenced by the organizational culture generated by contrasting management styles. When asked how he would characterize the store manager's role, the manager of one store talked a lot about the importance of employee development, including his capacity to alter and 'teach' the system. In contrast, the other store manager perceived the introduction of new information and communication technology as decreasing individual discretion and autonomy. She observed that 'most of the job really is policing, as it were, and checking that things are being done. I mean the system checks I carry out tells me whether they're doing their job right.'

The computerized stock system clearly has an important effect on employees' roles, and can both limit and change what they need to know. The introduction of the tools and devices of the SSM system is reconfiguring the network of relations embedded in this productive system. This case study provides an example of an organization which is trying to improve its performance by introducing new ways of working based on new technology.

The company's head office has not sought to impose a preferred management style or organizational culture. Attention is focused on performance outcomes rather than attempts to micro-manage how stores operate and employees utilized. The relationship between the corporate centre and the stores is mediated through the computerized SSM system, but it is apparent that senior managers are not always best placed to know how the system might be used most appropriately. This leaves open the possibility that the system can become all-powerful, or it can be manipulated and subverted. The challenge here would appear to be to design a productive system which facilitates knowledge sharing. This will involve an analysis of the work process as a whole, that is, across departments at the local level and between these and the 'centre.'

Company C: Software Engineering

Company C provides a contrast to the other two companies discussed in this chapter as it has the characteristics of a 'knowledge intensive' organization where the vast majority of employees are university graduates. The company, based in the south east of England, develops cutting-edge software and hardware products and solutions for a wide range of customers, including the U.S. and U.K. military and several multi-nationals. It employs 350 people, including 50 sales staff in the United States, where 90 per cent of the company's sales are generated. Some 30 people are based in Edinburgh and a small number of people work from home. A profit share scheme, involving all employees (including cleaning and catering staff) and determined through twice-yearly reviews of individual performance, plays a key role in cementing employee 'buy-in' to the corporate goals. The largest group of employees consists of software engineers recruited from Oxford and Cambridge and a small number of other top U.K. universities at the age of 21 or 22. They are nearly all male, reflecting the gender balance across the company where, currently, 69 out of 350 employees are female.

This company comes across as a strong community whose members are 'signed up' to the expectations in terms of performance, but also to the social ethos. A company director referred to the head office as the 'mother ship:'

All people who move to this company have been in [head office], have been in the mother ship if you like, and have got to know everybody else, have been brought up if you like with all the fundamentals of the mother ship and then they go out to the frontline offices.

Similarly, the chairman emphasizes the family atmosphere in which people are cared for and where the social life of the 'family' is seen as key to the company's success. The director of internet operations added to this by stressing that this is a 'long-lasting career driven company' in which people's careers are seen as the driving force. The company's physical environment, and devices such as a 'Morale Fund,' which pays for company outings help to sustain and enhance a strong spirit of collegiality. There is then an explicit management focus on developing and shaping the social relations of this productive system.

Many of the software engineers told us they had been attracted to the company because it would give them the chance to move from university to become a member of another community of 'bright people.' There seems to be a close alignment between their personal knowledge and the cultural knowledge of their occupation. The organization of work, including the management practices, further sustained and enhanced that alignment. This relates to Baldry et al.'s (2005) argument (see also Marks & Lockyer, 2004) that software workers demonstrate greater commitment to organizational goals in companies that respect their professional identity as software engineers and create working conditions that value worker discretion and autonomy.

The engineers rotate around project teams established for up to approximately nine months at a time. Knowledge and expertise are captured within the teams, as in Boreham et al.'s (2002) concept of work process knowledge, and disseminated through everyday interaction in the form of discussions and consultation across the teams. The performance review system acts as the main mechanism for capturing ideas and for facilitating what Boud et al. (2006) call 'productive reflection.' The review takes the form of a written report (around ten pages), compiled by the employee and their immediate manager, detailing the employee's strengths and weaknesses over the period in question. The reports are reviewed and graded by the chairman and senior managers in order for the profit share to be allocated. At the heart of the process is a commitment to individual career development and the role of the manager as the key facilitator of learning as advocated by Eraut et al. (2004). In this company, however, the concept of who is a manager and what form management should take has moved well beyond conventional notions of the management function. The vast majority of employees are expected to have a management role. The concept of 'managing' relates much more to a social relational model than the standard concept of managers as monitors of performance. In terms of the software engineers, once they have acquired the necessary technical competences, they are assigned a newcomer to manage, a process that is closely supervised by a team manager. The engineer has to show they can 'teach' their trainee as well as instil the corporate values, and this is recorded through the review process.

The growth and nurturing of managers reflects the company's privileging of on-the-job training and learning. Employees can, if they wish, participate in off-the-job training, but this is very rare. Knowledge is acquired and distributed throughout the company through the use of teams and the central role played by everyday interaction within and between teams and clients. This again reveals a much more dynamic fusion of the personal and the cultural than is perhaps envisaged by Eraut, and also the importance of identifying the full range of knowledge producers (with clients seen as key actors in the co-construction of knowledge and ideas). Senior managers lead workshops and seminars on specific topics and software engineers are encouraged to organize ad hoc presentations to colleagues when they want to get feedback on new ideas or long-standing problems.

Many of the interviewees stressed that there was little need for off-the-job training, as illustrated by this comment:

> The kind of people we have, this will sound arrogant and elitist, but they're sort of, a long way above the average you might encounter, if you go on a 'how to program course,' the people working on that course generally would be of a lot lower ability than the people here.

A small number of engineers, however, were concerned that the lack of off-the-job training meant that they were not able to acquire further work-related qualifications. Although they had no plans to leave the company and stressed that having worked there would probably impress another employer more than formal qualifications, they were aware that labour market conditions might change (see Marks & Lockyer, 2004).

Engineers spend 50 days of their first year learning the core technologies of the business from their mentor and manager. They become deeply immersed in real-work tasks and, hence, are involved in what Polanyi (1962) called 'participation through indwelling.' As ideas are developed and problems solved, engineers place this information in a series of 'public folders' on the company's intranet. This relates to Nonaka et al.'s (2005) concept of 'knowledge conversion' whereby tacit knowledge is 'externalized' and turned into an explicit form, then expanded, and then re-internalized through practice. In the case of Company C, the public folders also reflect Kerosuo and Engeström's (2003) requirements that such tools are powerful resources when they emerge from being part of an organization's collective routines and when they are interconnected with and implemented within workplace activity.

The metaphor of the 'mother ship' used by one of the directors is particularly apt when considering both the strengths and weaknesses of this company. The company's creative and sustained management of its physical, virtual, and mental space reflects Nonaka et al.'s (2002) concept of *ba*, one that potentially adapts the concept of communities of practice (CoP) to reflect contemporary organizational realities. On the one hand, the company has created a very prosperous, stable, and stimulating environment for its highly qualified crew. Cook and Brown's (2005) metaphor of the 'generative dance' between knowledge and 'knowing' is relevant here as the company has developed ways of working that produce a constant interaction between the engineers' expertise and the everyday problems they have to work on. This 'dance' occurs in all workplaces, and, hence, in all our case studies, but it varies in nature from the highly formalized and controlling to the haphazard. Some organizations, such as Company B, have centralized their knowledge management systems to the extent that, in some stores, employee knowledge is positively disregarded. In contrast, Company B relies on informal verbal exchanges to capture the knowledge of its van drivers. Company C has arrived at a potential 'tipping point' in terms of its size and its ability to innovate. The issue of size is significant, because the review process makes considerable demands on senior managers, including the chairman. The problem of innovation strikes at the heart of the belief that the generation and reproduction of skills and knowledge within the community of practice is sufficient. One of the directors voiced his concern about the propensity of the engineers, whom he referred to as 'propeller heads,' to be too inward looking and not interested in the business side of the company. It appears, then, that to maintain the success of this company, the continual ordering and organizing of the social relations of production needs to be extended to include the introduction of new actors and tools, with attendant effects on the development of the existing workforce.

CONCLUSION

This chapter argues that there is no easy 'read-across' between types of knowledge and their availability and distribution across particular organizational settings, or occupational groups. For example, depending on the occupational or professional context, scientific concepts or theoretical knowledge may or may not be just as crucial a resource in the workplace as in the educational institution. What is learned in what sorts of productive systems, how this is mediated and applied through the social relations of production, is highly relevant not only to gaining a better understanding of workplace learning, knowledge(s), and knowing, but also to their relationship with the organization and distribution of work and organizational outcomes. We are using this insight in order to strengthen the analytical capacity of the expansive–restrictive framework in two particular ways: firstly, in terms of its ability to conceptualize the significance of, and relationship between, forms of workplace learning and knowing, and forms of learning undertaken in 'specialist educational settings' (Young, 1998); and secondly, in terms of its ability to draw attention to the range and configuration of sources and types of knowledge in use in particular workplaces and by particular (groups of) employees.

The chapter also argues that empirically grounded case studies are vital in order to: (a) avoid making easy assumptions about the complexity and value of workplace learning based on employees' structural position in organizations, or the sectors in which they work; (b) expose the range of knowledge sources available (and not available) in the workplace; and (c) understand the relationship between personal and collective knowing, the social and technical relations of production (including job design and work organization), and organizational outcomes.

Our research shows that, as learning environments, workplaces have expansive and restrictive features. Their restrictive elements surface in factors such as the lack of opportunity for off-the-job learning, where employees might be exposed to new concepts and given the time to reflect critically on their practice. Their expansive elements can be detected in types of work organization which provide opportunities for discretion, exposure to a range of work processes, and a management style which encourages the creation and distribution of knowledge. Expansive and restrictive learning environments need to be viewed in two dimensions, that is, in terms of breadth and depth. This type of focus enables analyses which characterize environments in terms of their particular configurations of narrowness, breadth, depth, and shallowness, as well as the availability and location of different knowledge sources. Insights generated from such an approach could be developed to provide messages for skills policy as well as practitioners supporting employee development.

The case study evidence highlights the 'art' involved in applying knowledge effectively to fulfil occupational roles in diverse productive systems. For the department manager in Company B, there appeared to be an art to knowing how to manipulate the ordering system to continually hit three competing and dynamic performance targets. In Company A, the van drivers' complex job role, which contradicts stereotypical assumptions about what 'low-grade' employees know and can do, was shown to be to allow for considerable discretion and autonomy. It played a pivotal part in the network of relations which made up the productive process.

Management of a small business, such as Company A, called for 'knowledgeability' in everyday tasks as well as in how to manage for longer-term success. Having 'the art' (the knowing) to achieve this balance appeared critical to the sustainability of the firm. In contrast, Company C showed how organizations can construct powerful learning environments that suit the needs and circumstances of a given period in the lifecycle of a business. For this company, the challenge will be to take risks with the current community structure in order to adapt to changing market conditions, and will require a re-assessment of the inward-looking approach to learning and knowing that has been fostered hitherto. The aim of such a process would be the production of a more elastic 'community boundary' (see Fuller et al., 2005) allowing for the sorts of critical perspectives and external ideas associated with Engeström's (2001) concept of expansive organizational learning.

Finally, the illustrative material provides evidence of the different ways in which knowledge (of all types) is constructed, distributed, and put to use within the context of a productive system. This has implications for methodology. We would argue that case study researchers investigating workplace knowledge need to begin with an examination of the productive systems that underpin their research sites. As the research progresses, we are probing deeper into our case study organizations to create more detailed pictures of the learning and knowledge environments they are creating and re-creating.

ACKNOWLEDGEMENTS

We would like to thank the three anonymous referees for their useful and constructive comments on this paper.

NOTES

[1] The Learning as Work: Teaching and Learning Processes in the Contemporary Work Organisation (RES 139250110) project is funded under the ESRC's Teaching and Learning Research Programme. For more details, go to: http://learningaswork.cf.ac.uk. The case study sites referred to in this paper were all located in England. We would like to acknowledge the contributions of Peter Butler, Tracey Lee, and David Ashton who were involved in the data collection phase in the food processing, retail, and software engineering case studies.

REFERENCES

Ashton, D. & Sung, J. (2002). *Supporting workplace learning for high performance working.* Geneva: International Labour Office.

Baldry, C., Scholarios, D., & Hyman, J. (2005). Organisational commitment among software developers. In Barrett, R. (Ed.), *Management, labour process and software development* (pp. 149–172). London: Routledge.

Beckett, D. and Hager, P. (2002). *Life, work and learning.* Routledge: London.

Billett, S., (2001). *Learning in the workplace.* Crows Nest NSW: Allen & Unwin.

Blackler, F. (1995). Knowledge, knowledge work and organizations. *Organization Studies, 16*(6), 1021–1046.

Blanchard, K. and Johnson, S. (1981). *One minute manager.* New York: William Morrow.

Boreham, N., Samurçay, R., & Fischer, M. (Eds.). (2002). *Work process knowledge.* London: Routledge.

Boud, D., Cressey, P., & Docherty, P. (Eds.). (2006). *Productive reflection at work: Learning for changing organisations.* London: Routledge

Cook, S.D.N. & Brown, J.S. (2005). Bridging epistemologies: The generative dance between organisational knowledge and organisational knowing, In Little, S. & Ray, T. (Eds.), *Managing knowledge* (pp. 51–84). London: Sage.

Engeström, Y. (2001). Expansive learning at work: Toward an activity-theoretical reconceptualization. *Journal of Education and Work, 14*(1), 133–156.

Eraut, M, (2004). Transfer of knowledge between education and workplace settings. In Rainbird, H., Fuller, A., & Munro, A. (Eds.), *Workplace learning in context* (pp. 201–221). London: Routledge.

Eraut, M., Steadman, S., J. Furner, Maillardet, F., Miller, C., Ali, A., & Blackman, C. (2004). *Learning in the professional workplace: Relationships between learning factors and contextual factors.* Paper presented at the AERA Annual Conference, San Diego, California.

Evans, K., Hodkinson, P. Rainbird, H., & Unwin, L. (Eds.). (2006). *Improving workplace learning.* London: Routledge.

Felstead, A., Ashton, D., & Green, F. (2000). Are Britain's workplace skills becoming more unequal? *Cambridge Journal of Economics, 24*(6), 709–727.

Felstead, A., Bishop, D., Fuller, A., Jewson, N., Lee, T., & Unwin, L. (2006). *Moving to the music: Learning processes, training and productive systems – The case of exercise to music instruction.* Learning as work research paper no. 6. Cardiff: Cardiff School of Social Sciences, Cardiff University.

Felstead, A., Fuller, A., Unwin, L., Ashton, D., Butler, P., & Lee, T. (2005). Surveying the scene: Learning metaphors, survey design and the workplace context. *Journal of Education and Work, 18*(4), 359–383.

Fenwick, T. (2001). Questioning the concept of the learning organisation. In Paechter, C., Preedy, M., Scott, D., & Soler, J. (Eds.). *Knowledge, power and learning* (pp. 74–88). London: Paul Chapman.

Fuller, A. & Unwin, L. (2003). Learning as apprentices in the contemporary UK workplace: Creating and managing expansive and restrictive participation. *Journal of Education and Work, 16*(4), 407–426.

Fuller, A. & Unwin, L. (2004). Expansive learning environments. In Rainbird, H., Fuller, A., & Munro, A. (Eds.), *Workplace learning in context* (pp. 126–144). London: Routledge.

Fuller, A., Hodkinson, H., Hodkinson, P., & Unwin, L. (2005). Learning as peripheral participation in communities of practice: A reassessment of key concepts in workplace learning. *British Educational Research Journal, 31*(1), 49–68.

Kerosuo, H. & Engeström, Y. (2003). Boundary crossing and learning in creation of new work practice. *Journal of Workplace Learning, 15*(7–8), 345–351.

Lave, J. & Wenger, E. (1991). *Situated learning: Legitimate peripheral participation.* Cambridge: Cambridge University Press.

Law, J. (1994). *Organizing modernity.* Oxford: Blackwell.

Lloyd, C. & Payne, J. (2004). The political economy of skill: A theoretical approach to developing a high skills strategy in the UK. In C. Warhurst, C., Grugulis, I., & Keep, E. (Eds.), *The skills that matter* (pp. 207–224). Basingstoke: Palgrave Macmillan.

Marks, A. & Lockyer, C. (2004). Producing knowledge: The use of the project team as a vehicle for knowledge and skill acquisition for software employees. *Economic and Industrial Democracy, 25*(2), 219–245.

Mutch, A. (2002). Actors and networks or agents and structures: Towards a realist view of information systems. *Organization, 9*(3), 477–496.

Muller, J. (2000). *Reclaiming Knowledge.* London: Routledge Farmer.

Nonaka, I., Toyama, R., & Konno, N. (2005). SECI, *ba* and leadership: A unified model of dynamic knowledge creation. In Little, S. & Ray, T. (Eds.), *Managing knowledge* (pp. 23–50). London: Sage.

Polanyi, M. (1962). *Personal knowledge.* Chicago: Chicago University Press.

Sfard, A. (1998). On two metaphors for learning and the dangers of just choosing one. *Educational Researcher, 27*(2), 4–13.

Skule, S. (2004). Learning conditions at work: A framework to understand and assess informal learning in the workplace. *International Journal of Training and Development, 8*(1), 8–20.

Unwin, L., Felstead, A., Fuller, A., Bishop, D., Jewson, N., Kakavelakis, K., & Lee, T. (2007). Looking inside the Russian doll: The interconnections between context, learning and pedagogy in the workplace. *Pedagogy, Culture and Society,* 15(3), 333–348.

Whitfield, K. (2000). High-performance workplaces, training, and the distribution of skills. *Industrial Relations, 39*(1), 1–26.

Wilkinson, F. (2002). *Productive systems and the structuring role of economic and social theories.* Working paper no. 225. ESRC Centre for Business Research, Cambridge: University of Cambridge.

Young, M. (1998). The curriculum of the future: From the 'new sociology of education' to a critical theory of learning. London: Falmer.

Young, M. (2004). Conceptualizing vocational knowledge. In Rainbird, H., Fuller, A., & Munro, A. (Eds.), *Workplace learning in context* (pp. 185–200). London: Routledge.

MONIKA NERLAND

PROFESSIONS AS KNOWLEDGE CULTURES[1]

INTRODUCTION

The emphasis given to professionals' learning in today's society tends to focus the individual learner as the core object of debates and policies. Less attention has been paid to the role of knowledge domains and expert cultures in forming opportunities for learning. Within educational contexts, researchers have pointed to how different disciplines are marked by distinct knowledge practices, modes of inquiry, and principles for determining validity, which constitute students' learning in distinct ways (Becher & Trowler, 2001; Neumann, Parry, & Becher, 2002; Donald, 2002). However, the knowledge domains of professions are often interdisciplinary in character. Moreover, they comprise theoretical as well as experience-based knowledge that spans the education-work divide. Nevertheless, the professions also form distinct cultures that handle knowledge and constitute processes of learning and identity formation in distinct ways. Knowledge cultures may thus be seen as a constitutive force that operates in the intersection of political-economic efforts and individuals' agency.

A number of initiatives have been carried out to secure practitioners' opportunities for professional development. In some countries, efforts take the formal character of compulsory engagements (e.g., in the United Kingdom), while other countries frame their efforts within a rhetoric of rights (e.g., in Norway). In any case, learning in professional life is not only about meeting formal requirements. It is also about knowledge-related practices in which professionals engage in processes of improvement on a discretionary basis (Billett, 2004; Eraut, 2006). Such practices are encouraged and formed in specific ways by the knowledge culture in question.

This chapter examines the knowledge cultures of computer engineering and school teaching with regard to how they organize knowledge and frame opportunities for participation. How do these professional domains and their interrelated knowledge arrangements serve to construct the learning professional in specific ways? What kind of opportunities and demands are presented to individuals when it comes to continuous learning in working life? In order to explore these questions, this chapter draws on the concept of 'epistemic cultures' introduced by Knorr Cetina (1999, 2006), as well as the ideas articulated by Nespor (1994) about how organization of knowledge in space and time serves to mobilise actions and constitute opportunities for learning.

D.W. Livingstone and D. Guile (eds.), The Knowledge Economy and Lifelong Learning:
A Critical Reader, 207–228.

KNOWLEDGE CULTURES AND THEIR MANIFESTATIONS

One of the defining characteristics of a profession is its specific ways of handling knowledge. The forms of knowledge in use, the artefacts and tools provided for professional practice, the traditions and methods of knowledge production, and the collective models for knowledge application serve to give communities an integrative power.

In this respect, some organizational aspects of knowledge are of special interest: First, the ways in which knowledge is produced are constitutive of the knowledge domain. For instance, professional domains differ in the extent to which their collective ways of knowing rest upon scientific achievements, upon personal experiences and reflexivity, or upon processes of codification. Approaches to knowledge production are interlinked with strategies for knowledge verification. How, for instance, do professionals know that something is true or considered best practice? A second dimension relates to the ways in which knowledge is accumulated. This aspect concerns the extent to which knowledge is regarded as cumulative in character and built up within the logic of linearity. It also concerns the extent to which accumulation is seen as a collective and collaborative project or as an individualized matter of gaining rich experiences. Third, the ways of distributing knowledge within the professional community are a distinguishing aspect that is closely linked to the character of the tools and infrastructures provided. These may, for instance, be more or less locally bounded, more or less technological in character, more or less based upon the written language, and so forth. And fourth, the profession-specific patterns of applying knowledge and the ways of handling the relationship between general knowledge and its application in specific work settings are a constitutive dimension in professional knowledge cultures.

In practice, these dimensions mutually shape each other and operate together in structuring both work practices and approaches to learning. They form the discipline-specific temporal and spatial organizations of knowledge that constitute the professional field and that also provide the grounds for introducing newcomers to the professional practice (Nespor, 1994). In other words, they form a certain knowledge culture, which, borrowing the words of Knorr Cetina (1999, p. 1), may be defined as 'those amalgams of arrangements and mechanisms – bonded through affinity, necessity, and historical coincidence which, in a given field, make up how we know what we know.' Knorr Cetina points to the formative aspects of knowledge processes and utilises the metaphor of 'knowledge machineries' to illustrate how the different arrangements and mechanisms work together to constitute a certain domain (1999). Further, as Knorr Cetina points out, these machineries also serve to constitute the knower. Practitioners are shaped through and learn to see the world through the lenses of their knowledge culture. Following this line of thought, professional knowledge cultures express themselves in certain practices and are, at the same time, made possible through the ways in which knowledge is organized and with which it is (collectively) engaged. This does not mean that knowledge cannot be something 'real;' something materialized, something objectified, and something subjected to consensus. On the contrary, it is in processes of materialization, articulation, and codification that knowledge cultures manifest themselves; through these processes, they are brought into play, continued, and subjected to advancement. Moreover, as Nespor (1994) notes, the material and representational dimensions of a knowledge domain serve to produce the space and time relations through which practitioners move as learners. By examining how knowledge is developed and mediated by artefacts in collective practices, how these tools and activities are organized in time and space, how they are linked up with other structures of collective action, and how they invite certain kinds of engagement, we may reveal how the learning activities of practitioners are encouraged, directed, and perhaps restricted in certain ways.

The current chapter takes this perspective as a point of departure in portraying the general characteristics of the knowledge cultures of computer engineering and school teaching. These are contrasting fields in terms of modes of organizing work, societal mandate, relationships to other sectors in society, and types of expertise. At the same time, they share the position of being responsible for core services in modern society, they are practice-oriented occupational groups grounded in a certain field of expertise and, in countries such as Norway, the programmes for initial professional education are, in both cases, located at university colleges within a state-regulated educational framework. The differences and similarities make them interesting cases to compare, both for the sake of revealing contrasting positions within the landscape of professional knowledge cultures, and for the benefit of examining these cultures' potential for learning from each other.

The discussion draws upon data from the Norwegian research project, Professional Learning in a Changing Society (ProLearn). This project was a comparative study of learning in the transition from education to work among nurses, teachers, accountants and computer engineers, carried out in the period 2004-2008. Special attention was given to how ways of organizing knowledge in professional communities influence learning and identity formation. Early career professionals who graduated from Oslo University College in 2002 were selected from a larger survey study and followed in their first years in working life by means of individual interviews, group interviews, and learning logs. The project and its findings are described in a more detailed manner in Jensen, Lahn, and Nerland (2012). The discussion that follows draws primarily upon interviews and learning logs carried out among computer engineers and school teachers. In order to shed light on profession-specific ways of dealing with knowledge, these data are supplemented and related to an analysis of policy documents and recent debates within the professional bodies (Karseth & Nerland, 2007).

THE KNOWLEDGE CULTURE OF COMPUTER ENGINEERING

The empirical frame for this part of the discussion is the working domain of computer engineers whose main tasks and functions are related to software development or system administration. Although the division of labour in this professional field comprises a range of specialities where both expertise and working tasks are concerned, the ubiquitous presence of and interaction with technological objects form a common frame for this group. Such objects may, for instance, relate to a computer network in an organization, a programming language, or the user interface of electronic services provided by an organization. The constitutive power of the knowledge culture will be examined in terms of the key characteristics that premise the knowledge practices in this field.

Knowledge Production in Technological Markets

One distinctive feature is that notions of professional knowledge are closely linked to technological inventions and achievements. New computer programmes, platforms, and systems both premise the work of computer engineers and provide the foundation of the need for their expertise. Thus, to a large extent, the development of profession-specific knowledge pursues technological achievements. For the profession, this implies that the expert domain is characterized by dynamic interrelations with other parts of the industrial sector, making market orientation and co-operation an important dimension in advancement efforts. This comes into view, for instance, in the way in which the Norwegian Society of Engineers (NITO), the largest professional body of engineers and technologists in Norway, links its support services to recent inventions and allocates its courses to firms and arenas in the technological working field (Karseth & Nerland, 2007). The effects of this notion of knowledge production upon professional learning are, however, not clear-cut. While today's global markets might be said to undermine traditional professionalism based on jurisdiction within a certain field of expertise, they also require a widening of professional expertise along both vertical and horizontal dimensions (Beck & Young, 2005). Further, the market regulation of the domain contributes to the speeding up of the technological turnovers and to the intensification of the time and space relations of professional work. Some implications will be discussed below.

Distribution of Information in Global Networks

The ways in which the professional practice is embedded in a knowledge economy serve to generate modes of knowledge distribution that go beyond the boundaries of the profession. To a large extent, the epistemic infrastructures are given the character of information structures that are distributed in global networks, particularly by means of the Internet. Since technologies are subject to rapid shifts and changes, such information structures are regarded as the most reliable source of updating. As one engineer says about programming in Java; 'In Java, for example, all the information you need is on their homepage. If something new happens you will find it there. That's not the case in schoolbooks.'

Information structures provide a medium of transaction that cuts across institutional spaces and simultaneously allows for local embeddedness and global outreach (Knorr Cetina, 2006). Thus, when practising their work, the practitioners are linked up with wider movements of knowledge development. Further, the network mode of organization implies that the logic of knowledge distribution is characterized by multiplicity and non-linearity (Castells, 1996; van Loon, 2006). A diversity of connections is possible, as the information provided could be accessed in different orders and in ways that disrupt any predetermined chronology of time. At the same time, the knowledge domain is subject to increasing differentiation that follows from a growth in the number of programming languages and technologies. As a consequence, the request for specialization is increasing and a range of sub-networks for different technologies is emerging. In this regard, the thematic structure of forums provides practitioners with opportunities for focused inquiries, as described by this engineer:

> You find new knowledge on different websites where people have had the same problem as you before and where many have posted their solutions. I often look at the IRC [Internet Relay Chat] chat programme; the people who hang there know their stuff. It doesn't take long before you get an answer.

One implication of this mode of distributing and sharing knowledge is that there are close links between information structures and the application of knowledge in professional work. The information provided often has the character of codified procedures and recipes. The underlying logic reflects a way of reasoning that corresponds to what Schon describes as a *technical rationality*, in which practitioners are seen as 'technical problem solvers who select technical means best suited to particular purposes' (1987, p. 3). Thus, the kind of learning offered when accessing networks of information is often restricted to updating the repertoire of programming skills and codified knowledge as part of the activity of identifying appropriate means to deal with particular problems.

At the same time, the connections between knowledge production and dissemination, and the way in which these processes are linked to global information structures and market interests, serve to involve professionals in structures of innovation that go beyond local problem solving. The interdependency between the production and distribution of new technologies and the utilization of such inventions in engineering practice give rise to new arenas of participation in which the traditional distinction between market and profession (Freidson, 2001) is rather blurred. One example is the website of Sun Developers Network, a site that was mentioned as a main source of updating among our interviewees. Here, the producer of new technologies, Sun Microsystems, offers access to information and knowledge by providing online courses, conferences, catalogues of programming patterns that are regarded as 'best practices,' as well as software that can be downloaded by developers worldwide. What is interesting to note is the ways in which such distribution of knowledge and information are linked to social structures of participation and community alignment. By means of weblogs, forums, and discussion groups, members of the network are invited to share their personal as well as professional interests and to contribute to advancements in the field by testing technologies and sharing experiences. As Sun proclaims at one of its sub-sites for Java developers:

> java.net provides a common area for interesting conversations and innovative development projects related to Java technology. By participating on java.net, members learn from each other, discover solutions to programming challenges, find new colleagues and mentors, and have more fun with Java technology. (Oracle, 2007)

Thus, while certainly providing information about advancements in the field, these kinds of networks also offer developers professional identities that are grounded in certain technologies and which exceed the local work settings. The learning professional is constructed as a member of a technological community who is encouraged to commit him/herself to certain technologies and invited to contribute to the collective knowledge of the community. Moreover, the networks incorporate means of encouraging reciprocity and social commitment. As an engineer described in reference to one of the developer forums:

> On their websites, you find something called DukeDollars. If you have a question you want answered, you can use these. You just put three or four DukeDollars on the table and give these to the person that has the best answer. The other way around, you start with 25 dollars and if you want more you have to answer other people's questions and then pile up more, and then you can get people to answer your questions again. I think it's a neat system.

For the practitioners, these websites and information networks represent important arenas for sharing and updating their knowledge about current software and technologies. They also constitute learning processes in certain ways by giving priority to the application of codified knowledge and technical skills, within specific technological boundaries, and through patterns of interaction that mainly consist of structures of concrete questions and answers.

Accumulation by Standardization and Codification of Procedures

A powerful dimension in the knowledge culture of computer engineering is the emphasis given to the standardization of devices and codification of procedures. Standards serve as a precondition that allow the network structures described above to be efficient. Moreover, standardization is closely interlinked with the technical rationality characteristic of the field. Informal standards come into view in the way in which engineers assess the work of colleagues and possible solutions. In spite of the multiplicity of possible connections and technical solutions, there are established principles for good engineering work. One of our interviewees described it in the following way:

> I believe it is more generally accepted in this field [than in others] what a good solution looks like. If five code developers work individually on the same task they will probable all agree – or at least four of the five will agree – upon which solution is better.

Moreover, in approaching problem situations, the engineers often turn to codified 'best practices' that are distributed in the information networks. They also embrace these patterns as models for their own work as developers. As one engineer says, bearing in mind the ideal-typical approach to work; 'when you face a new challenge, you will [try to] solve it in ways that are so good, so generic, so recyclable and effective that it could have served as a best practice.'

The accumulation of knowledge in this professional domain, for instance through practices of developing and reprocessing programming codes, is also linked to the development and distribution of standards of a formal character. In contrast to many other arenas of everyday life, in which individuals constantly engage with standards without paying any attention because they are so taken for granted in their social practices, computer engineers are dealing with standards in a very explicit manner. This is, to a large extent, what their work is about: knowing the technological standards that are in play, knowing how they may or may not work together, and knowing how to perform different tasks within the different technological regimes. The commercial ways of advancing the knowledge domain by launching new versions of technologies serve to reinforce the importance of knowing and understanding the relevant standards.

Accordingly, technological and procedural standards are heavily present in the everyday language of computer engineers; in their ways of talking about their work, negotiating competence, and committing themselves to learning. For instance, our interviewees tell us about how the discussion among developers during the first phase of a new project is largely about deciding which standards to use when approaching the present task or problem. This phase is often marked by energetic negotiations of preferences that have an emotional dimension. As one engineer stated; 'Discussions among developers are often somewhat heated; however, disagreements are never long-lasting.' What seems to be discussed less are the ways in which the ever-present standards influence the social practices in the profession, including the practices of learning. Standards serve to create distinctions as regards competence, spaces for movements, differentiation of working tasks, and learning areas. Moreover, they serve to 'make up' kinds of engineers through their inscribed quests for specialization. In our data, this comes into view in the ways in which some engineers identify with certain technologies and standards. For instance, one engineer talks about himself as a 'J2EE developer,' while another describes himself as 'the Linux evangelist' in his workplace. The trend is also reflected in how employers tend to search for programmers who are specialized in certain technologies or programming languages.

This aspect of the knowledge culture is both supportive and challenging for the engineers. Standards open and close possibilities at the same time. As one engineer expresses it, there is a danger that you can 'get squeezed if the short-term interests of your employer make you less attractive on the labour market;' for instance, if the technologies preferred by the employer become out of date. Thus, in order to navigate as learners in this professional domain, the engineers are requested to monitor their engagement with standards and to secure their own position in relation to upcoming technologies.

Complex Artefacts and the Request for Creativity

At the same time as the knowledge culture of computer engineering highlights the need for standards and consistency, the practice is characterized by engagements with artefacts that have an ambiguous and open-ended character. Systems, programmes, and codes can always be improved to be more efficient, more widely applicable, or more complex in their functionalities. In the moment of resolving a technical problem by means of, e.g., applying distributed codes or patterns of practice, new possibilities and untried functionalities appear. The professional practice is thus characterized by a richness of what Knorr Cetina (1997, 2001) calls epistemic objects; that is, objects that are marked by their unfolding character and their lack of completeness of being. Such objects are characteristically open and question-generating, and when individuals try to reveal them, they typically increase rather than reduce their complexity (Knorr Cetina, 2006).

The presence of epistemic objects in a knowledge culture allows for an externalization of learning and knowledge engagements. This again constitutes the relationship between knowledge and practitioners in certain ways, where objectual relationships – that is, the relational dynamics between humans and their non-human material – define the knowledge processes. Knorr Cetina (2001) uses computer programmes as an example of objects that propel such dynamics by their way of being simultaneously both ready to be used and in a process of transformation. On the one hand, engineering work such as programming is heavily commodified and objectified in terms of standards, software, and platforms that are defined and materialized as physical things. On the other hand, the technology and computing practices are continuously changing. Following the arguments of Mackenzie (2005) and Bowker and Star (2000), complex technological objects and practices also resist commodification. The open-ended character of epistemic objects brings a creative dimension to work, which may serve as a primary driving force in work-based learning (Jensen, 2007; Nerland & Jensen, 2010).

As a consequence, it is not sufficient to understand the practice of computer engineers in terms of restricted problem solving and rule following. Engineering work also implies an interest in discovery and an ability to see the unfulfilled potential inherent in the technological scene. In a group interview, this came up as a topic when the engineers discussed challenges arising when routine-based actions are insufficient. One engineer, who works as a software developer in a large consulting company, provided the following example:

> In some cases, you have a customer who has a hybrid server park, and who, due to, e.g., new ownership structures, has received the message that no more money will be spent on that equipment. Then you have to make sure that what you do is compatible between the different systems, which may not speak the same language. Such situations require a lot more creativity than

214

just depending upon logic reasoning. You have to think broader and to think more freely than you would have done in a homogeneous technological environment.

This example points to how existing knowledge and standards are challenged both by the local work context and by the objects' inherent potential for change. Codified or materialized knowledge needs to be recontextualized in the specific context of problem solving. Moreover, this often takes the form of exploring the prospective opportunities of the technologies. As noted by Bucciarelli and Kuhn (1997, p. 211), engineers typically 'go about making up scenarios about things and principles, physical concepts and variables and how they relate.' While such scenario making requires creativity, the aim of the activity is to achieve closure by arriving at a solution that is 'fixed, repeatable, stable, unambiguous, and internally consistent' (Bucciarelli & Kuhn, 1997, p. 212). Thus, there is a paradox between the specified and the ambiguous in this knowledge culture, which allows practitioners to develop their competencies by constantly moving between the unfulfilled and the temporarily fixed. Interestingly, this dynamic is not only a case for developers, but also for engineers who mainly do system administration. As one of our interviewees belonging to the latter group stated; 'In fact the most important thing is to realise the potential of the system you are working with. As you learn more about it, you also see many new opportunities.'

For the professional, the relationships with objects require an experimental attitude in which the practitioner needs to be sensitive to the unfulfilled potential of the technology in question. That is, he/she needs to be sufficiently familiar with the field of knowledge to be able to interpret objects in terms of their ways of displaying not-yet-realized opportunities and to see their inherent potential for change (Knorr Cetina & Bruegger, 2002). At the same time, the objects may provide the learner with directions for further investigations and in this way also give the objects 'binding' functions that may propel learning forward (Jensen & Lahn, 2005; Jensen, 2007).

Knowledge Application within Series of Problem Solving

The ways in which the knowledge practices of everyday work are organized both reflect and constitute the knowledge culture of the profession. As in engineering cultures in general, the domain of computer engineering is characterized by a dominant pragmatist way of thinking. This implies a high value placed on the application of knowledge in dealing with practical problems, a focus on validating theoretical principles through activities of inquiry, and an overall emphasis given to making things work and getting the task done. The problem-oriented approach implies that engineering work is largely organized as a series of problem solving (Bucciarelli & Kuhn, 1997; Downey, 1998; Sørensen, 1998), either in terms of correcting malfunctions that occur in a technological system, or in terms of developing new functionalities in accordance with given specifications.

With regard to the question of work-based learning, the regulation of the problem-solving activities in time and space is important. The activities are characterized by restrictions in two ways. First, they are spatially limited in terms of *content*, as the engineers' responsibilities are often allocated to specific functions or parts of a project or a computer system. In larger firms, the practitioners are often organized in teams dealing with specific tasks that are linked together in a broader work structure. For instance, one of our interviewees is based in a 'user interface team' that develops functionalities that other teams use as a basis in their work:

> My team and another team develop modules that the business teams utilise to develop their logic … So, in a way, we provide the framework, or the components that the other teams use to, for example, make screen images.

Within the team, the tasks are further specialized. In this case, the user interface team comprises one leader who specifies the requests of the task; three code developers; one tester; and one person who is responsible for securing documentation. This division of tasks and responsibilities serves to constitute the space of learning opportunities in ways that are both enabling and constraining. On the one hand, one could argue that the engineers are involved in limited parts of the knowledge domain and, therefore, exposed to limited opportunities for learning. On the other hand, they are provided with opportunities to specialise their skills in ways that may enhance the opportunities for focused learning. Further, the ways in which additive structures of accumulation are developed through co-operative efforts allow for a sense of meaningfulness in the performance of limited tasks. One engineer links this to the performative character of the knowledge practices:

> You feel that you are part of a dynamic structure that, when working at its best, as it generally does, gives you an incredible feeling of satisfaction. Moreover, in my work situation, you see the results of what you have done in a very, very explicit manner. That really gives you a good feeling.

Second, the problem-solving activities are restricted in terms of *time*. The working days are often characterized by a series of 'short-term loops' where processes of inquiry and specific problem solving coalesce. The quest for quick solutions and knowledge application may give priority to surface forms of learning and undermine possibilities for more profound engagements with knowledge. Moreover, the dominant project organization characteristic of the field contributes to an intensification of time where the problems in question have to be resolved within a limited time frame (Ó Riain, 2000; Davies & Mathieu, 2005). In some cases, this may serve to undermine possibilities of work-based learning, as the timeframe does not allow for the development of new skills. In Ó Riain's ethnographic study of a software team, this came into view when the team found itself in need of new skills, and, due to time constraints, was forced to bring in an external consultant with the necessary competence instead of training current employees (2000, p. 196). Also, in our interviews, the ways in which the tight schedules restrict opportunities for learning was a recurrent theme. Quite a few of the interviewed engineers stated that they would have liked to engage more broadly in learning but that the time pressure of their work made this difficult.

Seen as a whole, the knowledge culture of computer engineering has distinctive characteristics that shape and encourage work-based learning in certain ways. Emphasis is given to the application of standards and codified knowledge in particular situations of problem solving and to the mediation of knowledge through complex artefacts and information structures in global networks. This gives learning in the workplace the character of inquiry-based activities that are partly internally driven by the problem setting at hand, and partly externally by the invention of new standards in the technological field. At the same time, the rapid shifts relate continuous learning to issues of career management. Our interviewees express a concern for staying informed about what is happening on the technological scene, and, by and large, they assume that this as an individual responsibility(see also Nerland, 2012b).

THE KNOWLEDGE CULTURE OF SCHOOL TEACHING

School teachers are, of course, working in a very different environment from computer engineers. Their profession is grounded in a societal mandate where supporting the intellectual and personal growth of the next generation is the prime concern. Teachers share the engineers' orientation towards practical issues and situated decision-making; however, their field of expertise constitutes a quite different knowledge culture, which also generates different ways of encouraging learning. Some general features will be explored in the following sections, within the context of teaching in primary and lower secondary schools in Norway.

Experience-Based Production and Accumulation of Knowledge

A major dimension in this knowledge culture is the notion of professional knowledge as acquired and developed by way of personal experience. A common narrative is that the individual teacher needs to build up a wide repertoire of first-hand experiences gained in a variety of teaching and learning situations. This view of knowledge and expertise is, for instance, reflected in the way in which teachers see themselves as being closer to craftsmen than to academics. As expressed by one teacher; 'The teaching profession is about craft, I think. It is a lot of knowledge that needs to be achieved by way of experience.' Another teacher shares this view, and relates the emphasis on personal experience to the nature of the knowledge itself. According to her, the knowledge is hard to define and to make explicit, and thus also difficult to extract from external sources: 'The knowledge is not very tangible,' she says, 'you have to build it up yourself.'

This way of thinking is manifested more broadly in the history of the teaching profession, which in Norway has been related to an egalitarian way of thinking as well as to a strong sense of individual autonomy within a national, unified, and curriculum-regulated school system (Lauglo, 1990; Hagerman, 1992; Michelsen, 2002; Karseth & Nerland, 2007). On a collective level, the emphasis on personal knowledge is reflected in the ways in which the teachers' union frames its efforts by protecting the opportunities for individual autonomy and by advocating a bottom-up strategy for knowledge development. In 2004, the Union of Education Norway launched a project on *Professional Awareness* as a means to strengthen the identity of the profession and develop collective ideals for professional practice. The president and vice-president of the union described the project as a matter of creating a shared platform for reflective practice by way of bringing the experiences of individual members to the fore:

> We are not going to create something entirely new. This is about articulating and summarising reflections about practices in the workplace. We want to disclose these reflections and turn them into a collective platform for member groups as well as for the entire organisation. This will provide the foundation for the Union's work on educational policy. (letter to the members of the union by President Hjetland and Vice-president Aahlin, 2004)

In this way, experience-based knowledge was highlighted as the basis for developing the profession's collective knowledge base. Teachers were asked to initiate group discussions in their workplace that aimed to reveal and verbalise tacit knowledge, and to bring the outcomes of their discussions 'upwards' in the organization. Moreover, the teachers' union underscored the need for respecting the individual teacher as a professional practitioner. As the president stated;

> Teachers are different and must find their own, personal way of teaching. We meet students with different needs of suitably adopted education. It is very important to maintain that teachers have the freedom to choose how they will proceed. (Hjetland, 2005)

Protecting teachers' rights to choose teaching methods has been a continuing concern for the teachers' union in Norway, as well as in later debates. For the learning professional, this way of thinking implies that work-based learning is individualized and closely related to the practitioner's reflective practice. At the same time, it is the individual teacher's responsibility to contribute to the development of a collective sense of identity and to feed one's experiences into the profession 'from below.'

Knowledge Distribution by Way of Human Interaction

A related facet of teachers' knowledge culture is the emphasis given to human interaction in strategies for knowledge distribution. Where the engineers are accessing sources of knowledge that are codified, technologically mediated, widely distributed, and open 'to all,' the access to professional knowledge for teachers is still heavily dependent upon chains of human interaction. Although teachers frequently access the Internet and written sources to seek out facts and information about specific themes (Caspersen, 2007), their engagement with profession-specific knowledge related to pedagogical issues is typically mediated by human interaction. For instance, a primary strategy for updating oneself in these domains is related to asking colleagues about their experiences and ways of doing things.

According to our interviewees, one reason for this is that the professional knowledge is not accumulated and provided in more structured ways. As one of them explained; 'You have to ask your colleagues, because it [the knowledge] is not systematized and made available in other ways.' Another teacher describes her experience in a similar way: 'It is oral transmission of knowledge all the way,' she says, 'that's the way it works.' In addition to the logic following from emphasising personal knowledge, they explain this situation by referring to time pressure and tight schedules at work, which leaves the practitioners with little space for documenting teaching procedures and experiences. As a consequence, learning in the workplace is related to informal interaction and knowledge sharing within the local school, in which the learning professional is implicitly asked to take personal responsibility for seeking out advice and ideas.

In recent years, the profession has shown an increased interest in developing more collective structures for professional development, e.g., by developing and offering courses around methodological topics. It is, however, interesting to note that efforts to provide more formal learning opportunities seem to employ a comparable strategy for person-mediated knowledge sharing. For instance, in some municipalities, the local educational authorities organize chains of person-to-person communication as a way of implementing new teaching methods:

At every school [in my district], there is one teacher who is called a reading teacher. He receives tuition from [name of specialist]. The research and method is built around his [the specialist's] approach. And then the reading teacher is responsible for training the staff at his school in this method.

This way of organizing knowledge distribution seems to rest upon the idea that professional development requires personal training in appropriate contexts, which provide opportunities for practical exploration and for dialogue around the knowledge issues. At the same time, it reflects an emerging interest in standardising and establishing a common knowledge base for teachers who are working in the same subject area. However, the ways and extent to which such collective learning is promoted varies from district to district and seems somewhat fortuitous. Another teacher tells of a related structure of knowledge sharing, which, in her case, is carried out within a more informal setting and based on the initiatives of individual teachers:

My colleague, who teaches in third grade, is currently involved in continuing education and participates in a network for math teachers. She does this on a voluntary basis, and then she is asked to share some of her knowledge with us. However, if she was not interested, no one would have done it. We don't have anyone in this role when it comes to teaching the Norwegian language.

The fact that several teachers express an interest in extending this model for knowledge distribution to other areas and subjects by way of a 'local tutor' indicates that this aspect of the profession's knowledge culture is well adopted at the level of individual practitioners. Many teachers seem to prefer to engage in learning within a context of human interaction.

The person-mediated way of distributing knowledge implies that the epistemic infrastructures are given a local profile in the sense that most teachers connect with profession-specific knowledge within the boundaries of their local community. The strength of this model is that engagement with knowledge takes place close to its application in practical teaching, and that it allows individual and organizational learning in the workplace to coalesce. The possible limitations include that it may be difficult to exceed the local boundaries and thus to reconceptualise current practice, and that the practitioners are not offered the sense of excitement that being in contact with wider structures of knowledge development may provide. As one of our interviewees expressed it; 'I feel that when I get to know about something new, it is from colleagues and those I am sharing working space with. And that's it, in a way.' In the long run, this limitation may contribute to undermining the professionals' drive for continuous learning.

Knowledge Application as a Matter of Differentiation

It follows from the notions above that this knowledge culture is marked by a resistance to standardization in terms of strict guidelines and codified procedures for how work is to be performed. This is related to three interlinked ways of understanding the application of knowledge in professional work: First, it emerges as a consequence of the complexity of the professional knowledge domain, which makes knowledge difficult to set permanently and to apply directly in practical settings. Teachers' field of expertise encompasses subject matter knowledge as well as knowledge about the cognitive, social, and emotional processes involved in learning (Klette, 2000). Thus, any idea about the direct application of knowledge becomes problematic. As one teacher says about knowledge related to teaching students how to read:

> It is a very wide-ranging domain of knowledge. Thus, you have to pick and choose from here and there, and try to use your own imagination. That's why I feel it would be very problematic to organize it [the knowledge] in a catalogue and state how exactly practice should be performed. Because, I don't believe the knowledge is fixed in that way.

The idea seems to be that general knowledge needs to be filtered and transformed through the individual teacher's judgment and personal approach to be applied efficiently in educational practice.

Second, there is a general concern that teachers work in very different settings that are dependent upon the actual students and educational context within which the teaching is to take place. The nature of work as being closely related to the needs and learning approaches of different students calls for a sense of carefulness and prudence that rejects the direct application of predefined standards. Thus, a constitutive facet of teachers' knowledge culture is the idea that knowledge has to be applied within an ethos of differentiation, in which the specificity of the situation at hand premises the best approach to teaching just as much as theoretical knowledge or predefined guidelines.

Third, at a collective level, the professional body has brought forward the argument that extensive use of standardized methods undermines the opportunity to accomplish their professional responsibility. As stated by the president of the teachers' union:

> Practice cannot hinge on so-called documented methods alone. For one, such overregulation will imply a dramatic loss in experience-based knowledge, which has traditionally been our basis for professional work. Second, it will undermine the freedom of methods and reduce our mandate as a profession. We will lose the right to practise qualified, professional discretion. In that case, we do not qualify for the term profession anymore. (Hjetland, 2006, speech to the general assembly of the Union of Education Norway)

Although efforts to strengthen the knowledge base by developing guidelines and collective repertoires of teaching strategies are increasingly coming up in this professional field in Norway, as in the professional sector in general, the concern for protecting individual autonomy by resisting standard-driven regulation of work is still very powerful. This may be related to the Norwegian history of regulating teachers' practice by means of a national curriculum that defines the content of schooling (Klette, 2000; Carlgren, 2000). For the learning professional, this way of thinking contributes further to an individualized responsibility for improvement and professional development. It generates an ideological space that encourages the continuous search for more efficient teaching methods and has the potential to stimulate reflexive learning on the basis of experience. At the same time, however, the resistance to standards may undermine the possibilities for linking local teaching and learning activities with other practices and levels of knowledge development. One function that standards may potentially assume is to mediate between scientific knowledge advancements and practical work. A lack of such mediating devices may leave the practitioners in a vacuum where secured guidelines for practice are concerned, and contribute to restricting the space of knowledge engagement to the boundaries of the local community.

Knowledge Engagements within Wide-ranging Tasks and Responsibilities

In contrast with computer engineers, whose work is often organized around specific technologies and thus also specific knowledge issues, the culture of school teachers is marked by indistinct boundaries and wide-ranging working tasks. Norway has a strong tradition for manning elementary schools with general teachers, thus both the educational programmes and the working tasks comprise responsibilities related to a wide range of subject curricula.[2] The idea is to follow the class and students instead of specific subjects as the principle for organizing work. Thus, knowledge practices in the workplace are traditionally discriminated in relation to grades and the age of the students, but teaching obligations typically comprise a range of subject matters and responsibilities within these frames. One teacher describes her work in this way:

I work with … everything, really … planning lessons, performing lessons, and not least monitoring and supporting students. It includes planning work in relation to different kind of students, because they are very different when it comes to knowledge and learning. And quite a lot of collaboration with other teachers. It is about everything, from following students to planning and administrative work. Quite different tasks. Marking …

In recent years, teachers' work has increasingly been subjected to team organization, which aims both to facilitate collaboration and to frame responsibilities in a more distinct way. The team organization is, however, also complex in structure, comprising teams formed around levels and classes, teams formed around subjects, and teams formed around specific projects. Thus, the knowledge demands are multiple, and individual teachers are often still left with the task of creating limits around their own work. Besides, teachers are given the responsibility to follow specific groups of students, a task that is not restricted to activities in the classroom but includes connecting to other areas of the student's life and staying in dialogue with the student and his/her parents or guardians.

As a consequence, teachers as learners are presented with multiple knowledge demands that span a range of subject-specific domains of knowledge and include complex social and emotional matters. Our interviewees express a general need for learning more about how to personalise teaching and how to support students with special needs. They also point to the unlimited areas of subject matter knowledge in which they feel they should have engaged themselves as learners. As one teacher expresses it:

I wish I had time enough to develop [my knowledge] in all these subject areas … there is so much more you wished you could learn in social science, in geography, in mathematics … I mean subject related. It's just so much … All world history and the history of Norway I wish I knew better. And I would really like to learn more about all the different religions … I would have liked to know more about everything, really.

Thus, in one sense, the knowledge culture of teachers provides a plenitude of open-ended questions and matters for further exploration that may invite learning. However, seen together with the lack of standardized procedures, and the time pressure and extensive demands for 'front stage performance' at work, the support structures around the learning professional may be too fluid and too open to provide clear directions for learning (for further discussion, see Klette & Carlsten, 2012). Teachers as learners are encouraged to engage in improvement and professional development by means of reflexivity and self-governed inquiry; however, the horizontal and multi-dimensional organization of knowledge may leave them with unclear support structures to cope with these demands.

The Primacy of Students' Learning

Last but not least, a powerful aspect of teachers' knowledge culture is the overall mission of supporting students' learning. The complexity involved in observing, assessing, understanding, and supporting students' learning presents constant challenges to teachers and requires their full attention. However, rather than leading to significant attention towards knowledge and professional procedures, many Norwegian teachers seem to be oriented towards the students as human beings. At the level of the profession, this comes through in the abovementioned emphasis on differentiation, as well as in a dominant construction of the teacher as 'pupil centered, caring and including' (Søreide, 2007). The attention towards the student is undoubtedly crucial for performing good work, but, at the same time, it may contribute to making teachers' own learning less visible and accessible. A typical tendency in our data is that teachers answer in terms of their students' learning when they are asked about their own experience of knowledge demands and learning needs. One teacher describes the challenges he faces as 'a matter of really coming through to the students. To reach them where they are. And to try to create teaching activities that really catch the students' attention.' Another teacher states that such processes entail continuing efforts in terms of trying out new approaches and methods, and that these processes of trying and assessing how the strategies work imply an ongoing creation of one's own teaching style:

> You learn new methods, new things all the time, see how it works. So that part you're in charge of yourself, and while travelling you see what works and not. So, in a way, you construct your own style and you continually strive to develop it further.

As these examples show, learning and professional development are closely linked to everyday teaching. Moreover, teachers' learning is mediated through the students' learning activities and learning requirements. The teachers' possible space for learning is largely framed by the content and form of the students' current learning tasks. These tasks are again premised and regulated by the national and local curricula for the specific subjects. Another example of how the learning requirements for students command teachers' learning comes into view in teachers' habits of seeking out new subject matter knowledge. One of our interviewees describes the circumstances that mobilized her to search for new knowledge. These are typically related to gaining insights into a topic scheduled to be taught in the near future: 'It happens when you see the topics coming up. In the planning period, you will try to read a bit about it, to check with colleagues how they have approached the issues, read what they have done...' She continues by providing an example from her reading about Egypt in a period when this topic was scheduled in the curriculum for her class. One consequence of this approach to learning may be that subject matter knowledge is brought to the fore as crucial for teaching and is subjected to deliberate learning. As discussed above, profession-specific knowledge related to pedagogical issues seems to be approached in different manners closely related to experience-based judgments and reflection embedded in practice.

On the positive side, the comprehensive orientation towards students' learning may serve to bring teachers' own learning close to practice and keep it relevant for the multiple working demands. At the same time, this way of thinking about professional development may undermine teachers' opportunities for dealing explicitly with learning in working life. Moreover, it may lead to an absence of knowledge objects for teachers to engage with that link their immediate work context to wider knowledge worlds.

Seen together, the powerful dimensions in the knowledge culture of school teachers construct work-based learning as forms of experiential learning, in which the professional is invited to embrace the position as a reflective practitioner who examines and intervenes in his/her own practice on a discretionary basis. The repertoire of approaches to teaching is subjected to individual accumulation and enacted within the logic of diversification. Moreover, learning opportunities are largely bound to the local context and school community. By virtue of the emphasis on students' current learning tasks and the requirements of the curriculum, teachers' own learning is mediated by the students' learning activities. This presents challenges to the professionals for dealing explicitly with their own competence development. Without stronger support structures for this mission at a collective level, teachers who are not fully capable of taking up the position as reflective and reflexive practitioners may be in danger of eroding themselves as learning subjects.

CONCLUDING DISCUSSION

The above exploration has revealed profound differences between the two professions in regard to their ways of organizing knowledge and positioning the knower. The two groups differ in the logics and arrangements through which knowledge is developed, circulated, accumulated, and applied in professional settings. These logics and arrangements also serve to form ways of envisioning knowledge and opportunities for learning. In this concluding section, I will relate the differences to three aspects that seem particularly relevant for our understanding of 'machineries of knowledge construction' (Knorr Cetina, 1999) in professional domains and their ways of influencing learning: 1) the temporal and spatial scale of knowledge practices and participation; 2) the types of intermediaries through which knowledge circulates; and 3) the collective belief systems and orientations that emerge through the former aspects.

The first issue concerns the space and time relations through which practitioners are invited to move as learners. As noted by Nespor (1994) in the context of educational programmes, (professional) communities are not only situated in space and time, they are also characterized by their ways of setting up patterns of movement and participation across space and time. This also seems to be highly relevant in the context of work-based learning. In the engineering culture, knowledge circulates in wider information networks in ways that bring spatial extension to work. The engineers move on these structures in multiple ways, and their knowledge practices may be simultaneously locally embedded and distributed. By connecting to other spheres of the knowledge world while exploring or solving present working tasks, the local-global divide becomes temporarily resolved and aspects of the wider infrastructure for engineering work become activated in local practices. Moreover, this co-presence of different spaces for engagement is also mirrored when it comes to time scales. Although work is often organized as series of problem solving within restricted time frames, the engineering culture is also geared towards the future. This comes into view, for instance, in the overall attention towards new technological advancements and unfulfilled opportunities. Hence, engineers may actively engage with future scenarios when performing current work and, in this way, move along different time scales simultaneously. Such heterochrony of practice is also described by Lemke (2000). However, while Lemke elucidates how the longer timescale processes related to human history produce effects on shorter timescale activities, the culture of computer engineering may turn this the other way around and allow ideas and visions of the future to influence activities in the present.

The space and time relations in the knowledge culture of school teachers are composed differently. In this culture, the professional practice is more locally bounded and relies more on local circuits of knowledge. The emphasis given to face-to-face communication and to experience-based knowledge makes the local work environment the prime setting for knowledge engagement. In one sense, the long-term commitment to students and their development provides extended time frames for teachers' engagement. In spatial terms, however, this engagement is still locally bounded and does not necessarily incorporate movements within extended knowledge worlds. Moreover, although teachers are also subjected to multiple and simultaneous demands, this simultaneity seems more related to the co-presence of concerns embedded in working tasks than to their own movement across space and time.

The second issue concerns the type of intermediaries that define the ways in which knowledge is produced, circulated, and approached. Such intermediaries may be of different material character, and include humans, artefacts, texts of various kinds, and forms of capital (Callon, 1991). In the culture of school teaching, knowledge tends to be mediated in personal interaction and enacted by the individual teacher with concern for the current needs of the student. Each professional accumulates his/her personal knowledge base, mainly by way of attaining teaching experiences and through the sharing of such experiences with colleagues in the local community. Profession-specific distributed knowledge is sparsely referred to in our data. Although the teachers engage quite extensively with codified knowledge, this is typically related to subject matter knowledge that is utilized to prepare lessons. In contrast, the knowledge culture in the field of computer engineering rests, to a great extent, on processes of commodification. This knowledge domain is heavily structured in terms of collectively shared knowledge objects and codified procedures. As also pointed out by Knorr Cetina (1997, 2001), a primary feature of object relations in expert cultures is the separateness of subject and object; that is, a distance that makes interpretation and exploration of something possible. It allows for abstraction, decontextualization, and recontextualization, which may be seen as core processes in learning (Guile, 2010). The richness of objects in the engineering culture may facilitate such processes to a larger extent than the more oral and person-oriented culture of school teaching.

The third issue is related to both the above, and concerns ways of envisioning knowledge and the collective belief systems that frame practitioners' orientation; that is, what Knorr Cetina (2006) terms 'epistementalities.' Different knowledge cultures will embody certain visions about how knowledge should be handled and inserted into personal and organizational life (Knorr Cetina, 2006). The explorations undertaken above show that both knowledge cultures emphasise applied knowledge and envision learning as embedded in current working tasks. Yet, there are significant differences in how knowledge application is envisioned. The knowledge culture of the teaching profession stresses the need for differentiation in the way in which the professional work is performed, whereas the culture of computer engineering advocates the need for standardization and consistency. In sum, the teaching culture is marked by an 'inwards' orientation, which highlights the particularities of the situation with reference to the present and the past, while the engineering culture is more 'outwards' and future oriented with attention given to new advancements that are externally introduced. These orientations contribute to constructing professional development as a matter of experiential learning in the teaching profession, whereas the access to and application of new and universal knowledge is given emphasis in the field of computer engineering.

The investigations undertaken in this chapter are explorative in character, and more empirical research is needed in order to develop a thorough understanding of how the characteristics play out in different settings, as well as how they may vary between local and national contexts. At the same time, the identified differences between the two professions demonstrate the relevance of conceptualising professional cultures as knowledge cultures marked by distinct heuristic practices and knowledge relations, and constituted by complex amalgams of instruments, strategies, practices, and ways of envisioning knowledge. These issues are further explored in Jensen, Lahn, and Nerland (2012). Hopefully, we will see more research that can complement the picture and increase our understanding of how knowledge, professional practice, and responsibilities are constructed in the interplay of local and extended knowledge worlds.

NOTES

[1] This chapter will also be published in Jensen, Lahn, & Nerland (2012).
[2] At the moment of writing this is about to change, as a new and more specialized national curriculum for teacher education was instigated in 2010.

REFERENCES

Becher, T. & Trowler, P.R. (2001). *Academic tribes and territories: Intellectual inquiry and the cultures of disciplines* (2nd ed.). Buckingham: Society for Research into Higher Education/Open University Press.

Beck, J. & Young, M. (2005). The assault on the professions and the restructuring of academic and professional identities: A Bernsteinian analysis. *British Journal of Sociology of Education, 26*(2), 183–199.

Billett, S. (2004). Learning through work: Participatory practices. In Rainbird, H., Fuller, A., & Munro, A. (Eds.), *Workplace learning in context* (pp. 109–125). London: Routledge.

Bowker, G., & Star, S.L. (2000). Invisible mediators of action: Classification and the ubiquity of standards. *Mind, Culture, and Activity, 7*(1–2), 147–163.

Bucciarelli, L. & Kuhn, S. (1997). Engineering education and engineering practice: Improving the fit. In Barley, S. & Orr, J. (Eds.), *Between craft and science: Technical work in U.S. settings* (pp. 210–229). Ithaca: Cornell University Press.

Carlgren, I. (2000).The implicit teacher. In Klette, K., Carlgren, I., Rasmussen, J., Simola, H., & Sundkvist, M. (Eds.), *Restructuring Nordic teachers: An analysis of policy texts from Finland, Denmark, Sweden and Norway* (pp. 325–362). Oslo: University of Oslo, Institute for Educational Research.

Caspersen, J. (2007). Kvalifiseringavnyutdannedesykepleiere – en undersøkelseavlæringsstrategie-rogopplæringavnyutdannedesykepleiereiarbeidslivet. [Qualifying novice nurses: A study of learning strategies and learning systems in working life]. Oslo: Oslo University College.

Castells, M. (1996). *The rise of the network society.* Oxford: Blackwell.

Davies, K. & Mathieu, C. (2005). *Gender inequality in the IT sector in Sweden and Ireland.* Stockholm: National Institute for Working Life.

Donald, J.G. (2002). *Learning to think: Disciplinary perspectives.* San Francisco: Jossey-Bass.

Downey, G.L. (1998). *The machine in me: An anthropologist sits among computer engineers.* New York: Routledge.

Eraut, M. (2006). Professional knowledge and learning at work. Knowledge. *Work & Society, 4*(3), 43–62.

Freidson, E. (2001). *Professionalism: The third logic.* London: Polity.

Guile, D. (2010). The learning challenge of the knowledge economy. Rotterdam: Sense.

Hagerman, G. (1992). *Skolefolk. Lærerneshistoriei Norge* [Teachers' history in Norway]. Oslo: Ad Notam Gyldendal.

Hjetland, H. & Aahlin, P. (2004). Kjæremedlemmerogtillitsvalgte [letter to members of the Union of Education]. Retrieved from www.utdanningsforbundet.no.

Hjetland, H. (2005). Helga Hjetland, President of the Union of Education Norway. Retrieved from www.utdanningsforbundet.no.

Hjetland, H. (2006). Speech to the general assembly. Retrieved from www.utdanningsforbundet.no.

Jensen, K. & Lahn, L. (2005). The binding role of knowledge: An analysis of nursing students' knowledge ties. *Journal of Education and Work, 18*(3), 305–320.

Jensen, K. (2007). The desire to learn: An analysis of knowledge-seeking practices among professionals. *Oxford Review of Education, 33*(4), 489–502.

Jensen, K., Lahn, L., & Nerland, M. (Eds.). (2012). *Professional learning in the knowledge society.* Rotterdam: Sense.

Karseth, B. & Nerland, M. (2007), Building professionalism in a knowledge society: Examining discourses of knowledge in four professional associations. *Journal of Education and Work, 20*(4), 335–355.

Klette, K. (2000).Towards a construction of a new teacher? Analyses of policy documents: The case of Norway. In Klette, K., Carlgren, I., Rasmussen, J., Simola, K., & Sundkvist, M. (Eds.), *Restructuring Nordic teachers: An analysis of policy texts from Finland, Denmark, Sweden and Norway* (pp. 263–324). Oslo: University of Oslo, Institute for Educational Research.

Klette, K. & Carlsten, T.C. (2012). Knowledge in teacher learning: New professional challenges. In Jensen, K., Lahn, L., & Nerland, M. (Eds.), *Professional learning in the knowledge economy.* Rotterdam: Sense.

Knorr Cetina, K. (1997). Sociality with objects: Social relations in post-social knowledge societies. *Theory, Culture and Society, 14*(4), pp. 1–30.

227

Knorr Cetina, K. (1999). *Epistemic cultures*. Cambridge, MA: Harvard University Press.

Knorr Cetina, K. (2001). Objectual practice. In Schatzki, T., Knorr Cetina, K., & von Savigny, E. (Eds.), *The practice turn in contemporary theory*. London: Routledge.

Knorr Cetina, K. (2006). Knowledge in a knowledge society: Five transitions. *Knowledge, Work and Society, 4*(3), 23–41.

Knorr Cetina, K. & Bruegger, U. (2002). Traders' engagement with markets: A postsocial relationship. *Theory, Culture & Society, 19*, 161–185.

Lauglo, J. (1990).A comparative perspective with special reference to Norway. In Granheim, M., Kogan, M., & Lundgren, U.P. (Eds.), *Evaluation as policymaking: Introducing evaluation into a national decentralized educational system* (pp. 66–88). London, Jessica Kingsley

Lemke, J. (2000). Across the scales of time: Artifacts, activities, and meanings in ecosocial systems. *Mind, Culture and Activity, 7*(4), 273–290.

Mackenzie, A. (2005). The performativity of code: Software and cultures of circulation. *Theory, Culture & Society, 22*(1), 71–92.

Michelsen, S. (2002). Nårstyringsambisjonermøter en profesjonsutdanning [About government and professional education]. In S. Michelsen & T. Halvorsen (Eds.), *Fagligeforbindelser. Profesjonsutdanningogkunnskapspolitikketterhøgskolereformen* (pp. 17–52). Bergen: Fagbokforlaget.

Nerland, M. & Jensen, K. (2010). Objectual practice and learning in professional work. In Billett, S. (Ed.), *Learning through practice: Models, traditions, orientations and approaches* (pp. 82–103). Dordrecht: Springer.

Nespor, J. (1994). *Knowledge in motion: Space, time and curriculum in undergraduate physics and management*. London: Falmer.

Neumann, T., Parry, S., & Becher, T. (2002). Teaching and learning in their disciplinary contexts: A conceptual analysis. *Higher Education, 25*(4), 405–417.

Oracle. (2007). Java. Retrieved from http://developers.sun.com/learning/academic.

Ó Riain, S. (2000). Net-working for a living: Irish software developers in the global workplace. In Burawoy, M., Blum, J.A., George, S., Gille, Z., Gowan, T., Haney, L., Klawiter, M., Lopez, S.H., Ó Riain, S., & Thayer, M. (Eds.), *Global ethnography: Forces, connections, and imaginations in a postmodern world* (pp. 175–202). Berkeley & Los Angeles: University of California Press.

Schon, D.A. (1987). *Educating the reflective practitioner*. San Francisco: Jossey-Bass.

Søreide, G.E. (2007). The public face of teacher identity: Narrative construction of teacher identity on public policy documents. *Journal of Educational Policy, 22*(2), 129–146.

Søreide, G.E. (2008). Teacher union and teacher identity. *Nordic Educational Research, 3*, 193–202.

Sørensen, K.H. (Ed.) (1998). The spectre of participation: Technology and work in the welfare state. Oslo: Scandinavian University Press.

Van Loon, J. (2006). Network. *Theory, Culture & Society, 23*(2–3), 307–322.

BETH A. BECHKY

OBJECT LESSONS

Workplace Artifacts as Representations of Occupational Jurisdiction[1]

The interdependence of occupations is a reality of organizational life, resulting from specialization within a division of labor (Durkheim, 1984). Because occupations vary in status, tasks, and goals, this interdependence may lead to discord, and certainly results in negotiation and accommodation between occupational groups. Such occupational conflict has an extensive tradition of study, primarily among analysts of the professions (Friedson, 1970; Abbott, 1981; Larson, 1977). Recent work on jurisdiction, the link between a profession and its work, presents a dynamic view of the competition between professions for dominance over areas of work. Jurisdiction is contested through public, legal, and workplace claims for control over task areas (Abbott, 1988). These jurisdictional claims act to shift both relations between professional groups and the boundaries of their core work domains. As Abbott (1988, p. 109) points out, 'the strength of task area boundaries is a central and problematic property of systems of professions.' Because the task domain is the means of continued livelihood, occupations fiercely guard their core task domains from potential incursions by competitors.

Competition for control of task areas has been well documented in the arena of legal and social institutions, but investigations of workplace occupational boundaries are rare. This is regrettable because it is through workplace interaction that many of the status dynamics between occupations are negotiated (Abbott, 1988), as the workplace is where claims are enacted and made real for particular occupation members. Studies suggest that occupational interrelations at the workplace can shift task areas, revise occupational scripts, and shake up organizational structures (Barley, 1986; Allen, 2000; Crozier, 1964). As occupational groups act to claim task areas in the legal or public realm, the consequences of such actions are enacted through workplace relations. Jurisdictional change also emerges through interactions initiated within organizations while members of occupations accomplish their daily work. We need to further investigate workplace interaction in order to be able to fully specify and explain the process by which occupational boundaries move and are shaped at the workplace.

In this chapter, I adopt such an approach to occupational competition by exploring the work of engineers, technicians, and assemblers at a manufacturer of semiconductor equipment. By examining their workplace interaction, I can describe how task boundaries are maintained and challenged in an organizational

D.W. Livingstone and D. Guile (eds.), The Knowledge Economy and Lifelong Learning: A Critical Reader, 229–256.

setting where specialization creates significant interdependence and the hierarchy generates differentials in status and power. Considering the interactions around two artifacts, engineering drawings and machines, provides an opportunity to see how claims of occupational status and challenges for control over the work process play out within an organizational hierarchy.

INTEROCCUPATIONAL JURISDICTION IN THE LITERATURE

Most analyses of interoccupational competition approach the negotiation of task areas from a macro-sociological perspective, looking at political boundaries rather than interactional ones. These studies provide a basis for our understanding of the channels for interoccupational conflict at the level of the professional field, but fall short of explaining how such processes take place within organizations, the setting for most occupational life. Studies in the tradition of the professional power approach to occupational conflict, for instance, locate the arena of negotiation between occupations in institutional structures (Friedson, 1970). These studies have shown that professions vary in their ability to control membership and practice through means such as certification, accreditation, or legislation (Kronus, 1976; Halpern, 1992; Begun & Lippincott, 1987).

Other examinations of occupational control derive from the professionalization approach (Etzioni, 1969; Ritzer, 1977), and point out that the composition of an occupation has a strong influence on its success in gaining jurisdiction. From this perspective, power results from the race, gender, or class composition of the occupation, which enables or restricts access to opportunity. Occupations that are primarily female, for example, such as teaching and nursing, have lower status and as a result do not have access to the educational, political, and bureaucratic systems needed to defend or expand their turf (Manley, 1995; Preston, 1995; Glazer, 1991; Kanter, 1977). Finally, research has also demonstrated that cognitive and representational strategies are influential in garnering and maintaining occupational jurisdiction. The framing of knowledge and expertise can shift public opinion in favor of a particular occupation (Power, 1997), and therefore occupations compete for jurisdiction 'by claims argued through abstract knowledge' (Abbott, 1989, p. 278) in attempts to make their control over a domain seem valid.

These studies demonstrate important institutional and cognitive dynamics in interoccupational conflict, and are the backdrop for our understanding of jurisdiction at the workplace. They suggest that access to resources, occupational composition and status, and representations of expertise can influence occupational boundaries. However, these theories of interoccupational conflict are incomplete; while macro-sociological processes influence jurisdictional outcomes, the task boundary is further specified through occupational interactions at the point at which the work takes place. Organizations are a social world in which task areas are susceptible to continual renegotiation as groups are faced with solving workplace problems as they arise. For instance, in manufacturing plants, specific engineers and technicians negotiate whether to allocate headcount to develop a wire harness or to have the assembly wired point-to-point on the production line. Similarly, the decision about how much medication is administered to a patient is enacted by particular doctors and nurses in the patient's room. It is by examining such workplace interactions that we more completely specify the processes of occupational competition.

Thus far, there has been little study of the interactional process by which these struggles happen within organizations. While many researchers note that workplace task boundaries differ from institutional strictures on task areas (Kronus, 1976; Abbott, 1988; Manley, 1995), they do not examine the work processes themselves to determine the consequences of the enactment of workplace task boundaries. However, a body of ethnographic literature about the professions, particularly in the medical field, suggests that the workplace is a consequential setting for jurisdictional struggles. In hospitals, workplaces with frequent cross-professional interaction, the informal practices and rhetorical strategies of professionals have been shown to blur and alter task boundaries (Mesler, 1991; Chambliss, 1997; Hughes, 1980). Allen (2000), for instance, has demonstrated that the everyday 'boundary work' of nurses is key to understanding how the division of labor in hospitals is accomplished.

One study that illustrates the unique insights provided by examinations of workplace interaction is Barley's (1986) examination of the changing interaction order of occupational groups within radiology departments. Barley found that the introduction of CT scanners into radiology departments changed the task area of radiologists and technologists; however, the roles ultimately adopted by the technologists in the two hospitals he studied differed. Macro-sociological approaches to occupational boundaries might predict that radiologists would maintain their status and task area in both settings as a result of their training, occupational composition, or framing of knowledge. Instead, Barley found that the mechanism that changed task area boundaries was the manner in which the occupations enacted their expertise in daily interaction: in one hospital the technologists exercised their knowledge through specific interactional scripts; in the other, the radiologists did. More work of this type is needed to extend our understanding of how the dynamics of occupational competition are created and enacted in the workplace, and how these dynamics relate to professional interaction in legal and public realms.

Investigating workplace boundaries is particularly important in light of the changing nature of the economy. Service work and white-collar work has become the mainstay of the economy; one of the largest American occupational segments is professional and technical workers (Barley, 1996a). With the development of progressively complex workplace technologies, technical knowledge has become an imperative of organizations (Barley, 1996b; Vallas, 1999; Zetka, 2001). If, as several analysts suggest, this leads to more organizing on the basis of occupation (Vallas & Beck, 1996; Barley, 1996a), occupational negotiations at the workplace will increasingly determine jurisdiction.

Investigating occupational jurisdiction at the workplace level requires gaining analytical purchase on the moments in organizations when such claims take place.

We need to document the relations that emerge when occupational groups intersect within an organizational structure. One such point is the creation, interpretation, and handoff of organizational artifacts. These artifacts cross occupational boundaries in the service of production, communication, and representation of every task area within an organization and thus are a vital element of the work process. Because occupations use physical objects not only for technical purposes, but also as a means of representing and instigating difference and conflict, an analysis of organizational artifacts provides a lever for understanding interoccupational dynamics at the workplace.

ARTIFACTS IN ORGANIZATIONAL LIFE

The display and use of objects is a key social mechanism for signaling and representation, particularly in the construction and maintenance of communities (Mauss, 1976; Douglas & Isherwood, 1979). Studies of commodity exchange, taste and consumption point to the function of artifacts, and people's stance toward them, for signaling membership in a particular class and expressing cultural categories and ideals (Veblen, 1979; Bourdieu, 1984; McCracken, 1988). People not only use objects as a means for presenting themselves as members of a culture, but also to invoke a particular definition of a situation (Goffman, 1959). These studies suggest that artifacts can symbolize an individual's membership in a particular social milieu, such as an occupational community.

Social dynamics also inhere in material objects, as several decades of study of science laboratories, socio-technical structures, and everyday life have demonstrated (Winner, 1980; Foucault, 1979; Knorr Cetina, 1999). For example, Latour demonstrates the social agency of artifacts as diverse as laboratory assays, automatic door closers and transportation systems (Latour, 1979, 1988, 1996). Artifacts embed the knowledge of their creators and can serve as boundary objects, conveying information between groups and mobilizing action (Star & Griesemer, 1989; Carlile, 2002; Henderson, 1999). Their function, therefore, is not only technical, but social.

These previous studies suggest that artifacts are an important aspect of organizational life: they symbolize social categories and influence and constrain social action. As such, they have the potential to influence social relations between occupational communities, and offer a means to fruitfully approach jurisdictional issues at the workplace. Examining artifacts provides a window into the social dynamics of occupational groups, because as artifacts cross occupational boundaries, they highlight the social interaction coalescing around them: people cooperating to solve problems, fighting to maintain status, and struggling to gain control of the work process. Below, I describe the ways in which two artifacts mediate the social relations of engineers, technicians and assemblers in a manufacturing firm. I find that in this organization, engineering drawings and machines embed knowledge and therefore are useful in problem solving across boundaries. At the same time, authority over these objects can reinforce or redistribute task area boundaries and, by symbolizing the work of occupational groups, the objects also represent and strengthen beliefs about the legitimacy of the work the groups perform. In particular, while the machines are occasionally employed to challenge the dominance of engineers, the use of drawings successfully maintains and reinforces the engineers' jurisdiction.

RESEARCH DESIGN

I conducted fieldwork for one year between November 1995 and November 1996 at EquipCo (a pseudonym), a semiconductor equipment manufacturing company located in Silicon Valley. EquipCo's employees built the large and complex pieces of equipment that other firms, such as Intel, use to fabricate semiconductor wafers. EquipCo primarily produced wafer-etching machines, many of which were customized to meet the requirements of a particular wafer fabrication facility. Of the firm's 5,000 employees, approximately 1,800 were directly involved in the production process: 570 design engineers, 90 drafters, 60 manufacturing engineers, 140 engineering and manufacturing technicians, 220 assemblers, and the remainder non-technical administrative support such as planners and schedulers. In the year of the study, EquipCo's revenues surpassed $1 billion, and the firm was named one of the top ten process equipment companies in the semiconductor industry for the seventh year running (VSLI Research, 1996).

While at EquipCo, I collected participant, observational, interview, and archival data. I was a participant-observer in the manufacturing technicians' lab for five months, followed by four months as a participant building machines as a member of a final assembly team and three months as an observer of a design engineering team. During this time, I collected copies of the documents that each of the groups used to support and perform their work, including engineering drawings, bills of materials, and meeting agendas and notes. I also closely studied the prototypes and products built by the technicians and assemblers. Finally, in addition to the spontaneous, informal interviews that regularly occurred while I was observing the work, I arranged formal interviews with several informants in each occupational group. I brought two sets of assembly drawings with bills of materials to each interview, and had each informant describe how they would use the drawings, either in designing or building a machine.

As a high-technology manufacturing firm, EquipCo provided fertile ground for studying the meaning and influence of artifacts in the social structure of the production process. New prototypes were frequently developed and built to meet the demands of a quickly changing market. EquipCo was characterized by closely interacting occupational communities as well as identifiable workplace artifacts. The different occupational groups involved in the production process communicated via interaction around two central artifacts – the formal engineering drawings and the prototype machines – which changed hands during product 'handoffs,' when responsibility shifted from engineering to prototyping to manufacturing. I chose EquipCo's new product line as the venue to study these handoffs, since the production process was less routine, which maximized the opportunities to witness the social interactions occurring between occupational communities in relation to these artifacts.

RESEARCH SITE

The new product development and production process at EquipCo progressed in phases, from design through prototyping and into final manufacturing, as displayed in Figure 1. In the design phase, a team of engineers designed a new product, working together and using drawings from previous designs. After designing the layout of a new machine as a group, the members of the engineering team divided up responsibility for the bills of materials and assembly and install drawings, and worked individually to complete them. Engineers' work centered on generating representations of the 'machine-to-be' on paper; while the process of building the machine was critical to the organization, knowledge about building was not emphasized in the engineering area. Although the engineers met weekly for updates on each product and frequently visited one another's cubicles to discuss projects, engineers spent most of their time alone, and the engineering area was generally quiet and calm.

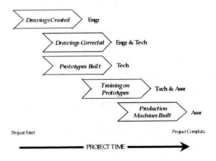

Figure 1. The production process at EquipCo

After the engineers created the basic structure for the drawings and sent the bills of materials to the planners to start ordering material, they would send the preliminary engineering drawings to the technicians' lab. This started the prototyping, or build verification, phase of the production process, in which the technicians verified and changed the engineering drawings. The technicians' lab was the central point in the prototyping of new products, where designs became reality and manufacturability became a consideration. The technicians started building from scratch using the preliminary engineering drawings, changing the drawings and the machine itself as they discovered ways to make it easier to manufacture. As they completed building, they provided feedback to engineers via 'redlines,' corrected engineering drawings. Their work, therefore, involved both concrete physical interactions with the machine, as they accumulated extensive hands-on product experience by building, and abstract understandings of the product, because they interpreted and redlined the drawings. The 27 technicians sat at benches in an open room, and built the machines on the floor space between their benches. The frequently changing designs and the lack of space resulted in a chaotic work environment in which parts piled up in boxes and tools were strewn across benches.

After several prototypes were built, and the engineers and technicians believed that the drawings were 95 per cent correct, the assemblers were brought into the process. Members of the new product assembly team trained in the technicians' lab, building the machine as instructed by the technicians. Often they would consult the technicians about how to build the machine properly. They had less discretion in building than technicians, assembling small discrete chunks and installing them on a frame to create the finished product. Assemblers had access to the technicians' binders of redlined drawings, and sometimes to the latest engineering drawings, and they were told to use only the drawings as a guide to building the machine. However, they rarely used them, as they found it more effective to ask the technicians or other assemblers for help, or to look at a prototype that was already built for guidance. After the training period, when the assemblers felt comfortable building a product on their own, they moved back into the final assembly clean room area to build the machines. The clean room environment in which the assemblers worked mandated that they wear a special clean room suit, known as a 'bunny suit,' along with gloves, boots, and a hood, in order to reduce the dust particles that could land on the machines and cause air leaks. The air circulation system in the spacious, particle-free clean area kept the room quite cold, while its constant whooshing noise made it somewhat difficult for assemblers to hear one another, as did the hoods worn by every member of the team.[2]

FINDINGS: JURISDICTION AND REPRESENTATIONS OF KNOWLEDGE, AUTHORITY AND LEGITIMACY

One can frame the work on EquipCo's new product line in terms of occupational jurisdiction, the engineers' jurisdiction was that of designing the machine, and the artifact associated with this jurisdiction was the engineering drawings. The assemblers' jurisdiction was that of building, a domain associated with the machines. As the group in the middle of the process, the technicians were responsible for the task area of prototyping, which included both building from scratch and changing drawings to match the new building process. The engineering jurisdiction symbolically encompassed the entire production process, the design through the finished product, because the engineering drawings were seen as the means of communication for the production process and guided the building of machines. Also, engineers were responsible for how the product looked and functioned after it was shipped. The engineers' task area therefore shaped the jurisdictions of the other two occupational groups.

Engineers were the superordinate occupation in the production process and had higher status in the organization. This status differential manifested in various ways, from engineers' exempt employment status to their higher pay. Technicians were non-exempt employees and were paid less than engineers. Assemblers, the lowest status occupation of the three communities, were not only lower paid non-exempt employees than technicians, but were also frequently hired as contract labourers. The red badges they wore symbolized their greater peril in the event of layoffs. A promotion ladder existed informally between the assemblers and technicians, with the most skilled and talented assemblers moving up the hierarchy to become technicians. This career ladder did not extend upward to engineering. When describing their career aspirations, technicians interested in engineering positions often recounted the story of Tyler, a technician skilled at drawing who had been promoted to test engineering. However, he was the only technician in the lab's history who had ever ascended to engineering.

As Table 1 summarizes, the interactions of engineers, technicians, and assemblers around the drawings and machines at EquipCo can be characterized as three analytically distinct but interrelated dynamics of jurisdictional conflict: knowledge, authority, and legitimacy. As representations of knowledge, these objects were both useful for solving problems and for reflecting the status of occupational knowledge. The occupational groups enacted claims of authority around drawings and machines by asserting their physical control over these objects and the processes used to create them. Finally, the objects represented occupational legitimacy: because they transmitted reputations, objects were used to claim standing as valid practitioners of a particular occupation. The social dynamics around the objects were not as tidy and distinct in practice as these analytic categories suggest but were simultaneously enacted and closely interrelated. I will begin below, however, by examining these representations separately and then I will address their interrelationship.

REPRESENTATIONS OF KNOWLEDGE

Since much of what assemblers, technicians, and engineers knew was inscribed into the drawings and machines, both of these artifacts were used at EquipCo as epistemic objects. Because these artifacts inscribed the knowledge of their creators and conveyed information to their users (Latour & Woolgar, 1979), they were useful in coordinating and communicating information about work tasks across occupational boundaries.

Engineering drawings epitomized this idea of an epistemic object; they were perceived as both showing designers how their ideas worked on paper and communicating to others, such as assemblers, all the information needed for building (cf. Ferguson, 1992). The drawings detailed the way to build a machine, from the precise terms calling out each part to notes standardizing the manner in which the parts should be assembled. Each drawing underwent many revisions on the way to becoming a final representation of the product, and because of this, during the design and prototyping process the drawings were viewed as open-ended projections of what the product would be.[3]

For instance, on my first day at EquipCo I helped Theresa, a technician, build a subassembly that Tom had built the previous week in the lab. We called Tom over to Theresa's bench several times, and he told us that in one case, we needed a longer screw than the size the documentation called for. At another point, he interpreted the diagram for us, and showed us that if you turned the assembly a certain way, you could see how it aligned with the diagram. 'Don't worry,' Tom said, 'I already called the [engineer] who drew the documentation to tell him that parts of it need to be exploded, and he said he is already working on it.'

Table 1. The impact of occupational artifacts on workplace jurisdiction

	Knowledge	*Authority*	*Legitimacy*
Drawings	Used by engineers and technicians to represent and communicate design, and to solve problems Discourse reinforced use as knowledge objects: "Build to the print"	Used by engineers to support their authority over the design process Engineers rebuffed assemblers' input and controlled technicians' feedback Engineers claimed "improper interpretation" of drawings to deflect blame for mistakes	Transmitted and reinforced reputation of individual engineers
Machines	Used by technicians and assemblers to represent and communicate about product and solve problems Used by engineers and assemblers to solve problems Not recognized by engineers and assemblers as an appropriate knowledge object	Both technicians and engineers felt they owned the machines Physical control over machine allowed technicians to challenge engineers' authority	Technician group reputation and survival depend-ed on well-built, manufacturable machines

The drawings served as a source of knowledge for two occupational communities at EquipCo. Engineers used them to represent their ideas about what the machine would look like and how the parts would fit together. Engineers at EquipCo rarely had a conversation about a design without pulling out a sheaf of engineering drawings. In addition, technicians used the drawings as an illustration of what the prototype should look like, so they could build it. Engineers and technicians also communicated with each other through the drawings, since the technicians provided feedback to the engineers via redlines. Technicians were 'the guinea pigs' working to catch the problems in the engineering drawings, as one technician described:

> What happens is you get to building it and discover that there were parts you weren't supposed to put together that you already did. So we redline it, correct the things that were wrong with the documentation and give ideas about what would help for when it is manufactured. We're the guinea pigs, its our job to find the problems and make everything flow smoothly.

Machines were also used as representations of knowledge at EquipCo. While the machine was intended to be the final outcome of the design process, the process of building the final product at EquipCo was in fact quite iterative. The assemblers built the first few as they trained in the technicians' lab, and with each version, they accumulated a better understanding of the building process. Therefore, during the process of building, the machine provided information and generated questions that the assemblers needed answered. In practice, assemblers used the machines as epistemic devices far more often than the drawings, because they did not understand the standardized language of the engineering drawings, and felt mistrustful of them as a result. The assemblers worked building machines every day, and saw the machines as being clearer and more concrete than the drawings. For instance, an assembler installing a cable compared his work with a technician's prototype machine rather than the engineering drawing, telling me:

> Looking at his [machine] is not only the short way. It's easier, but its also better because the percentage of mistakes you'll make is less. Because [the technician] is good, man, it's done right. If we do it from the print we can get confused, make mistakes.

Because the assemblers were not comfortable with the language and notation of the drawings, they preferred to use the machines as representations of knowledge.

Artifacts in Cross-Occupational Problem Solving

Artifacts were also used to mediate across occupational boundaries during episodes of problem solving. When problems arose in the building process, both drawings and machines were used as boundary objects between occupational communities to help solve them. Boundary objects are flexible epistemic artifacts that 'inhabit several intersecting social worlds and satisfy the information requirements of each of them' (Star & Griesemer, 1989, p. 393). In the case of EquipCo, the drawings were used as boundary objects between engineers and technicians, because both of these communities had working knowledge of them and were comfortable with communicating via the drawings. For the same reason, the machines were used for problem solving between technicians and assemblers. (Appendix A provides examples of these uses.)

However, when engineers and assemblers needed to solve a problem together, they frequently resolved such problems by using the machine rather than the drawings as an epistemic device. For instance, one day in final assembly, an engineer, Eric, came to the parts room in the assemblers' area with a handful of drawings to ask Abe about some scratches and chips on the inside of one of the chambers. Eric inquired, 'How did the chips get there?' Abe, gesturing upward with both hands, described the problem: 'When you lift the plate, a screw gets caught.' Eric looked puzzled. Abe said, 'I'll show you,' and went back into the lab, returning with the upper plate of the chamber cover. He showed the plate to Eric, pointing out the screw on the corner that moved and caused scratches inside the chamber.

The engineer did not understand Abe's response at first: he lacked the assembler's concrete physical understanding of the machine and knowledge about how the machine was assembled. However, neither Abe nor Eric thought of examining the drawings to help solve the problem; the drawings did not represent what happened when the plate was lifted. Instead, the assembler brought the part forward, which, as a concrete representation of assembly knowledge, provided an illustration of how the problem occurred in context.[4]

Boundary objects are most effective for problem solving when they are tangible and concrete, and are loosely enough defined to be usable by both groups (Bechky, 2003; Carlile, 2002). While the assumption at EquipCo was that the engineering drawings should be the best communication medium, in practice, the language of the drawings was too abstract and unfamiliar for assemblers to associate with their concrete understanding of the machine, since they lacked the contextual knowledge of drawings that comes from daily use. In contrast, the concrete nature of the machine engendered its usefulness as a boundary object for problem solving. Engineers did not understand assemblers' descriptions of the machines' problems, because they lacked the daily context of building machines and they approached the interaction with an abstract, schematic understanding of the drawings. However, when the machine (or a part) was presented to engineers, they were able to fit the concrete manifestation into their understanding of the product and get the information they needed. In essence, despite the multipurpose intention of drawings, the concrete machine, as the place where the 'rubber hit the road,' was more effective for problem solving between these two communities.

Discourse around Artifacts Reflected the Status of Engineers' Knowledge

The jurisdictional control that engineers maintained over their task area – the engineering drawings – had implications for the organization's emphasis on the value of both artifacts as representations of knowledge. As I describe in this section, the oft-repeated interpretation of these two artifacts was that only the drawings should be used to communicate knowledge. The engineering drawings were the legitimate means of communication between the occupations participating in the production process: all information needed for building was thought to pass through them.[5] In contrast, while machines were used in practice as boundary objects for the purpose of communicating knowledge, they were not perceived as a legitimate way to communicate within the organization. The perception of the legitimacy of these artifacts as epistemic objects reflects the contest for jurisdiction between the occupational communities at EquipCo. As Abbott (1988) points out, the image that an occupation presents in public discourse frequently diverges from the actual workplace jurisdiction. Similarly, at EquipCo, organizational discourse around representations of knowledge differed from the daily reality of their use.

The relative standing of the drawings and machines for communicating reflected the use of these artifacts as tools to reinforce knowledge claims. Because the technical purpose of the drawings was to communicate standardized information about designing and building the product, one might reasonably expect that they would be privileged as epistemic objects. However, their value in communicating knowledge cannot account for the rhetorical zeal surrounding the use of them, exemplified by the phrase I heard almost daily during my year working at EquipCo: 'Build to the print.' The drawings were considered the only authority in the design process; the organization's discourse reinforced the idea that drawings were the sole legitimate means of communication at EquipCo. This rhetoric served a jurisdictional purpose in addition to supporting the standardization of building methods. Because engineers controlled the drawings and the design process, promoting the use of the drawings supported their jurisdiction over their work and their place in the occupational hierarchy.

The discourse surrounding the drawings strengthened the jurisdiction of engineers in two ways: it invoked the superiority of the abstract knowledge of engineers and it reinforced the legitimacy of the representation of work that the drawings provided. Engineers created engineering drawings to communicate to one another specifically what the finished product should look like and to communicate to others how it should be built. As a result, the drawings were highly formal and abstract instructions about the product. Abstraction, in the sense of elaborated 'layers of increasingly formal discourse' about a narrow topic (Abbott, 1988, p. 102), can secure and strengthen jurisdiction. Although the engineering drawings were the formal means of communicating how to build, they did not always solve coordination problems across occupational boundaries. As the example above demonstrated, the machines were more effective at solving some of these problems, although their technical purpose was as a finished product. However, by regularly asserting that the standardization and formalization of the drawings made them the most effective way to coordinate the tasks of production, engineers could strengthen their jurisdiction by reinforcing the superiority of their abstract knowledge.

The importance of the drawings for use in building was reiterated continually. And this was not only a discourse of engineers; it also permeated the technicians' lab, where everyone understood that the goal was to create redlined drawings so that assemblers would be able to manufacture machines to the engineers' specifications. Similarly, when the technicians trained the assemblers, the rhetoric about 'building to the print' also predominated. For example, every time that Tony, a technician training a group of assemblers, left them to work unsupervised in the lab, he would bark out a variant of the following: 'Don't be looking at my machine! I'll kill you if I catch you doing that, just look at the print!' Technicians wanted assemblers to build the machine as the drawing indicated it should be built. At the same time, the technicians were well aware that the assemblers were more comfortable learning how to build by watching others or mimicking a finished machine. Additionally, they recognized that their own role was to improve the documentation, despite the fact that it might not be used fully. As one technician pointed out to me when I asked if his redlines would be used in the manufacturing area:

> No, they aren't supposed to, what will happen is on the next build, we'll have the manufacturing people come in so we can transfer knowledge that is not in the documentation. Then, when the machine really goes to be built in manufacturing it hopefully will have full documentation. It's not supposed to go over there without full and complete documentation.

Thus, the technicians, and even the engineers, were aware that the drawings would never truly represent how to build. The drawings needed to remain abstract not only for their use as an epistemic tool, but also for reasons of boundary maintenance and task control. For drawings to be powerful as a tool to maintain occupational jurisdiction, they must be somewhat unclear to other groups, because if every aspect of the work were easily codified and understood, engineers would be unable to maintain their status as experts. Therefore, the discourse emphasizing the exclusive use of drawings as an epistemic device was helpful in diverting attention from the less acceptable implications of their abstractness – the fact that drawings were incomplete and, further, not as useful in problem solving at occupational boundaries as the machines were. By appealing to the valued goal of efficiency, engineers could draw attention to the positive aspects of the drawings, thereby reinforcing the importance of the knowledge within their own domain. Thus, the discourse supporting the use of standardized drawings that efficiently solved problems and effectively communicated the best way to build reinforced the status of engineers and helped them to maintain their jurisdiction.

REPRESENTATIONS OF AUTHORITY

As the second column of Table 1 summarizes, artifacts served as representations of authority in the organization, effecting control over the work process. An important jurisdictional issue in the workplace is authority over the work itself; while formally granted through organizational hierarchy, authority is enacted through the control of organizational artifacts, helping to determine who has the right to participate in particular work tasks. At EquipCo, the control of engineering drawings was the well-established domain of engineers, while there was more conflict over control of the prototype machines.

The drawings and machines were central devices in maintaining the jurisdictional control of occupational communities over their work. Because engineering drawings directed the design and production process, engineers' legitimate control over drawings allowed them to directly influence the jurisdictions of the other groups, constraining the organization of the tasks of technicians and assemblers. Their control over the design jurisdiction also gave engineers the power to determine when the other communities could participate in the design process. In contrast, the machines were jurisdictional artifacts in dispute: engineers, technicians, and assemblers challenged each other for control over the machines.

Control of Drawings and Engineers' Jurisdictional Authority

Engineering drawings were the technical means of designing the product, and therefore they structured the design and production process. The content of the drawings circumscribed the work tasks of technicians and assemblers, whose work entailed building the machine that the drawings directed them to build. Drawings also served a jurisdictional purpose, as they were an instrument for engineers to maintain their authority over the design and manufacturing process. The engineers felt strongly that the only way they could design the machine effectively was by maintaining control over the drawings, and they had final approval over any changes to the design. Daily complaints in engineering centered on the fact that the document control department made it very difficult for them to produce drawings properly, or as one engineer grumbled when she was told about a new directive from the production control department, 'It is going to be sketches again, crap! They've made it so we can't do our job.' Engineers had developed a variety of work-arounds to skirt document control issues, from inserting placeholders on bills of materials to ordering parts through different planners outside the normal manufacturing system channels. These work-arounds made it possible for them to create the drawings the way they intended, in a timely manner, allowing them to complete their work and maintain control over the design. Similarly, engineers resented when members of subordinate occupational groups tried to encroach on their drawing domain, or as one engineer pointed out about a scheduler: 'He keeps getting involved in the Engineering Change Notice (ECN) packages, and it isn't his job. It is not his right to question ECN packages! If engineering says to do them, he should just be putting them through [the computer system].' By intruding on their jurisdiction and holding up the drawing packages needed to change the design, the scheduler was making it difficult for the engineers to perform their drawing work and get the design finished.

Participation in the design and drawing process was the seat of influence in the organization, and assemblers and technicians had different strategies for operating in the jurisdictional arena around the drawings. The assemblers were acutely aware that they had no capacity to contest control over the design, because they lacked the status to participate in the design process. For example, one morning when I was working in assembly, two of the assemblers were complaining about the problems they were having lifting an interface to install it on a machine. The interface required four men to lift it into place, and when the men were not there, the women could not lift it. As one assembler sketched out a drawing illustrating a fixture to lift the interface, he told me, 'We know how to build it, and we told the engineers months ago but they don't listen to us because we don't have the degree, we are just final assembly.'

Assemblers were made aware of their lack of influence because engineers repeatedly rebuffed their contributions, even in the infrequent instances when their involvement was requested. The following example, one of only two instances when I saw an engineer consult an assembler for design help, demonstrates how such discounting of input happened. In this meeting, an engineer had solicited an assembler's help in wording a note on a drawing indicating how to build a particular part, while the two of them looked at both the physical part and the drawing on the table between them. The engineer, Eric, said, 'We want to put "input of coil" … but you've done it, Angela, so you know what we mean. What if you hadn't done it?' Angela, the assembler, replied, 'Well, what we do on the floor when we train is have them read the notes and ask us questions about how to do it when they don't understand. For the little things, they go by the training we give them on the floor, they don't really listen to the notes, you have to show them how it is done on the line.' Eric responded, 'So you make up for our poor notes and we appreciate it, but I'd like them to be better.' They continued the discussion about the wording of the note for another 20 minutes. The engineer in this example was concerned that his drawings were perceived as clear and manufacturable, which was why he was soliciting the assembler's input. However, when Angela indicated that on the manufacturing floor the assemblers rarely use the drawings to show them how to build, the engineer discounted her statement and continued in his formalization of the drawings.

While this engineer was making an effort to include an assembler's perspective in his design process, ultimately the assemblers' actual practice was excluded from the drawings. The discounting of their perspective frustrated assemblers, some of whom opted not to try to participate as a result. As one assembler reflected about another, Abe, who was trying to present some feedback to engineering: 'Abe wants to talk to them, but they never listen. He is right; he wants to do [something] for the company. But he's stupid, why does he have to pay attention so much? I say one word, nobody listens, and forget it, I shut up.' Assemblers were discouraged when they offered input to engineers, which reinforced their belief that they had little to no influence in the organization.

Technicians, in contrast, while uncertain of their ability to successfully contest jurisdiction over the drawings, had more authority to do so than assemblers. The technicians regularly participated in the drawing process by providing redlined drawings to engineers; however, the changes they suggested had to be approved by the engineers. This left them relatively impotent as far as making their design changes a reality. The hierarchical structure of the design process protected engineers from technicians' interference; many meetings that occurred throughout the design and prototyping process were off-limits to technicians. For instance, while technicians provided feedback during 'install reviews,' they were often not welcome at 'redesign reviews.' Even when technicians were allowed to attend, the timing of such meetings could create barriers to their participation in the design process. For example, one day in December, Tony, a technician, mentioned to Ed, an engineer, that another technician had discovered a problem in building the emergency off (EMO) assembly. 'The problem is, you have to put it together and then at the next step, take it apart again, add a part, and put it back together.' Ed replied, 'Well, if it is a real issue he can come to us with it, but maybe he should save it for Phase Two, the February 15th meeting, because on my list it says the EMO is all completed.' It was too late for the engineer to incorporate the suggested change into the current round of drawings without significant effort, so he deflected the technician with the Phase Two alternative. As a result, the change would not even be considered for two more months, if at all. Here, the engineer buttressed his formal authority, maintaining his control over his own tasks by excluding the technician's input while deferring to the design process. Although technicians complained about their exclusion from participation in meetings, in the time I spent at EquipCo they never directly challenged the engineers' authority in this area.

In contrast to this more formal exclusion, many technicians would informally lobby individual engineers and get frustrated when their redlined suggestions to the drawings were not incorporated into the design, which was the source of some amusement to the engineers. For instance, while two engineers made changes to a technician's suggested redlines one afternoon, they joked about the technicians' reactions to the process: 'That Tam is so funny, he drives me crazy sometimes, always saying, "Don't change this, don't change that."' 'And Todd just glares at you: "I dare you to go ahead and change it."' Given this reception by engineers it is not surprising that while the technicians legitimately participated in some aspects of the design process, they were ambivalent about the impact that their participation might have. As one technician pointed out to me while I was building a subassembly, 'Remember that you are the expert on building this once you've finished it. You can make changes [to the drawing]. Well, you can at least send the changes to the engineer, they may not always get made, but you are the one in charge of how to build.'

Drawings and the Deflection of Blame

Engineers also used the drawings and their control over the design process to deflect blame when mistakes were made in the production process. The drawings were an easily manoeuvred tool for placing blame, because they were open-ended and in a state of flux, as new versions were continually being drawn. Therefore, engineers frequently referred to the improper interpretation of drawings when trying to direct responsibility elsewhere for mistakes that were made in the design and production process.

For instance, several months into his employment at EquipCo, a technician told me the story of the first project he built:

> On my print the engineer called out the wrong size screw in several places, he put 1032 when it was 632. He's mad because I told my supervisor and my supervisor pointed it out in a meeting. The engineer stood up in the meeting and said that we read it wrong, that it was our fault.

Because the drawing in question was not available at the meeting, and probably had gone through several revisions since the incident, the engineer was able to claim that the technician had made the mistake, not him. When other problems arose in the building of machines, or parts were delivered to EquipCo that were not built as expected, engineers often claimed that others read the drawings incorrectly or did not read them at all. As open-ended representations of knowledge, the drawings were susceptible to interpretation, and these interpretations were subject to dispute. Because the engineers were the occupational group of the highest status, their interpretation tended to prevail.

In contrast, machines were not used to deflect blame. While the machine also was absent from the meetings, machines were much easier to track down. Machines were fixed in a certain place and at a certain concrete material state. They also were perceived by the organization as a product, rather than as a tool for communicating knowledge and information. This made them more resistant to interpretation and concomitantly, to use in blame placing. Drawings were fluid and ambiguous, had many different versions, and were more mobile (Latour, 1986). Technicians were well-aware that drawings could disappear, and tried to prevent drawings from deflecting blame to them by keeping copies of all of their redlines in binders at their benches. When they did not do so, problems could arise, as they did in the case of some cable documentation that Tom, one technician, corrected. The engineer responsible for designing the cables claimed that he never got the documentation. As Tom's manager pointed out, 'We know that he got it. We have some of it, but Tom made the prime mistake of giving him some originals.' Having a record of their changes and the original drawings they received provided technicians with some protection when fingers were pointed in their direction. However, because they were excluded from design meetings, technicians and assemblers were often absent when the blame was directed at them via the drawings, and therefore they did not have much recourse.

In general, technicians and assemblers did not participate very often in cross-occupational finger pointing. Because the machines were less open to interpretation, and because engineers did not touch the machines, it would be difficult for technicians and assemblers to engage in blame deflection by utilizing the machine. And technicians and assemblers, constrained from participating in the drawing and design process, did not have the status or power to deflect blame through the engineering drawings. Also, as the jurisdictional incumbents, engineers' 'ability to define the problems and measures of success' (Abbott, 1988, p. 139) made them relatively resistant to attack on the front of the engineering drawings. The drawings both embodied and reinforced the hierarchical standing of engineers with respect to occupational knowledge and authority.

Control of Machines and Engineers' Authority

In contrast, the technicians' physical control of the machines allowed them to challenge the authority of engineers. As 'experts' who were 'in charge of how to build,' technicians were more comfortable exerting authority in the arena around the machines. While the machines were in their lab, the technicians had control over what work was done to build them. This direct control over the object conflicted with the jurisdictional claims of engineers, who also thought of the machines as belonging to them. One engineer in particular, Ernie, always referred to the parts of the machine that he designed as his 'baby,' entering the lab and exclaiming 'My baby looks better with the right parts!' and 'What happened to my baby?' However, because they were the ones considered experts at producing the material machine, the technicians could contest ownership.

For instance, when the engineer working on one product, Evan, went down to the lab and ordered the facilities workers to get the machine running, the technician responsible, Ted, became incensed, claiming that the relationship they had with the facilities workers, who were not EquipCo employees, was too fragile to give them orders. 'Too bad,' the engineer said, 'Ted thinks he's in charge of the machine and he's not. I can do whatever I want on the machine, I don't have to ask Ted what I can do.' In fact, Ted himself had already started the machine running and holding a vacuum the day before; he just did not tell Evan, saying to another technician, 'I didn't want him to know we could do that.' In practice, the machine was not ready to run and test until the technician approved it.

Therefore, while drawings seemed to be a successful means for engineers to uphold their authority, technicians effectively challenged engineers in the jurisdictional arena around the machines. The engineers had formal organizational authority over the machine, and their professional status also would suggest that they could regulate the management of the machine and the production process. However, technicians' practical control over the machine while it was being built provided them with the means to contest the engineers' influence over their work tasks.

Artifacts, as demonstrated above, therefore served as both the means to reinforce and contest authority over task areas. The drawings were used to reinforce engineers' authority over the task area of drawing, while control of the machines provided a way for technicians to challenge engineers and maintain authority over the building domain. Additionally, the knowledge and authority represented in artifacts were not separable, as some of the examples in this section demonstrate. For instance, by making claims about the interpretation of the drawings in order to blame others for mistakes, engineers were not only asserting their authority to make judgments about the drawings, but were leveraging their interpretations of the knowledge embedded in the drawings. The knowledge and the authority represented in these artifacts were not distinct from one another, but were drawn on simultaneously in their use at occupational boundaries.

REPRESENTATIONS OF LEGITIMACY

Finally, artifacts serve jurisdictional purposes as representations of legitimacy, as summarized in the third column of Table 1. Artifacts allow for judgments of worth, providing a reference point for valuing the work in the organization. As a result, individuals and groups can leverage artifacts to lay claim to the status of an occupational member in good standing. At EquipCo, individual and group reputations were established on the basis of producing good work. The means by which individual and group status was related to the objects differed on the basis of the work practices of the groups as well as how identifiable the origins of the object were. As Goodman (1978) explains, different types of social relations inhere in objects depending on whether their origins can be distinctly identified. He distinguishes between autographic objects, those with traceable origins that can be directly attributed to an individual, and allographic objects, those whose origins cannot. At EquipCo, drawings were autographic and machines were not.

Drawings were the means by which engineers' reputations were established. Every drawing was labelled with an engineer's name, which meant that anyone who read a drawing knew whose work it was. Engineers were proud of their drawings, and careful to make sure that they reflected their best effort. One engineer explained this to me while he was checking his drawings before releasing them to manufacturing: 'I don't like spending so much time checking, but if I designed it, it is going to be a certain way, and my name is on it. I check my drawings to EquipCo standards, but also to mine, and mine are higher.' Engineers' performance was evaluated on the basis of drawings and therefore engineers frequently exhibited concerns about others' impressions of their codified work.

Engineers were sensitive about their reputations among members of other groups as well as their status within their own occupational community. Engineers felt a responsibility to the design represented by their drawings and they had a desire to see the machine built precisely the way they intended. Therefore, their reputation among technicians and assemblers was also important for getting their job done. Because the assemblers and technicians had a measure of control over the actual build of the machine, their evaluations of the credibility of the work that the drawing represented could affect the implementation of the design. If an engineer's drawings were misinterpreted, poorly done, or wrong, the machine might not be completed as he expected. For example, as one technician pointed out: 'When an engineer puts "No Fomblin" (a type of grease) on the print, the assemblers will just laugh because it shows how little the engineer knows about how we build. The engineer who wrote it loses credibility and they'll put tons of it on [the machine].' The engineers know that pumping a chamber down to vacuum takes longer when there is too much Fomblin. Assemblers, on the other hand, know that it is difficult to get an o-ring to seal without Fomblin. Therefore, while any engineer had the formal positional authority to tell assemblers what to do via a drawing, if assemblers' knowledge of the production process differed from what was on the print, they might not see the work of a particular engineer as credible, and the engineers' expectations for building the machine might not be met.

Drawings not only represented the work and intentions of engineers, thereby creating their reputations, but they also inscribed the established reputation of the engineer into the drawing. As a design engineer reported:

> It is important to do these [drawings] right, you know, engineering doesn't stop at the computer, it goes through to the build, it's a matter of pride. So I tell people that they better not piss [the technicians] off, because you need to get along with them, your reputation precedes you. Because if they don't like you, they'll see your name on the drawing, and won't give it the same care you would.

Therefore, not only was an engineer's reputation at risk on the basis of the quality of his drawings, but if he was having problems with his reputation, the autographic nature of the drawings ensured that his reputation paved the way for his design.

Because the machines were not labelled by name at EquipCo, they conferred the status and reputation of those who created them in a different manner than drawings, and had a different effect as representations of legitimacy. Individual contributions were less evident, so reputation created and communicated via the machines was primarily at a group level. Among technicians, not only was the quality of production important, but consistency across a set of builds of the same machine also mattered. Every machine of a certain product line going to the same customer had to be built well, look aesthetically pleasing, and be identical to the others. Technicians went to great lengths to ensure that the machines all looked the same, which occasionally could even mean not building a particular machine completely to specifications. For example, when one technician, Tess, was sending out three machines to the testing lab, she noticed that a small part was missing on the last machine to leave the lab. She asked the assemblers who were building the machines, 'Why are we missing a clamp for the harness? Did we miss it on the others?' One assembler remembered putting the clamp on the other two machines, and Tess pressed him for reassurance. 'You're sure? Because if we did it on those, we'll put it on there, but if we forgot it, we'll forget it on this one too. We want them to be the same.' Shipping a consistent product to their customers was vital to maintaining the technicians' reputation. While consistency of drawings was important to engineers, they could evade responsibility for problems in the drawings, as described in the authority section. However, it was not possible for technicians to evade the consequences of perceptions of inconsistent or poor quality machines.

Because the technician group eked out its existence by garnering projects from different engineering groups, issues of reputation were particularly salient to technicians, and important for maintaining the legitimacy of their jurisdiction over prototyping. If the work of the group was not consistently good, the engineering groups would not send the department new projects. Therefore, good quality machine production was not only a technical imperative, but also a jurisdictional one. As a result, supervisors in the group regularly exhorted the technicians to think about pleasing their customers and be concerned about the quality of their work. As one manager reminded the group in a meeting:

> Although we are under the gun, always rushing, we need to think of our customers who are paying us to do this – the manufacturing units. When building more than one machine, always make sure the techs are using the same documentation so they all go out looking the same. It's not a quality issue, it's customer perception; we want them to be consistent.

Similarly, Terry, another manager, was appalled when he discovered that some circuit boards were not soldered properly and several integrated circuits fell out of the board while the technicians were showing their work to an engineering manager. He decided to develop a soldering training class and run every technician through it, because, as he explained in another meeting, 'We need to maintain our reputation, we don't want to be a group that engineers avoid working with. One "Oh shit" can outweigh a hundred "Atta boys!"' As these examples illustrate, the technicians depended upon the reputation established by their careful, consistent production of prototypes to generate more work for the group, thereby demonstrating that the prototyping work was of value to the organization.

Thus, artifacts served as a means for the occupational groups to enact both individual and group legitimacy. Drawings and machines reflected the value of the groups' work, and perceptions of these objects influenced the behaviour of other groups accordingly. These representations of legitimacy were also not separable from the representations of authority and knowledge analyzed earlier. For example, good quality prototyping not only ensured that the organization found the technicians' work valuable and legitimate, but if it caused engineering groups to continue to allocate the prototyping work to the technicians' lab, good prototyping also served to reinforce the technicians' authority over that jurisdiction. Similarly, by creating understandable drawings, an engineer could shore up his authority by asserting his legitimacy – if his drawing was perceived as legitimate, his 'baby' emerged looking as he expected. If, however, his drawing included information that assemblers regarded as invalid, as in the Fomblin example, the engineer might find that the knowledge represented in his drawing undermined his legitimacy. Because knowledge, legitimacy, and authority were interrelated, in the process of negotiating task areas, occupation members evoked them together, which could both fortify and dilute the strength of their jurisdictional claims.

'WORKMANSHIP:' ENACTMENTS OF KNOWLEDGE, AUTHORITY AND LEGITIMACY

The use of the term 'workmanship' at EquipCo provides an illustrative example of how jurisdictional issues around artifacts were simultaneously played out through dynamics of knowledge, authority and legitimacy. Workmanship generally referred to aspects of the practice of building, but it had contrasting meanings depending on the occupational groups' perspectives. When engineers used the term workmanship, they intended it to mean the 'tricks of the trade' or 'tribal knowledge' of building that was not called out on the blueprint. For example, when a technician questioned an engineer about why the notes for assembling the fibre optics in the chamber were absent from the drawing, he replied, 'Most of that is just workmanship; it doesn't need to be on the print.' Workmanship was the extra knowledge that did not need to be explained in the drawing, either because assemblers and technicians were expected to know how to build to a certain standard, or because the building process was seen to be elementary enough that it did not need directions.

Among technicians and assemblers, on the other hand, the workmanship exemplified in the machines represented their effort and skill in building well. In the technicians' lab, managers frequently reminded technicians to be careful about their workmanship, and both technicians and assemblers felt that a completed machine embodied their skill and technique. In one meeting of the technicians, for instance, the supervisor of the lab suggested that as a result of some feedback from the testing lab, he had three ideas for improvement: 'Workmanship, workmanship, workmanship.'

These differences in the treatment of workmanship reveal embedded representations of knowledge, authority, and legitimacy. First, the knowledge that was inscribed in the engineering drawings did not include representations of workmanship. Since workmanship was defined by engineers as 'what everyone knows about building,' it was not included as part of the design or instructions for building; similarly, many technicians and assemblers felt that their skill was not something that was incorporated into the drawings, but was transmitted through their practice. The treatment of workmanship also reflected the authority of the engineers – the engineer who created the drawing had the authority to decide what was included. Therefore, engineers decided what building practices qualified as 'workmanship' and were thus not included on the print. Finally, workmanship was an activity that embedded representations of legitimacy as well. For the technicians and assemblers, good work that produced high-quality machines required workmanship. In essence, workmanship was the effort that enhanced the legitimacy of the work each group performed. At the same time, because this work was not included on the drawing, its legitimacy was devalued.

By excluding the workmanship of technicians and assemblers from the drawings, engineers effectively excluded their work practice from the legitimate representation of work in the organization. As Bourdieu (1994, p. 239) notes, certain groups have 'monopoly of the legitimate – i.e. explicit and public – imposition of the legitimate vision of the social world,' and this 'official naming' garners them symbolic power. At EquipCo, engineers created the design and the structure of the production process within which everyone else had to work. The engineers not only had the authority to officially designate what work was legitimate within the organization, but also encouraged discourse supporting their claims of abstract knowledge. This helped them to strengthen their jurisdiction over their work and ensure their continuing high status in the organization.

CONCLUSIONS

Artifacts are an important part of organizational life: they surround us and our work and roles are dependent upon them. As an integral part of work processes, objects help us to accomplish tasks, but not in a merely technical manner. Artifacts, subject to interpretation, participate in the constitution of the social dynamics of organizations. In this paper, artifacts were shown to mediate the relationships between three occupational communities, symbolizing their knowledge, inciting their rhetoric, and defining task boundaries between them.

In particular, the study of EquipCo demonstrates how one set of artifacts – engineering drawings and machines – was used to both construct and reflect occupational jurisdictions in the workplace. As epistemic representations, they embodied the work and knowledge of the occupational communities, and were used for problem solving. As representations of authority, they provided the means for occupations to circumscribe and defend their task areas. As representations of legitimacy, artifacts signified value and were used to make judgments on occupational skill and worth. These properties were closely linked and mutually reinforcing.

These objects were used to reinforce occupational status and the organizational structure. For instance, assemblers' low occupational status was emphasized through the enactment of occupational conflict at the workplace. When engineers rebuffed assemblers' input, this served to support the assemblers' belief that they 'don't have the degree' and therefore cannot participate. Similarly, engineers' formal authority was enacted through workplace interaction with technicians and assemblers. The consistent repetition of 'Build to the print' emphasized the superiority of the engineers' abstract knowledge and supported their authority to control the design and building process. In this way, engineers used objects to support an important attribute of their professional power: the ability to pass blame on to lower status groups.

At the same time, workplace interaction granted leeway for movement at task area boundaries. While an engineer's education means he is the person in the hierarchy who knows how to draw, and thus formally controls the drawings, this knowledge was enacted every day at the workplace. On some occasions, training was not enough to gain control over the task area; for instance the engineer also had to keep his reputation intact and ward off input from others in order to have complete control over the drawing process. This study suggests that by challenging one another in the workplace, occupations can shift the lines that demarcate control over tasks.

The analysis of EquipCo demonstrates that interoccupational conflicts in the workplace are an important means for maintaining and justifying occupational jurisdiction, and suggests that we should pay closer attention to the interactional dynamics of occupations. While much of the literature about the professions hints that the workplace is important, it is rarely considered a significant force in the competition for jurisdiction. The hints offered by such studies, however, support my contention that examining workplace enactment provides a fuller picture of the process of occupational conflict. For instance, Halpern's (1992) study of four jurisdictional disputes among medical specialties demonstrates that political, institutional, and cognitive factors all played a role in the settlement of these jurisdictions. I would suggest that in addition to these factors, the enactment of occupational competition at the workplace was a means for settling such disputes.

Halpern points out that anesthesiology did not attain the level of jurisdictional control that other specialties were able to attain. While she focuses her analysis on the intraprofessional factors constraining anesthesiologists, her data also imply that workplace processes and interaction played a part in the struggle over who could anesthetize patients. For instance, anesthesiologists fell prey to 'politics' in the surgical suite (1992, p. 1013): surgeons were unwilling to cede authority to other physicians in the operating room, and preferred interacting with nurse anesthesiologists, who would acquiesce to their orders. While Halpern's intention was not to demonstrate the importance of workplace processes, her data that workplace interaction impacted anesthesiologists' ability to circumscribe their task area are consistent with my argument that examining the workplace provides us with a fuller picture of how occupational conflict is enacted in practice.[6]

Investigating the workplace interactions of professions yields greater explanatory power, illustrating how authority and legitimacy are enacted in organizations. Because this study is an ethnographic analysis of the occupational relations within one firm, it cannot directly address jurisdictional conflict at the level of the professional field. However, analyzing the occupational conflict at EquipCo further refines our understanding of the processes by which jurisdiction is claimed and maintained in the workplace. The results of this study suggest processes that are different than what a macro-sociological analysis focusing on political processes, institutional structures or representational strategies might predict. For instance, theories of professional power or occupational composition that rely on access to institutional resources as a lever for jurisdictional control might suggest that the engineers at EquipCo retained control over the design and production process via their education or occupational status. In contrast, my findings at EquipCo demonstrate that this picture is too simple – jurisdictional control is complicated by the daily interactions necessitated by organizational life.

While engineers were able to maintain control over the engineering drawings, they sometimes lost control over the design once the process moved into the arena of the machines. For instance, the technicians who physically controlled the machine in their lab also had authority over what happened to the machine in the production process. The engineers' higher status and education did not result in their full control over the process. Similarly, the engineers' design could be derailed via the reputational effects of the drawings. As the Fomblin example suggests, assemblers might change the way the machine was built on the basis of their reading of a drawing. While the engineer's abstracting of design principles into the drawing led him to add the note about Fomblin, the assemblers' knowledge of building attested to the efficacy of the grease. In this instance, the engineers' cognitive strategy of codifying their expert knowledge decreased their control, rather than solidifying it.

These examples suggest that another mechanism for challenging and maintaining occupational jurisdiction might be physical control over artifacts. We know that organizational objects are important for symbolizing status, identity, and elements of culture (Pratt & Rafaeli, 1997; Elsbach, 2000; Trice & Beyer, 1993). However, this study demonstrates that such objects are also used in social situations as a means for some groups to maintain control and power. At EquipCo, engineers used drawings as both technical objects and jurisdictional ones; technicians and assemblers did the same with machines. The use of artifacts described in this paper is specific to EquipCo; of course, social relations will coalesce around objects in different ways depending on the setting. However, while the occupational dynamics reported in this study would not be reproduced identically in other settings, the findings illustrate that artifacts can be useful jurisdictional tools.

Further, analyzing jurisdiction at the workplace level allows for the interplay of occupational and organizational status. While jurisdictional battles within systems of professions often occur at a legal or public level as professionals compete for a client base, most occupations encounter one another most frequently at the workplace itself. These groups interact on a daily basis within organizations, and the interdependence of their work makes occupational outcomes less predictable. Powerful occupational groups can accrue advantages due to status and superior resources, but still have to contend with control issues at the level of the task boundary.

The study of EquipCo demonstrated that the occupational group with the most hierarchical power and human capital, the engineers, was most effective in preserving its jurisdiction at the workplace. Power and position were influential factors in the definition of which artifacts and interpretations were significant. They also colored the perception of which groups had the ability to draw boundaries around their expertise and challenge the expertise of others. This power was partially a consequence of engineers' historical and institutional dominance; however, their location in the organizational hierarchy allowed them to leverage their status to support their claims in the workplace. Technicians' and assemblers' hierarchical position provided them with less power; at the same time, workplace interaction primarily around the control of machines allowed them to challenge the jurisdiction of engineers. It is only by looking closely at such workplace enactments that we can chart these relational dynamics, specifying the processes of occupational competition in greater detail.

APPENDIX A. EXAMPLES OF CROSS-OCCUPATIONAL PROBLEM SOLVING

Engineers and Technicians Used Drawings as Boundary Objects

The engineer, Evan, and Tim, the technician, were discussing the cable routing for an ACDC box, while looking at a drawing of it on the engineer's computer. Tim asked, 'Would it be better to have a little harness on the power supply? How long is the supply? That would be great for modularity.' Evan replied, 'There's the issue of reliability ...'

'We've done it that way before,' Tim interjected, 'although I think space is an issue.'

'Space wise I think you might be okay, if you go out in Z direction.' Evan indicated, 'This box is almost 11″ deep and there's nothing here.' Excited, Tim responded, 'Could you give me a copy of that top view?' 'Sure,' said Evan, 'and this is the interconnect diagram, you can get kind of the flow.'

Technicians and Assemblers Used Machines s Boundary Objects

Abe, an assembler, was building a power box. He lifted the box off the floor and pushed it into the enclosure, but it would not fit in all the way, and stuck out about a quarter of an inch. Abe said, 'It's stuck on something' and pulled it out to check inside. The pins seemed okay, and there was not anything obstructing the way. He tried again, but it still did not go all the way in. Pulling it out a little, he tries to see underneath. Another assembler, Andy, walked over to help, saying, 'It's like that, you have to jam it in.' Andy pushed it really hard, but it still stuck out of the enclosure.

Ted, the technician training them, approached and asked, 'Are you sure all the back is right, you checked?' Abe said yes, so Ted pulled it out, jiggled it and pushed it in hard, and it finally went in. He and Sam looked closely at the holes for the screws, which did not quite line up. Pointing at the enclosure, Ted said, 'This is sagging from all the weight, take the cover off and reach in with a wrench.' Abe removed the plastic cover and Ted used the wrench to push the enclosure upwards. The holes still did not align, so Ted suggested, 'You might have to slot these holes a little bit too. These are 632s, the design is messed up, the vendor messed up and it doesn't quite fit.'

NOTES

[1] For their helpful comments and advice, I thank Steve Barley, Nicole Biggart, Elizabeth Craig, Andy Hargadon, Julie Kmec, John Lafkas, Peter Levin, Gerardo Okhuysen, Wanda Orlikowski, Damon Phillips, Vicki Smith, Anand Swaminathan, Danielle Warren, Mark Zbaracki, the AJS reviewers, and participants in the University of Pennsylvania's Department of History and Sociology of Science seminar series. I am grateful to my informants at EquipCo for their friendship and patience.
[2] For additional detail about the site and methodology, see Bechky 2003.
[3] After the design was finalized, the drawings became closed and resistant to change. Because I was studying a new product line, most of the drawings had yet to reach this point.
[4] For further analysis of the use of these objects for problem solving across groups, see Bechky 2003.

[5] Drawings have several qualities that enhance their legitimacy and status as communication devices. Both Ferguson (1992) and Latour (1986) point out that drawings allow visual information to be reliably transferred across space and time. Additionally, Latour (1986) suggests that one source of the power of drawings is their creation of a common place for other information to come together (such as tolerances, sales information or task information), thereby joining realms of reality (mechanics, economics and the organization of work) that otherwise are difficult to bridge.

[6] As an anonymous reviewer pointed out, my analysis also confirms Halpern's study, in that the external hierarchy of occupations in this case is reinforced by workplace dynamics. Because of the large status imbalance of the occupations at EquipCo, the engineers' status is reinforced despite interactional challenges from technicians.

REFERENCES

Abbott, A. (1981). Status and status strain in the professions. *American Journal of Sociology, 86,* 819–835.

Abbott, A. (1988). *The system of professions: An essay on the division of expert labor.* Chicago: University of Chicago Press.

Abbott, A. (1989). The new occupational structure: What are the questions? *Work and Occupations, 16,* 273–291.

Allen, D. (2000). Doing occupational demarcation: The 'boundary-work' of nurse managers in a district general hospital. *Journal of Contemporary Ethnography, 29,* 326–356.

Barley, S.R. (1986). Technology as an occasion for structuring: Evidence from observations of CT scanners and the social order of radiology departments. *Administrative Science Quarterly, 31,* 78–108.

Barley, S.R. (1996a). *The new world of work.* British North-American Committee.

Barley, S.R. (1996b). Technicians in the workplace: Ethnographic evidence for bringing work into organization studies. *Administrative Science Quarterly, 41,* 404–441.

Bechky, B.A. (2003). Sharing meaning across occupational communities: The transformation of knowledge on a production floor. *Organization Science, 14,* 312–330.

Begun, J.W. & Lippincott, R.C. (1987). The origins and resolution of interoccupational conflict. *Work and Occupations, 14,* 368–386.

Bourdieu, P. (1984). *Distinction: A social critique of the judgment of taste.* Cambridge, MA: Harvard University Press.

Bourdieu, P. (1994). *Language and symbolic power.* Cambridge, MA: Harvard University Press.

Carlile, P.R. (2002). A pragmatic view of knowledge and boundaries: Boundary objects in new product development. *Organization Science, 13,* 442–455.

Chambliss, D.F. (1997). *Beyond caring: Hospitals, nurses and the social organization of ethics.* Chicago: University of Chicago Press.

Crozier, M. (1964). *The bureaucratic phenomenon.* Chicago: University of Chicago Press.

Douglas, M. & Isherwood, B. (1979). *The world of goods: Toward an anthropology of consumption.* New York: Basic Books.

Durkheim, E. (1984). *The division of labor in society.* New York: Free Press.

Elsbach, K.D. (2000). Affirming social identity through portable markers: A study of employee adaptation to a non-territorial work space. Working paper. Graduate School of Management, University of California, Davis.

Etzioni, A. (Ed.). (1969). *The semi-professions and their organization.* New York: Free Press.

Ferguson, E.S. (1992). *Engineering and the mind's eye.* Cambridge, MA: MIT Press.

Foucault, M. (1979). *Discipline and punish: The birth of the prison.* New York: Vintage.

Friedson, E. (1970). *Profession of medicine.* New York: Dodd Mead.

Glazer, N.Y. (1991). 'Between a rock and a hard place': Women's professional organizations of nursing and class, racial, and ethnic inequalities. *Gender and Society, 5,* 351–372.

Goffman, E. (1959). *The presentation of self in everyday life.* New York: Anchor.

Goodman, N. (1978. *Ways of worldmaking*. Indianapolis: Hackett.

Halpern, S.A. (1992). Dynamics of professional control: Internal coalitions and crossprofessional boundaries. *American Journal of Sociology, 97*, 994–1021.

Henderson, K. (1999). *On line and on paper: Visual representations, visual culture, and computer graphics in design engineering*. Cambridge, MA: MIT Press.

Hughes, D. (1980). The ambulance journey as an information generating process. *Sociology of Health and Illness, 2*(2), 115–132.

Kanter, R.M. (1977). *Men and women of the corporation*. New York: Basic Books.

Knorr Cetina, K. (1999). *Epistemic cultures: How the sciences make knowledge*. Cambridge, MA: Harvard University Press.

Kronus, C.L. (1976). The evolution of occupational power: An historical study of task boundaries between physicians and pharmacists. *Sociology of Work and Occupations, 3*, 3–37.

Larson, M.S. (1977). *The rise of professionalism*. Berkeley & Los Angeles: University of California Press.

Latour, B. (1986). Visualization and cognition: Thinking with eyes and hands. *Knowledge and Society, 6*, 1–40.

Latour, B. (1988). Mixing humans and non-humans together: Sociology of a door-closer. *Social Problems, 35*, 298–310.

Latour, B. (1996). *ARAMIS, or, The love of technology*. Cambridge, MA: Harvard University Press.

Latour, B. & Woolgar, S. (1979). Laboratory life: The construction of scientific facts. London: Sage.

Manley, J.E. (1995). Sex-segregated work in the system of professions: The development and stratification of nursing. *Sociological Quarterly, 36*, 297–314.

Mauss, M. (1976). The gift: Focus and functions of exchange in archaic societies. New York: Norton.

McCracken, G. (1988). *Culture and consumption*. Bloomington, IN: Indiana University Press.

Mesler, M.A. (1991). Boundary encroachment and task delegation: Clinical pharmacists on the medical team. *Sociology of Health and Illness, 13*, 310–331.

Power, M. (1997). Expertise and the construction of relevance: Accountants and environmental audit. *Accounting, Organization, and Society, 22*, 123–146.

Pratt, M.G. & Rafaeli, A. (1997). Organizational dress as a symbol of multilayered social identities. *Academy of Management Journal, 40*, 862–898.

Preston, J.A. (1995). Gender and the formation of a woman's profession. In Jacobs, J. (Ed.), *Gender inequality at work* (pp. 379–407). Thousand Oaks, CA: Sage.

Ritzer, G. (1977). *Working: Conflict and change*. Englewood Cliffs, NJ: Prentice-Hall.

Star, S.L. & Griesemer, J.R. (1989). Institutional ecology, 'translations' and boundary objects: Amateurs and professionals in Berkeley's Museum of Vertebrate Zoology, 1907–39. *Social Studies of Science, 19*, 387–420.

Trice, H.M. & Beyer, J.M. (1993). *The cultures of work organizations*. Englewood Cliffs, NJ: Prentice-Hall.

Vallas, S.P. (1999). Rethinking Post-Fordism: The meaning of workplace flexibility. *Sociological Theory, 17*, 68–101.

Vallas, S.P. & Beck, J. (1996). The transformation of work revisited: The limits of flexibility in American manufacturing. *Social Problems, 43*, 339–361.

Veblen, T. (1979 [1899]). *Theory of the leisure class*. New York: Viking Penguin

VSLI Research. (1996). *Ten best process equipment companies in 1995*. San Jose, CA: VSLI.

Winner, L. (1980). Do artifacts have politics? *Daedalus, 109*, 121–136.

Zetka, J.R. Jr. 2001. Occupational divisions of labor and their technology politics: The case of surgical scopes and gastrointestinal medicine. *Social Forces, 79*(4), 1495–1520.

ARTHUR BAKKER, CELIA HOYLES, PHILLIP KENT,
& RICHARD NOSS

IMPROVING WORK PROCESSES BY MAKING THE INVISIBLE VISIBLE[1]

THE NEED FOR TECHNO-MATHEMATICAL LITERACIES AT WORK

There is a growing movement for industrial companies to modify their production practices according to methodologies collectively known as process improvement. After World War II, Japanese companies such as Toyota developed new manufacturing paradigms (e.g., lean manufacturing) under the guidance of American experts, particularly W.E. Deming. Since the 1980s, the Japanese methodologies have been spreading to the West in a major way, in the form of programmes such as Total Quality Management (TQM) and Total Productive Maintenance (TPM) (Deming, 1986; Nakajima, 1988). Two American companies, Motorola and General Electric, became famous in the 1990s due to their successful development of the Six Sigma process improvement programme (e.g., Pyzdek, 2001). The core of all these programmes is a set of statistical techniques for the collection and interpretation of production data and the promotion of a workplace culture in which decisions are based on abstractions of work processes in the form of shared, and often computationally represented, data.

A key point that emerges in working with process improvement methodologies is that employees at almost all levels are faced with the need to participate in the procedures of data collection and to interpret the charts, tables, and graphs that are derived from the data. This faces companies with the question of what knowledge their employees need to participate effectively, and, particularly for our concerns, just how much of the mathematical and technical knowledge which underlies the production of these artefacts it is useful for them to know.

In this chapter, we will look closely at an example of a company attempting to address this issue with its employees.[2] Whatever the answer, we take the position that it is considerably more complex than any model based on 'skills' or 'competences.' For example, learning to read graphs is not a straightforward process. Roth and Bowen (2003), for instance, have shown that even professional scientists often misinterpret graphs from their own discipline if they are not sufficiently familiar with the context in which the data were collected. The idea, then, that we might engage employees either in general mathematical education in, say, graphical interpretation, in the hope that they will somehow 'apply' this knowledge at work, is unrealistic. More generally, we take it for granted that knowing cannot be separated from the activity in which it takes place (see, e.g.,

D.W. Livingstone and D. Guile (eds.), The Knowledge Economy and Lifelong Learning: A Critical Reader, 257–275.

Stevenson, 2002). Thus any simplistic attempt to characterize mathematical knowledge at work as simply a set of mathematical competences or skills runs the risk of ignoring just that element of the situation that provides meaning for employees – their often intimate familiarity with the work context, the behaviour of machines and materials, the quality of the outputs, and the routines of the work process.

It has been evident since the 1980s from studies of mathematical practices in workplaces that most workers use mathematics (in its broad meaning, including statistics) to make sense of situations in ways which differ quite radically from those of the formal mathematics of school and college curricula. Based on earlier work by Hoyles, Noss, and colleagues (Hoyles et al., 2002; Noss et al., 2002), we have coined the term 'Techno-mathematical Literacies' (TmL) as a way of conceptualizing mathematics as it exists in modern technology-based workplace practices. We have felt the need to adopt a new term to avoid the historical legacy of the term 'numeracy,' because it is often used to refer to basic mathematical skills, whereas the skills needs identified by Hoyles et al. (2002) clearly go beyond this basic numeracy (for a critique of the notion of numeracy itself, see Noss, 1998). Furthermore, we wanted to avoid the simple use of the term 'mathematics' itself, because in the workplace it bears the connotation of school mathematics. In fact, our use of the term 'literacies' is broadly convergent with the PISA definition of 'mathematical literacy' except for the explicit role of technology and workplace knowledge in TmL:

> Mathematical literacy is an individual's capacity to identify and understand the role that mathematics plays in the world, to make well-founded judgements and to use and engage with mathematics in ways that meet the needs of that individual's life as a constructive, concerned and reflective citizen. (OECD, 2003, p. 24)

What emerges from studies in workplaces is that people tend to develop mathematical techniques to carry out their work, which they generally situate by bringing to abstractions of the workplace their experiences, the tools they use, and the features and local regularities of the context. It is evident from research in workplaces that experienced employees come to use and interpret mathematical concepts as 'situated abstractions,' which are generalizable within the work context (see e.g., Noss & Hoyles, 1996).

Our previous research focused on a range of work contexts (including nurses, bank employees, and airline pilots). The study reported here stems from the *Techno-mathematical Literacies in the Workplace* project (Hoyles, Noss, Kent, & Bakker, 2010), which focused on several industry sectors: packaging, pharmaceutical manufacturing, automotive industry, food manufacturing, and the retail finance industry. In each of these sectors, the companies involved were deploying some form of process improvement at different points along the spectrum from initial steps (as in the food manufacturing case described here) to full deployment of lean manufacturing, Six Sigma, or a mixture of the two (in the pharmaceutical and automotive sectors). The companies also varied in terms of the embedding of information technology; food production – the subject of this chapter – rating relatively low in technology use, and, unsurprisingly, pharmaceuticals rating very high. In this chapter, we will demonstrate how TmL are emerging as a form of knowledge for employees as one company at the low end of both spectra seeks to modernize and improve its production processes by training process improvement teams in certain problem-solving techniques. The purpose of this chapter is to illustrate sets of TmL that prove useful in making processes more efficient, and thereby elaborate a small piece of the puzzle of how Techno-mathematical Literacies are needed in companies that are involved in some form of process improvement.

SOME REMARKS ON THE UTILITY OF ACTIVITY THEORY AND A SEMIOTIC APPROACH

In order to assist in identifying the nature of Techno-mathematical Literacies (TmL) in workplaces, we have employed *activity theory* as a means to gain a holistic, macro-level view on work processes. We share the view of workplaces as complex arrangements of interacting activity systems each characterized by their own object (i.e., the purpose of work), mediated by artefacts, and located in a context characterized by a specific division of labour, sets of rules of discourse, and inter-related workplace communities (see, e.g., Engeström, 2001). It is evident that shop-floor workers and managers can inhabit different activity systems with dissimilar goals expressed with diverse tools and following distinct rules. We will exploit the roles of different tools in achieving an object, and particularly the notion of boundary object (Star & Griesemer, 1989) that has recently been explored in the activity theory literature (Tuomi-Gröhn & Engeström, 2003) and many other bodies of literature (Akkerman & Bakker, 2011). A useful analytical technique in what follows will be to consider signs, such as numerical data and graphical information, as boundary objects that mediate communication between, and within, different communities.

Yet activity theory may not be quite sufficient for our purposes. The problem is that we will need to acknowledge the specificities of Techno-mathematical Literacies, including recognition of what constitutes the mathematical knowledge domain. In terms of its historical development, activity theory has maintained a rather different trajectory, starting with Vygotsky's distinction between everyday and scientific concepts, mainly focused on vertical development from everyday to scientific concepts – while later developments, due to the work of Leont'ev, introduced the distinction of activity, action, and operation, and Engeström (2001) focused attention on horizontal development between activity systems.

One of the merits of this latter approach is that it has drawn attention to such forms of development that previously have not been well described. Yet there is, in some of this work, less of a focus on the discipline-informed knowledge that we seek to characterize or a preference for general descriptions of individuals' attitudes rather than knowledge per se (see also Beach, 1999). Thus, recent developments in socio-cultural and activity-theoretical research have led to a focus on horizontal developments and forms of knowledge that appear to be learnable by participation in communities of practice (CoP); and as a backdrop, there is the associated attack from situated cognition on the very notion of disciplinary knowledge itself (Lave, 1988). Guile and Young (2003, p. 79) argue that 'the role of scientific concepts seems to have got lost in recent developments in activity theory with their stress on activities, context and horizontal development.' Since our interest is in the learning and use of mathematics, which typically involves generalization and abstraction, we seek to restore some balance to the question of knowledge while simultaneously taking into account recent insights from socio-cultural and activity-theoretical approaches.

A further imbalance in the evolution of activity theory, which has its origin in Soviet thinkers, relates to the question of semiotic mediation. According to Bakhurst (1996), in reflecting on activity theory, the notion of semiotic mediation was 'marginalized in the Soviet tradition since the Stalin era' (p. 215). In much recent workplace research, tools, artefacts, or instruments are broadly taken as mediating between subject and object of activity. But because mathematical 'tools' are often signs such as tables and graphs, symbolic tools that do more than merely represent or mediate, we also need a specific theory of semiotic mediation, which takes account of how particular mathematical signs are used at work and in the context of employee training. We have found it helpful to consider, therefore, some elements of Peirce's semiotics, which has its origins in mathematics and philosophy and which can be seen as complementary to Vygotsky's theory (see, e.g., Seeger, 2005).

In Peirce's (1976) terms, a *sign* is anything that stands for something (an *object*) for someone. His or her response is called the *interpretant* – the 'meaning' of the sign. Peirce distinguishes different types of interpretants: logical ('scientific' meanings), dynamic (actions), and emotive (emotions) interpretants. What allows people to interpret a sign is *collateral* knowledge, which sits 'by the side' and which consists of a network of knowledge forms including tacit, implicit, meta-cognitive, episodic, and codified knowledge forms (Hoffmann & Roth, 2005). Our own research focus has brought us closely into contact with the role of collateral knowledge and the peculiar mix of mathematical, scientific, and work context knowledge needed to use mathematical signs in solving production problems. In particular, we acknowledge Peirce's distinctions between several types of signs, the most important of which for our analysis is the *diagram*: a sign representing *relationships*. A diagram almost always is a complex sign, consisting of many elements with different functions, and it often functions as a model (for a more detailed account, see Bakker & Hoffmann, 2005).

The particular relevance of the semiotic approach for what follows is that: (1) signs are visible, whereas the objects they represent are often not (such as the cause of a problem); (2) people's responses to signs depend on their knowledge of them and their experiences with interpreting such signs in particular situations; and (3) signs mediate between subjects and the purpose of activity. We therefore make distinctions between:

– Sign: What is visible, whether as a physical or a mathematical sign.
– Object: What the sign represents in someone's interpretation or that someone wants to represent or measure. (Note that this Peircean notion of 'object' is different from the activity-theoretical one.)
– Interpretant: The response to the sign. The type of interpretant most relevant to our analysis is the 'dynamic interpretant,' the action taken in response to a sign, which can be the production of a new sign, such as a table or diagram.
– The TmL that are required to create and interpret the sign and respond to it appropriately in the workplace.

An additional rationale for our focus on semiotic mediation is methodological: TmL is most likely to become visible to us as researchers when employees use mathematical signs – signs with their origin in mathematical or scientific disciplines. As such, those signs can become boundary objects between activity systems.

METHODOLOGICAL REMARKS

The TmL project began with a phase of interviews combined with ethnographic observation of ten companies in the different sectors described earlier, in order to identify and categorize different forms of Techno-mathematical Literacies. Here we will focus on just one of the companies we observed, a biscuit manufacturing and packaging company. While we describe our observational methodology as ethnographic, we should be careful to state that we do not attempt the kind of engagement which is typical of ethnography amongst professional anthropologists, such as immersion of the researcher in the community under investigation over periods of months or years. As we noted above, the notion of TmL has developed out of our previous research on mathematics in workplaces, and thus, to a certain extent, our data collection has been driven by the motive of 'looking for' TmL, rather than merely 'looking at' workplaces in general. There has been, of course, a necessary balance between 'looking at' and 'looking for,' particularly in the early work of the project. One technique that we have found productive is to focus initial workplace observations on situations where routine working practice breaks down; this has brought into view the explicit problem-solving and communication strategies of employees – thus suggesting to us the TmL which might underlie those strategies, and suggesting issues to be looked for in subsequent observations. As illustrated in the next section, we often used 'mathematical' signs such as graphs as boundary objects to co-ordinate employees' and our own perspectives as researchers.

For each company that we have studied, interviews and observations (including artefacts collected) from workplace visits were written up as detailed reports and transcripts. Starting from these raw data sources, our analysis has proceeded by developing a preliminary categorization and description of TmL in order to identify significant work episodes that exemplify one or more elements of such knowledge. These work episodes were written up collaboratively by the project team, discussed and revised as appropriate. Similarly, the emerging TmL categorization and descriptions were collectively and iteratively examined and revised. The analytical schemes for the work episodes span various dimensions: routine or non-routine situation; the nature and role of the models, tools, and artefacts used or available; and the ways that TmL is mobilized (or not) to communicate between different groups or to make decisions. Note that, in general, we do not code individual 'chunks' of data, such as individual interview responses, since the understanding of how TmL is being used in practice requires a synthesis of different viewpoints and data sources. In fact, as we pointed out in the introductory section, we started from the presumption that TmL cannot be separated from the activity systems in which they are observed, a presumption which has been corroborated in each setting we have examined.

Triangulation is a key concern for our research (cf. Hammersley & Atkinson, 1995). In collecting data, we continuously seek to triangulate different views of the same workplace activity, seeking the perspectives of employees including shop-floor operators, supervisory managers, process engineers and process improvement specialists, maintenance engineers, and more senior managers. In analysing data, we share and elaborate interpretations of the raw data (audio transcripts, photographs of workplaces, artefacts in the form of paper documentation) amongst the project team. We further triangulate our findings by presenting provisional versions of them to the companies in which the research was carried out ('feedback meetings'), and by means of consultation with experts in the particular industrial sector involved ('validation meetings' in which sector experts are invited to learn about project findings, and comment on their validity and generality). The characterization of TmL presented in the next section was, in fact, one of the major topics addressed during a validation meeting with ten managers and technical consultants from the packaging sector and four researchers (workplace research, mathematics and statistics – excluding ourselves).

USING DATA TO SOLVE PROBLEMS IN FOOD PRODUCTION

In this section, we present some empirical findings that suggest what it means in practice to make visible key variables in the production process, to see what is important to be seen and to act accordingly, that is, actually solve a problem. After sketching the relevant activity systems as a broader context, we analyse the data on process improvement from a semiotic perspective and point out how the analysis suggests the need for a theoretical framework which can address more adequately the role of TmL in activity.

The example concerns a programme of process improvement work that is being carried out in food factory, with the overall goal of improving efficiency (less waste, more production) and hence increasing profitability. Among the aims of the programme are, first, dealing with obvious process deficiencies, and second, build-ing, in the long term, a culture among employees of thinking about process improvement and simultaneously upskilling employees at all levels to support this change. One part of the programme is the formation of 'process improvement teams' (PI teams), which spend several weeks working full-time on one particular production line. Each team consists of volunteers who have different roles across the company – managers, maintenance engineers, and shop-floor operators – with the idea that by interacting in detail with the managers and engineers, the operators will become stakeholders in process improvement. We focus on one PI team as the subjects, trying, as the object of activity, to reduce the waste problem in one production area, using a series of graphs, tables, diagrams, and data as mediating signs.

From our point of view – though not necessarily that of the PI team – the process improvement exercise was an attempt to make visible and explicit the relationships between elements and variables of the process. As such, its key component can be seen as a form of modelling – making relationships visible with signs such as diagrams. This process is often cyclical, as it involves several steps of measuring variables, representing them, and deciding what to do next. The analysis presented below is an attempt to clarify one defining characteristic of TmL as rendering the invisible visible through the use of mathematical signs and developing meanings for action from their interpretation. We highlight the interpretants of signs since these appear to be critical in revealing the TmL that the members of the PI team used to solve problems.

Capacity Profile Chart as a Boundary Object

The PI team that we observed began with several days of classroom training. After this, the first problem-solving activity of the team was to collect data about the whole production line and assemble it into a single chart, known as the 'capacity profile chart' (see Figure 1). The intention of this chart was to reveal any 'bottlenecks' in the production process, so that the PI team could prioritize a programme of tasks to remedy the most important sources of inefficiency. However, the meanings drawn from reading this chart are not unproblematic. From the point of view of the PI team, the chart was to serve as a problem-solving tool, but also to get a better overview of the whole process, which many operators needed:

> They run a packaging machine far faster than the production so that misalignments are very likely – so the machine will miss cartons and pile-up, and if you say, 'Why don't you turn it down a bit,' they've already accumulated stackwork because of the pile-ups, so they say, 'We can't turn it down we've got to deal with this stackwork.' They get into a cycle of running the machine faster than needed, which creates a problem, which creates stackwork to deal with. (engineer in the PI team)

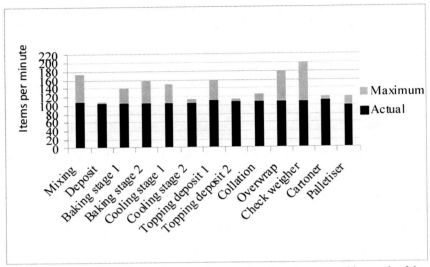

Figure 1. Capacity profile chart showing the actual and maximum possible speeds of the different stages in a baking process.

Also notable about the capacity profile chart is the way that it served as a boundary object between us as researchers trying to understand what we were observing and the industrial context. As mathematical experts, we experienced some confusion as we tried to make sense of the chart: it became clear on trying to understand it that we needed contextual knowledge. Mathematically speaking, Figure 1 looks like a bar chart of the different components in the baking process. Yet implicit in the horizontal axis is a *time* dimension, which is the sequence of baking and packing stages. Thus the chart should be read from left to right through the baking process (mixing of raw ingredients, baking, cooling, adding toppings, and packaging of the finished biscuit). Furthermore, we expected that the heights of all the 'actual' bars would be the same through the process (that is, there is one overall production rate). The fact that there is not, as we learnt by talking about this chart to employees, is in part due to the approximate nature of many of the measurements taken, and in part due to the fact that the process is not continuous in practice (there are breaks between stages where biscuits may be removed from the process for temporary storage).

During the feedback meeting, employees (including the PI facilitator) were shocked that we did not really understand their graphs; they assumed that their graphs must in some way be faulty as they could not be read by 'the mathematicians.' Our own experience of reading the capacity profile chart contrasted nicely with the response of an experienced packaging manager (from a different company) when we presented the chart at the validation meeting. To him the process, and the location of the bottleneck, was obvious:

It is a very complex science marrying all the equipment in a factory, like a jigsaw puzzle that needs many calculations. The maximum capacity has to be measured by the marriage of all the machines, and whichever one is producing the lowest is the point of action [the 'Depositor' bar in Figure 1, second from left]. If the investment is not made at that particular point, then that is the maximum that can be achieved.

Returning to the PI team, the depositor was identified as the major bottleneck, but another variable was brought into play: senior managers noted that the cost of fixing this bottleneck was so high that it would require a high-level decision that could not be made within the time frame of the PI exercise. Consequently, the team decided to shift its attention away from bottlenecks; the PI facilitator with the team judged the waste issue in the production line to be a manageable set of problems within the available time span of a few weeks.

From our point of view, as exemplified by the chart example, the process improvement exercise was an attempt to make explicit the relationships between elements and variables of the process, and it is for this reason that it makes sense to regard it as a form of modelling. Though seen scientifically, the depositor was the main problem in the work flow, the contextual constraints and collateral knowledge accompanying the graph demanded the PI team to work at a more manageable problem. In this sense, the abstraction of the work process instantiated as the capacity profile chart could only be interpreted within the specificities of the workplace situation: it is a *situated* abstraction of the work process.

We now analyse the solving of the waste problem in three steps, illustrating the cyclical nature of producing and interpreting mathematical signs to make explicit the implicit causes of problems.

Step 1: Measuring waste (Table 1). Having decided to focus on waste, the PI team wished to obtain a clearer image of the problem, and the areas to prioritize in solving it, by measuring the quantity of wasted biscuits in a more detailed way than hitherto existed. Instead of weighing the waste collected over an entire day and coming from several different areas of the production line (which was the routine practice), they separately measured the waste arising from particular areas and for the particular different types of biscuits being produced during the day. As one manager said: 'With better collection of information, we should be able to highlight where the problems are.' These measurements were recorded in a table (see Table 1).

From this table, it was clear to the team that most waste was generated in Area 3, the topping depositor, where jam and other toppings are deposited onto biscuits from a set of nozzles (see Figure 2). At this point it is worth noting that there is not always a need to use the mediation of mathematical signs to see the cause of a problem. As a team member said: 'Sometimes you can see it straight away' (although, in this case what is obviously 'visible' is only visible when one looks for it!). As we have seen in other companies as well, data representations often serve to confirm what people have already seen, but the availability of quantified data can help prioritize the different actions to be taken. In this case, once the

265

topping depositor had been identified as a priority area, it was investigated further to find out the causes of the waste.

Table 1. The waste table produced by the PI team (machine names have been replaced by Area 1, 2, etc.)

Product (type of biscuit)	Area 1 (after baking) (waste in kg)	Area 2 (waste in kg)	Area 3 (topping) (waste in kg)	Area 4 (waste in kg)	Area 5 (packing)
Jam	10	31	134	20	576 packs
Vanilla	30	87	141	59	2304 packs
Chocolate	-	22	131	120	
Total	40	140	406	199	

In short, Table 1 helped the team to know on which area to focus in reducing the waste. The TmL involved in this interpretation and action are identifying and measuring key variables, representing and interpreting data, and thus refining the definition of the problem (i.e., its location in the topping depositor as opposed to general 'waste' from the production line).

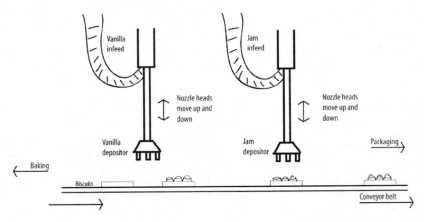

Figure 2: Schematic drawing of the topping depositor area: two nozzles, one for vanilla and one for jam, deposit toppings onto biscuits.

Step 2: Making a cause-and-effect diagram (Figure 3). Alongside both the numbers in the tables and observations from the topping depositor area, the team discussed how the problem could 'be broken down into manageable sub-problems' (as one team member phrased it) and from this produced a cause-and-effect diagram of the part of the process around 'topping deposit' (Figure 3). This diagram was used as a 'dynamic' tool by the PI team; it was drawn on a whiteboard and revised daily as the work progressed. Each day, sub-teams of two or three people were assigned to look at different problem areas, with a feedback meeting held at the end of each day. The version of the diagram shown here comes from part way through the work; we have added divisions into 'first level,' 'second level' problems, etc., in order to make the diagram more readable. There are three main problem areas (first level), which have been broken down for investigation into sub-problems (second level), and several of these have been further broken down (third/fourth level). For each problem box, the optimum and actual states are indicated (many of these are shown incomplete, since they were as yet not investigated); an X indicates that the problem is still unsolved, and a tick indicates a problem solved (there is only one tick, so much work remains to be done!); problems without X or tick are still to be investigated at this stage of the work.

This diagram helped the team to co-ordinate their actions of assessing and prioritizing sub-problems and of measuring actual values. This involves similar TmL as in the previous step, but also conjecturing on the relationships at issue. Moreover, systematic measurement of key variables is crucial.

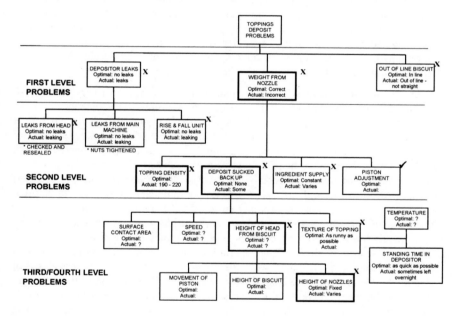

Figure 3. Cause-and-effect diagram of the topping deposit problems. The bold boxes show the line of investigation we analyse here.

In the first and second step, the mathematical knowledge at stake is mainly measuring and methodically presenting data and relationships. The cause-and-effect diagram can be seen as a model of the problem, representing the key variables and their relationships. Much more important than its representational function, however, is the fact that it is action-oriented. In the experience of the

267

team members, the diagram tells them what to do. This emphasizes the highly situated nature of such a model; having the scientific and general analytical skills to make this model and visualize the salient features and relationships of the process is only part of the story, complementary to its mediational function in solving the problem. The next step more explicitly highlights the lack of and need for TmL.

Step 3: Tackling sub-problems. We were able to observe directly the work of the team as it tackled the 'Deposit sucked back up' and 'Topping density' sub-problems:

> We are trying to work out why we are getting a lot of waste ... [Currently] we are looking at one aspect of that, the topping weight ... the deposit head, which is trying to stick topping onto the biscuit ... it is the surface area of contact between topping and biscuit which determines if the topping stays on the biscuit or gets sucked back up again ... so we are trying to increase that surface contact area ... The team are trying to reduce the density of the topping, so that same weight will deposit at a lot higher volume. At the moment, they are gradually introducing more air into the topping to see if they improve the surface contact. (process improvement facilitator)

As part of this work, several operators had been given the task of trying to work out both an optimum height of the delivery of toppings onto biscuits, and the density of the topping material, controlled by the amount of air injected into it (these were both sub-problems as identified in Figure 3). There was a significant complexity regarding the meaning of optimum in this situation; there were multiple variables to consider – height of delivery nozzles, density of topping ingredients, and temperature of the ingredients – and we suspect that even the more expert members of the team did not have a very good understanding of the optimal solution that might be achieved. (Note that 'optimal' here implies something rather different than a mathematically optimal construction, since it depends on many factors within the work context, only some of which may be quantifiable.)

We were struck by the fact that operators – in seeking some kind of optimal value – did not use a consistent way of measuring the height of the nozzles. For instance, they would measure from the top of the biscuit to the ring of the nozzle in some cases, but from the bottom of the biscuit in other cases. This, of course, made it hard to make reliable judgements on the data. Moreover, they recorded their data using very rough and loosely organized pen-and-paper notes.

This example suggests the role of TmL which are concerned with combining and co-ordinating different data sources to assess the relative effects of key variables, but it also points to a lack of TmL in systematic measurement and optimization. Scientific disciplines such as mathematics and statistics provide powerful techniques to assist this optimization process, ranging from simple graphical displays to sophisticated techniques such as designs of experiments (Montgomery, 1997), although the latter are clearly beyond the scope of operators and even most managers. Nevertheless, it is worth remarking that using such a scientifically sound technique would probably have quickly delivered a reliable optimum, perhaps saving the company a lot of waste.

We speculate that the measuring and recording tasks would have been more successful if the operators had had spreadsheet software available to organize their data and look for relationships between variables. This, however, was explicitly ruled out by the Process improvement facilitator:

> We [the facilitators] do the number crunching part, and use graphs to communicate ... It would be helpful if everyone could design and use their own spreadsheets, but they can't so we do it – it would save us a lot of time and we could get more done in the time available. We try to keep things simple so everyone can progress at the same speed – it is really bad to have people left behind and lose interest.

Apart from this choice in division of labour, it obviously would not be enough to give spreadsheets to operators: there is a need for them to acquire common TmL, such as systematic measurement, through using the tools and techniques that a spreadsheet provides.

Summary

In semiotic terms, this sequence of sign production and developing meaning for action can be summarized as in Table 2. *Sign* refers to any visible issue, whether physical or mathematical. *Object* refers to the mostly invisible issue that is represented by the sign or, seen from the user perspective, the issue that employees wanted to measure and tackle. *Actions* are the responses (interpretants) to the sign or a combination of signs. The TmL refer to what is required to interpret the signs and act upon them. Note that the TmL in 'Coming to a decision and identifying an action' (Table 3) are required at all stages of the sequence. In brief, the waste table (Table 1) served to make visible the point at which the major waste problem was located. The actions that followed from this interpretation involved looking at the major waste area and analysing how to break down the overall problem into manageable sub-problems, which was supported by a cause-and-effect diagram (Figure 3). Next, systematic measurement had to lead to optimizing certain key settings (e.g., height from nozzle to biscuit).

The data we have presented here exemplify TmL, part of a broader set of literacies, which we have observed in process improvement activity in other contexts besides the bakery. Overall, these TmL fall into two categories: *making the invisible visible* and *coming to an informed action*. The TmL commonly required in *making the invisible visible* are: defining a problem; seeing the need to quantify; identifying and measuring key variables; and representing and interpreting data. In our list of common TmL, we have left out the optimization issue mentioned in step 3, because this is more specific to certain situations. The TmL involved in *coming to an action* are conjecturing about possible causes and communicating about the data to come to a decision (see Table 3). We would like to stress two points:

269

- The nature of TmL is that these cannot be seen as generic competences or general problem-solving skills; they require constant recontextualization as well as 'webbing' (Noss & Hoyles, 1996) of contextual and mathematical knowledge.
- The TmL listed do not provide exhaustive or exclusive sets of steps that have to be taken in a specific order; for example, the definition of a problem is often refined during other steps.

Table 2. A sequence of sign production and developing meaning for action

Sign	Object	Actions	TmL required
1. Waste table (Table 1)	Total weight of wasted biscuits in different areas	Focus on highest numbers first: at topping depositor; Make a cause and effect diagram	Identifying and measuring key variables; Representing and interpreting data
2. Cause and effect diagram (Figure 3)	Relationships between causes, and manageable sub-problems	Assess and prioritise sub-problems; Measuring actual values	As above, plus: Conjecturing Systematic measurement of key variables
3. Data about sub-problems	Relationships within and between sub-problems	*Cycles of sign production leading to further actions and signs*: Defining and trying to find optimal values for each sub-problem (e.g., height from nozzle to biscuit)	As above, plus: Combining and co-ordinating different data sources; optimization

Table 3. Common TmL for situated modelling in context

Making the invisible visible

Posing a problem
Identifying key variables
Appreciating the need to quantify
Systematic measurement and sampling
Representing data
Combining and co-ordinating different data sources to assess relative effects of key variables

Coming to a decision and identifying an action

Interpreting, conjecturing and communicating with data
Making a decision based on information
Judging implications of possible decisions and deciding action

– mediated by available technology and situated in the work context

270

The two sets of TmL can be grouped under one heading of 'situated modelling:' the problem-solving activity of the PI team exemplifies the development of knowledge about models of processes represented in diagrams (in this case, the processes in a manufacturing production line), in order to identify and understand the problems and the relationships between problems inherent in different processes. We characterize these models as situated because their understanding depends on a combination of contextual and mathematical issues, and because the meanings of signs for the different actors are contingent on work experience as well as expertise with mathematical signs. As such, the modelling described here is rather different from the standard type of mathematical modelling in which a real-world situation is 'translated' into a mathematical model so that it can be used to solve a (now) mathematical problem or make a prediction that is translated back to the real world, while neglecting any 'noise' from the context. On the contrary, the situated approach takes the 'noise' (from a mathematical perspective) as providing much of the meaning to the diagram or model and thus the basis for decision making.

DISCUSSION

The episodes reported here illustrate the nature of Techno-mathematical Literacies during process improvement, specifically those needed by employees with relatively little formal education. Compared to other companies we have investigated, the bakery in which we observed this particular waste problem being solved was at an early stage of implementing a process improvement programme and was comparatively 'low-tech.' In later work, we have compared more high-technology settings with that of the bakery and assessed the extent to which technology affords different kinds of uses of mathematical signs such as tables, diagrams, and graphs to make problems visible and prioritize actions (Bakker, Kent, Noss, & Hoyles, 2009; Hoyles et al., 2010; Noss, Bakker, Hoyles, & Kent, 2007). Based on workplace research literature (e.g., Kim, 2002; Reich, 1991; Zuboff, 1988) and our own observations, we would think that companies at the higher end of the spectrum of deploying process improvement programmes and high-tech tools require a higher level of TmL for many of their employees. As a signal of this trend towards scientifically based business programmes, we cite the general manager from this bakery: 'We are an engineering business that happens to make biscuits.' Compare this with one of the operators of one production line with many years' experience who confessed to us that in moving from one biscuit line to another (which to us, looked more or less identical), she felt 'lost.' She certainly did not think – or want to think – of her job as engineering, preferring instead to maintain a craft-based approach to her work. We do not comment on whose perspective – hers or the general manager's – is preferable; only that the manager is pointing to an abstraction of the work process he wants to share, and we remark on the possible role of symbolic boundary objects in achieving this outcome.

As the bakery example points out, it is not just mathematical or statistical knowledge and computer skills that are needed. One manager said to us: 'People

271

will be able to make more decisions from the data at their fingertips and they will need more skills to do that – not really computer skills, more decision-making skills.' When we have asked managers how they recruit and develop new employees, they often speak of looking at processes and making decisions. What is needed, said one manager, is 'the ability for people to look at things and react.' From a semiotic perspective this implies that people need to interpret signs and know what to do in response. To interpret information and make data-informed decisions requires a mixture of collateral knowledge forms, including mathematical knowledge, while crucially webbing this knowledge with invaluable familiarity of the work system.

A word more about webbing and collateral knowledge. We have emphasized that TmL cannot be seen as generic competences, and have illustrated how there is an organic link between context and the signs used to represent the workplace. Elsewhere we have commented on this linkage as a fundamental characteristic for developing mathematical meaning, and referred to it as webbing. The idea of webbing evokes the ways that people can come to construct mathematically based knowledge by forging internal connections in interaction of internal and external resources (cognitive and artefactual tools) during activity and in reflection upon it. The notion of webbing aims, therefore, to recognize the central significance of signs and tools as external resources that shape the nature of the mathematical resources constructed. The notion of webbing also resonates with Peirce's idea of collateral knowledge as the many different knowledge forms that allow people to interpret and use signs (cf. Hoffmann & Roth, 2005), and Brandom's (1994) idea of 'web of reasons,' which has made its way into educational research (Bakker & Derry, 2011).

We have taken activity theory as a theoretical background framework, and attempted to complement it with elements of a semiotic perspective in order to analyse how mathematical signs mediate within those systems. The fundamental idea is that signs do more than merely represent and mediate – they create for themselves a voice in the system, a voice which can only be heard, or at least understood, as part of a broad set of Techno-mathematical Literacies whose existence cannot be taken for granted.

In the examples we have 'zoomed in' on semiotic mediation to identify the nature of TmL, but we would like to remark that 'zooming out' to activity systems is equally important, particularly if we are interested in engendering change in the workplace. For example, it was apparent from our observations that it is not enough to educate other operators on the production line by simply presenting to them the results of the PI team. One of the operators from the PI team reported that: 'We changed things while we were working on the plant, and people have gone back to doing things as before.' He gave an example of how they had found an optimal speed for a conveyor belt, but operators (who had not been in the PI team) changed it back to what they were used to: 'We slowed down the conveyor belts so people could be more productive putting biscuits on, and now they have speeded it back up. They think about getting more biscuits out, but they sometimes struggle getting the biscuits on.' This is not surprising if we realize that only a subset of the operators have undergone the same process of sign production and developing meanings or taken part in the activity system of the PI team. As an extreme example of the struggle between craft and scientific approaches, we heard of another company in which operators use *fake* control panels. They think they have the freedom to manipulate certain variables, but in fact the settings are fixed by the engineers!

An extreme example, perhaps, but it highlights a crucial specificity in the role of mathematically derived symbols. The special property of mathematical symbols is that in order to deal with them, to infuse them with meaning, it is necessary to situate them internally as part of a system of relationships between signs as well as externally, as part of a system of more or less familiar relationships between things (some of which might, of course, be symbolic). The balance between this internal and external system of relationships is one of the ways to recognize 'mathematical' activity of a professional kind. The symbols seem to have a life of their own, they are constitutive of meaning, but only when an appropriate balance is achieved (appropriate, that is, for the object of activity). When this integration fails (as in the case of the operators who did not participate in the PI team) or is deliberately fractured (in the case of the operators 'duped' into using fake control panels) the abstractions of the work process they represent remain just that, unsituated and non-constitutive of meaning.

After our ethnographic case studies the TmL project shifted to intervention – via the development and evaluation of learning opportunities (Hoyles et al., 2010) – and although this lies outside the scope of the current chapter, it is worth enquiring why the PI team trainers were so reticent to introduce a tool such as a spreadsheet into their work. In part, we conjecture that this is part of a cultural assumption that spreadsheets are just 'too much maths' – and they may be right. But our experience so far, for example in mortgage pricing (Bakker, Kent, Hoyles, & Noss, 2011), suggests that this is short-sighted view, and one that excludes some important – and, it seems so far, approachable – ways to link collateral knowledge with mathematical and technical knowledge. In this short-sighted view, technology is something which automates the workplace, and 'de-skills' the production employees rather than 'informates' the workplace (Zuboff, 1988), that is, provides information to employees such that they develop a greater knowledge of the production process and become more effective controllers of it.

NOTES

[1] We gratefully acknowledge funding by the United Kingdom Economic and Social Research Council's Teaching and Learning Research Programme (www.tlrp.org), Award Number L139-25-0119. See also www.ioe.ac.uk/trlp/technomaths. We are grateful to our colleague Dr David Guile for his contributions to our research and for discussions of an earlier version of this chapter.
[2] We do not naïvely believe that the interests and – by implication – the 'needs' of employees and employers are coincident, or even convergent, but consideration of this and similar sociological issues lie outside both our professional competence and the scope of this chapter.

REFERENCES

Akkerman, S.F. & Bakker, A. (2011). Boundary crossing and boundary objects. *Review of Educational Research, 81*, 132–169.

Bakhurst, D. (1996). Social memory in Soviet thought. In Daniels, H. (Ed.), *An introduction to Vygotsky*, pp. 196–218. London: Routledge).

Bakker, A. & Derry, J. (2011). Lessons from inferentialism for statistics education. *Mathematical Thinking and Learning, 13*, 5–26.

Bakker, A., & Hoffmann, M. (2005). Diagrammatic reasoning as the basis for developing concepts: A semiotic analysis of students' learning about statistical distribution. *Educational Studies in Mathematics, 60*, 333–358.

Bakker, A, Kent, P, Noss, R., & Hoyles, C. (2009). Alternative representations of statistical measures in computer tools to promote communication between employees in automotive manufacturing. *Technology Innovations in Statistics Education, 3*(2), 1–31. Retrieved from www.escholarship.org/uc/item/53b9122r.

Bakker, A., Kent, P., Hoyles, C., & Noss, R. (2011). Designing for communication at work: A case for technology-enhanced boundary objects. *International Journal of Educational Research, 50*(1), 26–32.

Beach, K.D. (1999). Consequential transitions: A sociocultural expedition beyond transfer in education. *Review of Research in Education, 24*, 101–139.

Brandom, R.B. (1994). *Making it explicit*. Cambridge, MA: Harvard University Press.

Deming, W.E. (1986). *Out of the crisis*. Cambridge, MA: MIT Press.

Engeström, Y. (2001). Expansive learning at work: Toward an activity theoretical reconceptualization. *Journal of Education and Work, 14*(1), 133–156.

Guile, D. & Young, M. (2003) Transfer and transition in vocational education: Some theoretical considerations. In Tuomi-Gröhn, T. & Engeström, Y. (Eds.), *Between school and work: New perspectives on transfer and boundary-crossing* (pp. 63–81). Amsterdam: Pergamon.

Hammersley, M. & Atkinson, P. (1995). *Ethnography: Principles and practice*. London: Routledge-Falmer.

Hoffmann, M.H.G. & Roth, W.-M. (2005). What should you know to survive in knowledge societies: On a semiotic understanding of 'knowledge.' *Semiotica, 156*, 101–138.

Hoyles, C., Noss, R., Kent, P., & Bakker, A. (2010). Improving mathematics at work: The need for techno-mathematical literacies. London: Routledge.

Hoyles, C., Wolf, A., Molyneux-Hodgson, S., & Kent, P. (2002). *Mathematical skills in the workplace*. London: Science, Technology and Mathematics Council.

Lave, J. (1988). *Cognition in practice: Mind, mathematics and culture in everyday life*. Cambridge: Cambridge University Press.

Kim, Y.-H. (2002). A state of the art review on the impact of technology on skill demand in OECD countries. *Journal of Education and Work, 15*(1), 89–109.

Montgomery, D. C. (1997). *Design and analysis of experiments* (4th ed.). New York: John Wiley.

Nakajima, S. (1988). *TPM: Introduction to Total Productive Maintenance*. Portland, OR: Productivity Press.

Noss, R. (1998). New numeracies for a technological culture. *For the Learning of Mathematics, 18*(2), 2–12.

Noss, R., Bakker, A., Hoyles, C., & Kent, P. (2007). Situating graphs as workplace knowledge. *Educational Studies in Mathematics, 65*, 367–384.

Noss, R. & Hoyles, C. (1996). *Windows on mathematical meanings*. Dordrecht: Kluwer Academic.

Noss, R., Hoyles, C., & Pozzi, S. (2002). Abstraction in expertise: A study of nurses' conceptions of concentration. *Journal for Research in Mathematics Education, 33*, 204–229.

Organisation for Economic Co-operation and Development (OECD). (2003). *PISA 2003 assessment framework*. Paris: OECD.

Peirce, C.S. (1976). *The new elements of mathematics* (4 vols.) (Eisele, C., Ed.). Atlantic Highlands, NJ: Humanities Press.

Pyzdek, T. (2001). *The six sigma handbook*. New York: McGraw-Hill.

Reich, R.B. (1991). *The work of nations: Preparing ourselves for 21st century capitalism*. London: Simon & Schuster.

Roth, W.-M. & Bowen, G.M. (2003). When are graphs worth ten thousand words? An expert-expert study. *Cognition and Instruction, 21*(4), 429–473.

Seeger, F. (2005). Notes on a semiotically inspired theory of teaching and learning. In Hoffmann, M., Lenhard, J., & Seeger, F. (Eds.), *Activity and sign – Grounding mathematics education* (pp. 67–76). New York: Springer.

Star, S.L. & Griesemer, J. (1989). Institutional ecology, 'translations,' and boundary objects: Amateurs and professionals in Berkeley's museum of vertebrate zoology, 1907–1939. *Social Studies of Science, 19*, 387–420.

Stevenson, J. (2002). Concepts of workplace knowledge. *International Journal of Educational Research, 37*, 1–15.

Tuomi-Gröhn, T. & Engeström, Y. (Eds.). (2003). *Between school and work: New perspectives on transfer and boundary-crossing*. Amsterdam: Pergamon.

Zuboff, S. (1988). *In the age of the smart machine: The future of work and power*. New York: Basic Books.

PETER H. SAWCHUK

DIVERGENT WORKING AND LEARNING TRAJECTORIES IN SOCIAL SERVICES

Insights from a Use-Value Perspective

INTRODUCTION

In this chapter, I argue that a critical understanding of the notion of a knowledge-based economy (KBE) in advanced capitalism requires attention to the ways that the details of everyday occupational life and learning represent an important arena of political economic struggle. As elsewhere in this volume, the discussion below relates to questions defining the nature of a KBE. For example, I respond to the very real impacts of the *increasing speed of innovation and change* in work processes which often, as is the case in the research below, is mediated by new forms of production technology and work design. Likewise, as conventional notions of a KBE might predict, we will see that *intensified learning and knowledge production* efforts are required (see Introduction). And yet, many other assumptions of KBE thinking can also be seriously questioned. 'Knowledge' continues to be central to production and control, as has traditionally been the case. This has not changed. What else has not changed? Part of the answer to this question involves human 'use-values' – the direct satisfaction of individual and collective need. In myriad ways, at multiple levels of social and economic life, use-value production and mediation continue to clash with the forces of commodification, surplus value, capital accumulation and exchange-value. Below I address how practical needs stemming from use-value generation and mediation continue to drive knowledge production in a variety of ways. This need for use-value in one's working life, along with the objects that motivate the learning and practices that spring from it, are *not* new. In the course of the intensification of learning and change however, the contradictions that emerge may provide an important point of departure for analysis of occupational change.

In this context, the general claim is that the making and re-making of occupations must ultimately be accomplished through the agentive learning of workers. Yet this learning is mediated by many things. It is mediated by the organizational premises and the work/technological designs that are dropped into workers' lives. It is also mediated by the elements of occupational culture and knowledge, real and imagined, inherited from the past. To pursue these types of general claims, I outline a synthesizing approach to the labour/learning process, its implications, and then provide empirical illustrations of its application.

D.W. Livingstone and D. Guile (eds.), The Knowledge Economy and Lifelong Learning:
A Critical Reader, 277–300.

I draw on research about the changing occupational lives of state welfare workers in Ontario (Canada) which underwent radical re-organization in 2002. This re-organizing included the introduction of a new division of labour that disassembled a single holistic occupation into a series of more specialized jobs; the implementation of a new technology called Service Delivery Model Technology (SDMT) that re-sequenced, re-routed and centralized information on clients, workers and output; the introduction of new measures of performance, forms of management, training and occupational socialization. The re-organization fundamentally altered the occupational lives of over 7,000 workers and through them the lives of over 650,000 welfare recipients; the latter being a number that has continued to grow. In understanding the role of occupational learning in advanced capitalist countries today, the public sector and state welfare workers specifically, is not an unlikely focal point. Expanding state austerity that leads to the types of labour process changes addressed here, rising poverty and economic polarization, as well as questions concerning the role of the state in society intersect directly in the lives of workers in this occupation.

This extended occupational case study began with the implementation of the new labour process in 2002 and continued to 2009.[1] The data sets it produced have been described a number of times, in detail, elsewhere (e.g., Hennessy & Sawchuk, 2003; Sawchuk, 2010a, 2010b, forthcoming). To summarize however, it includes ethnographic work, 75 in depth, semi-structured occupational learning/life-history interviews, as well as large survey of the population of state welfare workers in Ontario. In this chapter, I focus on key examples from amongst the qualitative data only (for a fuller account see Sawchuk, forthcoming).

The analysis is guided by a synthesizing approach I refer to as a *use-value thesis* (UVT) (see Sawchuk, 2006a). This approach constructs a dialogical engagement between a specific sociocultural approach to learning and human development (Marxist Cultural Historical Activity Theory, or CHAT) and a Marxist approach to the sociology of work (Labour Process Theory, or LPT).[2] I suggest that it is through this type of dialogical integration of analytic capacities that we can see how particular *relations of contradiction* endemic to advanced capitalism drive skill and knowledge formation; and, that without explicit attention to these relations, other more specified depictions of the learning/labour process including the identification of skill/knowledge types and processes are ultimately limited. Indeed, I suggest this approach places front-and-centre how the learning/labour process can likely only be fully understood in relation to its broader historical, political and economic character: that is, as a generalized, daily struggle under advanced capitalism to re-humanize economic life. The active struggle to *learn* to re-humanize oneself and one's occupation in the context of a given labour process is essential to a historical and transformational view of work and society.

In this context, we see why it may be necessary to forefront not simply challenges, tensions, and contradictions of employment in general, but rather the contradictions between people's everyday production of *use-values* (the direct satisfaction of individual or collective human need in activity) and their production of *exchange-values* (the satisfaction of human need as mediated by the logic of capital accumulation in activity). A UVT approach synthesizes how use-value and exchange-value production are central to the making and re-making of occupations. In this chapter specifically we see this in terms of how divergent trajectories and dynamics of learning, skill and knowledge production emerge, how some knowledge forms must be seen as partial while others can be considered more expansive, whole and transformational.

Obviously, workers are never mere appendages to the machineries of work or knowledge construction at work. This has been true throughout the histories of work as much as it is today. Workers continue to actively and creatively respond to change and bring change about. In terms of learning, skill and knowledge formation, in the empirical illustrations I provide below, particular attention is paid to how creative responses to work change revolve around workers' abilities to make what the CHAT tradition has generally referred to as both *personal sense* and *collective meaning*. I will argue that attention to these matters makes an important contribution to understandings of divergent trajectories of learning and occupational knowledge formation as a contradictory struggle across the many mediations of use-value and exchange-value in activity.

I specifically illustrate below two major trajectories of occupational learning within activity defined either by the production of what I term state welfare work *administrative knowledge* or *craft knowledge*. Through these distinctions, we see how workers in the same objective conditions learn and re-learn in different ways. The first trajectory implicates what in the CHAT tradition is understood as operational expertise. It also implicates what I define here as *repair-work/skill* and *sense-repair-work/skill*, and the processes of occupational accommodation and consent. The example I present in these terms demonstrates how there is clearly a set of workers who – far from any bureaucratic caricature of rule-following we might care to imagine – struggle to learn and establish richly complex, if structurally limiting, occupational learning lives. In particular we see that the trajectory of this learning is defined by the dominance of the *relations of contradiction between operations and goals* in activity that channel the human capacities for engrossment, and establish particular modes of participation and specific patterns of object-relatedness in labour process activity.

Other workers learn something different and learn differently in their work. In contrast to the type of re-skilling, administrative identity and object-relatedness of activity associated with administrative knowledge, amongst these other workers learning revolves around the active struggle to construct, re-inherit and maintain alternative orientations to their work in welfare services. Something identifiable as a welfare work craft trajectory of learning is seen. Once again, we encounter learning as occupational struggle, but here workers struggle to construct service to the client and client/worker relations as having an inherent *use-value*. These practices illustrate how specific goals and object/motives unfold with active interventions of a different kind. Of particular relevance, the trajectory of this learning is defined by the active engagement of *relations of contradiction across goals and object/motive levels* of activity, and here what I term repair-work and sense-repair-work explored previously is joined, and governed, by what is termed *object-work/skill*.

Each of these terms as well as findings will be defined and illustrated below. However, to be clear, I do *not* treat the basic fact that workers experience and construct different lives and purposes within their occupation as a particularly novel claim. There is a long tradition of studies noting this that has emerged drawing on a variety of analytic traditions (some dealing with social services specifically). What is novel is, in the first instance, *how* these differences emerge in terms of agentive, contradictory and mediated *learning*. More novel still are the claims concerning how this learning encapsulates the political economic struggles endemic to knowledge economies in advanced capitalism.

Having previewed the basic types of claims and findings, I begin below with further details on this notion of a use-value thesis. Central to it are the relations of contradiction in learning. Then, I move on to illustrate and discuss the divergent trajectories of occupational knowledge development in the case of state welfare workers specifically.

CONTRADICTIONS AND A USE-VALUE THESIS APPROACH

The dialogical integration of Marxist LPT and Marxist CHAT is important because it deals effectively with a series of analytic gaps. On the one hand we find CHAT's relative under-development of a sustained, critical approach to the implications of divisions of labour, forms of control and autonomy, and, in general, the political economic dimensions of skill, knowledge and learning. In this regard, where CHAT fails, LPT responds. On the other hand, we find in LPT research a general lack of robust conceptual tools for analysing occupational learning, development and activity itself, beyond proxies (see Warhurst & Thompson in this volume). Here, CHAT offers a particular effective response.

At the same time, however, a UVT approach highlights another related gap as well. This gap concerns the dynamics of the lived, occupational contradictions of capitalism, understood in relation to everyday forms of commodification, alienation, and de-humanization. Absent in particular is an appreciation of the role of the contradiction of use-value and exchange-value in the commodity form *within the learning process*. From the type of Marxist humanist orientation I take, this third gap contributes toward obscuring understanding of how workers make, re-make and have the potential to transform their work.

A *UVT approach* begins with this recognition of dialectical contradictions within capitalism. For the same reasons that Marx embraced the human/historical complexity of capitalism by beginning his analysis in the first volume of *Capital* (1990) with the commodity form, I suggest that understanding the contradictions of human learning under capitalism is also suitable. This type of beginning is useful for its analytic power at multiple levels of generality (what non-dialectical social sciences mis-construe as separate micro, meso and macro levels of analysis). It supports the claim that capitalism does not simply exist *out there*, but *in here*; in our daily lives as citizens, mothers, consumers and, of course, *as workers*. In this sense, given the disproportionate role of work in the waking hours of our lives, we might say that our jobs remain one of the origins of political resistance as well as reproduction of capitalism.

Still, it may seem odd that the notion of use-value takes centre-stage in the title of this recommended approach; after all, we are talking about economic life, and economic life in capitalism remains dominated by commodification and exchange-value. However, this is a matter of emphasizing what is both definitive of labour process activity and yet systematically obscured. Our human capacities for use-value generation remain as foundational to economic life as they are foundational to social change more broadly. Within our jobs as well as beyond, the motive to directly satisfying the needs of ourselves and others within activity is powerful; whether this is taking pride in our work for its own sake, helping and being recognized by others for its own sake, and even our efforts to reclaim use-value in our lives when we say that our work is for something more than a paycheque. A focus in this way suggests an approach to learning, in other words, that explicitly is aimed at revealing the capacities – frustrated and re-directed as well as occasionally realized – to transcend capitalism. Across historical epochs and political economic arrangements prior to and beyond capitalism, it is use-value production that is the true common denominator of humanized existence. Thus, at minimum, a UVT approach suggests that no analysis of occupational life can be complete without recognition of how use-value mediates our potential. Among other things, a UVT approach provides a coherent way of theorizing how conflict and co-operation, satisfaction, enchantment and alienation, de-skilling, re-skilling and up-skilling necessarily co-exist. A UVT approach seeks to explain why each of these phenomena have a deeply human as well as a deeply developmental and political economic relationship with historical change, even when shrunk down to the size of our daily lives.

Thought of in terms of the dialectical contradiction of use- and exchange-values in people's learning lives, from a CHAT perspective, the notion of need is only a gloss. Needs, even many of those we think of as fundamental, are mediated phenomena. Indeed, we can each recognize the many needs – large and small – in our lives that go under-realized; that quite separate from the barriers we encounter cannot seem to effectively move us to action. As Leontiev (1978) demonstrated: a need becomes a motive for practice in activity only when it finds its object. Thus, the satisfaction of needs is a dialectical construction of needs/objects/motives in changing forms of activity. In a capitalist society specifically, this dialectic of needs/objects/motives can be understood to take two general forms without which the details of skill and knowledge construction cannot be properly understood. In this sense, the basic definitions of use-value and exchange-value must be carefully qualified as involving myriad configurations of mediations that rapidly evolve into patterns of object-relatedness and potentially divergent purposes within an occupation.

Looking more carefully at the implications of the claim that mediations of use-value and exchange-value are central to understanding occupational learning, we can note that one of the defining features of capitalist society, as Marx observed, is that as the system develops and expands, more and more of our use-value production is governed by the principles of exchange-value production. They must co-exist, but in an increasingly hierarchical relationship. This expresses the basic contradiction between the forces of production and relations of production. We can see this easily in our everyday lives at work. The economic needs of capital are realized as it find objects, such as specific work designs or technologies, that provide form and motivate its practices. And still, activity, skill and knowledge oriented to some greater or lesser degree by use-value production persist. Use-value continues to be realized in instances of co-operative achievement, friendships and dignities amongst workers (and between workers, supervisors and management in some instances); it is also realized in purposes and object/motives of activity more broadly. Each form of realization bears on analyses of occupational learning. Indeed, in many ways it is use-value generation that underwrites our collective abilities to persist, *despite the contradictions* of capitalism.

These comments paint a picture in broad strokes. However, as we consider the way these contradictory dynamics inform an analysis of learning within activity more specifically, it makes some sense to recall the comments of Ilyenkov (1982), the contemporary dialectical philosopher perhaps most closely associated with the CHAT tradition.

> The dialectical materialist method of resolution of contradiction in theoretical definitions thus consists in tracing the process by which the movement of reality itself resolves them in a new form of expression. Expressed objectively, the goal lies in tracing, through analysis of new empirical materials, the emergence of reality in which an earlier established contradiction finds its relative resolution in a new objective form of its realization. (p. 263)

A UVT approach has the capacity to follow these suggestions by empirically tracing the emerging ways that, under conditions of aggressive state austerity in the case of social services generally and state welfare services specifically, the contradictions of class struggles in occupational learning unfold.

The same concern is expressed in the work of a leading voice in CHAT analyses of work as well. For Engeström (1987), contradiction in activity can be distinguished in a number of ways. *Secondary* and *tertiary* (or in general, *peripheral*) contradictions, for example, refer to those rooted in role conflict in the contingencies and conditions of work practices at the level of work team, office or organizational practices. The broader purpose and political economic dimensions are, strictly speaking, left to one side, and brought to the fore are relations of operations and goals within activity. However, there are also *primary* contradictions which Engeström and Sannino explain, following Marx, are rooted in the commodity form.

> Activity theory is a dialectical theory, and the dialectical concept of contra-diction plays a crucial part in it ... In capitalism, the pervasive primary contradiction between use value and exchange value is inherent to every

commodity, and all spheres of life are subject to commoditization. This pervasive primary contradiction takes its specific shape and acquires its particular contents differently in every historical phase and every activity system. Most importantly, contradictions are the driving force of transformation. The object of an activity is always internally contradictory. It is these internal contradictions that make the object a moving, motivating and future-generating target. (Engeström & Sannino, 2010, pp. 4–5)

Attending adequately to the significance of both peripheral and primary contradictions is a point of contention in CHAT research.[3] As pointed out by a variety of researchers (e.g., Avis, 2007; Langemeyer & Roth, 2006; Niewolny & Wilson, 2009; Sawchuk, 2006a, 2006b, 2007; Sawchuk & Setsenko, 2008), empirical exploration of primary contradictions within activity are remarkably inconsistent. Avis notes that even when some CHAT scholars analyse contradictions it is typically within narrow organizational confines, in terms of peripheral contradictions. This inadequacy, he explains, gives rise to a tendency to privilege, for example, reproductive rather than contested and potentially more radical learning dynamics. Taking the example of Engeström's work specifically, Avis (2007) argues:

Processes of transformation are Janus-like; they can both secure the interest of capital or align with radical interests. Whilst Engeström argues 'the mightiest, most impersonal societal structures can be seen as consisting of local activities carried out by concrete human beings with the help of mediating artefacts' (1999a, p. 36). This insight fails to be translated into wider societal interventions that challenge capitalist relations. Although the notion of social practice is fully theorized, with respect to the activity system(s) under investigation, in its application it is *truncated* and veers towards a conservative practice, becoming in effect '*bourgeoisie*' *transformation*, or in Gramsci's terms, a form of transformism. Whilst change occurs, it secures the interests of capital rather than being forcibly tied to an emancipatory project (Gramsci, 1971, pp. 58, 106; Johnson & Steinberg, 2004, p. 13). This tendency is in part a consequence of the focus upon secondary contradictions but is also a failure to engage in a wider politics … Although the *recognition of primary contradictions could herald wider emancipatory possibilities, these are effectively bracketed.* (p. 163; emphasis added)

Warmington (2008) likewise explains that reinvigorating the Marxist elements in the CHAT tradition would guard it from becoming 'domesticated' (p. 17). To do this, he argues, it is necessary to indelibly fore-front the forms of dialectical contradictions within the labour process that in fact define it *as capitalist*. It is with these types of concerns in mind that a UVT approach offers a position that abandons neither the broader contradictory relations of occupational life under capitalism, nor the additional complexity of coping, accommodation and consent that must simultaneously be addressed as well.

At the centre of a UVT approach is a struggle inherent to the capitalist project. In the case of public sector services such as those addressed in the data set I draw upon, the implications of this project are expanding at an accelerated pace. Global austerity places new levels of pressure on occupations such as state welfare work. Yet, there is no avoiding the fact that workers have their own views on the matter. As such and in addition to broader forms of social mobilization – the occupational learning of consent, accommodation and resistance may prove ever more important. Below I outline responses to the question of why and how workers find themselves investing *and* not investing their considerable capacities in new forms of public sector work. In this context, we can more effectively inquire into the ways that consent permits 'the degradation of work to pursue its course without continuing crisis' (Burawoy, 1979, p. 94). Likewise, we can explore the relationship between these the degradations and resistance. In either instance, we attempt to view these dynamics through the lens of thinking, feeling, knowing, choosing and changing workers at the fault-line of capitalism's ever-deepening failures: the place where poverty meets the labour process charged with its management – state welfare work.

LEARNING AS STRUGGLE OVER OCCUPATIONAL PURPOSE AND ITS RELATION TO A UVT APPROACH

A UVT approach can be applied in many ways. One of these ways illuminates the processes and significance of potentially *divergent trajectories* of learning that bubble beneath the surface of an occupation; trajectories that speak to how the future meanings and purposes of an occupation may unfold. For some time, a variety of traditions have shed light on the existence of significant variability and divergence within a single occupation. Stretching back at least as far a Blau (1955), we can see that objectively similar labour processes give rise to different styles, types, or rather trajectories of participation. However, few have offered detailed discussion of the processes of knowledge and expertise formation that define such distinctions, divergences and struggles.

Two key, contemporary exceptions to this rule are found in the work of Felstead, Fuller, Jewson and Unwin (2009) and Hampson and Junor (2010). Felstead et al. (2009) report on a number of sectors to develop their WALF (Work as Learning Framework) approach drawing on sociocultural perspectives and in particular CHAT. As in this chapter, they attempt to establish an integrated analysis across the concerns of the field of sociology of work and those of fields dealing with occupational learning processes specifically. The many (vertical and horizontal) dimensions of production systems mediate the potential directions that workplace learning takes. Important for the discussion here is their recognition that individual workers experience the production system, and hence construct their learning lives in distinct ways. Taking a step closer still to the analysis offered here, however, is the work of Hampson and Junor (2010) who deal specifically with public (as well as community) sector work in an attempt to *put the process back in*. As with Felstead et al. (2009), we learn how one can look long and hard, but conventional notions of skill remain difficult to truly locate empirically. Processes and practices, on the other hand, abound. Indeed, in moving in a direction similar to a UVT approach advocated here, Hampson and Junor (2010) reference the struggles, conflict and symbolic violence of the hidden injuries of skill formation that are inherent to learning in occupational life. They turn toward notions of 'staged assimilation' and 'work process knowledge' in fore-fronting the importance of 'situational and process awareness as foundational skills' (p. 532) for example: when they do so, they employ the language of *arcs* and *trajectories* of occupational learning.

In the following section I deal with the contradictory machineries of knowledge construction of state welfare workers in similar ways. These are machineries that themselves must to be constructed and re-constructed in the course of the many transformations within activity. Here it is important to recognize how an occupation in transition is composed of contradictions between alternative trajectories of knowledge and skill development. However, as distinct from the works cited above, I emphasize that the differences between these trajectories account for something dramatic: the struggle for the soul of an occupation. This struggle is traced in a variety of ways below. However, I pay particular attention to three basic types of practices: repair-work/skill, sense-repair-work/skill and object-work/skill.

By way of introduction, *repair-work/skill* is defined as learned occupational practices associated with the repair of conditions that do not necessarily involve the relationship between what I earlier referenced as organizational meanings and personal sense in activity. All workers necessarily engage in these processes. They form the common everyday practices of coping with the general contingencies of all labour processes, but are particularly pronounced in the context of labour process re-organization under examination here. Destined to become tacit and un-self-conscious in nature, these practices emerge from and return to what in CHAT theory is referred as operations and the conditions of work. *Sense-repair-work/skill* refers to learned practices associated with the repair of the relationship between the organizational meanings and personal sense in activity specifically. In itself, particularly under conditions of labour process change (as opposed to simply the ongoing contingency of an established labour process), this revolves around the *contradictory relations between operations and goal-directed action.* It is signalled by the processes of workers actively constructing a new place for themselves in a labour process; whether that process challenges or confirms the domination of exchange-value generation. Finally, *object-work/skill* involves learned practices associated with the dynamic and *contradictory relations across operation, actions and object/motive of activity as a whole.* What distinguish the practices of object-work/skill are processes in which workers question or otherwise agentively incorporate concerns for the broader purposes of their work. This often involves actively resisting, for example, pre-given or designed organizational arrangements and meanings. In this formulation, object-work cannot proceed without sense-repair-work. But, incorporating agency across activity as a whole, the practices of

285

object-work actively integrate – as an object of mundane struggle – the most primary contradictory dynamics of capitalist labour processes.

Finally, a UVT approach suggests a particular perspective on skills and knowledge. It suggests that conventional notions of skill or knowledge *content* (e.g., technical, literacy, language, inter-personal, emotional, aesthetic, articulation skills/knowledge, etc.) are not meaningful categories outside of their relation to contradictions within activity in general, and the practices of repair-work, sense-repair-work and object-work specifically. Much the same can be said of the conventional notions of learning *processes* (e.g., formal, non-formal, informal, tacit, experiential, self-directed, etc.).

MULTIPLE TRAJECTORIES OF OCCUPATIONAL LEARNING IN STATE WELFARE WORK

Officially what we do is dictated by others. We are to just follow what we are told. And according to our own compassions or just that kind of commitment that you're dedicated to, if I want to make a decision and it does not fit the system, it is simply, no. In this field I think it must be made flexible. I mean that's worth fighting for I'd say. (John, case manager)[4]

Purposes 'dictated by others,' their relationship with occupational commitments, and things 'worth fighting for' are key elements of what is discussed below. They provide basic terms of reference for appreciating the concrete dynamics and the significance of divergent trajectories of learning in relation to a UVT approach. Yet, as we will see, concerns, criticisms and intentions, in themselves, tell us only a small part of the story of the struggles of occupational knowledge production.

The administrative and craft trajectories of learning I outline below revolve around how modes of participation in activity produce an accumulation of experience and skill which may someday become expert judgment, and yet which are not immune to change; that is, they are not realized structures of learning but only trajectories of the ongoing structurations of learning. At their heart is a struggle in relation to artefacts that mediate the learning of accommodation, consent (i.e., administrative trajectories) or resistance (i.e., craft trajectories). What artefacts come to mediate practice are important; so too, are the ways these mediations are configured (their object-relatedness as a whole). This is so, in particular, in terms of worker/client relations and the dominance of relations of either peripheral or primary contradictions within activity. Overall, I illustrate how it is that thinking, feeling, knowing, choosing and acting people come to construct these divergent trajectories of skill and knowledge development, and why this represents the terrain over which the meaning, purposes and soul of an occupation are eventually established over time.

In basic terms, administrative trajectories of knowledge production account for the agentive problem-solving and learning that reproduces, in creative ways, the received organizational order, meanings and purposes. Predictably, one of the key casualties in this process is the individual client; a person who must be reconstituted as a *case* and, in turn, aggregated into a *caseload*. Alternatively, craft trajectories of skill and knowledge formation entail attempts to re-humanize the state welfare work process, the client/person as well as the client/worker relationship, often requiring particularly creative artefact production that supports workers in re-inheriting the best of past traditions of the welfare work.[5] Below, we meet only two illustrations from the qualitative data set. Yet, given sustained attention, even these illustrations offer, I suggest, an important, empirical glimpse into the dynamics of *learning to become* a certain type of state welfare worker from a UVT perspective.

Notably, I have selected two experienced case managers who have similar professional and educational backgrounds.[6] An expanded analysis would reveal many other distinctions, but for now it can be said that each has a raft of occupational skills, resources and work relationships at their disposal for retaining elements of autonomy and control. And yet, they do so in different ways. A generalized reading of their quotations on their own might tempt the claim that what we are seeing is some notion of different personality types; and yet, as CHAT theory has so vigorously demonstrated from the beginning, psycho-biological explanations of this type (whether they echo from the works of Piaget or Freud for example) do not provide adequate explanations. Rather, a CHAT approach maintains that the appearance of personality and identity emerge from, as well as act upon, the specific dynamics of *concrete activity* even as we admit a biological self.

As we will see, *learning to become* a particular *type* of state welfare worker requires localized development of object-related operational expertise, requiring forms of judgement and creative problem-solving. These types of expertise seem to become most clearly visible in the context of rule-bending/breaking (see Glisson & Hemmelgarn, 1998; Daniels et al., 2007) and *workarounds* (see also Bowker & Star, 1999; Hennessy & Sawchuk, 2003). Repairing situations, and using unconventional means and workarounds (many which are shared through local management; others which are distinct to individuals or groups) to do so, are crucial. Workarounds in this context can even include a worker choosing to leave required work undone or doing things that violate, rather than merely re-interpret, procedure. In this way, workarounds have an ambiguous status: some represent pragmatic, tacit co-operation between management and workers in response to contingency (a common feature of most workplaces); others represent more whole-sale departures which lie in opposition to managerial interests. Taken together, these are terms of reference, however, that describe sustained practices involving personal as well as broader occupational struggle as much as they reference generalized creativity and expertise. And analytic points such as these raise additional questions about how the conscious critiques and intentions of workers may pale in comparison to the effects of the more minute, moment-by-moment machinations of occupational knowledge production. As in Marxist theory generally, these are questions that inquire into how it is that (occupational) being determines consciousness much more than the reverse.

Administrative Trajectories of Occupational Learning

In the following illustration of the emergence of administrative trajectories of occupational expertise, we obtain a fine-grained snap-shot of skill and knowledge formation in process. The focal point of the excerpt is the very common problem, in this form of state welfare work, of repairing what are known as 'client overpayments.' This refers to the situation in which the computer system (called SDMT) signals an improper amount of payment has been issued to a client. In the new labour process, when this occurs a case file is automatically flagged for attention, client letters are automatically printed and mailed without the aid of the case manager, and a sequence of repair-work practices is triggered. Overpayments are a key instance in workers coming to establish a distinctive trajectory of learning. In responding to this repair-work, *prior* work experience, values and judgements as well as the learning and application of *new* procedural skills are all set in motion in activity. With this in mind, the excerpt below begins with a premise that goes unstated: that a worker has established in her own mind that the client *is qualified* to receive a certain welfare payment, and yet the computer system is suggesting something else. This is not insignificant. Things must be *learned* as well as *unlearned* in the establishment of an administrative trajectory of occupational learning.

The examples of work practice described were common in the data set of this research overall. Sometimes the discrepancy leading to overpayment is obvious to a case manager; its origins can be quickly traced, basic repair-work initiated and repair-work skill and knowledge developed. Frequently, however, the origins of overpayments are not obvious, and a range of judgments leading toward distinctive forms of occupational expertise are involved in carrying out the repair-work. Specifically, we see how specific forms of expert judgement are generated through shifts in the structure of activity, and importantly, how this may contribute to ongoing trajectories of skill and knowledge development. In the moment-to-moment dynamics of activity, a worker's attention/dis-attention, skill, knowledge and expertise formation become oriented by contradictions of a particular type. In these instances, the mode of participation and the object-relatedness of welfare work reflect the dominance of contradictions *defined by relations between operations and goals* in activity.

The learning this case manager describes is not only social, it is collective, as we will see in a brief but significant set of statements. In fact, what Vygtosky called a Zone of Proximal Development is a collective accomplishment easily recognizable in the account (e.g., when the worker explains how she will 'yell over to the person next door' to her cubicle; or, she speaks of the importance of the 'help you get' from co-workers). And yet, it is a collective practice aimed at resolving individuated contradictions of autonomy and control, and in this sense implicates a particular means/end (value-generating) formula. It is just as thoroughly rooted in the new division of labour and technology which deeply shape the limits of autonomy and control. All of these, we can recall, are expressions of austerity measures and the broader political economy of the state.

INTERVIEWER: What would happen with a new worker then who didn't figure out what happened to that file? The Case Worker would do what?

ALISON: The client would either be overpaid or underpaid and that worker would be *ripping their hair* out trying to figure it out and have to probably take it to a supervisor or somebody.

INTERVIEWER: Can you paint me a picture of that?

ALISON: I can give you an instance with overpayments because an overpayment will come on the file and you could have done something, and *you have no idea what's even created the overpayment,* and a letter comes out and the client calls you and says 'I have this overpayment. It says to call you.' And so, you go 'Alrighty then.' You go in and you look, 'Yes, that overpayment was created on such and such a day and I can see that the total is two thousand some odd dollars.' And you look and there it is: February, March, April, May; it's calculated at $511 each one of those months. And you go, 'Okay $511,' and *it doesn't tell you it's the shelter component of that cheque. It just shows the amount* and there's nowhere on that system that you can look to figure that out, to figure out how that overpayment was created. You just *come to know by looking at that figure.* You look at the *type of number it is, is it an uneven or even type of number, and you look at the size, and you start to go 'Yeah, it's got something to do with accommodation costs.' So you and look, and you think, and you start to know.* It's like this *detective work* at first, and then eventually *it becomes second nature.*

INTERVIEWER: So then what do you do? Take me step by step. You'd see the $511 and you'd go, 'Okay, that has to have something to do with accommodation.' But, how does that work? What's next?

ALISON: Accommodation cost, yeah, so now you're off and running. You'd go into a different screen and look at accommodation and what date that was changed, and you can't even always figure out why the system did it, but at that point you'd *have some clues* but then you'd probably first think to go looking around the office for a [training support worker], but since they disappeared officially, you would *yell over to the person next door, 'How do you fix such-and-such? Ever heard of that?'* I don't think there's many of us who could figure that out *on our own.* It gets better and you can go in and fix it with workarounds, but often times there's some that you just have no idea.

INTERVIEWER: So, how many, one out of five, one out of 10? How many cases do you need help with on a regular basis?

ALISON: It's just the difficult ones, so maybe *20 percent of the cases* I'd say.

INTERVIEWER: So it's not just like it happens once in a blue moon?

ALISON: No.

INTERVIEWER: And so there's this *ongoing, sort of long learning curve* part of it that's been going on for a while now since SDMT came in?

ALISON: Well, part of it's an initial *learning curve,* if say you were new to the work, but *we're way past that so it's more than just that* ... The worst part of this system is that the errors are compound errors. In any other computer system I've worked on, when you do something you didn't mean to do you can always back up a step and then with this one *you can't back up* that step. Well, ninety per cent of the time you can't back up, you just can't take it back. Because you go obviously, 'Hey, that wasn't the right thing to do, let me think about what might be the right way.' But you can't do that since *you can't retrace your steps backward.* So you're in this *crazy situation* where the only way I can describe it is that it's like you have to keep *moving forward in the system, first here, and then here and then here until you're way out in left field,* and you can't ever come back to that starting point *where you know that you are where you know.*

INTERVIEWER: That doesn't sound like a very good situation to be in.

ALISON: No, that would be a nice way to put it. It really *plays with your mind,* but you keep trying and trying and things get better with *the help you get.*

Difficulties in dealing with an overpayment are as serious as they are ubiquitous in workers' (as well as clients') lives in the new welfare system. Moreover, these are difficulties that can reverberate through the rest of a person's work including dealings with a specific client going forward. Disproportionately, choice-making, setting self-conscious goals and taking action in the context of the broader, evolving conditions of the welfare office are premised on these specific sets of difficulties. Linked to them is a common unfolding series of events. For example, the client does not receive an accurate cheque, the client inquires and not infrequently submits a complaint or the occasional yelling match emerges, and so on. For many welfare workers, the gravity of knowing that a client or a family will go without necessities invests a series of everyday operations with additional professional and ethical weight. For others, the daily frustrations and feelings of not knowing their job come to weigh them down. The accumulation of difficulties also bears on one's career, and on one's formal and informal occupational standing in the office adding additional intensities to the mix. In each instance, these additional weights implicate what Vygotsky (e.g., 1994) referred to as *perezhivanie* (emotional experience) and Leontiev (e.g., 1978) wrote about in terms of *contradictory emotional colouring* in activity. All this inherently stands behind the daily practice of state welfare work and learning.

The worker quoted above, Alison, has over a decade of experience as a case manager. By all accounts, she is considered by co-workers to be an expert case manager. She and colleagues are beyond the initial 'learning curve' of their dealings with the new technology and labour process, as she notes above. And yet the details of her account illustrate how it is that expertise can take many forms and how the labour process activity shapes her thinking and feeling. As she puts it, the work 'plays with' her mind. What we can begin to see is that the skill formation process is engaging for her *despite* its frustrations and *because of its challenges.* The account provides a near-classic allusion to a type of expert problem-solving. This performance initially demands conscious attention and develops into expert judgment that culminates in intuition and the automaticity of repair-work/skill: a process of 'just com[ing] to know ... by looking at that figure ... the type of number it is,' the 'clues' it can offer. Her description of practice as 'detective work' in a 'crazy situation' ('that plays with your mind') and which can inspire people to 'start ripping their hair out trying to figure it out' is not inconsequential. It points to what Knorr Cetina (1999) describes as a process of *engrossment*. There is, of course, the alarming frequency in which such problem-solving is required, but this also means that her work is engrossing on a regular basis. In terms of attentive studies of learning and work, very little of this is surprising. Perhaps less surprising still, we see reference to the general value of co-worker communication, of informalized on-the-job, incidental learning, and so on.

More importantly, we see the significance of the unidirectional character of the computer software that is designed to dictate (what in traditional work design language is referred to as) work routing, process control and information centralization. At first glance, these appear to be dynamics associated with classic de-skilling. And yet, in listening to Alison we see that notions of de-skilling remain relevant as a premise rather than a practice. In fact, the dynamics of labour process design discipline by playing a persistent pedagogical role. Indeed, especially when work practice is mediated by substantial prior professional experience, travelling down the one-way rabbit-hole only to end up 'way out in left field' offers an example of a powerful disciplinary pedagogy in action.

Of even greater importance are some additional observations. Each suggests processes of not simply engrossment but what we might call the *channelling of engrossment*. And yet, Alison is not simply adapting to the SDMT computer system and labour process, rather is an *active agent in her engrossment*. In comparison to the worker we hear from below, Alison derives relative satisfactions from fixing things and working around problems. We can thus ask: what is the structure of activity, the configurations within the machineries of occupational knowledge construction, involved in this agentive process resulting in channelling?

I argue Alison's mode of participation in activity and her new needs in the labour process as a case manager indicate an object-relatedness in activity that shape ongoing motivation in a particular way. That is, while the object of state welfare work remains recognizably *shared amongst different workers*, for workers like Alison the specific relations to the object of activity are *shifting*. A powerfully emergent goal-directed action has become *putting a stop to an overpayment*. The difficulties associated with it engross her on an ongoing basis. The result is that *the contradictory relations of this goal-directed action and operational practice* are becoming embedded as a key, orienting feature of her learning in activity. Operational contradictions are becoming a fixture of a specific trajectory of learning over time.

Re-skilling of the form I am describing here is expressed as the process of becoming successfully channelled and captured by specific forms of engrossment. It is a mode of participation in activity – a trajectory of occupational learning – in which peripheral contradictions become central. I say *captured* because the process is mediated by a labour process design. Here it is helpful to recall that the conditions of the labour process are the most direct expressions of the intentions of the designers (and employer who commissioned them). Indeed, the establishment of the operational conditions of the labour process lay legally within the purview and are the most direct expression of the standpoint of the employer, in this case the capitalist state. The mediations this design is meant to afford are based on principles of productivity and, ultimately, exchange-value generation in the form of austerity goals and harsher forms of regulation of the poor.

Workers must still bring a labour process to life. In doing this, we see creativity and expertise are necessary in the use workarounds to fix persistent problems. At the centre of the matter, however, is the reconfiguration and transformation of the object-relatedness of one's activity in order to regain a stable relation between *personal sense* and the pre-conceived organizational *meaning*; the latter rooted in labour process design. In Leontiev's (1978) terms, this is a stability which also reduces the *emotional colouring* of activity. Repair-work learning becomes sense-repair-work learning as shaped by Alison's daily engrossments. It is further supported by the construction of a particular type of Zone of Proximal Development with co-workers, at least amongst those workers within yelling distance. Vis-à-vis processes of engrossment, for workers like Alison, self-conscious goal-directed actions have become fused with the premises of the newly designed and implemented labour process and its organizational meaning beginning from their many expressions in the mediations of operations. Without such agentive learning accomplishments, the needs of the state are under-realized.

At the general level, it might be easy to simply conclude that a colourful and challenging instance of re-skilling is occurring within an occupation undergoing change. However, looking closer we might also see that there is a form of expertise emerging in which a veteran welfare worker is finding specific new ways to cope with the fact she can neither see, nor understand what exactly is transpiring in her work. Indeed, Alison cannot even 're-trace' her steps to obtain an overview. As such she begins from the premise of a loss of personal sense of her work. It matters less that she holds general concerns about the new character of her work. She does recall a more preferred way of working. Yet, in collaboration with co-workers, she finds her capacities channelled. She describes, in fact, actively producing and becoming engrossed in the object of her work in a distinctive way that begins to forefront consent and accommodation, and which provides relative satisfactions of its own.

Craft Trajectories of Occupational Learning

Although state welfare work was designed by others and consent emerged in countless instances, according to the type of analysis I use here we see also how consent was not achieved amongst a significant proportion of workers. These workers lived and perceived their work, perceived themselves and their place in their work, in ways that challenged not only the premises of de-skilling but forms of administrative re-skilling as well. It is crucial to the argument, in this sense, that the excerpts above and below be considered comparatively.

Wendy is a case manager who also has over a decade of experience. At a general level, the account speaks for itself and solidifies some relevant points of departure for analysis. It is a continuous strip of talk, but since it is lengthy I break it into parts to aid referencing specific comments in the account. Parts A and C explicitly illustrate issues central to the sub-set of welfare workers who see, and continue to struggle to create their job in the mould of a type of welfare craft ideal. To do this requires a constant effort to re-configure her place, mode of participation and object-relatedness within labour process activity in a particular way.

[Part A]

INTERVIEWER: Can you tell me your thoughts on the way your tasks are divided up?
WENDY: Well I mean this job by its nature isn't always conducive to keep it in a manageable *little square box because you're dealing with the people*. For me, I mean there are case managers who like to operate in a *very structured environment*. It's like they'll sacrifice everything to just get that structure. They really get into that. I'm really not one of them. I'm more *loose ended*. I guess I'm kind of not as organized as I should be. I really shouldn't say that because I am organized in a lot of other ways. You can be super organized and you would not survive in this job for a week if you didn't have some organizational skills because it's become too big of a job. *There's your phone, your messages, your walk-ins, you know, all the support that you give other staff, and your supervisor's demands, and your manager's demands,* the community demands for the rapport and referrals we have and like you know you couldn't possibly not be organized at some level or you'd flounder. In a month you'd be like, 'Oh shit,' so I think my organizational skills, I leave them *kind of loose ended* because *now that I'm thinking about it* I actually kind of think *that's really important to the way I actually deal with clients*. I don't want a *structured little box* where I say 'Okay 15 or 20 minutes,' and then go 'Next,' kind of thing. And I've been really kind of *afraid*, especially coming into the *office and the cubicle scenario* that we've become like that, like this *cattle herding of clients*. *Lots of us, we* are all *afraid* of that. So I've sort of intentionally left it that so okay, this might pile up but I'm *prioritizing my time face-to-face with a client or telephone calls* or whatever. *Client contact, that's the thing. Knowing what's really going on with people*. So, *it might look like I'm disorganized because I've got this load over here* but on this other side I'm *very organized as far as meeting client needs*. I'm not saying I'm a super case manager and all my clients are super happy because we all have our complaints but that's just sort of the way I organize.

[Part B]

INTERVIEWER: And what about the workarounds?
WENDY: Oh I *hate the workarounds*.
INTERVIEWER: Don't they make it easier for you?

WENDY: Yeah, but *we've got a million of them.* Try to remember them all! I've said to myself again and again that I *won't even try because you know that's not what it's all about.* But oh my god, we've got workarounds for everything. It's you know, you have to know the system well enough half the time to even do the workarounds because the system is so unreliable. We're always pulling out sheets, we just got a list of new workarounds the other day with about eight or nine, what *we call 'The way SDMT should work' scenario.* We're *constantly getting them coming our way.*

INTERVIEWER: So who gives them to you? Do your supervisors and everybody supply you with the workarounds? What do you mean you got a list?

WENDY: Supervisors won't admit it really. I mean that's just their management role, to sort of keep it on the low-down because they know some people would be just so much more disgruntled at the idea.

INTERVIEWER: So are these survival skills or what?

WENDY: They are but it's just that there's too many problems within the system that the *workarounds get to be a problem too.* I mean we're just too busy to be constantly figuring them out, and just again the nature of the job, I mean you could have a case today that would present almost every foreseeable form that you're going to have in your cabinets to use and then you might not have that form for that situation for five or six or seven weeks or longer in a lot of cases so in others words if you run into some little SDMT glitch that you have to use a workaround solution to deal with, like I've decided *I'm not going to keep them in my mind every day.* It's just *not even a practical thing that you can do.* You know *you learn them just because.* It's one of those workarounds, or whatever. So *you could spend time flying through your manuals* to see what the workaround is for this or that. Or, what memo did we get on that, or what are we supposed to do in this situation. Well the way I look at it, that's not very time effective to be having to do that stuff *given what we need to do in reality.* And it's not only that, it frustrating, it's extremely frustrating in your work day when you've got client after client back to back you know, demands of meetings and whatever else that management puts on you and then you've got to look up a workaround for the most recent glitch that SDMT is throwing at you which is constant and continual.

[Part C]

WENDY: I mean *if you interviewed everyone here I think they'd say the same thing.* I mean I'm ticked at the system and I'm probably voicing that pretty noticeably and I go to the supervisors too. I tell them. If they could get the glitches out of it, and if it were a little more friendly, just for case managers, then it probably would be not a bad system but we've been waiting for years for them to get some glitches out of it that are well, and I don't see anything but more glitches ... I mean *you walk out of here most nights I think, I'm really buzzing.* I tell you, a lot of us *go home and wake up through the night* and go, 'Oh my god, that cheque is not going to go out!,' or, 'I forgot to pull that! That client was told to come in and pick up the cheque tomorrow and I forgot to pull it!' The fact is you're constantly multi-tasking on the computer and the phone and the paperwork. There's *a real pull to make it like you're just shuffling papers,* you're just constantly shoving a piece of paper in a file and *clearing out your Task List.* Like that's so *unprofessional as far as getting to the grips with your client's issues. It's not me.*

The illustration above speaks to the specific, agentive means of re-structuring one's mode of participation in activity – the construction of a specific type of object-relatedness within activity – that successfully resists the channelling of expertise in one direction while allowing it to unfold and develop in another. We see that this depends significantly on Wendy's active production (and recovery from past practices) of particular symbolic artefacts that mediate this learning to resist in the state welfare work labour process design. In CHAT this process can be referenced as a particular form of externalization. Discursive artefacts (like the self-talk Wendy describes above) are regularly rehearsed not simply in the account, but, according to this analysis of the account, in the course of work activity itself.

The discursive constructions/externalizations described in the account serve many specific functions that are mutually supportive in the development of alternative trajectories of occupational learning over time. In fact, they can be categorized as those artefacts that construct a target of resistance (e.g., a 'very structured environment,' 'little square box' or 'structured little box;' 'cattle herding of clients' [Part A] or the 'way SDMT should work scenario' [Part B]), as well as artefacts that describe specific means to resist these newly constructed targets such as the style of organizing one's work (e.g., 'loose ended' [Part A]). These comments may appear at first glance to be un-remarkable, but I argue that they are not. They provide a portal into the symbolic and material organization and re-organization of both conscious and tacit dimensions of work and learning that Wendy undertakes. Together, these artefacts create new configurations of mediations more broadly: new object-relatedness within activity. These mediations fundamentally alter a particularly important sequence of practices in activity which, as we saw in the section above, was central to the type of channelling of engrossments. Notably, these new artefacts, mediations and object-relatedness in activity allow a re-construction of the notion of legitimate work performance: for example, 'it might look like I'm disorganized because I've got this load over here but on this other side I'm very organized' (Part A).

Activity is, in this context, a socio-cognitive as well as a political economic battle ground on which the purposes of an occupation are fought. There is, as Wendy states at the close of the excerpt, 'a real pull to make it like you're just shuffling papers, you're just constantly shoving a piece of paper in a file and clearing out your task list' (Part C). This is the constant pull of the premises of de-skilling and the constant potential for administrative re-skilling. It is relevant to our understanding of activity that Wendy explicitly says, 'now that I'm thinking about it' in reference to many of her key practices (Part A). This begins to confirm the

295

notion that in key places she is talking about operations and object/motives which, according to a CHAT analysis, are not available to one's conscious awareness in the course of participation in activity. In terms of operations specifically, beyond her gloss ('paper shuffling'), the 'pull' is made up of 'your phone, your messages, your walk-ins' (Part A). Again, we find warrant to take operations seriously. The pull also originates from the spatio-material arrangements of the labour process activity; something for which Wendy and co-workers have constructed a specific artefact to describe, i.e., the 'office and cubicle scenario' (Part A).

Importantly, in Part B we see illustrated how *operational workarounds and problem-solving* must be actively made un-engrossing. These practices are unavoidable in the new labour process. New workarounds are constantly 'coming our way.' She tells us, 'There's too many problems within the system that the workarounds get to be a problem too.' In response, Wendy explains how she self-consciously repeats to herself 'I won't even try' to remember all the workarounds for they are simply 'constant and continual.' In so doing she keeps them from becoming an object of problem-solving that may engross. Indeed, the 'way SDMT should work scenario,' for example, serves as a type of symbolic container for these potentially engrossing concerns.

Just like in the case of Alison above, we see that a Zone of Proximal Development is involved. Wendy indicates that the types of new artefacts she describes are used in conversation – that is, they are *collectively* externalized – to organize the ongoing unfolding of social relations of her work. We can note her multiple references to shared meaning-making in fact: for example, 'lots of us;' the regular use of 'we' (Parts A and B) including in reference to the use of the 'way SDMT should work scenario' (Part B). Wendy even states that 'if you interviewed everyone here I think they'd say the same thing' (Part C). The fact that everyone does *not* say the same thing further suggests the role of meaning-making specific to groups and distinct spheres of communication within the occupation rather than across workers the occupation generally. There is, in other words, evidence available which suggests significant forms of variation between the two accounts in terms of the processes of internalization, the production of alternative artefacts, configurations of mediations, and collective externalization within activity.

In the end, the account provides evidence of a resolution for peripheral contradictions between the pull of the operations and her goal-directed actions: 'you *could* spend time flying through your manuals' (Part B) but it is 'not very time effective to be having to do that stuff *given what we need to do in reality*' (Part B). The use-value of clients and client/worker relations and contradictions related to the broader object/motive of welfare-work activity begin to emerge as a driver and *sense-maker* (Kaptelinin, 2005) for learning. Unlike workers like Alison above, despite similar levels of work experience (and, in fact, similar concerns for the current state of their occupation), for Wendy a specific type of 'reality' is constructed through the myriad moment-by-moment constructions of mediating artefacts and their object-relatedness within activity. Wendy undertakes repair-work, but remains un-engrossed by it. Her sense-repair work is therefore undertaken more as a process of recovery and re-inheritance of occupational culture in resistance to the labour process as designed. In carrying out practice in this way, she is enveloping repair-work learning and sense-repair-work learning in something broader: *object-work learning*. The very purposes of her work – its object – and, most importantly, the contradictions associated with it, have been constructed for active rather than passive forms of mediation.

In Wendy's case, we find the establishment of a particular object/motive of, *and* occupational identity within, activity. This revolves around 'client contact' and 'what's really going on with people' (Part A). She concludes that 'paper-shuffling' is 'unprofessional as far as getting to the grips with your client's issues. It's not me' (Part C). The object-relatedness of Wendy's mode of participation in activity allows her to admit that the contingencies of clients' lives is – *and perhaps should be* – legitimately reflected contingency in workers' lives; this mode represents a fundamentally more comprehensive and expansive perspective on state welfare work, the forms of value production which could or should govern it, and her place in it.

CONCLUSIONS

The aim of this chapter was to seek to understand how a synthesizing use-value thesis approach that takes seriously the *political economic identity of learning/labour process activity as capitalist* reveals important dynamics in the moment-by-moment world of *occupational learning*; and, vice versa. I refer to *trajectories* of occupational learning to do this. This is because the concept of trajectories confirms knowledge production as an ongoing process based on the accumulation of moment-by-moment achievements – both internally and externally – that construct potentially divergent horizons or endpoints.

However in order to fully assess the implications of the approach I have summarized, it worth quoting the work of A.N. Leontiev (1978) on the differences between forms of knowledge production in activity.

> The mobility of separate 'forming' systems of activity is expressed ... in the fact that each of them may become a smaller fraction or, conversely, may incorporate in itself units that were formerly relatively independent. Thus, in the course of achieving an isolated general goal there may occur a separation of intermediate goals as a result of which the whole action is divided into a series of separate sequential actions; this is especially characteristic for cases where the action takes place under conditions that inhibit its being carried out by means of already formulated operations. The opposite process consists of consolidating isolated units of activity. This is the case when objectively attained intermediate results flow one into another and the subject loses conscious awareness of them. In a corresponding manner there is a *fractionation or, conversely, a consolidation* also of 'units' of psychic images: A text copied by the inexperienced hand of a child breaks up in his perception into separate letters and even into their graphic elements; later in this process the units of perception become for him [*sic*] whole words or even sentences. Before the naked eye the process of fractionation or consolidation

of units of activity and psychic reflection – in external observation as well as introspectively – is hardly distinguishable. (p. 67; emphasis added)

Building on these comments, I suggest that the pathways and destinations of these trajectories of occupational learning are not simply different from one another. *Trajectories of administrative knowledge production* in welfare work involve the engrossment of workers' learning in the premises of labour process design. This design aims at meeting the needs of state austerity (profitability of another kind), and by extension the broader interests of the capitalist state to discipline the poor by disciplining the workers who administer the rights of the poor. This labour process encourages a mode of participation and a type of object-relatedness in activity in which the contradiction between capitalist economic logic (exchange-value generation) comes to obscure and dominate the use-value of learning and work, workers and clients. In this sense, it is *fractionalized* (and fractionalizing) occupational learning. Its emerging trajectory does not allow intervention in terms of the full range of contradictions that might possibly drive a more expansive form of occupational knowledge production.

Alternatively, what I have called *trajectories of welfare craft knowledge production* suggests a form of more *consolidated* (and more consolidating) occupational learning. Here, the skills of repair-work and sense-repair-work become consolidated within a type of activity in which the primary contradictions of activity, those involving the object/motive and thus object-work/skill, may begin to unfold. In short, craft trajectories offer the potential for *more whole* forms of occupational knowledge since they are encompassing of a broader, interrelated range of contradictions. As such, trajectories of craft knowledge production give rise to the potential, over time, to undertake resolutions that are fundamentally more complex and more far-reaching.

I claimed above that in times of change the very meaning, purpose and 'soul' of an occupation are placed in question. Such questions are not only answered by employers and work designers. In the end, all forms of work must be brought to life by workers, and it is ultimately in the collective lives of workers that important answers to why work changes in the way it does can to be found. In this regard, applying this type of UVT approach can shed new light on how the basic defining features of capitalism are both made, re-made, accommodated and consented to, as well as resisted in occupational life. This approach offers an additional, critical perspective on knowledge economies in which the most generalized political economic principles of capitalism can be more effectively located in the minutiae of work and learning.

NOTES

[1] The study was linked to a large national research network called the Work and Lifelong Learning Network (WALL) (www.wallnetwork.ca), housed at the University of Toronto's Centre for the Study of Education and Work headed by Professor D.W. Livingstone. It was funded by the Social Science and Humanities Research Council of Canada.

[2] I do not spend time introducing either of these traditions here; for that see Engeström, Miettinen, and Punamäki (1999) and Thompson (1997) respectively.

[3] Using different terms of reference, this point is likewise contentious in LPT research where questions of retaining analysis of the labour process as capitalist in nature remain hotly debated.

[4] The names of workers quoted in this chapter are pseudonyms.

[5] In Sawchuk (forthcoming) there is a third trajectory that is explored called floundering occupational learning which refers to those workers busy developing expertise related to hiding poor job performance and retaining their job (often through practices of social withdrawal), and/or workers actively negotiating choice-making in terms of the two trajectories of occupational learning discussed in this chapter.

[6] Moreover, the interviewees were middle-aged and born less than ten years apart; both were moderately involved with their local union; and, each grew up in a working-class household (household heads were truck driver and construction worker).

REFERENCES

Avis, J. (2007). Engeström's version of activity theory: A conservative praxis? *Journal of Education and Work, 20*(3), 161–177.

Blau, P (1955). *The dynamics of bureaucracy: A study of interpersonal relationships in two government agencies.* London: University of Chicago Press.

Bowker, G.C. & Star, S.L. (1999). *Sorting things out: Classification and its consequences.* Cambridge, MA: MIT Press.

Burawoy, M. (1979). *Manufacturing consent: Changes in the labour process under monopoly capitalism.* Chicago: University of Chicago Press.

Daniels, H., Leadbetter, J., Warmington, P., Edwards, A., Martin, D., Popova, A., Apostolov, A., Middleton, D., & Brown, S. (2007). Learning in and for multi-agency working. *Oxford Review of Education, 33*(4), 521–538.

Engeström, Y. (1987). *Learning by expanding: An activity-theoretical approach to development research.* Helsinki: Orienta-Konsultit.

Engeström Y, Miettinen R., & Punamäki, R.-L. (1999). *Perspectives on activity theory.* New York: Cambridge University Press.

Engestrom, Y. & Sannino, A. (2010). Studies of Expansive Learning: Foundations, findings and future challenges. *Educational Research Review, 5,* 1–24.

Felstead, A., Fuller, A., Jewson, N., & Unwin, L. (2009). *Improving working as learning.* Abingdon: Routledge.

Glisson, C. & Hemmelgarn, A. (1998). The effects of organizational climate and interorganisational coordination on the quality and outcomes of children's service system. *Child Abuse and Neglect, 22*(5), 401–421.

Hampson, I. & Junor, A. (2010). Putting the process back in: Rethinking service sector skill. *Work, Employment and Society, 24*(3), 526–545.

Hennessy, T. & Sawchuk, P.H. (2003). Worker responses to technological change in the Canadian public sector: Issues of learning and labour process. *Journal of Workplace Learning, 15*(7), 319–325.

Ilyenkov, E.V. (1982). *The dialectics of the abstract and the concrete in Marx's Capital.* Moscow: Progress.

Kaptelinin, V. (2005). The object of activity: Making sense of the sense-maker. *Mind, Culture and Activity, 12*(1), 4–18.

Knorr Cetina, K (1999). *Epistemic cultures: How the sciences make knowledge.* Cambridge: Harvard University Press.

Langemeyer, I. & Roth, W.-M. (2006). Is cultural–historical activity theory threatened to fall short of its own principles and possibilities as a dialectical social science? *Critical Social Studies – Outlines, 8*(2), 20–42.

Leontiev, A.N. (1978). *Activity, consciousness, and personality.* Englewood Cliffs, NJ: Prentice Hall.

Marx, K. (1990). *Capital* (Vol. 1). New York: International.

Niewolny, K. & Wilson, A. (2009). What happened to the promise? A critical (re)orientation of two sociocultural learning traditions. *Adult Education Quarterly*, *60*(1), 26–45.

Sawchuk, P.H. (2006a). 'Use-value' and the re-thinking of skills, learning and the labour process. *Journal of Industrial Relations*, *48*(5), 593–617.

Sawchuk, P.H. (2006b). Activity and power: Everyday life and development of working-class groups. In Sawchuk, P.H., Duarte, N., & Elhammoumi, M. (Eds.), *Critical perspectives on activity: Explorations across education, work and everyday life* (pp. 238–267). New York: Cambridge University Press.

Sawchuk, P.H. (2007). Understanding diverse outcomes for working-class learning: Conceptualizing class consciousness as knowledge activity. *Economic and Labour Relations Review*, *17*(2), 199–216.

Sawchuk, P.H. (2010a). Re-visiting Taylorism: Conceptual implications for studies of lifelong learning, technology and work in the Canadian public sector. In Livingstone, D.W. (Ed.), *Lifelong learning in paid and unpaid work* (pp. 101–118). New York: Routledge.

Sawchuk, P.H. (2010b). Occupational transitions within workplaces undergoing change: A case from the public sector. In Sawchuk, P. & Taylor, A. (Eds.), *Challenging transitions in learning and work: Perspectives on policy and practice* (pp. 189–208). Rotterdam: Sense.

Sawchuk, P.H. (Forthcoming). Working knowledge and the limits of control: Social services, technology and the pathways of occupational expertise.

Sawchuk, P.H. & Stetsenko, A. (2008). Sociological understandings of conduct for a non-canonical activity theory: Exploring intersections and complementarities. *Mind, Culture and Activity*, *15*(4), 339–360.

Thompson, P. (1997). *The nature of work: An introduction to debates on the labour process*. London: Palgrave.

Vygotsky, L.S. (1994). The problem of the environment. In Vander Veer, R. & Vlasiner, J. (Eds.), *The Vygotsky reader* (pp. 338–354). Cambridge, MA: Blackwell.

Warhurst, C. & Thompson, P. (2006). Mapping knowledge in work: Proxies or practices? *Work, Employment and Society*, *20*(4), 787–800.

Warmington, P. (2008). From 'activity' to 'labour': Commodification, labour power and contradiction in Engeström's activity theory. *Critical Social Studies – Outlines*, *10*(2), 4–19.

DAVID GUILE

WORKING AND LEARNING IN THE 'KNOWLEDGE-BASED' CREATIVE AND CULTURAL SECTOR

Vocational Practice, Social Capital, and Entrepreneurability

INTRODUCTION

The profile of the creative and cultural (C&C) sector has risen worldwide over the last twenty years for a combination of economic and social reasons. Economic gurus have argued that the industries that comprise the sector are paradigmatic examples of the type of knowledge-based industries that will constitute the basis of nation states' prosperity in the twenty-first century (Porter & Ketels, 2003). Socially, the sector symbolizes the transactional freedom to work creatively, unencumbered by bureaucratic work regimes that many people claim they are looking for (Hesmondhalgh & Baker, 2011), as well as an opportunity to design products and services that reflect the forms of cultural diversity which are an increasing feature of advanced industrial economies (Bilton, 2007). It is hardly surprising therefore that an increasing number of young people in Europe aspire to enter the sector (KEA, 2006).

Viewed from the educational policies that have emerged worldwide as the idea of the knowledge economy has captured the collective imagination of policy makers (EU, 2000) and transnational agencies (OECD, 1996; World Bank, 2003), the issue of access to the C&C sector should simply be a matter of acquiring a higher level qualification. This chapter shows, however, that the link policy makers and transnational agencies assume exists between qualifications and access to employment does not apply in the ways they imagine in this sector.

In making that argument, policy makers and transnational agencies first assumed the existence of firm-specific and occupational labour markets with transparent policies and practices for recruitment. Secondly, they assumed that the knowledge learnt through studying for a qualification constitutes a proxy measure for the knowledge required for a job. The chapter, however, reveals that the C&C sector is characterized by: (a) external labour markets (i.e., contract-based) where employment opportunities emerge as people participate in occupational networks; and (b) cultures and practices that require two forms of knowledge, namely, vocational practice (i.e., mix of knowledge, skill and judgement) and social capital (i.e., knowledge of networks to secure contracts for employment). The chapter coins the term 'Moebius-strip' expertise to refer to the way in which individuals use their social capital networks to secure contracts to enable them to deploy their

D.W. Livingstone and D. Guile (eds.), The Knowledge Economy and Lifelong Learning: A Critical Reader, 301–316.

vocational practice (Guile, 2007). In doing so, it highlights the role of 'intermediary agencies' in assisting young people gain experience of work and work cultures to assist them to enter the sector. The chapter also uses what Kennedy (this volume) refers to as the perspective of the logic of labour – in other words, a focus on people's reasons for wanting to work in an occupational field and the sacrifices and strategies they make in order to do so – as a guiding principle to structure the presentation of four case studies of young people who are attempting to develop the expertise, connections, and self-promotional skills to gain opportunities to work in the C&C sector.

The chapter concludes by suggesting that policy makers should rebalance existing educational polices based on the acquisition of higher level qualifications with policies that assist intermediary organizations (i.e., local bodies) to devise programmes that provide young people with opportunities to develop their vocational practice and social capital and to develop insights into how to deploy the latter entrepreneurially to secure contracts for their services. The chapter sets the scene for this argument by initially discussing policy makers' assumptions about the knowledge economy and the role of education in assisting young people to secure work in such an economy.

THE KNOWLEDGE ECONOMY AND EDUCATION

The Conventional Wisdom

The origins of the argument that the emergence of the knowledge economy poses a new challenge for education was fuelled by the claim that knowledge rather than land, labour, and capital was now the most important factor of production and hence the idea of a 'knowledge economy.' This term was first coined in the late 1960s by Drucker (1969, p. 263) to refer to the application of knowledge from any field or source, new or old, to spur economic development. The subsequent debate about the role of knowledge in the economy, which only took root from the late 1970s, has fractured over the years. The dominant strand follows the argument first promulgated by Bell (1973), namely, that theoretical knowledge is the most important form of knowledge in the economy; this is the position that underpins the current global concern for supporting science, technology, engineering, and mathematical (STEM) research. A parallel strand follows the argument first put forward by management theorists, such as Lundvall (1996), that tacit knowledge is the most important form of knowledge because it is not subject to codification and therefore constitutes a resource that other firms cannot replicate.

Despite the existence of these two views concerning which type of knowledge is important in the economy, policy makers internationally have tended to accept the former position. At the present time, the most obvious manifestation is the general consensus that STEM subjects are critical to economic prosperity and hence scientists should be the major targets for research grants.

A major influence on policy makers' thinking as regards the educational response to the knowledge economy was Robert Reich's book *The work of nations*

(1991). Reich fused the social theorists' case for the new role of knowledge in the economy and the emerging case for globalization into a compelling argument that the challenge for advanced industrial nations was to position themselves to secure 'high skill' work, because they could no longer compete with newly industrializing nations on the basis of price alone. Reich advanced the distinctive thesis that the economies of the future would be education-led and, as a consequence, that the challenge for national education and training systems would be to develop the new forms of human capital – to develop 'symbolic analysts' (i.e., people with degrees who had acquired the ability to manipulate abstract forms of knowledge) – which he maintained were integral to high-skill work.

The idea that we now live and work in a knowledge economy and/or society has gained increasing prominence over the last decade or so amongst national and supranational policy makers worldwide (European Commission, 2000) and amongst transnational organizations concerned with economic growth (OECD, 1996; World Bank, 2003). The concept of the knowledge economy has come to constitute, paradoxically, both an 'imaginary' (Jessop et al., this volume) and a 'pre-given' reality (Guile, 2010a), a quasi-enlightenment vision of economic progress and a new reality that we must adapt to through attaining a higher level of qualification.

One of the most well known expressions of the 'learning' policy position is found in the European Commission's Lisbon Memorandum (European Commission, 2000). This memorandum led to the concept of a knowledge economy being deployed in European Union (EU) policy literature in two senses. It provided a vision of the purpose of all future European economic activity, but also intertwined this vision with a policy for lifelong learning. The most highly influential expression of the readiness position is the development by the World Bank (2008) of its Knowledge for Development (K4D): Knowledge Assessment Methodology (KAM). The KAM is an interactive, diagnostic, and benchmarking tool that the World Bank is actively encouraging countries and regions to use, in order to provide a preliminary assessment of the knowledge base of their economies. This will be expressed in terms of the volumes of knowledge-based products and services generated by their economies and qualifications held by their populaces (Robertson, 2008).

Problems with the Conventional Wisdom

Although there clearly is a considerable grain of truth in the above argument, the problem with it is that policy makers and transnational agencies, along with social and management theorists, have failed to recognize that economies that are purportedly knowledge-based pre-suppose the existence of 'epistemic' (i.e., knowledge) cultures and activities (Knorr Cetina, 1999). These are, according to Knorr Cetina, the types of cultures and practices that are an embedded feature of workplaces (universities, corporations, and networks) and which foster the production and utilization of knowledge in both research and development (R&D) and in professional practice. Hence, it is epistemic cultures and the economic, political, and social goals for how the knowledge those cultures produce should be used – not just knowledge itself – that are central not only to the economy but also to societies that purportedly 'run on' knowledge and expertise. These cultures constitute the settings in which new theories or new forms of knowledge are produced, and where existing forms of knowledge are 'recontextualized' and 'reconfigured' in new ways to support and/or challenge economic, social, and political goals (Guile, 2010a). Without these cultures and goals, there would be no knowledge economy, no experts whose knowledge can be tapped into, nor any debate about the future direction of advanced industrial societies. Furthermore, once we focus on epistemic cultures and practices, we are able to see what is distinctive about the use of knowledge in the economy at the present time: it is the way in which those cultures and practices facilitate all forms of knowledge to increasingly play a central role in the production of goods and services.

This argument is therefore consistent with, and yet slightly different from, the arguments advanced by the critics of the knowledge economy in Section 1 of this book. Stated simply, knowledge that can be treated as a tangible asset and quantifiable in terms of economic return on the investment in research and development has always been viewed as important in capitalist economies. There is now, however, a greater recognition than at any other point in history of the contribution that the more intangible forms of knowledge (i.e., those ones that are difficult to quantify) make to the creation of products and services. The conceptual basis and an empirical exemplification of this claim are explored in the first part of the next section by considering the way in which the C&C sector offers a tangible and intangible contribution to the economy.

THE CREATIVE AND CULTURAL SECTOR AND THE KNOWLEDGE ECONOMY

The Concept of the Creative and Cultural Sector (C&C)

Many of the industries that comprise the C&C sector – for example, art and design, broadcasting, film, music, and so on – have been a long-standing feature of the U.K., the U.S., and the European and Pacific Rim economies. Two developments have, however, resulted in the convergence of those industries and the introduction and widespread use of the term 'creative and cultural' to define the outcome of this process. The first one was the development of 'digital technology,' that is, software programmes which can be continually developed and combined in different ways (Quah, 2003). The emergence of digital technologies has facilitated the creation of new industries (e.g., web development and design), as well as offering people working in industries which previously had been separate from one another a resource they could use to establish the conditions for those industries to be gradually intertwined economically and technologically in radically new ways, as with, for example, software animation as an integral element of films, etc. (Tapscot, 1995; Coffey, 1996).

The second development follows from the first. The process of industrial convergence led to the recognition that the C&C sector was dependent on both tangible and intangible 'knowledge' inputs (Lash & Urry, 1994). Many firms in the sector have, as noted above, utilized digital technology that had been funded as part of research and development programmes either by national governments or by private sector companies to enhance their products and services. The distinctive feature of their use of such technologies, as Lash and Urry (1994, p. 123) pointed out some time ago, was to use 'cultural knowledge,' by which they meant a mix of knowledge of aesthetics and cultural trends, to' 'design' or 're-design' products and services so they appealed to consumers. Design here refers to both the idea for and marketing of a product or service as much as the interplay between technical and aesthetic features of that product or service. Hence, the critical challenge for firms in the C&C sector, as Ross (2003) has acknowledged, has been to support this creative process by establishing workplace cultures and practices that facilitate the interplay of tangible and intangible knowledge. In light of this, many writers have maintained that the C&C sector should be considered part of the knowledge economy because cultural knowledge is as important as STEM knowledge in facilitating economic development (Bilton, 2007; Florida, 2000).

The above developments have resulted in the thirteen industries – crafts, design, fashion, film, music, performing arts, publishing, research and development, software, toys, TV, radio, and video games – being defined as the C&C sector (Howkins, 2001, and also resulted in the people who generate new ideas that enable those industrial segments to flourish being defined as creative knowledge workers (Florida, 2002). It is generally agreed that the C&C sector is now worth about $2.2 trillion worldwide and, according to the World Bank (2008), is growing at 5 per cent per year. In the case of the U.K., the C&C sector now accounts for £1 in every £10 of GDP and employs up to 2 million people (U.K. Treasury, 2005, p. 14).

The Organization of Work in the C&C Sector

The profile of the clusters and industries that comprise the C&C sector are, however, rather different from the historical profile of conventional economic sectors such as the automobile and pharmaceutical industries. These latter industries tended to be characterized by strong national identities and vibrant corporate sectors with strong 'strategies,' 'structures,' and 'systems' which facilitated the manufacture of mass-volume standardized products and services (Ghoshal & Bartlett, 2001), and had well-established systems to train new personnel and re-train existing ones (Green, 2006). Whilst globalization has transformed competitive strategies and work organization in those industries significantly, they still tend to be involved with large-scale mass production.

In contrast, the profile and structure of the C&C sector in Europe is characterized by a mix of a small number of global corporations and national organizations and a very large number of small and medium size (SME) enterprises/organizations and freelance work (Bilton, 2007; Deuze, 2007). This mix of organizations and freelancers tends to be concentrated in specific regions and they continually form value chains and networks, often for a short duration;

sometimes they are involved with the continual evolution and marketing of a mass-produced product (e.g., Microsoft Windows) and on other occasions they are involved with creating and promoting new products or services for particular market niches (e.g., the Harry Potter films) (Hesmondhalgh, 2002). Furthermore, unlike industrial sectors such as the automobile, engineering, and medical sectors, which have historically been characterized by very strong 'occupational labour markets' (OLMs) and firm-specific 'internal labour markets' (ILMs) (Ashton, 1995), the C&C sector is characterized predominantly by 'external labour markets' (ELMs). These labour markets function in rather different ways from one another. OLMs enable new entrants to be trained in a range of skills, which provide competence in specific occupations and recognized qualifications for registration, as well as membership of professional bodies. This process of occupational socialization results in the development of an identification with an occupation (e.g., engineering, nursing, mechanics) as well as a 'skill base' that can be enhanced through further training within firms. In addition, ILMs provide a series of job or career ladders which, following further training, enable young employees to be promoted and progress within an organization.

These labour market conditions are only really found in those segments of the C&C sector which have developed equivalent professional identities and education and training traditions, (e.g., broadcasting and printing), although even here ELMs/OLMs are no longer as entrenched a feature of these industries as they were in the 1960s, 1970s, and 1980s (KEA, 2006). Large swathes of the C&C sector, such as design, music, and games, are characterized by ELMs, where the buying and selling of labour is not linked to jobs which form part of an ILM or a long-standing and clearly defined OLM. Movement of labour in ELMs is determined by the price attached to the job and/or contract on offer. The qualifications of the individual concerned and such jobs/contracts in the creative and cultural industries tend to run the gamut from high to low skill.

Traditionally, ELMs were seen by labour market economists as constituting the secondary, rather than primary, labour market and were treated by them as less desirable work contexts for young people as compared to OLMs and ILMs because they did not offer the same form of employment protection and structured opportunities for development (Ashton, 1995). The use of 'projects' and 'cost-based funding' as guiding principles for the organization of work inside large companies as much as in partnership activity between companies, irrespective of their size, has profoundly increased the prevalence of ELM employment contracts, with the result that contracts are now increasingly given to people only for the life of a funded project (Bilton, 2007). The net effect has been to position existing workers and aspiring entrants to the C&C sector in the United Kingdom (and increasingly in Europe) as 'workers'/'entrepreneurs' between capital and labour because:

> The traditional categories of the 'full-time job society' ('here the worker, there the employer') no longer apply; the cultural content worker is suddenly also a (cultural) entrepreneur (without capital). In academic literature the

'new worker' is described as multi-skilled, multifunctional and flexible in working time as well as often being self-employed. (KEA, 2006, p. 91)

Operating in this in-between position is particularly challenging because it requires a distinctive form of entrepreneurial and vocational expertise. This expertise has been characterized by Guile (2007) as 'Moebius-strip' expertise. I have characterized this expertise through the image of a looped ribbon twisted once to convey two ideas about SMEs and freelancers. On the one hand, they have to use the social capital (i.e., networks and connections) that they have accumulated *entrepreneurially* in order to search and tender for sources of funding to realize their creative aspirations. On the other hand, they must deploy their vocational expertise flexibly to suit each commission they successfully secure or to which they are invited by other SMEs/freelancers to contribute.

This depiction of how experienced members of the C&C sector continually gain new contracts for their services begs the following question: How do aspiring entrants develop Moebius-strip expertise to gain access to the C&C sector? This is because it is crystal clear that in external labour markets qualifications by themselves are insufficient.

THE DEVELOPMENT OF MOEBIUS-STRIP EXPERTISE

Based on research in different industries in the C&C sector over the last few years, it is apparent that aspiring entrants have recourse to two main strategies to gain access to the sector so as to begin to develop Moebius-strip expertise. They either can exercise their own agency and identify and negotiate internships and work placements or they can participate in the development activities offered by 'intermediary agencies' (Guile, 2010b). The term 'intermediary agencies' encompasses a diverse range of organizations. Some are found in: (a) the formal education sector, for example, education-industry liaison units in universities; (b) the not-for-profit sector, specifically companies with a sectoral specialization, and possibly some industry funding, that provides a range of learning and development programmes for aspiring entrants and longstanding members of their field; (c) the non-formal sector, colleges that do not receive statutory funding; and (d) the public sector, for example, local government-funded community-liaison agencies.

Intermediary agencies are therefore rather different from the traditional forms of community education that are usually delivered by cohorts of trained educators employed by local authorities. In contrast to the latter, intermediary agencies attempt to co-ordinate segments of the labour market by acting as catalysts to bring conglomerates, SMEs, freelancers, and networks together to forge partnerships. The aim of these partnerships is to assist aspiring entrants to supplement their qualifications or prior experience in developing the forms of Moebius-strip expertise that will help them enter the C&C sector. Over the last decade, many intermediary agencies have achieved this goal by securing funds from sources such as the European Union, U.K. government departments, charitable foundations, and the private sector to provide new spaces for learning. These can include: (a) the provision of short courses that usually do not result in a recognized qualification;

(b) offering access to master classes, sometimes with bursaries; (c) negotiating internships/work placements with companies and employing experienced professionals as tutors/mentors to support aspiring entrants in ways that are appropriate to the needs of the sector; and (d) working closely with employers and educational institutions to design innovative forms of education and training that address pressing skill needs. In each case, these programmes help people who hold qualifications but who have not yet acquired much work experience to move into the C&C sector.

The next section of the chapter summarizes research from four case studies undertaken between 2005 and 2007 as part of *The Last Mile* Project (Guile 2010b). The case studies were based in the film industry, the jewellery industry, the performing arts sector, and the theatre/live entertainment sector, all of which have a number of features in common in the United Kingdom. The features are: (a) external labour markets and hence freelance work; (b) individualized rather than unionized work practices; and (c) multi-faceted conceptions of expertise (i.e., knowledge and skill, connections and self-promotion). The aim of this three-year project, which was funded via the EU's EQUAL Programme, was to identify learning strategies that assist people to develop their Moebius-strip expertise. Two ideas underpin the presentation of the case studies: one is Kennedy's notion of the logic of labour, and the other is Lave and Wenger's (1991) distinction between two varieties of curriculum: the 'teaching' (i.e., formally designed sessions) and 'learning' (i.e., opportunities to participate in routine and stretching activities) curriculums. The former is used to allow the perspective of the learner, who is seeking to either gain a starting position or to broaden the basis of their expertise in their chosen niche in the C&C sector, to manifest itself in each case study. The latter is employed to describe the strategies that intermediary organizations, employers, and individuals use to build upon learners' prior knowledge and skill to facilitate the development of Moebius-strip expertise.

Jewellery Industry Innovation Centre (JIIC)

The Jewellery Industry Innovation Centre (JIIC) is an industry-education funded intermediary agency attached to the University of Central England, Birmingham with a remit to provide support in research and development in the U.K. jewellery industry. The jewellery industry presents aspiring entrants with a very specific kind of challenge. Much of this sector depends upon a value network of 'horizontal' collaboration between SMEs and freelancers who create new products and services and vertical collaboration between SMEs/freelancers and large retail firms who act as suppliers and distributors. This generates a pattern of economic activity and epistemic culture based on local ties wherein SMEs and freelancers create new jewellery products and the larger firms are concerned with their manufacture and distribution.

Working in partnership with the Innovation Unit (IU), part of Birmingham City Council's Economic and Development Department, and with funds secured from the European Social Fund (ESF), the JIIC in 2005 designed a new unaccredited initiative – the Design Work Placement Project. This project ran for six months and was based on a three-way partnership. First, participating manufacturers gave recently qualified jewellers an opportunity to develop a new range of commercial products based on their research because they had faith in the JIIC's track record in identifying new talent. Second, recently qualified jewellers who choose to use the placement and the small bursary it provided learn how to supplement aspects of their vocational practice that could not be developed in university. Specifically, they learnt how to incubate (i.e., create, cost, and monitor the fabrication of) their designs and, by working for and in jewellery companies, started to develop their social capital which they could later use to secure contracts for their services as freelancers; and (c) the JIIC acted as project managers and mentors for the participant jewellers.

The JIIC ran workshops (i.e., teaching rather than learning curriculum) to support the recently qualified jewellers in developing an industry-relevant approach to designing new jewellery collections. It introduced them to more commercially-orientated methods of working, encouraging them to attune themselves more to the way in which cultural trends influence how people incorporate jewellery into their fashion style; supported the process through one-to-one mentoring; and ran showcasing events with industry representatives for the participants at the end of the project. The jewellery companies provided the participating jewellers with their learning curriculum. This consisted of, on the one hand, very demanding commercial projects. For example, graduates enrolled in jewellery degrees usually have a whole term to produce the final design for their degree, whereas the companies expected forty new designs to be produced within twelve weeks and then expected the majority of them to be manufactured within the next twelve weeks. And on the other hand, the new jewellers were presented with opportunities to become familiar with up-to-date techniques of production that they had never encountered in college and to participate in production planning meetings. The aspiring jewellers used the JIIC's teaching curriculum and the employers' learning curriculum to formulate and instantiate the new designs they created.

The Design Work Placement Project (DPP) assisted the participating jewellers to develop what was referred to earlier as Moebius-strip expertise by developing their vocational practice and their vocational identity. Specifically, the DWP assisted the participating jewellers in deciding whether to remain a jewellery designer and, as a consequence, become a freelance worker, or to enter management within a jewellery company and, therefore, be in a better position to secure a full-time position. Moreover, the jewellers who took the former decision recognized that life as a freelancer meant being prepared to demonstrate to national and international jewellery companies that they are sufficiently versatile to turn their expertise to meet the requirements of any contract.

Slough's Creative Academy (CA)

Slough Borough Council's Arts Development Team is a regional arts partnership that receives some core funding from the local council to ensure that the arts in Slough have the best resources, and connections (Guile, 2010b). Because the U.K.'s four largest film studios are located within fifteen minutes of Slough, the Creative Academy, one of the Art Development Team's partners, prioritized film as an industrial sector where they were keen to secure employer support to assist young people from the Slough area in gaining access to the industry. This led the director of CA to use networking opportunities to meet the director of Aria Films and negotiate work placements for ten aspiring entrants on one of their forthcoming productions.

Aria's director was responsive to the CA's pitch for work placements because he was aware that 'the film production community is not a nurturing one' and that it is difficult 'to establish a career in the industry unless one can find an opportunity to work within the industry' (Guile, 2010b, p. 478). The aim of the partnership between Aria and CA was to enable people with a degree in a film-related field (e.g., special effects, make-up design or television and production, or people who did not have a degree but who had experience of working in television and/or on the production of advertisements) to move into the film industry. To realize this goal, Aria offered them a two-week work placement on either the 'shoot' or the post-production for the film he was producing, *Kill Kill Faster Faster*. The film was shot in Rotterdam over six weeks in June–July 2006 with a budget of £3.7 million. Seven participants undertook technical positions in Rotterdam, while three were involved in post-production work in London once the filming was complete. All the participants received small bursaries from funding the CA had obtained from one of the European Union's education and training funds.

Given that Aria's film crew had no previous experience of supporting people on work placement on a film shoot and the participants equally lacked any experience of such work, its director and the CA's director devised a multi-faceted teaching and learning curriculum to support both parties. Prior to the Rotterdam shoot, the CA ran a series of workshops in order to support the participants' understanding of the aims of the scheme and to prepare for their roles through one-to-one meetings with experienced professionals in the fields of lighting, filming, and sound. During the shooting, the CA offered on-site mentoring support by visiting the participants and helping to iron-out any misunderstandings and/or difficulties that arose. Prior to the participants arriving in Rotterdam, Aria's director briefed the experienced technical staff recruited to work on the film about the rationale for providing work placements, and encouraged them to model their vocational practice so the people undertaking work placements could visualize what had to be done and step in at moments the experienced staff deemed appropriate, to film a scene, adjust the sound, etc.

The work placement occurred on-set for an actual film and therefore it supported the appreciation of the participants about how, although film-related qualifications can provide a conceptual understanding and orient aspirant entrants towards key issues about the history and social conventions that inform film-making, such knowledge has to be supplemented by the experience of practice. This is because much of the knowledge that is an integral feature of forms of vocational practice, such as sound, lighting, and direction, is invested in action and involves developing the forms of judgement that arise when engaging in professional activity. The placement therefore provided the participants with opportunities which would otherwise not exist for aspiring entrants unless they already had contacts in the film industry. In addition, the placement also provided the aspiring entrants with an opportunity to hear experienced professionals' 'war stories' about which film events to attend and which networks to join and, in the process, assisted participants in their coming to appreciate that to flourish in the film industry, it is as important to deploy one's vocational expertise flexibly in a range of situations as it is to use one's social capital entrepreneurially to acquire freelance contracts.

WAC

WAC – a non-formal performing arts and media college – specializes in the field of performing arts and raises its income from a mix of U.K. and European education funding streams. In recognition that many of its graduates, who were active in the field of world arts, were unable to supplement their freelance income streams through securing employment as a teacher/teaching assistant because they lacked a recognized qualification, WAC decided to create a degree in world art forms. To do so, WAC turned to the framework provided by U.K.'s Foundation Degree (FD). This framework allows agencies that have not previously run a degree to design one and to form a partnership with a university to oversee the validation and assessment of the degree.

WAC designed its FD as an integrated learning-teaching curriculum. WAC achieved this goal by mobilizing its accumulated social capital (i.e., the former WAC graduates who were experienced professionals in the field of world arts forms) to work as teachers. Their involvement enabled participants to develop their vocational practice to industry standards as well as to expand their network of contacts and thus position them to gain access to the performing arts' external labour markets. WAC used the expertise of its staff and former graduates first, to explain the discipline-based knowledge and skill that underpins different world art forms in ways that extended their existing vocational practice and developed their professional identity and confidence. Second it provided opportunities for learners to plan and then perform in a wide range of contexts and for culturally diverse audiences. This opportunity to participate legitimately, albeit peripherally, within a range of different world art forms in authentic settings enabled participants to develop the forms of judgement that are integral to the development of their practice. Lastly, it provided opportunities for learners to bridge and link their existing fledgling network to other existing and successful networks.

The wide variety of learning opportunities in the college and in the field of performing arts enabled FD participants to first, extend their existing vocational practice and bridge and link their existing and new social capital in ways that could potentially result in them being invited to contribute their specific vocational expertise to a contract that others had secured. Secondly, these learning opportunities positioned participants to develop entrepreneurial expertise by encouraging them to look at themselves as not just performers searching for contracts for their specific world art expertise, but also as arts' practitioners who have developed broader based capabilities that could assist them to secure employment in art-based project management and/or community education.

Birmingham's Innovation Unit and Repertory Theatre

Birmingham's Innovation Unit and the city's Repertory Theatre (Rep) formed a partnership to secure European Social Funding to develop a 'Technical Apprenticeship' (TA) that offered eight apprentices, none of whom held a qualification above U.K.'s Level 3, to successfully enter the C&C sector. The Rep devised the TA outside the national framework for apprenticeship because it felt that the framework had been designed to serve the 'educational' goal of enhancing academic progression more than the vocational goal of developing sector-specific knowledge and skill. The Rep also felt that work in the theatre (and for that matter live events in general) is characterized by a 'project culture.' This work context caused particular problems for the framework's mandatory features, namely NVQ assessment and attendance at a Further Education College. The Rep felt that it was impracticable to release apprentices to attend courses or to stop and assess apprentices' competence in the middle of a production. To do so would deny the apprentices the opportunity to develop key aspects of vocational practice which are unlikely to surface again within the life span of a production.

To realize its vision of creating a modern, culturally diverse and inclusive traditional craft apprenticeship which reflects the realities of the new work context in which it operates, the Rep appointed a project co-ordinator (PC) who had worked as production manager previously in the Rep as well as having extensive knowledge and experience in training and development. Working with the technical heads of departments (HoDs), for example, lighting, costume, wigs, sound, and so on, the PC designed an apprenticeship that immersed apprentices in the 'work flow' of the Rep's life so that they were involved in every stage of mounting a production. The PC negotiated with the HoDs for the apprentices to have the opportunity to be: (a) 'legitimate peripheral participants' (Lave & Wenger, 1991) within their department, that is, actively engaged with the production process and supported *in situ* by modeling and demonstration activities in order to develop their technical expertise; and (b) 'boundary crossers' (Tuomi-Gröhn & Engeström, 2003) between departments, that is, provided with opportunities to grasp the connections between different forms of vocational practice that exist within the Rep and how they all contribute to the success of a performance.

The PC also arranged for the apprentices to enhance their on-the-job learning in the down-time between productions by offering them access to a custom-made teaching curriculum consisting of a mix of generic knowledge and skill about the process of production, and occupationally-specific knowledge and skill relating to their technical specialism. Furthermore, a programme of limited work rotation and visits was arranged to other theatres and events across the country. These experiences enabled the apprentices to locate their understanding of vocational practice in a wider industry context and lay the foundation for them to transfer their knowledge and skill into other theatrical settings.

The Rep's model supported the apprentices' skill formation and transfer because it not only developed distinctive forms of occupationally-specific knowledge and skill which are in short supply and hence for which there is a high demand in the global C&C economy, but it also developed their social capital and entrepreneurial ability. Recognising that the U.K.'s national system of repertory theatres is characterized by strong, mutually self-supporting networks, with high levels of trust amongst all levels of specialism and seniority, the Rep bridged and linked their apprentices into as many of these networks as possible. They did so in the knowledge that, on the one hand, these networks would accept that an apprentice 'trained' at Birmingham Rep was well-trained and sufficiently experienced to be offered a contract for their services and, on the other hand, that the apprentices had acquired fledgling Moebius-strip expertise and could pitch for contracts by demonstrating to prospective employers that they were sufficiently versatile to operate in a range of settings, for example, theatres, television studios and live events.

CONCLUSION

The trend away from occupational and internal and towards external labour markets is likely to continue rather than diminish in the C&C sector for a number of reasons. The use of projects as an organizing principle for work inside corporations as much as in partnerships between corporations, SMEs and freelancers is increasingly occurring globally in many industrial sectors (Doz, Santos, & Williamson, 2000), as well as intensifying in the C&C sector (Grabner, 2003). This development, on the one hand, assists firms to simultaneously maximize profits and minimize costs. Firms can contract with whichever company and/or individual they feel offers them the expertise they require at a given moment, rather than try to anticipate all the types of expertise they may need at some point and develop that expertise internally. On the other hand, a project model enables SMEs and freelancers to exercise their transactional freedom and creative aspirations by tendering for contracts for their services or accepting portions of contracts that other SMEs/freelancers have secured but which lack the necessary expertise to fulfill all the requirements of the contract. In each case, the SMEs and freelancers are in a position to exercise choice about which contract to accept rather than being required by an employer to work in a particular way on a contract. This development represents, as Boltanski and Chiapello (2005, p. 5) observe, the emergence of a 'new value relation' as SMEs and freelancers chose to exercise control over of their labour and creativity in the marketplace rather than accede that control and creativity to an employer.

The above labour market conditions suggest that the transition of young people into the C&C labour market, which researchers had noted even before the impact of the 'credit crunch' became more extended during the 1990s than in the previous two decades (McRobbie, forthcoming), is likely to become even more extended in the future. Moreover, given the opacity of the C&C labour market and the fact that access is dependent on the development of the forms of social capital that provide people with access to the networks that gate-keep and facilitate employment in the C&C sector, access is likely to become even more competitive as the C&C sector gradually comes to terms with the implications of the 'credit crunch.'

Assuming that the depiction of the above trends is correct and that policy makers' assumptions that qualifications are a proxy measure for the knowledge employers require continues, aspiring entrants are still going to struggle to gain access to the C&C labour market. In the case of graduates, this is partly because many are financially cushioned by their families or are prepared to engage in multiple job-holding or to accept fairly insecure and temporary positions in an attempt to develop the forms of vocational practice and social capital to gain access to the C&C labour market (Raffo et al., 2000). In the case of individuals holding pre-degree qualifications, access to employment in the C&C sector via network connection, coupled with employers in the C&C sector increasingly using what Marsden (2007) has referred to as 'tournament contests,' is exerting considerable 'downward' pressure on them. This term refers to the tendency of employers in the C&C sector to offer people starting positions on a temporary basis or as unpaid interns and then to determine whom they will retain after they have observed them working. Given the aforementioned forms of support that graduates can often call on, it is hardly surprising that they are in a stronger position to take advantage of such tournament contests.

In combination, these developments are likely in the current financial climate to exercise a suppression effect on the aspirations of people who lack financial and emotional forms of support and to position those who do have access to such support to take advantage of the port-of-entry positions that are either advertised in the C&C sector or uncovered from participating in C&C networks. Given policy makers' stated intention to use education to foster employability in the global knowledge-based economy and social mobility in society, a good way to begin to combat the preceding inequalities and to support the development of Moebius-strip expertise among all sections of the population is to consider how to use intermediary organizations to broker and advertise port-of-entry positions on a regional basis. This suggestion implies a radical re-thinking of transnational and national policies for education and training. The implications of the suggestion are explored in the concluding chapter of this book.

REFERENCES

Ashton, D. (1995). Understanding change in youth labour markets: A conceptual framework. *Journal of Education and Work, 6*(3), 5–23.

Bell, D. (1973). *The coming of post-industrial society: A venture in social forecasting.* New York: Basic Books.

Bilton, C. (2007). *Management and creativity: From creative industries to creative management.* London: Blackwell.

Boltanski, L. & Chiapello, E. (2005). *The new spirit of capitalism.* London: Verso.

Coffe, D. (1996). *Competing in the age of digital convergence.* San Franscisco: Jossey Bass.

Deuze, M. (2007). *Media work.* London: Sage.

Doz, Y., Santos, J., & Williamson, P. (2001). *From global to metanational: How companies win in the knowledge economy.* Harvard: Harvard Business Press.

Drucker, P. (1969). *The age of discontinuities.* London: Transaction.

European Commission (EC). (2000). *Memorandum on lifelong learning.* Brussels: EU.

Florida, R. (2002). *The rise of the creative class.* New York: Basic Books.

Ghoshal, S. & Bartlett, C.A. (1997). *The individualized corporation.* New York: Harper Business.

Grabher, G. (2003). Learning in projects, remembering in networks? Commonality, sociality, and connectivity in project ecologies. *European Journal of Regional Studies, 11*(1), 103–120.

Green, F. (2006). *Demanding work: The paradox of job quality in the affluent economy.* Princeton, NJ: University of Princeton Press.

Guile, D. (2007). Moebius-strip enterprises and expertise: Challenges for lifelong learning. *International Journal of Lifelong Education, 26*(3), 241–261.

Guile, D. (2010a). *The learning challenge of the knowledge economy.* Rotterdam: Sense.

Guile, D. (2010b). Learning to work in the creative and cultural sector: New spaces, pedagogies and expertise. *Journal of Education Policy, 25*(5), 465–484.

Hesmondhalgh, D. (2002). *The cultural industries.* London: Sage.

Hesmondhalgh, D. (Forthcoming). Cultural and creative industries. In Bennett, T. & Frow, J. (Eds.), *The Sage handbook of cultural analysis.* London: Sage.

Hesmondhalgh, D. & Baker, S. (2011). *Creative labour.* London: Routledge.

Howkins, J. (2001). *The creative economy.* London: Penguin.

KEA European Affairs. (2006). *The economy of culture in Europe.* Retrieved from http://ec.europa.eu/culture/eac/sources_info/studies/economy_en.html.

Knorr Cetina, K. (1999). *Epistemic communities.* Harvard: Harvard Education Press.

Lash, S. & Urry, J. (1994). *Signs and spaces.* London: Sage.

Lave, J. & Wenger, E. (1991). *Situated learning: Legitimate peripheral participation.* Cambridge: Cambridge University Press.

Lundvall, B.-Å. (1996). *The social dimensions of the learning economy.* Working papers. DRUID: Copenhagen Business School, Department of Industrial Economics and Strategy & Aalborg University, Department of Business Studies.

Marsden, D. (2007). Labour market segmentation in Britain: The decline of occupational labour markets and the spread of 'entry tournaments.' *Economies and Societies, 28,* 965–998.

McRobbie, A. (Forthcoming). Be creative: Making a living in the new culture industries. London: Sage.

Organisation for Economic Co-operation and Development (OECD). (1996). *The knowledge-based economy.* Paris: OECD.

Porter, M. & Ketels, C.H.M. (2003). *UK competitiveness: Moving to the next stage.* London: DTI.

Quah, D. (2003). Digital goods and the new economy. In Jones, D. (Ed.), *New economy handbook.* San Diego: Academic Press.

Raffo, C., O'Connor, J., Lovatt, A., & Banks, M. (2000). Attitudes to formal business training amongst entrepreneurs in the cultural industries: Situated business learning through 'doing it with others.' *Journal of Education and Work, 13*(2), 215–230.

Reich, R. (1991). The work of nations: Preparing ourselves for 21st century capitalism. New York: Vintage.

Robertson, S. (2008). 'Producing' the global knowledge economy: The World Bank, the knowledge assessment methodology and education. In Simons, M., Olssen, M., & Peters, M. (Eds.), *Re-reading education policies: Studying the policy agenda of the 21st century* (pp. 235–256). Rotterdam: Sense.

Ross, A. (2003). No-collar: The humane workplace and its hidden costs. New York: Basic Books.

Tapscot, D. (1995). *The digital economy*. New York: McGraw Hill.

Tuomi-Gröhn, T., & Engeström, Y. (Eds). (2003). Between school and work: New perspectives on transfer and boundary crossing. Amsterdam: Pergamon.

U.K. Treasury. (2005). *The UK financial services sector: Rising to the challenges and opportunities of globalisation*. Retrieved from www.guidance-research.org/future-trends/ banking/links.

Work Foundation. (2008). *The knowledge economy: How knowledge is reshaping the economic life of nations*. Retrieved from www.theworkfoundation.com/research/publications/.

World Bank. (2003).*Lifelong learning for a global knowledge economy*. Washington, DC: World Bank.

World Bank. (2008). Knowledge for development (K4D): Knowledge Assessment Methodology (KAM). Retrieved from http://web.worldbank.org/kam/.

CATHERINE CASEY

THE LEARNING WORKER, ORGANIZATIONS AND DEMOCRACY

INTRODUCTION

The modern cultural aspiration toward participatory democratic citizenship continues to be highly valued and striven for in the contemporary West. Although there is much recognition of democracy's many imperfections and everyday political practices that fall well short of democratic ideals, many social and political theorists argue for the continued applicability of models of democratic civil society to our present times (Archibugi et al., 1998; Held, 1993; Touraine, 1997). They argue that a revision and revitalization of democratic ideas and practices enables a crucial response to contemporary counter-modern and counter-democratic forces, such as fundamentalisms and authoritarian regimes, and their powerful effects. Similarly, debates over the meaning and role of citizenship in contemporary society, especially through the current course of European integration, are robust (Alexander, 1998: Andrews, 1991; Shafir, 1998; Turner, 1993) and efforts continue toward advancement of effective civil society. Further contributions to these debates are found in discourses on lifelong learning and education for persons, for communities, and societies (Delors, 1996; Demaine & Entwistle, 1996; Forrester, 2003).

Yet, notwithstanding these efforts to retrieve and revitalize democratic ideas and citizenship rights, some powerful currents of thought and practice in the everyday world of work and organizations at the present time serve not so much to extend and encourage democratic civil society values and practices but – perhaps unwittingly – to oppose them. In comparison with two or three decades ago in the West many workplaces, especially large and corporate ones, are *less* rather than more, conducive to the expansion of worker participation, the democratization of systems of authority and control, and lifelong educational and developmental opportunities for workers. Many production organizations require workers' integration not through democratic citizenship, but through conformity to elite-established rules and systems. Movements toward industrial and organizational democracy effective through much of twentieth century (Blumberg, 1973: Crouch & Heller, 1983; Durand, 1994), which sought the education of workers for their participation in management practices – including rule-setting, job design, and reward systems – and for the expansion of civil society rights and responsibilities, have manifestly lost ground. A decline in trade union membership and political effectiveness, and new obstructions to putting in place workplace participatory

D.W. Livingstone and D. Guile (eds.), The Knowledge Economy and Lifelong Learning: A Critical Reader, 317–333.

structures and self-management which seemed in the 1960s and 1970s realizable goals (Gorz, 1985; Kester & Pinaud, 1996; Szell, 2001) are apparent in many industrial sectors.

At the same time, economic and political leaders currently espouse a drive toward learning economies and learning societies as the key to success in rapidly expanding knowledge-based economies of production and exchange. In view of this heightened interest in learning economies and learning societies, which Western governments in particular are now emphasizing (e.g., Archibugi & Lundvall, 2001; European Commission 1999, 2000; Reich, 1991), it may seem paradoxical that there is a decline in forms of workplace learning highly valued a generation ago. These workplace learnings include not only advancement of practical occupational and job skills but education and learning for democratic participation and for human development within and beyond the workplace (Dewey, 1966 [1916]; Freire, 1973; Hoggart, 1957; Leyman & Kornbluh, 1989).

The reasons for the decline in older models of worker learning for the democratization of organizations and for lifelong human development, and for the rise of knowledge-based economies and demands for 'learning organizations' are complex. While a full discussion of these matters is beyond my task here, I wish in this article to discuss two matters arising from recent economic and technological developments that have direct bearing on conceptualizations of lifelong education and on democratic citizenship. The first is an exposition of some crucial flaws in current demands for learning organizations that are set in economic and managerial discourses and the conceptions of worker-learners these models espouse. The second poses an alternative construct to the managerial framework that restores the working person to the centre of concerns, and which may restore avenues for a renewed congruence between socio-political notions of democracy and citizenship, and the workplace. Both of these aspects have many implications for the theory and practice of lifelong education. It is helpful to offer first an explanatory discussion of the organizational level of focus in the learning economy debates, especially as this level is under-addressed in lifelong learning discourses. A fuller discussion of the learning worker then follows.

KNOWLEDGE-BASED ECONOMIES, ORGANIZATIONS AND LEARNING

In recent decades many observers have theorized the expansion of a post-industrializing economy that has altered many of the production practices and social structures of modern industrial society. The rapid advance of new electronic and computer technologies of production, communication, and financial exchange and the rise of post-Fordist, flexible and contingent organizational forms and deregulated labour markets (Castells, 1996; Harvey, 1989; Heckscher, 1988; Kochan et al., 1995) are effecting considerable changes to the world of work and organizations. These economic developments, characterized by an intense drive for rationalization and efficiencies, are generating changes to organizational practices, to workplace life, and to workers' experiences of work. At the everyday level, they manifest, for example, in demands for organizational restructuring, for downsizing, for flexible employment relations, such as temporary jobs, longer or shorter working hours, and for intensified worker productivity. Many of these developments occur in conflict with other social and cultural aspirations, such as for secure employment, social inclusion, community development, and quality of working life.

The impact of advanced production and information technologies, and the neo-liberal economic reforms of the 1980s that encouraged a deregulation of economic institutions, have stimulated a globalization of markets for production and exchange. In market environments characterized by heightened complexity and uncertainty, economic and business leaders now promote a drive toward product and process innovation and for knowledge-rich production of goods and services. At the political level, these developments are expressed in demands for developed countries to become 'learning economies/learning societies.' At the organizational level of this discourse, new theories of organization and management place emphatic attention on generating 'learning organizations' for the achievement of innovation and advantage (Boisot, 1998; Senge, 1999; Stewart, 1997).

The complex impact of these economic, technological, and organizational developments includes alterations to modern conceptions of organization and workers, and of workers' education and learning. Mid-twentieth century organization theory conceived workers, like other parts of the organization, as functionaries for organizational purposes and ends.[1] But they also held an implicit recognition that organizations were contested terrain and that workers had divergent and potentially counter-organizational rationalities of their own. Hence organization theorists focused considerable attention on the problems of control, compliance and integration. These were practical organizational problems with respect to problematic workers – and their trade unions – which rational organizational design and management structure could functionally negotiate and manage. However, these approaches to organizational analysis and management practice were also practically influenced by currents of thought and action in the broader society.

Notwithstanding organizational management's interest in achieving worker compliance and control and persuading workers of the superior functionality of rational organizations, organizations also responded, for several decades, to political demands expressed in social democratic movements in the wider civil society. Among these demands were calls for humanistic workplace relations, for participatory workplace structures and for the advance of industrial democracy sensibilities. Across most Western societies worker education movements gained both at-work and paid-leave opportunities for education and training from job training, health and safety, negotiation and management skills, to self-directed learning for human and social development (Burns, 1995; Casey, 1995; Charnley, 1975). Among their accomplishments were reforms to enforced systems of labour process and many vital improvements in workplace conditions and quality of life (Heckscher, 1988; Kester & Pinaud, 1996; Szell, 2001). The famous models of worker participation and self-management structures, notably in Sweden and Germany, reached their heyday in the 1970s and 1980s.

But these decades were also experiencing the effects of the application of advanced electronic and computer technologies in production, communication, and financial exchange. Heightened competition, market uncertainty, and rapid innovation exacerbated managerial anxiety and stimulated retrenchment. Under the guise of a liberalizing deregulation, reassertion of management power and control consequently arose. Management theorists argued that new practices of organizational design and management were required to respond to the new economic and production environment. The result has been the emergence of a neo-rational *strategic* management. Contemporary strategic management endeavours to pragmatically deal with increased organizational complexity in highly informated and globalizing market environments (Harvey, 1989; Preece et al., 2000; Senge, 1990; Storey, 1989). The model, which privileges rational strategic action exclusively on the part of managerial elites, demands internal organizational conformity to hyper-efficiency, contingency, and innovation. It favours a dynamic management of contingent and flexible organizational forms and employment relations. Accordingly the model deals, too, with the management-perceived inefficient and disruptive competing intra-organizational currents of organizational democracy, workers' participatory demands, and worker education and learning for plural personal and socio-cultural ends.

It is within this trajectory of post-industrial, knowledge-based and continuously innovating production, and strategic neo-rational management, that notions of the learning organization have arisen and gained much contemporary currency. The concept of the 'learning organization' is premised on an idea that human knowledge as human capital is now the principal productive force in contemporary capitalism (Boisot, 1998; Harvey, 1989; Senge, 1990, 1999; Stewart, 1997; Reich, 1991). The learning organization is now extolled as the pivotal agent in technological innovation and competitive success. A heightened re-privileging of managerial agency in organizational design and behaviour represses or ignores the implicit recognition and legitimacy of the role of political action on the part of workers' unions and their demands for participatory forms of industrial organization and for individual lifelong learning.

The humanistic, participatory reforms which industrial democracy and adult education movements advocated, in which worker education enhanced both practical skills and personal development, now give way to *strategic organizational learning* models serving singular organizational business imperatives. These find expression, for instance, in management decisions, including about the retention or discarding of labour, with decisions being oriented solely according to the business organization's 'core business' of profit making and shareholder satisfaction. At the same time strategic models champion innovation in production and process in order to gain strategic advantage. The logic of hyper-rationalization simultaneously requires organizational and worker learning to accomplish strategic innovation in production and conformity to contingency. These are immense demands of both workers and organizations.

Strategic management's emphasis on learning in organizations privileges the organization as the learner – it is abstracted, collective learning in order for the organization to respond and innovate that is regarded as the singular imperative of learning organizations. The learning needs of the organization, as defined by management, override or occlude attention to the needs of individual learning workers. Individual learning is legitimated solely according to criteria for its contribution to organizational learning. Moreover, in the managerial model, even attention to interactive learning, which one might assume to be learning occurring among interacting human actors, has largely concentrated on the institutional level – on the effects of inter-organizational interactions on the functioning of economic institutions, particularly industrial organizations (e.g., Lundvall, 1988; Lundvall & Borras, 1997).

These current conceptions of organizational learning, which entail an acute abstraction of the individual person as learner, eschew competing approaches to work and organization, especially those that envision work, and workers, as more than instrumental economic activity. The definition and legitimation by managerial elites of key concepts in contemporary debates on learning workers and learning organizations has immense implications for the theory and practice of lifelong education, and for the prospects of revitalizing a correspondence between social notions of citizenship and democratic participation in the workplace. Most pressingly, are the implications ensuing from a further pivotal element in the hyper-rational managerial model, that of the 'human resource.'

THE HUMAN RESOURCE

The trend toward hyper-rationalized models of production, organization and management, and for lean, tightly controlled operations, requires a correspondingly altered conception of the worker, and of worker learning. A principal concept of the learning organization, which underpins the successful shift of worker-focused lifelong learning to a managerial one, is the notion of the 'human resource.' The concept emerged in the 1980s (see discussions in, e.g., Guest, 1987; Kochan et al., 1995; Whittington, 1993; Wright & McMahan, 1992) and gained rapid popularity in economic, management, and organizational theory and practice. Although the concept clearly manifests a privileging of organizational system rationalities and managerial priorities, its use is now widespread and virtually taken for granted. It is even employed in traditionally more humanistic adult education literature (e.g., Knowles et al., 1998). The term has displaced former concepts such as personnel and staff, and encouraged a view of management as the legitimately dominant party in industrial management. With respect to current policies and programmes toward the development of learning organizations and learning workers, the widespread utilization of the concept of the human resource affects conceptions of knowledge and learning and narrows the options for worker education.

The managerially-framed model of learning organizations conceives the worker, (which is a term evoking older connotations of an integrated relation between the person, her knowledge and skill, and the doing of work) as being more readily strategically utilized by rendering as a 'human resource.' As an abstracted component in the organizational production process, like other production resources of material and plant, the worker is rationalized into correspondence with rational management. As a human resource, the worker is an object of utility for the organization, and accordingly of its overtly privileged stratum of agentic management. The worker's human needs, interests, aspirations and irrationalities are eclipsed and rationalized by the technical resource imperative of the organization. The needs of the organization are, in this model, determined and normalized by a managerial cadre, which practices a strategic utilization and management of resources toward their attainment (Porter, 1991; Whittington, 1993; Storey, 1989).

The managerial organizational concept of human resource has direct implications for contemporary understandings of organizational learning and worker learning in a politically promoted learning economy. Within the apparently widely accepted logic of instrumentally rational organization, the concept of human resource is put forward as a sensible, pragmatic organizational concept. An implicit convergence of managerial interests with organizational ones – a common ideology in contemporary managerialist organization studies – presents the concept as legitimate, descriptive and neutral. Indeed, while it may well serve to delegitimize or marginalize the demands of workers and trade unions for humanistic conceptions of the worker, the term is regularly employed by trade unions and worker educators.

The model of the ideal learning organization proposes a rational alignment of workers with the organization's rational techno-economic imperatives. The organizational level of learning in the managerial perspective requires institutional reform toward facilitating the strategic selection of innovative ideas, knowledge pursuits, technological developments and ways of doing things. Consequently, organizational learning is framed by a focus on learning directed to the tasks of selection, coordination and retention of practical and theoretical productive knowledge. It includes the extraction and codification of workers' personal capacities, tacit knowledge and affective creativity. It also includes strategic containment of worker knowledge. The strategic championing of selected knowledge forms is directed toward instrumentally-defined organizational goals pursued in organizational environments conceived as highly competitive and increasingly global. Illustrations of this approach are readily found in training programmes for organizational and workplace learning (e.g., Garvin, 2000; Marquardt, 1996; Senge, 1990, 1999; see also Boud & Garrick, 1999 for further discussion on this point).

However, the idealized managerial model of the learning human resource rationally aligned with the learning organization in a learning economy contains a fundamental oversight. Notwithstanding strong demands for technological innovations and economic efficiencies at the organizational level in the forced correspondence of the rationalized worker, organizations are also sites of myriad human activities and learning agenda. As numerous studies have shown workers, who rarely behave as ideal human resources, try to exercise various forms and degrees of control over their learning processes and those of the collective organization (Burawoy, 1985; Casey, 2002; Jermier et al., 1994; Kunda, 1992). As long as workers with the demonstrated propensity for diverse learning at work and in other arenas of adult life are reduced to the status of human resource for distant others' ends, and denied recognition of their multiple needs and motivations, underlying tensions will frustrate and delimit their learning potential – for themselves and the organization. Irrespective of remunerative incentives, soft motivation campaigns, or more overt disciplinary and coercive means, workers performing a resource-defined role will find ways to contain and withhold not only their expertise but their commitment.

A widening and reframing of the currently dominant management approach allows for a re-imagination of organizations as sites for the development and practice of innovative human relations in the organization of production, work, and self-creation. Such a re-conception of the managerially framed notion proposes more convivial concrete organizations and personnel, and importantly enables a substantive realignment of the notion of the learning economy, currently extolled by the advanced industrialized countries, with socio-cultural development and democratic citizenship in which learning and education are more broadly conceived.

Recognizing the limits of abstract instrumental rationalities embedded in the managerially focused agenda for enhanced organizational learning allows for a response to diverse expressions of workers' interests and demands in their organizational experiences. Such recognition motivates a turn away from human resource concepts. It allows for a re-conceptualization of knowledge beyond monological instrumental terms. It elevates a more complex notion of the learning person working in and co-constituting a learning organization. A conceptual shift of this magnitude may have advantageous consequences in both practical techno-economic outcomes and in socio-cultural goods particularly those of lifelong learning for human developmental ends.

Immediately, a fundamental problem presents to worker educators: the task of encouraging organizational learning beyond its conventionally delimited frameworks of resource dependency, role socialization, and instrumental utility. Turning to consider the individual learner sheds some light on this task.

INDIVIDUAL LEARNERS AND LEARNING

The technical reduction of humans to organizational utility abstracts *instrumental* rationality from a *substantive* rationality of socio-cultural ends. It elides an ethic of human subjectivity as end in itself into an undifferentiated instrumental rationality. This ethically devoid utility not only debases the human experience of organizational work – even if production efficiencies and market advantage are expanded – it ultimately truncates the potential for human initiative and creative imagination. It is the latter that comprise rich resources not only for innovation and organizational success in strict economic terms, but for organizational transformation in more comprehensive ways. The facilitation of greater development of persons working for more than a singular rational and economic imperative recognizes work as potentially self-fulfilling and socially participatory.

323

Although contemporary managerial organization theory exerts a strong hold over concepts of learning and knowledge in organizational life – subjugating contrary conceptions in adult education discourses – an interruption of its one-dimensional trajectory is conceivable and practicable. The everyday life of organizations readily exhibits to any close observer myriad competing rationalities among individuals and groups of workers. These competing rationalities and currents of interest manifestly challenge and interrupt the officially, solely privileged instrumental rationalities of economy. As adult educators have long known, the learning gained and pursued by workers is diverse and oftentimes contradictory to that desired by organizational managers and trainers (Boud & Garrick, 1999; Casey, 2002; Lewin & Rigine, 2000). The challenge in the arena of education for workers within a learning-seeking organization is to recognize, address and accommodate multiple motivations and agenda in learning needs and aspirations.

This suggestion does not require that the realist recognition that an organization comes together by and large for the pursuit of a primary set of rational purposes be set aside. But it does require recognition that the pursuit of a primary set of purposes – especially when those purposes are determined by controlling elites – is always in relation to intersecting and competing unofficial purposes with varying attachments and investments. A managerial view of this form of organizational diversity regards it as a problem for organizational managers faced daily with the task of achieving more or less a rational order of things and outcomes. But recognition of these diverse interests is a necessary step for a creative repositioning of the dominant and impoverished managerial view. Surrendering the singular privileging of instrumental rationality, and its concomitant conceptions of organizational design and process, which drives contemporary learning economy and learning organization imperatives opens up rich possibilities for organizational life. A concept of the learning organization that goes beyond an instrumental logic entails a restoration of person-centeredness to learning. It recognizes that workers have multiple life interests in which their performance of organizational labour is just one.

A RE-CONCEPTUALIZATION OF THE LEARNER AS WORKER–SUBJECT

As a first step in moving organizational learning and worker training away from conventional managerial models, and in opening up possibilities for richer lifelong educational opportunities in the workplace and beyond it, I propose a new, or perhaps it is revitalized, concept of the learner as a worker and as a subject. This concept imagines the learner, not as rationalized, abstracted human resource and object of organizational utility, but as a subject who works, desires, and learns. I turn now to elaborate this concept and explain its vital role in organizational innovation and in the restoration of democratic citizenship in the so-called learning economies. The questions orienting this discussion are: Who is the learning worker? What is her/his relationship with the learning organization?

The conventional answer to those questions can be readily discerned in prevailing organizational approaches to education and training of workers. In privileging the organization's needs for particular developmental trajectories, for skills and competencies generating product innovation and production efficiency (Garvin, 2000; Marquardt, 1996; Senge, 1990, 1999) the learning worker is rendered simply as a smart component. Moreover, in serving economic organization needs, the majority of vocational education, worker training, and human resource development has focused on socialization and training of individuals for participation in industrial institutional roles specifically for employing organizations and generally in a work-based society. As critics have pointed out, these approaches have practised a schooling-type socialization function of the under-socialized adult worker into either occupational roles or, more specifically, predetermined organization roles as employees (Boud & Garrick, 1999; Casey, 1995; Leymann & Kornbluh, 1989; Littler & Salaman, 1984). This social reproductive model has been much criticized in recent decades in the education of children (Bourdieu & Passeron, 1990; Popkewitz, 1987; Wexler, 1987). But the discourses on organizational learning and worker education and training – as human resource training – have largely ignored the critical arguments in education. Instead, a heightened emphasis is placed on organizational systemic needs for specific learning and knowledge utilization directed toward optimization of production.

The contemporary hyper-rational model of organization, which reduces human actors in organizational activity to objects of utility, runs contrary to humanistic theories and practices of education, especially the principles of lifelong education. For lifelong education to include learning and development in the workplace – where the vast majority of adults spend much of their lives – these impoverished and one-sided conceptions must be redressed and surpassed. But the challenge to surpass the hyper-rationalized conceptions is considerable. Not only are hyper-rational economic and managerial discourses powerfully effective, but other immensely influential currents of thought in recent decades pose distinctive challenges. Postmodern theories in particular have both contested and aggravated modernity's rationalization trajectories. Postmodern theories have thoroughly deconstructed the humanist 'man'[2] conceived within the frame of modernist rationalization. But postmodernism poses an anti-humanism and risks a totalizing system of subjectification, a no-self alternative to autonomous, rationally acting man. Neither conception is satisfactory. Notwithstanding the considerable influence of the postmodern turn, a number of philosophers and social theorists argue, notably since the 1980s, for a critical alternative that rejects both exclusive humanism and anti-humanism. Among these important currents of thought (of which space precludes elaboration) is the postulation of a notion of a non-autonomous, relational subject acting within and against currents of social dynamics. These theories argue for a reintegration of humanity with nature (Toulmin, 1990) and a restoration of ethical ideals in the domain of human institutions (Bauman, 1993; Melucci, 1996; Taylor, 1989; Touraine, 1995).

Drawing on this body of thought I endeavour to outline below a re-conceptualization of the person at work, and of the learning worker. In particular, I draw on the thought of French sociologist Alain Touraine (1995, 1996) in ways that bear direct application to the tasks of organizational re-conceptualization beyond the neo-rational model, to the education of workers and the revitalization of democracy. Touraine's comprehensive critique of modernity and his rejection of postmodern subjectification (1995) lead to his theorization of a concept of the Subject. The Subject, for Touraine, is an idea of the human person that refuses reduction to rationalization. The subject is neither a product of power as conceived by contemporary structuralist and Foucauldian theorizations, nor is it reduced to a rationally choosing economic agent as neo-liberal theorists purport. Touraine's subject refuses both traditional identifications and subjectifications *and* the rationalization and instrumentalization of personal and collective life (1996, p. 297). Rather, the human subject is, for Touraine, one who seeks freedom and creation, autonomy and relatedness, reason and affect and spirit. It is this subject – the resistor of the demands of instrumentality – who is able to act and to create.

Subjectivation – the process by which one becomes an acting, self-creating, subject – is achieved through 'an individual's will to act and to be recognized as an actor' (Touraine, 1995, p. 207). Subject–actors construct personal self–projects through the events of their lives and strive to create spaces for autonomy and freedom. Furthermore, for Touraine, in the process of subjectivation the individual constructs its individuation against the world of economic rationalities and commodities and the world of community, and it succeeds in its individuation as it is able to unite instrumental rationality and relational identity. The subject strives for its subjectivation in all dimensions of life, not least in its working life.

This notion of a complex subject who resists and appropriates rationality and affectivity is an important one for the theory and practice of lifelong education. The recognition of contemporary workers seeking subjectivation – against long class histories of *subjectification* at work – demands a substantive shift in the conception of workers and in organizational arrangements accommodating them. Notwithstanding, or in spite of, the demands of hyper-rationalized organizational workplaces, my own research (Casey, 2002) and that of other analysts of contemporary work practices (Handy, 1997: Lewin & Rigine, 2000; Rifkin, 2000) observes much evidence that many people are demanding, often in idiosyncratic ways, self-expressive, self-creating space. These include efforts toward bodily and affective well being (as in various mind–body therapies, Yoga, alternative health practices and so forth), spiritual quests, and identity constructions around sexualities, ethnicities, and ecological sensibilities, and community building. These efforts indicate self–creation struggles and alternative value setting to that privileged in an overly rationalized technocratic workplace. Their practitioners are seeking agentic subjectivation in creating their lives and acting in the world.

If we take this notion of the subject into organizational life, we are faced with a very different notion of the worker, as an agentic, learning, relational person whose actions and choices are more than instrumentally rational. The managerially defined human resource, a notion that epitomizes the reduction of the person to a commodified object of instrumental utility is disrupted. The conventional strategic management conception of the human resource and its concomitant conceptions of organizational learning and human resource development must be rescinded. A re-conceptualization of the learning worker as a self–creating subject at work – as a subject–worker – makes possible the stimulation of new concepts and forms of knowledge. It demands theoretical and institutional changes toward a more complex grasp of learning and development in a social economy. This turn of the subject–actor, for which there appears growing evidence in the rise, for instance, of identity movements, religio-cultural value demands, and political–economic pluralisms (Casey, 2002; Castells, 1997; Lewin & Rigine, 2000; Melucci, 1996; Rifkin, 2000), makes possible the stimulation of participatory processes in organizational life which are vital to the reinvention of organizations and work practices, and of democracy in post-industrial societies.

SUBJECTS, ORGANIZATIONS, LIFELONG EDUCATION, AND DEMOCRACY

Having sketched out a moral ideal for organizational worker–learners to be re-conceptualized as subjects, possessing complex desires and imperatives for agency and creation, let us turn to consider how production organizations – and educators working at the organizational level – may accommodate and utilize a new concept of learning workers, and of learning organizations. Managerial approaches to learning and knowledge creation focus on rational and strategic learning. A richer conception confronts the challenge of facilitating and shaping multiple learning agenda. A vision of lifelong education encompassing workplace learning recognizes the validity of both rationally useful and intrinsically developmental learning. As such it demands a congruence of organizational and production activity with substantive socio-cultural values. That is, rational production imperatives must be met alongside the subject–worker's demands for personal value and active participation in organizational life. Organizations which continue to practise a narrow agenda of management-defined instrumental learning among workers, and retain the transmission of education and training of workers in traditional ways, for example, via expert professional to deficient worker, the learning accomplished will reflect that model. It will typically produce specific and delimited knowledge for problem solving within conventional frameworks. Conformity and compliance to alienating production systems generate expected outcomes which include a measure of productivity gain, but exacerbate rebelliousness, dissent, and strategic withholding of worker commitment and intelligence.[3]

A conventional managerial approach to worker learning which fails to recognize the more complex needs and interests of worker learners and obstructs efforts toward worker participation and organizational democracy produces only conventional learning outcomes. As a consequence, neither the organization nor the worker learns in ways more appropriate to contemporary post-industrial conditions. In other words, despite growing complexity in production and trading systems in globalizing markets, the expansion of post-Fordist, flexible, contingent organizations, and growing socio-cultural diversity, a narrowly conceived instrumental, resource-based model of organizational learning fails to deal with contemporary complexities and diverse currents of demands – in effect denying or suppressing the realities of both.

For Touraine, the idea of the subject and its relation to social institutions requires in the first instance a refusal. The worker as Subject refuses the monological instrumental rationality privileged in the organization's reduction of labour to an apparatus of production. This refusal entails a rejection of concomitant notions of worker learning. Notions of worker learning and organizational learning which are conceived solely in terms of their strategic functionality or dysfunctionality for the organizational system are rendered grossly inadequate and redundant. A more appropriate conception for the development of education and training in organizations recognizes that the worker is neither an anonymous object of utility, nor a disengaged, a – social individualist. Rather, the worker conceived as a subject is a relational person with individual and collective desires and goals, selectively employing instrumental rationalities, affective sensibilities and substantive socio-cultural values toward her/his self-creation projects.

The recognition and facilitation of a complex learning agenda, rather than its suppression and denial as in managerial models of organization and human resource learning, enables a conception of production organizations which are constructed according to the dynamics of participation, negotiation and collective goal setting. The rejection of human resource models opens admission to organizational complexity beyond both functionalist utility and elite ideological control. It conceives the ability of individuals to combine their diverse skills and imaginations for the attainment of common, collectively negotiated, goals. Their collective productive intelligence depends on coordination, mutual adjustments and personal initiatives in common work. This alternative ideal of learning workers and their production organizations – as an accomplishment of revitalized models of lifelong education in conjunction with organizations – engenders an expansion and revitalization of democratic process within organizational life and potentially in social life more broadly.

Relinquishing concepts of knowledge as solely an instrumental resource that must be abstracted from commodified workers enables a vital organizational innovation. Concomitantly, the admission of an ideal in which the person at work is conceived as a subject with life interests and personal projects beyond those of the world of work and employing organizations allows for a legitimate but morally delimited role of instrumental rationalities and their institutionalization in contemporary organizations. It delimits the demands for education and training for innovation and organizational competitiveness. And it repositions the elevated, ideological position of managerial control over worker knowledge.

The organization that integrates these cognizances and institutionalizes these values produces and allows dynamic action capable of transforming the organization beyond the industrial vision. It breaks with the instrumentally congealed modernist conceptions of organizations and takes up the collective task of creating learning organizations appropriate to a post-industrial society. It makes possible not only new forms of socially constructed organizational action for productive and economic goals, but action admitting new dynamics of creativity. These dynamics are the key to practical innovations in technology and labour process, as they are key to socio-cultural innovations resulting from the value demands of subject–workers, and subject–citizens. A generative interface between political notions of a learning economy and socio-political aspirations for participatory citizenship beyond juridically defined notions is consequently opened up.

Of course, these demands for organizational re-conceptualization and relinquishment of managerial holds over the terms of debate are scarcely palatable to managerial interests and to organizational learning models conceived in that framework. But a dynamic conception of organizations recognizes that setting the terms and agenda of organizational learning is a political process and not necessarily a forgone conclusion that workers must accept. When participatory avenues are closed, consequences manifest in the passive demands of disaffected employees in the withholding of competence and the pursuit of alternative self-satisfying expression.[4] Such outcomes are typically seen as obstructions to organizational learning and innovation. But a re-conceptualization of organizational knowledge and worker learning in accordance with the recognition of the subject status of the working person can mitigate those obstructions and contribute to the construction of new organizational institutions, including those for participatory structures of governance and management. Recognition, rather than suppression, of the political contest over the stakes of organizational life is a key condition of these changes.

A learning organization conceived as comprising learning worker–subjects is capable of institutional transformation of a nature rarely admissible by instrumentally driven conventional organizations. The implications for the theory and practice of lifelong education are immediate. Adult educators must fully enter the debates on learning occurring at the level of production organizations. Their vital contribution to re-setting the agenda for the education of workers for agentic, political participation toward plural goals, which include economic goals and non-economic, cultural goals; emancipation and self-determination, rests on a full recognition of the needs of workers in plural, democratic societies. Furthermore, a re-conceptualization of 'human resources' and of learning in organizations to reflect the moral ideal of the Subject makes possible a renewed and effective link of organizational practice with broader cultural notions of citizenship. The revitalization of citizenship and of civil society is given further strength by demanding a correspondence between citizens of civil society and citizenship in organizational workplaces. Development of capacities for self-directedness, cooperative endeavour, trusted utilization of expertise, and for participatory management relations in the workplace reflects and encourages the revitalization of models of civil, democratic society.

CONCLUSION

The subjugation of notions of personhood at work, and of substantive socio-cultural ends of rational economic activity, is widely commonplace in today's workplaces. For many analysts and practitioners, including those most closely involved with workers through education and training, an apparent acceptance of dominant rationalization imperatives relegates discussion of human – and planetary – interests to an abstract, impractical, philosophy. Others, too, may dismiss an appeal for a reintegration of rationality and causality, humanity and nature, as a seeming reiteration of Enlightenment or modernist humanism. But the propositions I have sketched out are neither. Re-conceptualizing the learning worker is vital for both the articulation of a moral ideal, and for the imagination of learning organizations and learning economies beyond their currently truncated conceptions.

The idea of the subject is a principal key in the conceptualization of both new forms of knowledge and the substantive socio-cultural ends of knowledge. This subject, which modernity in part both inspired and repressed, is increasingly demanding new and re-imagined social arrangements. Cultural currents of self-expressivism, identity movements, ecology and ethical debates represent some iterations of the newly demanding subject (Casey, 2002; Lewin & Rigine, 2000; Melucci, 1996; Rifkin, 2000). It is this subject who demands lifelong learning in diverse interests and pursuits. Within a movement toward a globalizing learning economy a sophisticated organizational strategy arises in the recognition of the demands of the would-be subject and a strategic alignment with the moral ideal struggling for articulation in these demands. The attention of theorists of lifelong education to the goings-on of economic organizations and to the organizational level of learning is vital. Their involvement has the potential to assist organizational practices, particularly educational ones, to serve more than instrumentally rational economic ends and to restore human workers to a central focus. A conception of lifelong education for active, desiring, creating subjects may contribute to the development of innovative and sophisticated organizations. Both may stimulate renewed potential for a revitalization of democracy and the reduction of social fragmentation. In a globalizing economy, political and organizational competency in managing complex socio-cultural demands may prove a key factor in shaping the nature of economic globalization. Such competency requires the crucial recognition that workers are, above all, people whose capacities for knowledge, action and life far exceed those required by production.

NOTES

[1] There is, of course, an extensive literature on organization theory in sociological, economic, and management traditions. Structural-functionalist theories exerted considerable influence for many decades; see notable works such as Bendix (1974 [1956]), Blauner (1964), Etzioni (1970), Parsons (1960), or Casey (2002) for further discussion.

[2] See, in particular, the works of Michel Foucault and subsequent Foucauldian theorists criticizing the conception of humanist man as an autonomous individual acting in rational self-interest as though abstracted from and unconstrained by social and cultural institutions.

[3] Note the rise of 'open sourcing' knowledge sharing among computer workers and software programmers that belies the corporate boundaries of organizational knowledge and intellectual property.

[4] Numerous examples of these include deliberate mediocre performance, elaborate practical joking, and playing fantasy games on the internet. See, e.g., Casey (2002), Jermier et al. (1994), Kunda (1992) for further discussion.

REFERENCES

Alexander, J. (1998). *Real civil societies: Dilemmas of institutionalization*. London: Sage.

Andrews, G. (Ed.). (1991). *Citizenship*. London: Lawrence & Wishart.

Archibugi, D., Held, D., & Kohler, M. (Eds.). (1998). *Re-imagining political community*. Stanford, CA: Stanford University Press.

Archibugi, D. & Lundvall, B. (Eds.). (2001). *The globalising learning economy*. New York: Oxford University Press.

Bauman, Z. (1993). *Postmodern ethics*. Oxford: Blackwell.

Bendix, R. (1974 [1956]). *Work and authority in industry*. Berkeley & Los Angeles: University of California Press.

Blauner, R. (1964). *Alienation, freedom and technology*. Chicago: University of Chicago Press.

Blumberg, P. (1973). *Industrial democracy*. New York: Schocken.

Boisot, M. (1998). *Knowledge assets: Securing competitive advantage in the information economy*. Oxford: Oxford University Press.

Boud, D. & Garrick, J. (Eds.). (1999). *Understanding learning at work*. London: Routledge.

Bourdieu, P. & Passeron, J.C. (1990). *Reproduction in education, society and culture*. London: Sage.

Burawoy, M. (1985). *The politics of production*. New York: Verso.

Burns, R. (1995). *The adult learner at work*. Chatswood, AUS: Business and Professional Publishers.

Casey, C. (1995). *Work, self and society: After industrialism*. London: Routledge.

Casey, C. (2002). *Critical analysis of organizations: Theory, practice, revitalization*. London: Sage.

Castells, M. (1996). *The rise of the network society*. Oxford: Blackwell.

Castells, M. (1997). *The power of identity*. Oxford: Blackwell.

Charnley, A. (Ed.). (1975). *Paid educational leave: A report of practice in France, Germany and Sweden*. Frogmore, UK: Hart Davis Educational.

Crouch, C. & Heller, F.A. (Eds.). (1983). *Organizational democracy and political processes*. Chichester: John Wiley.

Delors, J. (1996). *Learning: The treasure within*. Paris: UNESCO.

Demain, J. & Entwistle, M. (Eds.). (1996). *Beyond communitarianism: Citizenship, politics, education*. London: MacMillan.

Dewey, J. (1966 [1916]). *Education and democracy*. New York: Free Press.

Durand, J.-P. (Ed.). (1994). *La fin du modele Suedois*. Paris: Syros.

Etzioni, A. (1970). *Complex organizations*. New York: Holt, Rinehart, Winston.

European Commission (EC). (1999). *The European employment strategy*. Luxembourg: Office for Official Publications of the European Communities.

European Commission (EC). (2000). *A Memorandum on lifelong learning*. Working paper, SEC (2000)1832. Brussels: European Commission.

Forrester, K. (2003). Leaving the academic towers: The Council of Europe and the Education for Democratic Citizenship Project. *International Journal of Lifelong Education, 22*(3), 221–234.

Freire, P. (1973). *Education for critical consciousness*. New York: Continuum.

Garvin, D. (2000). *Learning in action*. Boston: Harvard Business School Press.

Gorz, A. (1985). *Paths to paradise*. London: Pluto.

Guest, D. (1987). Human resource management and industrial relations. *Journal of Management Studies, 24*(5), 503–521.

Handy, C. (1997). *The hungry spirit: Beyond capitalism*. London: Hutchinson.

Harvey, D. (1989). *The condition of postmodernity*. Oxford: Blackwell.

Heckscher, C. (1988). *The new unionism*. New York: Basic Books.

Held, D. (Ed.) (1993). *Prospects for democracy*. Cambridge: Polity.

Hoggart, R. (1957). *The uses of literacy*. London: Penguin.

Jermier, J., Knights, D., & Nord, W. (Eds.) (1994). *Resistance and power in organizations*. London: Routledge.

Kester, G. & Pinaud, H. (1996). *Trade unions and democratic participation in Europe*. Aldershot: Avebury.

Knowles, M., Swanson, R., & Holton, E. (1998). *The adult learner: The definitive classic in adult education and human resource development*. Houston: Gulf.

Kochan, T., Locke, R., & Piore, M. (Eds.). (1995). *Employment relations in a changing world economy*. Cambridge: MIT Press.

Kunda, G. (1992). *Engineering culture*. Philadelphia: Temple University Press.

Lewin, R. & Rigine, B. (2000). *The soul at work*. New York: Simon & Schuster.

Leymann, H. & Kornbluh, H. (1989). *Socialization and learning at work*. Aldershot: Avebury.

Littler, C. & Salaman, G. (1984). *Class at work*. London: Batsford Academic.

Lundvall, B.-A. (1988). Innovation as an interactive process. In Dosi, G., Freeman, C., Nelson, R., & Silverberg, G. (Eds.), *Technical change and economic theory* (pp. 349–369). London: Pinter.

Lundvall, B.-A. & Borras, S. (1997). *The globalising learning economy: Implications for innovation policy*. Report DGXII. Brussells: European Union Commission.

Marquardt, M. (1996). *Building the learning organization*. New York: McGraw Hill.

Melucci, A. (1996). *The playing self: Person and meaning the planetary society*. Cambridge: Cambridge University Press.

Parsons, T. (1960). *Structure and process in modern societies*. Glencoe, IL: Free Press.

Popkewitz, T. (Ed.). (1987). *The formation of the school subjects*. New York: Falmer.

Porter, M. (1991). Toward a dynamic theory of strategy. *Strategic Management Journal, 12*(S), 95–117.

Preece, D., McLoughlan, I., & Dawson, P. (Eds.). (2000). *Technology, organizations and innovation*. London: Routledge.

Reich, R. (1991). *The work of nations: Preparing ourselves for 21st century capitalism*. New York: Alfred Knopf.

Rifkin, J. (2000). *The age of access*. New York: Tarcher Putman.

Senge, P. (1990). *The fifth discipline: The art and practice of the learning organization*. New York: Random House.

Senge, P. (1999). *Challenges of sustaining momentum in learning organizations*. New York: Doubleday.

Shafir, G. (1998). (Ed.). *The citizenship debates*. Minneapolis: University of Minnesota Press.

Stewart, T. (1997). *Intellectual capital: The new wealth of organizations*. New York: Doubleday.

Storey, J. (Ed.). (1989). *New perspectives on human resource management*. London: Routledge.

Szell, G. (2001). *European labour relations*. Aldershot: Gower/Ashgate.

Taylor, C. (1989). *Sources of the self: The making of modern identity*. Cambridge, MA: Harvard University Press.

Toulmin, Stephen. (1990). *Cosmopolis: The hidden agenda of modernity*. Chicago: University of Chicago Press.

Touraine, A. (1995). *Critique of modernity* (Macey, D., Trans.). Oxford: Blackwell.

Touraine, A. (1996). A sociology of the Subject. In Touraine, A., Clark, J., & Diani, M. (Eds.), *Alain Touraine*, (pp. 291–342). London: Falmer.

Touraine, A. (1997). *What is democracy?* (Macey, D., Trans.) Boulder, CO: Westview.

Turner, B. (1993). *Citizenship and social theory*. London: Sage.

Wexler, P. (1987). *The social analysis of education*. New York: Routledge.

Whittington, R. (1993). *What is strategy – And does it matter?* London: Routledge.
Wright, P. & McMahan, G. (1992). Theoretical perspectives for strategic human resource management. *Journal of Management, 18*(2), 259–320.

MICHAEL YOUNG

EDUCATION, GLOBALIZATION AND THE 'VOICE OF KNOWLEDGE'[1]

INTRODUCTION

This paper starts from a problem that is perhaps better expressed as a contradiction. On the one hand 'Knowledge' has undoubtedly become the major organizing category in the educational policies of international organizations and many national governments. Global similarities are increasingly apparent – whether they are expressed with reference to knowledge itself, to the knowledge society, to knowledge workers, or to The Knowledge Promotion,[2] as the recent reforms of Norwegian secondary education are referred to. On the other hand the category 'knowledge' appears to be used in an almost entirely rhetorical way; the meaning of knowledge is at best implicit[3] and at worst virtually empty of content. One consequence is that such policies deny or disregard the idea that access to knowledge in the strong sense that involves its claims to reliability is central to the whole purpose of education. Thus, what I shall refer to in this paper as the 'voice of knowledge' (following Moore, 2007) as a distinctive factor shaping educational policy, is lost. If I have accurately identified this trend and it continues, it is a highly problematic heritage that we leave to future generations – namely, that there is no explicit knowledge that it is important enough to be 'transmitted' to the next generation. It is a heritage that has none of the visibility of the environmental or sustainability crises, although arguably, addressing it is fundamental to whether we are able to deal with either.

The aim of this paper is to explore this apparent contradiction and to begin to develop an alternative that takes the idea of the 'voice of knowledge' seriously. An issue that I touch on, but only by implication, is whether significant strands of the social sciences (and sociology in particular) may be part of the problem of denying a 'voice' for knowledge rather than being the basis for offering a viable alternative for the future (Young & Muller, 2007, p. 2009).

The paper has five sections. Section 1 provides a number of examples of how knowledge is interpreted in international educational policies and raises the question, 'Why knowledge?' What purpose does such a focus on knowledge have in today's educational policies? My examples are drawn from the educational policies of international organizations such as the World Bank and new national curricula and national education policies (my illustrations are from Norway and England). I also refer briefly to the work of the Portuguese sociologist, Buoaventura de Sousa Santos, a leading critic of globalization, to indicate the

D.W. Livingstone and D. Guile (eds.), The Knowledge Economy and Lifelong Learning:
A Critical Reader, 335–347.

terms within which the debate about education and the knowledge economy among globalizers and anti-globalizers has largely been set. My argument is that, despite treating knowledge as a main organizing category, international and national policy makers *and their critics* in effect by-pass what I (following Rob Moore) mean by the 'voice of knowledge.'

Section 2 begins to make explicit what the idea of the 'voice of knowledge' in educational policy might mean. It starts from a paper by Moore (2006) in which he draws on the critical realist tradition in the philosophy of science and establishes the epistemological basis for the idea of the 'voice of knowledge' in education. However, in my view, despite its strengths, critical realism does not move us very far towards conceptualizing a more adequate role for knowledge in educational policy.

Section 3 builds on Moore's ideas by arguing that the key idea implicit in a realist theory of knowledge is *knowledge differentiation*. This idea is elaborated through a brief account[4] of the ideas of the French philosopher, Gaston Bachelard. Section 4 considers the educational implications of the idea of the social differentiation of knowledge with reference to the work of Durkheim, Vygotsky, and Bernstein. Section 5 builds on Section 4 to explore five forms of knowledge differentiation as they apply to the curriculum. Section 6 concludes the paper by returning to the idea of the 'voice of knowledge' as a shaper of educational policy.

KNOWLEDGE AS THE NEW GLOBAL NARRATIVE

The striking thing about the many publications of international organizations and governments that refer to knowledge and the knowledge economy is that they don't feel the need to ask the question 'What is this knowledge that we are referring to?' Its meaning is simply taken for granted. As Susan Robertson (Robertson, 2007) puts it in a recent paper which started me thinking about this issue: 'Who can be against knowledge?' It is not therefore surprising, she writes 'that the idea of knowledge articulates with the left as well as the right.' In U.K. terms, this use of 'knowledge' is an example of a characteristic New Labour or 'third way' doctrine – it includes everything, it sounds progressive (or at least modernizing) but it says nothing substantive.

It is the word knowledge, rather than the related term 'information' that has caught on as the key category in the new education policy literature. I suspect that the reason for this is that, despite its multiple meanings and absence of any referents, the word *knowledge* does retain a public association with ideas such as certainty, reliability, and objectivity and even truth. Reference to knowledge therefore provides a kind of authority for policies that do not have to be justified in other ways. The authority of the term knowledge is taken over but not the basis of its claims.

A brief glance at documents produced by international organizations and governments indicates that the idea of knowledge acts as a license for a whole range of educational policies that have little directly to do with knowledge in the more specifically epistemological sense. Two examples of widely supported educational policies illustrate this point. The first is the emphasis on maximizing learner choice and the associated tendency for learning to become little more than another form of consumption. In a world dominated by learner choice knowledge looses all its authority. The second example is the popularity of the slogans 'personalized learning' and 'individual learning styles' and the gradual replacement of the terms education, school and college with their assumed elitism by learning and learning centres. This is not to underplay the importance of learners having an active role in any educational process as any level. It is rather to highlight the importance of distinguishing between the everyday or common sense knowledge that is acquired by individual learners in specific contexts and the idea that we acquire powerful knowledge (Young, 2009) to take us beyond our everyday experiences (Karpov & Heywood, 1998). If this distinction is blurred or seen as unimportant, the role of teachers is reduced to little more than facilitation and support and we are not a million miles away from the idea of 'user-generated knowledge' that is associated with YouTube and Facebook (Keen, 2007).

My argument is that an empty and rhetorical notion of knowledge and the increasing tendency to blur distinctions between the production of knowledge and its acquisition and between knowledge and skills – the latter unlike the former being something measurable and targetable – becomes a way of denying a distinct 'voice' for knowledge in education. Furthermore excluding such a 'voice' from educational policy most disadvantages those learners (and whole societies, in the case of developing countries), who are already disadvantaged by circumstances beyond the school.

Illustrations of this 'emptying of content' can be found in the educational policies of many countries; I will mention two briefly: England and Norway. Since the end of the 1980s, but increasingly in the last decade the control of public education in England has been centralized under the Department of Education and Skills (DFES). Schools, local authorities, examination boards and research councils have increasingly taken on the role of agencies delivering government policy. The DFES now has two departments – the Department of Innovation, Universities and Skills (DIUS) and the Department for Children, Schools and Families(DCSF) – that as with all government departments are now regulated under a public service agreement (PSA) which governs the funds they receive from the Treasury.[5] The PSA for Education has five objectives broken up into 14 sub-objectives. All refer to generic targets and none make reference to any specific knowledge or curriculum content. Another illustration that is more obviously closer to what goes on in schools and colleges comes from the requirements laid down by the government for the new diplomas for 14–18 year olds.[6] These requirements set out in considerable detail the packaging, module combinations, credit levels and pathways for the diplomas, but make only minimal reference to content. Targets which are based on a common set of levels, and common units for measuring volume of learning have priority over reference to specific contents. The implications are that what might be assumed to be distinctive to formal education – the acquisition of specific knowledge – is treated as relatively unimportant. Institutions are held accountable and students assessed in terms of outcomes that are not content-specific.

The new Norwegian[7] curriculum reforms follow a similar trend. They are known, significantly, as The Knowledge Promotion;[8] the new Norwegian curriculum is defined by five basic skills and a seven-part quality framework; each of the twelve criteria have to be reflected in the teaching of the different subjects; subject syllabuses no longer prescribe specific contents. It is this combination of basic (generic) skills and a quality framework, not the knowledge content of subjects which is built into the legislation, drives teaching, and defines what students have opportunities to learn, and how they are assessed.

A rather different example of the evacuation of knowledge, is found in the publications of the radical Portuguese sociologist, Buoventura de Sousa Santos, now largely based at Wisconsin. It illustrates how the approach taken to knowledge by at least some the Left-wing critics of globalization and the role of international agencies leads to a similar evacuation of content. De Sousa Santos works are widely read in Brazil and he has played a key role in the Global Social Forum. In Brazil I have heard him spoken of as the new Paulo Freire. What he refers to as his 'epistemology of absent knowledges' claims to goes beyond what he sees as the 'blindness' of western science. He refers to it in a paper in the *European Journal of Social Theory* in the following terms:

the epistemology of absent knowledges starts from the premise that *social practices are knowledge practices*. The nonscience-based practices, rather than being ignorant practices, *are practices of alternative rival knowledges*. There is *no a priori reason to favour one form of knowledge against another*. (Sousa de Santos, 2001, p. 270, emphasis added)

Starting from a critique of mainstream economics, de Sousa Santos is trapped in a framework that associates epistemologies with particular social groups or world regions. The result is a concept of knowledge that equates it over-simplistically with power,[9] and is as empty, despite its radical rhetoric, as that of the World Bank.

THE 'VOICE OF KNOWLEDGE'

What then might the idea of the 'voice of knowledge' that I have argued is increasingly absent in educational policies mean? I begin with what Moore (2007) identifies as its four elements; it must be, he argues:

- First, *critical*: that is, open to revision and embody a fallibilist notion of truth;
- Second, *emergentist*: in recognizing that knowledge is not reducible to the conditions of its production or the activities and interests of those involved;
- Third, *realist*: in recognizing that the objects of knowledge of both the natural and social worlds are realities that (a) are independent of our perception of the world and (b) provide limits to how we can know about the world; and

- Fourth, *materialist*: in recognizing that knowledge is produced (and acquired) in specific historically created modes of production, or in Bourdieu's terms, intellectual fields.

Knowledge, it follows, from a realist perspective and in the sense that I as an educationalist use the word,[10] can be differentiated from the meanings we construct to make sense of the word in our everyday lives; it is not created by learners or even by learners with their teachers; it is acquired.

Although these propositions form a sound basis for any serious enquiry into the role of knowledge in education, the terms in which they are set are too general for them to be a basis on their own, for drawing any conclusions about educational and more specifically, curriculum policy. I will comment briefly on each proposition and suggest that the key underlying concept that can be derived from them and needs developing is the *differentiation of knowledge*.

Proposition 1 refers to fallibility. The idea of fallibility or 'openness to critique and revision' is usually associated with the natural sciences. However it is no less important in the humanities and social sciences. Different concepts of fallibility arise from the ways in which different knowledge domains subsume the particular under the general.[11] However fallibility is always understood as being 'within a tradition or a discipline' The dangers of breaking the link between 'openness to critique' and a tradition within which critique is located are well demonstrated by Anthony Kronman, the former Dean of Humanities at Yale. In his book *Education's Ends: Why have American universities given up on the meaning of life?* (Kronman, 2007) Kronman describes how after the 1960s many humanities faculties in the United States rejected any notion of tradition and focused only on critique; this left them, he argues, open to the most extreme forms of relativism and political correctness.

Proposition 2 refers to Emergence. This is the idea that powerful knowledge is the product of social conditions or contexts that do not wholly determine it. Examples might be the science laboratory or the classroom. Archives, libraries and the internet can also be conditions for the emergent properties of knowledge to be generated. However this does not take place, as is sometimes assumed, in isolation from teachers or members of other 'communities of specialists.' These originating 'contexts' will leave their mark on the knowledge acquired and produced in them. However what makes powerful knowledge' powerful is its independence or autonomy from the specific contexts of its origin. Let's take an example. The English chemist Robert Boyle needed to be wealthy enough to build the laboratory on his estate in which he discovered what became known as Boyles' Law. However today's aircraft designers do not need to read Steven Shapin's (1995) account of the gentry culture of which Boyle was a part to understand and apply his law about how gas volumes change under pressure.

Emergence is a less straightforward idea in the social sciences. For example, Max Weber's concept of ideal types has emergent properties that account for why it remains fruitful to this day. However only a few sociologists will be familiar with the debates Weber had with the Marxists in the German Social Democratic Party which led him to formulate the idea. Contemporary sociologists could well

339

gain additional sociological insights into Weber's ideas by reading Marianne Weber's account of his life in ways that would not be true for physicists reading Shapin's account of Boyle's life, however interesting they might find it.

Proposition 3 refers to the *real* basis of knowledge; in other words that our claims to knowledge are not just claims; they say something about the world that is not dependent on how we conceive of it. If the sociology of knowledge is to say anything about the curriculum it must provide a theory that distinguishes between knowledge and non-knowledge-whether this is expressed as experience, opinion, belief or common sense. Likewise, if the nature of the objects of knowledge (our theories) limits what we can know about reality, we need to know how they are differentiated between different domains when we come to make decisions about the curriculum.

Proposition 4 refers to the *materiality* of knowledge production and acquisition – that these processes do not take place anywhere but in particular social contexts with specific rules and forms of organization. This idea of the materiality of knowledge production points to the importance of research into different forms of specialist knowledge communities and their role (and often their lack of role) in the design of curricula. In the United Kingdom, vocational education programmes preparing students for different occupational fields vary widely in how they interpret their knowledge base. Much of this variation can be explained in terms of the different roles that professional associations have in the design of programmes at pre- or non-professional levels.[12]

The conclusion that I draw from this brief discussion of Moore's four propositions about knowledge is that they have to be developed further. One way of doing this is through the idea, implicit in each proposition, that knowledge is socially differentiated. Section 3 draws on the French philosopher, Gaston Bachelard's historical epistemology to present an way of developing this idea.

THE SOCIAL DIFFERENTIATION OF KNOWLEDGE

The idea that there are real structured differences between types of knowledge that are not dependent on our perceptions – in particular between scientific and non-scientific knowledge – lies at the heart of the work of Gaston Bachelard, the French philosopher of science. In the United Kingdom, his work has been largely associated with Louis Althusser's flawed attempt to construct a 'scientific' Marxism. However, and here I draw largely on Christopher Norris' account, this is to miss the broader importance of Bachelard's work. Norris (2000) points out, rightly, I think, that Althusser, presumably for political reasons, misinterprets Bachelard and relied on 'a misplaced "scientific" rigour that seeks to emulate the physical sciences in fields where different criteria apply' (p. 190). This habit, Norris argues, gives rise to 'various kinds of false analogy and wire-drawn metaphors' which find no justification in Bachelard's own work. Furthermore, Bachelard's epistemology is more historically grounded than that of critical realists such as Bhaskar; it focuses on distinct episodes in the history of the physical sciences. For this reason it is more useful for clarifying what the 'differentiation of knowledge' might mean in sociological terms.

The following points are a necessarily over-simplified summary of the aspects of Bachelard's theory of knowledge which have particular relevance for the concerns of this paper; they are drawn largely from Norris' discussions:[13]

- Bachelard establishes a basis for distinguishing science from pre- (or non-) science that has parallels with Lakatos' distinction between 'progressive' and 'degenerating' research programmes;

- he has a theory of how knowledge progresses from 'less efficient' to 'more efficient' concepts through the process of 'conceptual rectification and critique,'

- he provides examples from the history of science of how knowledge 'progresses' by tracing the discontinuous development of ideas such as the 'atom' from the Greeks 'atomism' to modern atomic theory. In each case he shows how ideas are transformed from being largely metaphorical into increasingly precise and testable 'scientific' concepts;

- he recognizes that a theory of knowledge must begin from 'the current best state of knowledge in the field concerned' – in other words, where a discipline is currently at;

- he proposes a methodology for distinguishing between two kinds of historical enquiry which Norris argues are often confused in contemporary discussions – *histoire sanctionee* – the history of the growth of science (this focuses on those early steps, like Lavoisier's discovery of the role of oxygen in combustion, which led to further advances) and *histoire perimee* – the history of past scientific beliefs (those which were later rejected as leading nowhere. One of Bachelard's examples in this case was Priestley's attempt to explain combustion with the idea of phlogiston; and

- his historical epistemology is underpinned by a trans-historical set of principles associated with rigour, clarity, conceptual precision, and logical consistency.

None of these proposals can be easily applied to the social sciences[14] and I am not aware of any attempt by Bachelard to extend his theory beyond the physical sciences.[15] However his focus on the *historical* conditions for the growth of knowledge in any discipline does not imply that it must be restricted to the physical sciences or that the idea of a historical epistemology must take physics or any particular science as its model. Also for Bachelard concepts are not just theoretical propositions; they are simultaneously embedded in technical and *pedagogic* activity – the material conditions for producing them. Thus he opens the possibility of a realist account of the differentiation and growth of knowledge and the role of educational institutions.

APPROACHES TO THE SOCIAL DIFFERENTIATION OF KNOWLEDGE:
DURKHEIM, VYGOTSKY, AND BERNSTEIN

This section takes further the idea of knowledge differentiation by drawing briefly on the work of Durkheim, Vygotsky, and Bernstein, three theorists who focus specifically on the differentiation of educational knowledge. Their analyses form

341

the basis, I suggest, for a research programme into the differentiation of educational knowledge as the principles for a theory of the curriculum. The significance and range of work of the three theorists is only touched on briefly here. I have explored their ideas in more detail elsewhere (Young, 2007).

Durkheim

As a sociologist rather than a philosopher of science, Durkheim's theory of knowledge is broader than Bachelard's; he does not limit himself to the physical sciences and he does not differentiate between scientific knowledge and knowledge in any broader sense. The differences that he identifies between knowledge and experience can be traced back to his early rejection of Kant's transcendentalism and to the concepts – 'sacred' and 'profane' – that he developed in his studies of religion in primitive societies. Durkheim initially used the sacred/profane distinction to describe the separation of religion and everyday life that he found in primitive societies. However the 'sacred' and the 'profane' became, for Durkheim, a basic distinction at the heart of all societies, even those that have become largely secularized. He saw the distinction as a form of social organization that was basic to science and intellectual thought; hence his reference to primitive religions 'proto-sciences.' Without the conceptual and social moves from the everyday world of survival to the sacred world of totemic religion that those early societies made, Durkheim argued, no science and no knowledge, and indeed no society, would be possible.

Vygotsky

Entering adult life and beginning his short career at the start of the Soviet Revolution, Vygotsky inevitably focused on the immediate problems facing teachers in the new society. His primary concern was with how teachers could help students to develop the higher order concepts that they would not have access to in their everyday lives. Like Durkheim, his theory was about the differentiation of knowledge and he also relied on a binary distinction – between two kinds of concepts – the theoretical (or scientific) and the everyday. For Vygotsky, the task of the curriculum, and schooling more generally, was to provide students with access to theoretical concepts in all their different forms – from history and literature to the sciences and mathematics. Furthermore, he saw that access to higher order concepts was not a simple one-way process of transmission but a complex pedagogic process in which a learner's everyday concepts are extended and transformed by theoretical concepts. From the point of the role of knowledge in education, the implications of Vygotsky's ideas are most clearly expressed in the work of the Russian Vasily Davidoff and his ideas of 'kernel knowledge' and learning as moving beyond the abstract and gaining a grasp of the concrete 'real' nature of things.

Bernstein

Bernstein (1971, p. 2000)[16] took Durkheim's ideas of knowledge differentiation further in a number of important ways. Here I will only refer to three brief points which focus on the issue of knowledge differentiation:

- With his concepts of 'classification' and 'framing' Bernstein developed Durkheim's idea of boundaries as the key social category separating types of symbolic meanings. He used these concepts to show how boundaries in education play a major role in the development of learner and teacher identities;
- Bernstein distinguished two types of educational boundary that are crucial for any curriculum theory – those between knowledge domains and those between school and everyday knowledge. He analysed the implications of both these types of boundary being blurred or dissolved; and
- Bernstein drew on Durkheim's concepts of the 'sacred' and the 'profane,' and his argument that the 'sacred' represented a kind of 'proto-science' to develop a distinction between forms of the 'sacred' which he expressed as vertical and horizontal discourses. In his last work (Bernstein 2000), he began to analyse the curriculum implications of these distinctions.

FORMS OF KNOWLEDGE DIFFERENTIATION AND THE CURRICULUM

In this section I want to comment briefly on *five* aspects of the social differentiation of knowledge that can be derived from the ideas of Durkheim, Vygotsky, and Bernstein and suggest that they could provide the basis for a theory of the curriculum that is based on the idea of the 'voice of knowledge.' Although aspect each has a distinct focus, there are overlaps between them and further conceptual clarification could no doubt reduce the number of types listed and define them more precisely.

The fundamental difference between knowledge and experience: Without this difference, which lies at the heart of Durkheim's social theory of knowledge, the idea of a curriculum is impossible. This has been demonstrated by the failed attempts of successive generations of progressive and radical educators to collapse the categories and construct an experience-based curriculum. The problems of the South African and Australian outcomes-based curricula, the English child-centred curriculum that followed Plowden and the more radical Queensland-based 'new basics curriculum' are among the many examples. Less publicized, but in social justice terms, even more damaging is the extent to which curricula based on the work experience of young people have been the basis of a wide range of vocational programmes which claim to offer educational possibilities to slow learners and those disaffected from schooling.

The conceptual separation of knowledge from experience was Durkheim's major point in his most explicitly philosophical book *Pragmatism and Sociology* (Durkheim, 1984). In that book he praised William James and the pragmatists for bringing philosophical questions about truth back to where he felt they should be located – in social life (or as he expressed it, in society) and not in academic philosophy. However, he criticized James and the pragmatists for having an

343

undifferentiated concept of the social and society and therefore at least implicitly equating it with experience. For Durkheim, experience is a powerful force but inadequate as an epistemological principle and no basis for reliable knowledge or for the curriculum.

The differences between theoretical and everyday knowledge: This is a narrower and more concrete expression of the first difference. If these differences are dismissed of blurred, it becomes increasingly difficult to make reliable decisions about what to include and exclude in the curriculum or indeed to say what formal education is for. There are two possible consequences of blurring the distinction between theoretical and everyday concepts. The first is that many kinds of knowledge are included in the curriculum, for broadly political reasons, which schools may not provide the conditions for acquiring sex and moral education as well as employment-related skills are examples. The second consequence is that the contents that may be the condition for acquiring theoretical knowledge are excluded or replaced (as in the recent proposals for the secondary science curriculum in England). Thus on the grounds of popular relevance or pupil interest, the opportunities that students have for acquiring systematic theoretical knowledge that can not be acquired elsewhere are restricted.

Without a specification of the differences between theoretical and everyday concepts as well as a focus on the relationships between them that go beyond the moral or political standpoints of those involved, curriculum decisions are inevitably reduced to politics.

The differences between knowledge domains: These differences refer to horizontal aspects of the intellectual division of labour in Durkheim's terms and what Bernstein describes as the classification of educational knowledge. A theory of knowledge differentiation presupposes that domain differences are not arbitrary but in some degree are the product of Bachelard's historical processes of 'rectification and critique.' An understanding of the extent to which domain differences such as those between disciplines and subjects have an epistemological as opposed to a merely conventional basis is crucial to the analysis of the links between domain boundaries, learner identities, and learner progress and to addressing the debate around multi-, trans- and inter-disciplinarity and the limits of modularization and student choice.

The differences between school and non-school knowledge: These differences follow from Vygotsky's distinction between theoretical and everyday concepts and my interpretation of Bernstein's concept of the framing of educational knowledge. However the differences between school and non-school knowledge have a specific importance in that they indicate why it is important to distinguish between the curriculum – as the conditions for acquiring new knowledge, and pedagogy – which refers to the activities of teaching and learning involved in the process of acquisition. This is a distinction that both Durkheim and Bernstein were somewhat ambiguous about. Both, but explicitly Durkheim, relied on an over-deterministic transmission model of education which played down the active role of the learner in transmission and the extent to which the recontextualization of school knowledge lies at the heart of pedagogy.[17] Vygotsky, on the other hand, was more sensitive to the complexity of pedagogic issues, but was less explicit about exactly what he meant by theoretical (or scientific) concepts. This maybe why the socio-cultural and socio historical activity theories of learning which locate their origins in Vygotsky's work have largely neglected the role of knowledge in formal education. From the perspective being developed in this paper, while pedagogy necessarily involves the teacher in taking account of the non-school knowledge that her/his students bring to school, the curriculum explicitly does not.

CONCLUSIONS

This paper began by noting the emptying of the concept of knowledge in the increasingly globalized debates about education and the knowledge economy and explored some of the implications of this trend in contemporary educational policy. In endeavouring to recapture knowledge as lying at the heart of the goals of all education, the idea of the 'voice of knowledge' does not divorce knowledge from knowers and hence from thinking and judgment. Rather it offers a counter to this divorce in much contemporary writing where thinking and learning are treated as if they were processes that can be conceptualized as educational goals independently of what the thinking and learning is about.

I have argued that the idea of the structured differentiation of knowledge is central to a more adequate conceptualization of its role in education. The paper focused primarily on the differentiation of school and non-school knowledge and discussed some of the dimensions of this differentiation and their educational significance. The growth of knowledge, whether in a subject like physics or history, or in an occupational field like engineering or financial management, and hence the opportunities for acquisition open to new learners whatever their age, will depend on the continued process of 'rectification and critique,' to return to Bachelard's apt phrase, by the various specialists involved. Making this process explicit is the task of a realist sociology of knowledge in relation to the curriculum, if the 'voice' of knowledge' is to shape educational policy and knowledge is not to continue to be an empty category. There is much to do.

NOTES

[1] I would like to thank Suzy Harris (Roehampton University) for her helpful comments on an earlier draft.

[2] See www.utdanningsdirektoratet.no/templates/udir/TM_Artikkel.aspx?id=2376.

[3] As in the case I recently came across of a lawyer whose new post was Head of Knowledge.

[4] My account draws on Christopher Norris' (2000:2005) excellent accounts of Bachelard's ideas.

[5] I am grateful to Professor Alison Wolf (Kings College, University of London) for pointing out to me the important role of Public Service Agreements and their potential influence on what counts as successful learning in school.

[6] See www.dcsf.gov.uk/14-19/index.cfm?go=site.home&sid=52.

[7] I mention Norway for two reasons; one is that I have recently visited two Norwegian universities and the other because Norway has often been celebrated by English researchers as representing a model of strong educational policy making (Payne 2002). My point is not to disagree with Payne but to suggest that this 'emptying of knowledge content' under the guise of promoting knowledge can be found even in a country as little prone to 'marketizing' and 'individualizing' tendencies as Norway.

[8] See note 1 above.

[9] Of course, knowledge is about power and 'the powerful' will always try to define what counts as knowledge. However it is not only about power; some types of knowledge *are* more reliable than others and we cannot afford to forget either aspect.

[10] It is what I and I imagine most teachers (and parents) want their students/children to acquire at school that they will be unlikely to be able to acquire at home.

[11] Joe Muller and I discuss this in an earlier paper (see Young & Muller, 2007).

[12] One of the most successful programmes of vocational education in England (in terms of progression both to employment and to higher education and professional level programmes) is that developed by the Association of Accountancy Technicians (AAT). A major reason for this is the key role played by the Institute of Chartered Accountants in England and Wales (the professional association of chartered accountants) with which the AAT is associated.

[13] A much more detailed account of Bachelard's epistemological theory is given by Mary Tiles (Tiles 1984) and by Christina Chimisso(2001) who locates her account in the context of Bachelard's work as a whole.

[14] Althusser's failed attempt to apply Bachelard's proposals to Marxism as a theory of capitalism and his use of Bachelard's idea of an 'epistemological break' are an illustration of the difficulties.

[15] George Canguilhem, who succeeded Bachelard at the Sorbonne, developed an influential historical epistemology with a focus on biology. However I have not considered his work in this paper.

[16] I have only referred to two of Bernstein's many publications here.

[17] Bernstein was the originator of the concept of 'recontextualization;' however he was more concerned with its role in the structuring of pedagogic discourse than as a way of conceptualizing pedagogy.

REFERENCES

Bernstein, B. (1971). *Class, codes and control* (Vol. 1). London: Routledge.

Bernstein, B. (2000). *Pedagogy, symbolic control and identity*. London: Taylor & Francis.

Chimisso, C. (2001). *Gaston Bachelard: Critic of science and the imagination*. London: Routledge.

De Sousa Santos, B. (2001). Towards an epistemology of blindness. *European Journal of Social Theory*, *4*(3), 251–279.

Durkheim, E. (1984). *Pragmatism and sociology* (Alcock, J., Trans.). Cambridge: Cambridge University Press.

Karpov, Y.V. & Heywood, H.C. (1998). Two ways to elaborate Vygotsky's concept of mediation: Implications for instruction. *American Psychologist*, *53*(1), 27–36.

Keen, A. (2007). *The cult of the amateur*. London: Nicholas Brealey.

Kronman, A. (2007). *Education's end: Why our colleges and universities have given up on the meaning of life*. New Haven: Yale University Press.

Moore, R. (2006). Going critical: The problems of problematising knowedge in educational studies. *Critical Education Studies*, *48*(1), 25–41.

Moore, R. (2007). *The sociology of knowledge and education*. London: Continuum.

Norris, C. (2000). *Deconstruction and the unfinished project of modernity*. London: Routedge.

Norris, C. (2005). *Epistemology*. London: Continuum.

Payne, J. (2002). A tale of two curriculums. *Journal of Education and Work*, *15*(2), 117–143.

Robertson, S. (2007). *Teachers matter ... Don't they?* Bristol: Centre for Globalisation, Education & Societies, University of Bristol.

Shapin, S. (1995). *The social history of truth*. Chicago: Chicago University Press.

Tiles, M. (1984). *Bachelard: Science and objectivity*. Cambridge: Cambridge University Press.

Young, M. (2007). *Bringing knowledge back in*. London: Routledge.

Young, M. (2009). What are schools for? In Daniels, H., Lauder, H., & Porter, J. (Eds.), *Knowledge, values and educational policy* (pp. 10–18). London: Routledge.

Young, M. & Muller, J. (2007). Truth and truthfulness in sociology of educational knowledge. *Theory and Research in Education, 5*(2), 173–201.

Young, M. & Muller, J. (2009). *Three scenarios for the future: Lessons from the sociology of knowledge*. London: London Knowledge Lab.

347

CONCLUSION

What is distinctive about this collection is that it has problematized – conceptually and empirically – the claims that a smooth transition to a knowledge-based economy (KBE) has occurred over the last forty years. In this final chapter, we draw together the strands of the different arguments presented and suggest that policy makers need to rethink the way in which polices for lifelong learning (LLL) are formulated so that: (1) individuals, employers and other interested parties (such as trade unions and local government) can contribute actively to the policy formation process to support the needs of labour as well as capital; and as a result, (2) such policies can articulate in a more meaningful way with the expanded conception of the KBE that emerges from our analysis.

Cumulatively, the contributions to this collection have provided ample evidence that the claims and assumptions of transformation to a knowledge economy are at least overstated. In terms of economic change, in spite of an acceleration of the information content of production systems, and in spite of much effort to construct the knowledge economy as a new 'imaginary,' inter-firm competition for profits continues to drive production relations, firm owners continue to negotiate with employees over profits and wages, and there is continual change in the techniques of production in a quest for greater efficiency. These defining features of the capitalist mode of production remain evident across all private enterprises, from steel mills to software companies. Of course, many specific aspects of production relations have shifted with the declining materials content, the increasing information content of many commodities, and the increasing cross hierarchical collaboration, as illustrated by the case studies in Section Two. Equally, there may be somewhat more discretion in task performance for more workers by dint of engagement of their minds in information processing and the emergence of greater entrepreneurial and epistemic activity on behalf of workers in some sectors of the economy. But there is little evidence in our case studies or the empirical research literature in general that 'knowledge workers' such as computer engineers and software designers have gained greater power over such policy matters as making decisions about the types of products or services delivered, employee hiring and firing, budgeting, or workload.

Secondly, in terms of educational requirements for jobs, the intensification of competitive labour markets, the growth of neo-liberal social policies, and policy makers' advocacy of qualifications as a proxy measure for the knowledge and skill required in the KBE have encouraged workers to engage in an educational arms race. One consequence has been that formal educational attainments have attained a paradoxical status. On the one hand, employers use qualification and the status of the institution in which they were acquired to screen job entrants irrespective of whether they are recruiting new or experienced staff. On the other hand, aspiring and experienced workers seek to diversify their qualifications by securing paid and unpaid work while they are still studying or on completion of their studies to

D.W. Livingstone and D. Guile (eds.), The Knowledge Economy and Lifelong Learning: A Critical Reader, 349–360.

enhance their status with employers. At the same time, external labour markets are growing either as a result of employers choosing to make employment contract-based or because the contracts that employers' secure are for a shorter duration than in the past, or both. Hence, primary coping strategies for workers are continually escalating as they struggle to obtain as many formal credentials and other qualifications and experiences as possible to enhance their own prospects. In this context, the line between over-qualification and oversupply of skilled applicants for available work has become increasingly blurred. Although a well-established line of empirical research in contemporary paid work settings confirms that formal qualifications increasingly exceed job requirements (Berg, 2003; Felstead et al., 2002; Livingstone, 2009), a preoccupation with qualifications deflects researchers and policy makers' attention away from the diverse forms of knowledge, or intangible capital, that workers need and accumulate from their ongoing lifelong learning.

PERSISTENCE OF LIFELONG LEARNING

Well-established fields of empirical research on adult learning (e.g., Tough, 1971), workplace learning (e.g., Billett et al., 2008; Boreham et al., 2002; Evans et al., 2006; Felstead et al., 2009; Hoyles et al., 2010; Livingstone et al., 2010; Rainbird et al., 2004) and working knowledge (e.g., Gherardi, 2006; Harper, 1987; Johnson, 1979) all suggest that informal learning has been of overwhelmingly greater magnitude than formal training in learning how to perform most jobs as well as many other adult activities. This claim can, however, be deceptive; all too often it appears to imply that there is little or no relation between formal and informal learning. The reality is more complex. Specialized formal knowledge is becoming more prevalent in most forms of paid employment, but informal learning in occupational fields that require specialist knowledge is also becoming more salient. Informal working cultures in occupational fields and the interplay between different occupational cultures are becoming increasingly critical, both for effective performance of productive work, as many of our case studies (e.g., the Bechky chapter) illustrate, and also to facilitate the development of individuals or fields and tools of practice, as other case studies (e.g., the chapter by Nerland) illustrate. Yet, policy makers regrettably continue to miss the significance of this issue when formulating policies for lifelong learning and employers are inclined to ignore or take it for granted (see Casey's chapter).

We can agree with knowledge economy theorists that decreasing focus on material handling and increasing focus on information processing involve a greater proportion of the labour force engaging in more sustained cognitive activity at work, as well as greater reliance on cognitive formal qualifications for jobs. This means that there are greater cognitive requirements for remaining material handling jobs (e.g., as with the biscuit makers in Bakker et al.'s chapter). But most employed and prospective workers are managing to keep up to or ahead of most of these requirements through continuing formal and informal 'lifelong' learning (e.g., the computer literacy of many workers that is greater than that which their jobs require), even though this is unrecognized by most policy makers. In the case studies in this book and in a growing body of empirical research literature (e.g., Livingstone, 2009, 2010), workers' informal job learning continues to be much more extensive than formal training. A few recent studies suggest that informal learning related to unpaid housework and community work may be even more relatively extensive as well as significant for paid work (Livingstone, 2010). Through 'expansive' learning on or off job (e.g., the chapter by Fuller et al.), in response to general life conditions ('use-value' in the Sawchuk chapter), and in interplay with other colleagues, social networks, and widely accessible information forums (in all case study chapters), workers are continually gaining more really useful knowledge. The bulk of the direct evidence here and elsewhere indicates that the labour force in most advanced industrial societies is managing to keep up to or ahead of the changing knowledge requirements for jobs in these societies. This is because workers can in the main, unless they require access to highly specialized technological resources, use their work-based lifelong learning to enhance their knowledge and skill. Problems crop up, however, for people who have either not yet entered the labour market or who have been made redundant because they lack the work-based opportunities to engage in forms of lifelong learning relevant to employment opportunities. We return to this issue below.

INTELLECTUAL PROPERTY VERSUS KNOWLEDGE ACCESS

At the same time as workers engage in more advanced formal education and extensive informal learning related to their jobs, the contest among private firms to gain and protect intellectual property rights for profit maximizing grows apace (as the Carlaw et al. chapter traces). Hence, a contradiction between widely accessible public knowledge and restricted access to knowledge for private gain tends to increase. There are at least three general directions and a more circumscribed direction that workers can take in order to deal with this contradiction. The general directions are:

1. to continue to accept the knowledge economy imaginary that insists on greater learning efforts from the labour force as an inherent demand in future jobs. This entails a continuing escalation of the educational arms race and increasing individual competition for available jobs;

2. to use existing and emergent social networks to nurture and increase recognition for working knowledge and to share working knowledge with employers in reformed 'learning organizations' in hope of ensuring continuing firm profitability and decent wages with new knowledge-intensive commodities; and

3. to use increasingly widely accessible production knowledge to mobilize for workplace democratization with greater power to workers, for worker self-management, or for worker ownership, any of which might eventually lead to transformation from the capitalist mode of production to forms of economic democracy.

The latter more specific direction is to:

4.   act entrepreneurially and establish small/micro businesses to secure contracts for work. This option is to some considerable extent sector- and experience-specific, but is nevertheless a viable option for workers who have accumulated the right mix of vocational practice and social capital.

As the critical analyses throughout this book suggest, option (1) is currently predominant. In terms of option (2), the case studies illustrate some of the expansive learning environments that have been developed effectively in some current organizations. Option (3), genuine workplace democratization, appears to be less imminent, although various recent instances have occurred (see Ness & Azzellini, 2011). Option (4) is restricted to sectors, such as the creative and cultural (C&C) sector, where the growth of external labour markets and contract-based commissions and employment is prevalent. The basic point is that the contradiction between growing accessibility to strategic knowledge for socially useful production and restricted access to such knowledge for private profit must be resolved in some fashion for information-rich production systems to continue to function. This clearly means that, firstly, the knowledge-based economy is not, as Jessop (this volume) noted, an organic economic development. Secondly, whatever one's political desires, a primary objective surely should be the fuller realization of workers' capacity to use their formal and informal working knowledge in the less idealized, more complicated view of a knowledge-based economy advanced in this collection.

FURTHER RESEARCH

Although we believe that these conclusions are generally accurate, they are still based on limited empirical research. While the basic arguments made in Section One about relations between economic conditions and educational requirements appear to be accurate for advanced industrial economies and their formal educational systems generally, further empirical research is needed to test their applicability across sectors. For example, there are still few grounded studies of the actual array of learning practices in new 'creative' sectors of the economy. There is growing attention to informal learning in paid workplaces (Malloch et al., 2010) and there are now some critical studies of relations between formal schooling and the actual needs of knowledge economies (e.g., Lauder et al., 2012). But there has been almost no recent research on the interrelations between formal education and informal learning in paid workplaces, learning related to unpaid work, or the interrelations between formal and informal learning in paid and unpaid work as these might affect conclusions about relations between job requirements and workers' actual knowledge in settings considered to be part of knowledge economies (see Livingstone, 2010).

The case studies in Section Two suggest that the interplay between formal qualifications and on-the-job informal learning as well as the interplay between occupational cultures are vital for the formation of workers' knowledge competencies and productivity. But the interplay between workers' competencies and their job requirements may be equally vital. The preoccupation of prior research has been on how workers' respond to and cope with job requirements imposed by an emergent knowledge economy. But in light of the general finding that many workers may have accumulated not only more qualifications, but also more work process knowledge (Boreham et al., 2003) than is formally required by their current jobs, an equally pertinent question is how workers' knowledge can positively affect job design, extent of skill utilization, and the sustainability of paid workplaces. Reversing this research optic may shed new light on the relations between workers' knowledge and job requirements in current paid workplaces, as well as prospects for *re*design of jobs.

LIFELONG LEARNING AND THE KNOWLEDGE-BASED ECONOMY: FUTURE DIRECTION FOR POLICY

The editors of this book have both acknowledged and criticized policy makers' prioritising and matching of formal learning and qualifications for entry to, and progress within, labour markets. In doing so, we recognize that there is a credible and plausible argument behind policy makers' actions, namely that the division of labour is predicated upon specialist qualifications and that employers do use qualifications as a proxy measure for the knowledge they require. Unfortunately, this fixation on qualification provides a very partial view of the role of knowledge in the economy, as all the contributors to this collection have demonstrated. A focus on qualifications has the effect of diverting attention away from the critical role that informal learning plays at work. Section 2 of this collection has highlighted the different guises of informal learning as a key resource for assisting firms to prosper and therefore generate employment. We are not alone in pointing this out. The contribution that informal learning, and by extension tacit knowledge, makes to economic development has been recognized and explored empirically in fields such as economic geography (Amin & Roberts, 2006; Gertler, 2003). Where research in this field adds substance to our argument is that it demonstrates the global scale and impact of what we referred to earlier as informal learning in specialist occupations. In combination with our argument, this suggests that informal learning is as vital to access as well as to development within the labour market.

In stating this conclusion, it is important to clarify the relationship between formal and informal learning and what was referred to in Section 2 as epistemic cultures (see the Nerland & Guile chapters) and the organization of work. In a nutshell, our argument is that the knowledge economy would not exist without such cultures. These cultures are, however, multifaceted rather than singular. They can be characterized, at a minimum, as discipline-based and occupation-based cultures. The former are responsible for generating the knowledge that constitutes the bedrock of curricula in formal learning, irrespective of the phase (primary, secondary, higher) or foci (professional, vocational). In contrast, the occupational epistemic cultures arise through an interplay between experts' desire to continue their individual learning (Jensen, 2012) and organizations nurturing that desire (see the Nerland chapter) or experts forming networks to address personal and occupational interests (Grabher, 2004; Grabher & Isbert, 2006).

Once we focus on the latter type of epistemic cultures and practices, we are able to see: (1) what is distinctive about the use of knowledge in the economy at the present time – it is the way in which all forms of knowledge, not just science, technology, engineering, and mathematical (STEM) research-based knowledge, are used to support the production of goods and services; (2) the contribution that tangible and intangible forms of knowledge make to the development of products and services; and (3) the use of knowledge to facilitate economic development is not a technical matter. It presupposes social and political debate about what knowledge is used and in what way: an issue that policy makers continually shy away from discussing with their electorates.

In the case of the former, policy makers may feel that they have addressed this issue. For example, the European Commission (EC) has developed a three-fold definition of learning: formal learning (i.e., learning that occurs in a structured context and that results in nationally recognized qualifications); non-formal learning (i.e., learning that is embedded in planned activities that are not explicitly designated as learning); and informal learning (i.e., learning that arises from daily life experiences and that traditionally does not lead to certification but may be subject to some form of accreditation/recognition) (Colardyn & Bjornavöld, 2004). This may appear to be the type of progressive development – because it offers a way to acknowledge the importance of different types of knowledge and learning – that addresses our concerns. However, at best, the EC's policy amounts to little more than a technical exercise of accrediting and agglomerating forms of knowledge and skill that are gained formally and/or informally, ones that had been previously disregarded (Guile, 2010).

This approach is a world away from offering encouragement for firms and individuals and other interested parties (such as trade unions and local government) to develop the type of epistemic cultures discussed above. From our perspective, the challenge for policy makers is to rebalance policies for lifelong learning so that they strike a better balance between: (1) encouraging the demand for, and the supply of, accredited skills, irrespective of their mode of learning; and (2) spreading epistemic cultures and their modes of informal learning through more companies and industrial sectors.

Addressing this challenge will involve policy makers in all countries re-thinking their top-down policies for lifelong learning. The great strength of this mode of policy making, as Sabel and Zeitlin (2008) have highlighted in an article on governance regimes within the European Union, is that it ensures clarity and consistency in both policy goals and mechanisms of delivery and evaluation. The downside, however, is that it can lead to rigid standardization and the presumption that centrally set policy goals can meet the needs of each region, firm, and individual as they struggle to survive in a fiercely competitive global market-based economy. Therefore, we put forward a series of new principles for policy makers to consider to help them to rebalance the tension between what can be referred to as the *logics of capital and labour*, and now supplement with the notion of the *logic of the market (i.e., 'demand-led) and state (i.e., supply-led) provision.* The principles are as follows:

1. To introduce 'heterarchical' (Jessop, 1998) modes of planning and delivery for educational policies.

At the macro government level, the state–market dichotomy in governance strategies, as Jessop (1998, 2000) has observed, has resulted at the macro government level in the constant substitution of one of these policies for the other. He argues that rather than trying to manage the relative change between states, markets, and globalization within one overall structure, what is required is the introduction of 'new balancing points' that enable policy makers to involve stakeholders more directly in the co-ordination process involved in managing that change Jessop offers suggest that this greater degree of collective-organization, which he refers to as, 'heterarchy' – constitutes the basis of an alternative mode of governance. From Jessop's perspective, heterarchical governance, coupled with autonomy at the regional level for determining how to deploy national funding streams, offers a potential key for unlocking the totality of the state-market interface at the macro-level.

There is insufficient space here to do justice to the complexity of Jessop's argument. We suggest, however, that his notion of heterarchical governance can be usefully extended to a way in which policy and provision for lifelong learning could be rethought. To illustrate what we mean, we here extrapolate from the case study on the development of apprenticeship in Guile's chapter and made a more general argument about the design, or more accurately the co-production, of workplace training. It is our contention that this approach is vital not only to the transformation of training in existing industries, but also to ensure that emerging industries, such as the 'green' industry that will have to be developed over the next decade to counteract the environmental downside of late capitalism, are sustainable.

The use of heterarchical principles of governance to rebalance the design of workplace training would provide opportunities for all stakeholders (employers, workers, trade unions, representatives from local government, etc.) to contribute to the co-production of new models of training. This approach is very different from the well-known 'social partnership' tradition that exists in Germany and some other European countries. That tradition is based on the principle of national frameworks that are implemented and monitored regionally. `In contrast, the heterarchical principle implies custom-made firm- and/or region-specific approaches to, and models of, workplace training which respond to all parties' needs. To enshrine this principle in practice, it would be important for all parties to agree to devise regional 'kite marking' systems. These systems would be based on clearly defined criteria for skill formation, skill transfer, and employability such that workers developed requisite form of vocational practice and social capital. Arguably, the kite marking systems would reassure employers that the schemes were providing value-for-money, local government that the scheme would support economic prosperity in the region, and trade unions would see the new models of training contributing to the consolidation of and/or growing opportunities for employment.

2. Reconceptualize the transition from formal education to work and from present work or unemployment to future work as the development of vocational practice and social capital.

Although qualifications are important because they are the longstanding way to certify the forms of knowledge and skill acquired in education, throughout this collection we have pointed out that policy makers' affirmation of the role of qualifications in facilitating access to the labour market has overlooked that these do not necessarily constitute adequate proxy measures for all the forms of knowledge and other competences required in workplaces. In parallel, policy makers have also been inclined to suggest that the knowledge and skill required for work can be broken down into discrete units of study and taught independent of any contact with workplaces. While there is a grain of truth in the idea that study and simulation can provide a grounding and inspiration for learners, the case studies contained in Section 2 have clearly demonstrated that vocational practice – in other words, knowledge, skill and, most importantly, the ability to discern when and how to use them (i.e., judgement) – has to be developed *in situ*, that is, in conditions of work or through the provision of opportunities to gain access to networks and specialist advice.

The mention of networks presupposes the issue of social capital. An increasing feature of working life is that workers have to develop the capability to mobilize resources, that is, other people/institutions/ technologies, and so on, to help them to address the challenges they confront. The development of vocational practice and social capital is equally a concern for students who have not yet made the transition to work and for workers who have been made redundant. These observations offer further grounds to consolidate our argument in favour of a more nuanced conception of lifelong learning and the way in which people develop, hold, and use knowledge (Duguid, this volume). Its development will, however, entail a further shift in policy makers' thinking about lifelong learning policy.

What is required is the introduction of a more multifaceted and differentiated strategy based on an explicit recognition of the respective contributions that the following activities play in facilitating access to work. They are:
– *accreditation* activities (i.e., academic or vocational qualifications);
– *industry-recognized* activities (i.e., knowledge and skill acquired from informal and non-accredited activities, such as experience at work, work placements, internships, master classes, etc.); and
– *network* activities (i.e., the development through the working life course of a personal range of contacts that can be mobilized to address needs as they emerge).

Assuming that policy makers have already relaxed the reins of policy and offered all stakeholders the opportunity to broker custom-made education and training solutions (see Principle 1), the next step is to identify how to incorporate what we have referred to above as access to industry-recognized and networked activities

356

either as integral parts of accredited programmes (see, e.g., the WAC case study in Guile's chapter) or as part of non-accredited programmes (see the CA and JIIC case studies in Guile's chapter). These activities can develop vocational practice and social capital in highly effective ways and need to become an explicit feature of supporting transition into the labour market.

3. A shift from conceiving learning as consisting of the accumulation of pre-specified outcomes to seeing it as the development of judgement.

In addition to the global tendency, which we have noted in this collection, to conceive learning as consisting of the accumulation of pre-specified outcomes, the widespread introduction of National Qualification Frameworks (NQFs) is resulting in pressure on educational institutions to standardize qualifications through the use of programme specifications and learning outcomes (see Young & Allais, 2011). Unless this development is countered, it is likely to re-affirm the idea worldwide that qualifications constitute a proxy measure for vocational practice and hence for employment in the knowledge economy. This is deeply worrying because, as the case studies presented in Section 2 demonstrate, the knowledge associated with any field of vocational practice is always broader than any qualification. Developing such knowledge requires opportunities for workers to 'conduct inquiries' and 'rehearse and revise procedures' and, in the process, to develop the capability to make occupationally-relevant judgements (Sennett, 2008a).

What is required, therefore, is the formulation of a language of description for vocational practice that will offer researchers, policy makers and practitioners a resource to identify the different contributions that accredited, industry-recognized, and network activities make to supporting transitions into, and sustaining work in, the labour market. The first step towards such a language of description has already been taken (Guile, 2010). It has resulted in the formulation of three conceptions of vocational practice. They are: *evolutionary* (i.e., the gradual development of a practice through individual and collective agentic activity); *laterally branching* (i.e., the explicit use of professional/vocational field-specific forms of knowledge and skill (i.e., codified and non-codified) to develop a practice in ways that can be recognized in the field; and *envisioning* (i.e., inter-professional activity to envision a new form of practice).

These conceptions offer, in principle, a way to capture the different modalities of practice and the forms of judgement associated with them and, therefore, offer ways for policy makers to support the four ways in which we have identified workers may respond to securing their employability in the expanded conception of the global knowledge-based economy described in this book. The enactment of this principle of conceiving of learning as the development of judgement presupposes that policy makers have relaxed the reigns of policy for lifelong learning so that stakeholders at the regional level have the autonomy and funding to establish strong and sustained partnerships. The aim of these partnerships is: (1) to identify the forms of working and learning that have to occur outside of educational institutions to facilitate the development of the above conceptions of vocational practice; (2) to agree on strategies to provide existing and aspiring workers with access to these forms of working and learning; and (3) to press the case for the greater recognition for wider range of pedagogic activities in paid and unpaid work settings in the realms of national and international lifelong learning policy formation. These activities, as the case studies in Section 2 have demonstrated, create the conditions for positive epistemic cultures in all type of workplaces and, in doing so, assist workers to develop and to share the knowledge essential for learning and working effectively in a knowledge-based economy.

FINAL REMARKS

Overall, the contributions in this reader lead us to the following conclusions:
- the extent of the emergence of the knowledge-based economy has been exaggerated and simplified; the reality is more complicated and uneven; familiar profit-driven capitalist relations of production still prevail and knowledge workers are not driving the ship.
- the presumption that a knowledge-based economy needs a more qualified labour force than is currently available is demonstrably false in terms of formal qualifications, as workers in advanced capitalist societies are becoming increasing overqualified in these terms; however, many aspects of informal job-related learning are increasingly found to be essential to becoming and remaining knowledgeable workers, and more informed policies and practices enabling the recognition and accessibility of such informal knowledges are much needed in many sectors. The submerged part of the 'iceberg' of lifelong learning is increasingly vital to the further development of a KBE.
- the co-production of workplace training, involving such stakeholders as employers, workers, and their trade unions/associations and representatives from local government, can enable sensitive and effective design of new models of training and job-related lifelong learning and should be widely encouraged; however, in light of the growing contingency of jobs in many sectors and the continual learning efforts of most people, similar forms of co-operation are likely needed to design new jobs and economic reforms to ensure that most people have access to meaningful work in which to apply their knowledge.

Finally, whichever directions may be ascendant in the continuing contest between intellectual property rights and workers' access to formal qualification and useful knowledge through lifelong learning, this contest is likely to persist however fully developed the knowledge-based economy becomes.

REFERENCES

Amin, A. & Roberts, J. (2008). *Community, economic creativity and organisation*. Oxford: Oxford University Press.

Berg, I. (2003). *Education and jobs: The great training robbery*. Clinton Corners, NY: Percheron.

Billett, S., Harteis, C., & Eteläpelto E. (2008). *Emerging perspectives of workplace learning*. Rotterdam: Sense.

Boreham, N., Samurçay, R., & Fischer, M. (Eds.). (2002). *Work process knowledge*. London: Routledge.

Colardyn, D., & Bjornavöld, J. (2004). Validation of formal, non-formal and informal learning: Policy and practices in EU-member states. *European Journal of Education, 39*, 69–89.

Edwards, A., Daniels, H., Leadbetter, J., Martin, D., & Warmington, P. (2009). *Interagency working*. London: Routledge.

Evans, K., Hodkinson, P., Rainbird, H., & Unwin, L. (2006). *Improving workplace learning*. London: Routledge.

Evans, K., Hodkinson, P., & Unwin, L. (Eds.). (2002). *Working to learn: Making learning visible*. London: Kogan Page.

Felstead, A., Gallie, D., & Green, F. (2002). *Work skills in Britain 1986–2001*. Nottingham: Department for Education and Skills.

Felstead, A., Fuller, A., Jewson, N., & Unwin, L. (2009). *Improving working for learning*. London: Routledge.

Gertler, M. (2003). Tacit knowledge and the economic geography of context, or The indefinable tacitness of being (there). *Journal of Economic Geography, 3*(1), 75–99.

Gherardi, S. (2006). *Organizational knowledge: The texture of workplace learning*. Oxford: Blackwell.

Guile, D. (2010). *The learning challenge of the knowledge economy*. Rotterdam: Sense.

Grabher G. (2004). Learning in projects, remembering in networks? Communality, sociality, and connectivity in project ecologies. *European Urban and Regional Studies, 11*(1), 103–123.

Grabher, G., & Ibert, O. (2006). Bad company? The ambiguity of personal knowledge networks. *Journal of Economic Geography, 6*(1), 251–271.

Harper, D. (1987). *Working knowledge: Skill and community in a small shop*. Chicago: University of Chicago Press.

Hoyles, C., Noss, R., Kent, P., & Bakker, P. (2010). *Improving mathematics at work*. London: Routledge.

Jensen, K., Lahn, L., & Nerland, M. (Eds.). (2012). *Professional learning in the knowledge society*. Rotterdam: Sense.

Jessop, B. (1998). The rise of governance and the risks of failure: The case of economic development. *International Social Science Journal, 50*(155), 29–45.

Jessop, B. (2000). Governance failure. In Stoker, G. (Ed.), *The new politics of British local government* (pp. 11–32). London: Macmillan.

Johnson, R. (1979). 'Really useful knowledge:' Radical education and working-class culture, 1790–1848. In Clarke, J., Critcher, C., & Johnson, R. (Eds.), *Working class culture: Studies in history and theory* (pp. 75–102). London: Hutchinson.

Lauder, H., Young, M., Daniels, H., Balarin, M., & Lowe, J. (Eds.). (2012). *Educating for the knowledge economy: Critical perspectives*. London: Routledge.

Livingstone, D.W. (Ed.). (2009). *Education and jobs: Exploring the gaps*. Toronto: University of Toronto Press.

Livingstone, D.W. (Ed.). (2010). *Lifelong learning in paid and unpaid work*. New York: Routledge.

Livingstone, D.W., Mirchandani, K., & Sawchuk, P. (Eds.). (2008). *The future of lifelong learning and work*. Rotterdam: Sense.

Malloch, M., Cairns, L., Evans, K., & O'Connor, B.N. (Eds.) (2010). *The Sage handbook of workplace learning*. Los Angeles: Sage.

Ness, I. & Azzellini, D. (Eds.). (2011). *Ours to master and to own: Workers' councils from the Commune to the present*. Chicago: Haymarket.

Nijof, W. & Nieuwenhuis, L. (2007). *The learning potential of the workplace*. Rotterdam: Sense.

Rainbird, H., Fuller, A., & Munro, A. (Eds.). (2004). *Workplace learning in context*. London: Routledge.

Sabel, C. & Zeitlin, J. (2008). Learning from difference: The new architecture of experimentalist governance in the European Union. *European Law Journal, 14*(3), 271–327.

Sennett, R. (2008, February 11). *The craftsman*. Lecture at the Royal Society of the Arts.

Tough, A.M. (1971). *The adult's learning projects: A fresh approach to theory and practice in adult learning*. Research in Education Series, 1. Toronto: Institute for Studies in Education.

CONCLUSION

Tuomi-Gröhn, T., & Engeström, Y. (2003). *Between school and work: New perspectives on transfer and boundary crossing*. Amsterdam: Pergamon.
Young, M. & Allais, S. (Eds.). (2011). Special issue on National Qualification Frameworks. *Journal of Education and Work, 24*(3–4), 209–429.

Lightning Source UK Ltd.
Milton Keynes UK
UKOW04f1058060414

229468UK00001B/29/P